I0759526

SLOW POISON

SLOW POISON

IDI AMIN, YOWERI MUSEVENI, *and the* MAKING *of the* UGANDAN STATE

MAHMOOD MAMDANI

THE BELKNAP PRESS OF HARVARD UNIVERSITY PRESS
Cambridge, Massachusetts
London, England *2025*

Printed in the United States of America

Second printing

EU GPSR Authorised Representative
LOGOS EUROPE, 9 rue Nicolas Poussin, 17000, LA ROCHELLE, France
E-mail: Contact@logoseurope.eu

Library of Congress Cataloging-in-Publication Data
Names: Mamdani, Mahmood, 1946– author
Title: Slow poison : Idi Amin, Yoweri Museveni, and the making of the Ugandan state / Mahmood Mamdani.
Description: Cambridge, Massachusetts : Harvard University Press, 2025. | Includes bibliographical references and index. |
Identifiers: LCCN 2025000591 | ISBN 9780674299870 cloth | ISBN 9780674301757 pdf | ISBN 9780674301764 epub
Subjects: LCSH: Uganda—Politics and government—1971–1979 | Amin, Idi, 1925–2003 | Uganda—Politics and government—1979– | Museveni, Yoweri, 1944– | South Asians—Uganda—History—20th century | Deportation—Uganda—History—20th century | Uganda—Colonial influence
Classification: LCC DT433.283 .M354 2025 | DDC 967.6/03—dc23/eng/20250325
LC record available at https://lccn.loc.gov/2025000591

For those who worked selflessly above ground:

Augustine Ruzindana, Wafula Oguttu, Wabwire Kwoba,
John Musinguzi, Okot Nyormoi, and Margaret Odeke

The Sun is not always Dead at Midnight,
And Fire does not always Beget Ash.

—Okello Oculi, *The Orphan*

Contents

Preface

ETHNICITY AND TRIBE

Africa has always been a collection of tribes, goes the conventional refrain. The speaker will point to the multitude of language groups on the continent, their numbers more or less constant over time. But is a language group the same as a tribe? This book argues otherwise: a language group is a cultural community, an ethnic group. An ethnic group becomes a tribe when politicized, and identified with a fixed territory ("homeland"), a hierarchical authority ("customary authority"), and a set of laws that apply only to members of the tribe ("customary laws"). A tribe is a political community.

In the African countries, the politicization of culture took place over the colonial period. Modern colonialism created the tribes of Africa. It is colonial power that translated linguistic boundaries into political ones, and language groups into "nations," claiming that these were really a carryover of premodern units.

To see through these claims, we need to focus on three critical changes under colonialism. First was the creation of a power structure in the new units: "traditional authorities" were empowered by colonial authorities to run the newly bounded "traditional societies." Second was the creation of "customary law." This law claimed to be a continuation of precolonial custom, but at the same time distinguished between two kinds of residents: indigenous and migrants. Traditional authorities were said to be empowered by customary law to discriminate between those indigenous and those not—the former tracing their genealogy to the time before colonialism and the latter to colonization or after. Even when colonial migrants had come to speak the language of the locality ("culture"), they were considered not indigenous to the area. And even when culturally assimilated, they were treated as political strangers. They were considered not part of the tribe. Finally, in a continent where most ethnic groups had historically been mobile, moving in search of productive land and water sources, these same ethnic groups were now fixed to a territory ("tribal homeland") and said to have been fixed to it eternally.

Colonial power built the colonial state on tribal building blocks. Recruitment into all colonial institutions was based on tribal identities. Every institution—from the army to the police to the prisons, even plantation or factory or domestic labor—was identified with particular tribes. When members of a tribe demanded increased representation in any institution, their calculation was inevitably based on a tribal arithmetic. Tribalism was a representation of colonial logic.

Idi Amin and Yoweri Museveni have been defined by their opposed relationship to tribalism: Amin as the father of the nation, and Museveni as one who has sought to resurrect tribe as a political identity and make it permanent.

SLOW POISON

INTRODUCTION

I first saw Idi Amin in 1972, after I returned home to Kampala from the United States to begin research on my doctoral thesis. Ali Mazrui, the head of the Political Science Department at Kampala's Makerere University, had suggested I join the department as a teaching assistant, which I was delighted to do. That same year, Amin came to Makerere to preside over the university's fiftieth anniversary celebrations. From the moment he arrived, Amin was the center of attention. As he took the podium, Amin's remarks had the effect of a tremor: "I came here with a battalion of soldiers so that when you lift your heads from books, you know who has power." We were stunned. Then came an even more outrageous statement: "On my way to the main hall, I stopped at Mulago (the university hospital). I looked at your records. I see that most of you are suffering from gonorrhea. I will not tolerate you spreading political gonorrhea in Uganda." This was my introduction to Amin's many uses of public buffoonery as political performance.

A year later, I joined the University of Dar es Salaam as a young lecturer. There, I met Yoweri Museveni who had graduated from the university and taken a job as an instructor at the Cooperative College in Moshi, Tanzania. I had heard of him as the charismatic head of the University Students' African Revolutionary Front (USARF) at the University of Dar es Salaam. Perched on a hill several miles from the city center, the university campus was generally known as "The Hill." Never a shortage of anecdotal stories when it came to Museveni, one went like this. In the week after Mao's death, Museveni was teaching at the

Cooperative College. Before class began, he walked to the blackboard and wrote something like,

> Marx was a great man. Marx is dead.
> Lenin was a great man. Lenin is dead.
> Mao was a great man. Mao too is dead.
> I, too, am not feeling so well . . .

There was little reason to think of Museveni as modest.

Like other subjects in the colony, both Amin and Museveni were products of British colonialism in at least one sense: they were both publicly identified as members of a race or a tribe. And so was I. The British were master classifiers. They understood that to be modern was to be master of all; the power to define would lead the way to other powers, to arrange and rearrange everything, in nature and in society. This hubris would ultimately lead the British to cleanse and reorder areas of the world as part of a larger effort to remake the world as a whole. Not surprisingly, their first act after conquest was to classify all plants and animals. Humans, too, were classified, into natives and non-natives. Non-natives like myself (I was of South Asian descent) were persons of no fixed abode. In contrast, natives, like Amin and Museveni, were defined by place. Classified into a variety of species, each belonged to a "tribe" with a designated territory ("tribal homeland"), under charge of a single "traditional authority." The "tribe" was different from the precolonial "ethnic group" in two ways. First, it was identified with a fixed territory and, second, every tribe had a hierarchical authority with the right to mete corporal punishment to native subjects as the exercise of a "customary" right. The person in charge of maintaining order and gathering taxes in this territory was known as the tribal chief, as distinct from the clan head. By fixing cultural identity to a territorial space, colonialism politicized culture as "tribe" and organized it under a single traditional authority. By the time of Uganda's independence in 1962, the colony represented a patchwork of tribes.

The colonial economy that Britain created was powered by migrant labor. In Uganda, migrant workers came from across several borders, including Rwanda, Sudan, and Kenya, and small traders came from the older British colony of India. Having brought these migrants to Uganda without any restriction on the duration of their stay, the colonial authority at the same time barred them from owning land in their new home. The prohibition on owning land was extended to denial of birthright citizenship at independence. As part of the preparation for independence, Britain finalized a list of "indigenous tribes" (communities) in the colony so as to leave no doubt as to who was considered officially "indigenous" and who was not. The constitution at independence (that is, the 1962 Constitution) reserved citizenship by birth to members of "indigenous tribes" in the country. The first government, led by Milton Obote, the then–prime minister and second president of Uganda, followed Britain's lead when it expelled all Luo persons living within the country as non-indigenous—regardless of how many years they had lived there. The distinction between "indigenous" and "non-indigenous" became critical when it came to staffing the modern sector emerging in the colonial period—the army, the police, large-scale trade. The power to define and distinguish the "indigenous" from those not was the *first* lever of power wielded by postindependence governments. It was at the heart of the politics of "tribalism." Though invented by Britain, we shall see that none perfected it as did Museveni. As part of an attempt to stabilize his rule and vanquish all opposition, Museveni subdivided existing districts into many, doubling, tripling, and even quadrupling the number of districts. Now, each district had its "native" tribes (sometimes more than one) alongside "non-native" or settler tribes. Continuous fragmentation of the subject population, an ongoing and seemingly endless process, reinforced by official violence and institutionalized corruption—that is, different ways of disciplining resisters and rewarding collaborators—is what I call "slow poison."

A decade after independence, in 1971, Amin became president in an orgy of violence, wielding one part of the colonial army as a hammer against the part that remained loyal to the ousted Obote government. The colonial army had been recruited from groups marginal to the country's administration and the economy and was marked by two features. First, the army came mostly from the area north of the Nile River, which gave it a regional character. Cash crop–producing peasants south of the Nile River were carefully kept out of the army, even though they had a long tradition of participating in military service in different centralized kingdoms of the south. The reason was simple: after all, the army was likely to be used against them. Second, the colonial army was recruited from particular ethnic groups. The mixing of persons from different "tribes" was discouraged. Britain tagged the administrative units from which they drew soldiers and police as "martial tribes." Company solidarity and spirit was hailed as tribal solidarity, a form of patriotism befitting natives.

The politicians, too, represented different "tribal homelands." So, when the coup took place in 1971, everyone knew which side they were on. In the colonial world, there had been little freedom. As with ethnic and religious identity, so with politics, your side was assigned to you at birth. At the time of the Amin coup, the "northerners" were on one side, and those from the Northwest—including the Nubi, a group whose members possessed a hyphenated identity, one part ethnic, the other linguistic (more on this later)—were on the other side. Though a minority in the army, Amin's group won because they enjoyed predominant support from the civilian majority in the south, where the capital was located, and from key outside powers, Britain and Israel.

Foreign advisors disagreed on the course the coup makers should pursue: the British argued for a straightforward assassination of Milton Obote; the Israelis said it would only serve to warn the president's tribal support in the army, and thus was likely to be counterproductive. They proposed to begin the coup by neutralizing Obote's supporters in the army. That led to massive violence in the barracks.

The first wave of violence was the largest: Amin's group, which carried out the coup of 1971, annihilated large sections of the army. Many who survived either left with Obote, the ousted president, or followed him, to Tanzania or Sudan. The army would continue to be a collection of glorified tribal militias, drawing its personnel, particularly its leadership, from two regions: West Nile, Amin's home region; and South Sudan. South Sudanese soldiers (the Anyanya) were incorporated into Amin's army following the 1972 Addis Ababa peace accords that brought the civil war in Sudan to an end.

The tribal nature of the army persisted, both with the government army in Uganda and the rebel armies in Tanzania. After the fall of the Amin regime in 1979, two armed tribal militias, one led by Obote (Kikosi Maalum) and the other by Museveni (Front for National Salvation, FRONASA), would confront one another, the former drawing its soldiers mainly from "the North," the latter from "the West." So long as governance revolved around "tribe" as its fulcrum, as it did since the colonial period, every institution in the country would reflect a tribal arithmetic.

I ask the reader to shed certain media-driven preconceptions before reading this book. The first of these is that Amin was a Hitlerite presence in Africa. Amin's public performance—especially his buffoonery—was an integral part of his style of governance. He invited his adversaries to underestimate him, even to think of his as a buffoon. His rhetoric included Hitlerite proclamations (including actual praise of Hitler), but that was not the same as committing Hitlerite atrocities. The Asian expulsion is said to have been a Hitlerite act. Yet, as we shall see, even as Amin ethnically cleansed Uganda of Asians and expropriated them, he did everything in his power to spare Asian lives.

The second media-driven preconception is that Museveni has been an effective antidote to Amin, promising a return to a rule of law, and a guarantee of a return of Asians, previously exiled, and of international capital, allowing the way for an era of prosperity.

I began writing this book as a witness, as Georg Wilhelm Friedrich Hegel's proverbial Owl of Minerva who takes flight at dusk, trying to make sense of events in retrospect. As I continued to write, I realized that I had been a participant and not just an observer in many of the events I was narrating. Some may think it self-indulgent to straddle the position of an observer and a participant. But the recognition of "dirty hands" is also an opportunity for self-reflection. It has led me to formulate a set of fresh questions.

One of twenty-three beneficiaries of scholarships America gifted to Uganda at independence in 1962, I was also among the Asians expelled in 1972. I took my first academic job at the University of Dar es Salaam in 1973, became part of exile politics until the overthrow of Amin in 1979, and finally returned to Uganda in 1980. Turning down FRONASA's offer to go to the bush that same year, I chose to pursue politics above ground with comrades who had come back from Tanzania after the fall of Amin, working alongside the Museveni-led National Resistance Movement (NRM) when it came to power in 1986, but without joining it, only to part ways soon after. Rather than risk a second and a third expulsion, I chose to leave and to take on academic jobs in South Africa and the United States. I returned home every summer, finally to work as director of Makerere Institute of Social Research for twelve years (2010–2022). The lesson I had learned was to continue to work above ground to preserve life and pass on its lessons to the next generation.

I introduce the immediate protagonists in the Asian expulsion of 1972, the Nubi and the Bayindi (Indians), in the opening two chapters of this book. Both the Nubi and the Bayindi had come to colonial Uganda with the advent of British colonialism, and both had sheltered under its spreading wings, as either soldiers in the military or traders in the economy, but they faced different futures. The Nubi found a place in the postcolonial nation, the Bayindi found themselves outside the nation. Like the Nubi, the Bayindi had been colonized; but, unlike the Nubi, the Bayindi had come to be defined by colonial law as the racial other of the nation. I grew up in a racialized neighborhood in Kampala, played in race-exclusive fields, and prayed in racialized mosques. My father had a literary sensibility, but it seldom translated into a political one. My mother had a passion for justice, but it was channeled within narrow horizons, fighting for women's rights within our small religious community. How does the offspring of a middle-class Asian family break from their race-tinted and narrow political horizons? My political awakening began in the United States and matured in Dar es Salaam.

This book focuses on the Amin and the Museveni eras, both critical to the making of contemporary Uganda. The research for this book has depended on multiple sources: archival, historical, and ethnographic. My understanding of Amin has been a product of direct encounters in life and the travails of a scholar in search of primary sources—starting with the 1972 Asian expulsion. Some of those sources have been official, such as minutes of cabinet meetings under Amin and the report of Amin's 1975 commission into "disappearances." I also benefited from reading the then–unpublished memoir of Idi Amin's son, Jaffar Amin.

Above all, this book rests on firsthand ethnographic knowledge, comprised of my upbringing in Uganda until the age of seventeen and my later return to Uganda from the US to teach at Makerere University in 1972 and again from roughly 1980 to 1995. Then every academic summer since 1995, I returned to Uganda until I took over the directorship of the Makerere Institute of Social Research for twelve years (2010 to 2022).

My understanding of the Museveni years has been a product of face-to-face encounters, from the time I first met Museveni in Dar es Salaam in 1973 to the early years of his presidency. My understanding was immediate until I put together and contextualized the fragments of information from the Ugandan daily and weekly media. Only when the blood emerged did the picture become clear.

I present this narrative as an opportunity for the reader to see through the standard academic claim to "objectivity" and "neutrality." I have come to question any claim of a single objective truth. It is more illuminating to think along the lines of Ibn Khaldun, who suggests that we see objective truth as an attribute we give God, for only an omniscient power can be privy to one objective truth. The truth we strive for and glimpse as humans is inevitably colored by our location and perspective. I invite the reader to share these changing vantage points, both social and political, that have shaped my own point of view.

1

IDI AMIN

The Parental Heritage

Amin was born on one of Islam's biggest festivals, Eid al-Adha, and his father named him Eidi in honor of it, a name later simplified to Idi. Amin was Idi's father's name. His father also gave the name Dada to both Idi and his older brother. At Uganda's independence in 1962, Idi officially added this name to his. He would henceforth be known as Idi Amin Dada.

There is no agreement on the year of Idi Amin's birth. According to Jaffar, Idi's son, the family has regularly observed 1928 as the year of his father's birth. Anxious that they not be remembered as having recruited a child soldier, British official documents recorded 1925 as his year of birth.

Idi's mother, Aate, was a Lugbara, married to a Kakwa, two small neighboring ethnic groups in the northwest of what would become the British colony of Uganda. Amin's parents also belonged to the Nubi community, a multiethnic group with a historical and linguistic foundation. Most writings on the Nubi see them as Sudanese who came to Uganda during colonization. Often they are described as "mercenaries" or as "slave-soldiers." They were neither.

The Nubi originated around the late eighteenth century when European powers (including the Ottoman) moved to take over Northeast Africa.[1] As the European "Scramble for Africa" moved southward, so did the Nubi, and as the existing political order changed, armed custodians of the old order, previously organized as *zariba*—"a band of armed men with a commander"—scattered in several directions.[2] Over time, they attached themselves to different groups. As they moved from one to another, they developed a common identity with a distinctive language, shared practices, and a collective history. In nineteenth-century Eastern Africa, this group came to be known as the Nubi.

Part of the human debris of the old order, the Nubi were neither an ethnic group nor a multiethnic formation. They came out of a mix of conscripts and runaway refugees drawn from many ethnic groups. Toward the end of the nineteenth century, the Nubi came to live in the Lado Enclave, a cross-roads territory that passed between two British colonies, Uganda and Sudan. In the words of Omari Kokole, a Nubi Kakwa scholar, the Nubi have neither an indigenous language nor a tribal myth of origin, neither indigenous African names nor an ancestral home.[3] Their shared language was a colloquial, or creole, Arabic.[4] This language was named Kinubi by the Swahili (the prefix *ki-* refers to the language of the Nubi). If Swahili is an African language whose linguistic structure is entirely Bantu, and roughly a quarter to a third of its vocabulary consists of loanwords from Arabic, Kinubi is its mirror opposite. Kinubi has the grammatical structure of Arabic, and much of its vocabulary comprises loanwords from Bantu languages. Kokole cites the position of Major Chauncey Hugh Stigand (1877–1919), a part-time linguist who served in both military and civilian capacities in the Lado Enclave, that the origins of Kinubi lay in the Arabic introduced into the region by the old Egyptian government and the Dangala traders, likely in the late eighteenth century.

The Nubi were predominantly Muslims—a Muslim identity that incorporated a variety of spirit possession cults derived from the countryside.[5] Besides Kinubi, the colloquial lingua, the Nubi also speak Swahili, if not always fluently, and often several languages of the region. Over time, they gelled into an officer corps spread over the entire Eastern African region. In Uganda, for example, the four top officers of the country's army at independence in 1962 were all Muslim, multilingual, and Kinubi speaking.[6]

The arrival of Nubis in East Africa is traced to the work of Emin Pasha. Born Eduard Schnitzer, an Austrian Jew of German descent who had converted to Islam, Emin Pasha was a doctor who worked in the employ of the Anglo-Egyptian administration in Cairo and was assigned the responsibility of organizing the British-Ottoman colonial effort in the southern regions. He followed a string of European officers who had been posted to the region before:

Sir Samuel Baker, governor of Sudan's Equatorial Province; the British General Charles George Gordon who "deployed Egyptian troops on the frontier of Buganda and set up a military post in 1876"; and Eduard Schnitzer, governor of Equatoria province. Known at the time as gentlemen-agents, they would today be called mercenaries.[7] Schnitzer converted to Islam, took on the name Emin (Amin) Pasha, and prayed regularly. When he visited Buganda in 1876, Emin Pasha introduced himself to Kabaka Mutesa I as a Muslim.[8] According to Omari Kokole, we should think of Emin Pasha, a German who converted to Islam and spoke Kinubi, as a Nubi.[9]

The Mahdists—followers or descendants of al-Mahdi, the Sudanese who believed himself a prophet divinely endowed with the gift to restore Islam—killed General Gordon and took Khartoum on January 26, 1885. As a result, Emin and his four thousand Nubi troops were effectively isolated from British-controlled territories at Wadelai, which lay in what became the colonial-era West Nile district. The British mounted several organized campaigns, claiming these to be so many "humanitarian" efforts, to reach Emin Pasha. One group in Europe formed the Emin Relief Expedition. Its chairman, William Mackinnon, also chaired the board of Imperial British East Africa (IBEA) Company, which spearheaded the British colonization effort in the region. The Company hoped to rescue Emin and "persuade" him to become its agent, with terms that would include employing his troops to capture and transport ivory to the coast.

The opportunity came in 1888, when two different sections—one under Fadhil al-Mullah (Fodumula), a Nubi Lugbara; and another under Selim Bey—were both asked to accompany Emin and Stanley to Zanzibar the following year, but refused. Nubi troops mutinied; they deserted Emin and Stanley, but they also refused to join the Mahdi's rebellion. When the Mahdists were defeated in 1889, Emin left with Stanley for the East African coast.[10] Two years later, on September 13, 1891, Emin Pasha signed an agreement handing over charge of his Nubi troops to the IBEA. The second signatory to this accord was Selim Bey, the Nubi representative of Pasha's Sudanese troops, an indication that this was hardly an army of slave soldiers. Almost a thousand troops were transferred to the IBEA. They formed the core of the standing army Frederick Lugard would use to conquer Uganda.

For Lugard, who later became the governor-general of Nigeria (1914–1919), the Nubi were "the best material for soldiery in Africa."[11] The British called the Nubi "Sudanese," using the term to refer to people recruited from across the northern state border. But that, too, was not true. Emin Pasha had done the bulk of his recruitment in the Lado Enclave in Equatoria, which then included the West Nile region.[12] Like a moving piece in a game of chess, the Lado Enclave, first a part of Sudan, was leased by Britain to the Belgian King Leopold II, then returned to Sudan when the lease expired in 1910, finally becoming a part of Uganda in 1914.[13] As is said of Mexicans (Chicanos) in the Southwest of the United States, the Nubi had not crossed the border; the border had crossed them, not just once but several times.

The Nubi do not fit the colonial stereotype of an African "tribe" with a fixed "homeland." A Nubi elder once told a young Nubi researcher at Makerere: "The Nubi . . . lived everywhere, just like birds that keep flying from one place to another."[14] British officers made several attempts to territorialize or localize the Nubi: settling Nubi ex-soldiers in designated areas, the *mulkis,* and those not in the colonial army among native communities.[15] As a result, most Nubi developed hyphenated identities: Fadhil al-Mullah (Fadmullah) was a Nubi Lugbara, and Idi Amin a Nubi Kakwa.

Ama Aate, Amin's mother, was a renowned practitioner of herbal medicine and an experienced midwife in the community. Among Aate's clients was Irene Drusilla Namaganda, the *Nnabagereka* (a Luganda title translated as queen in English) of Buganda. The British had installed her husband, Daudi Chwa, as the kabaka of Buganda at the tender age of six months. The British tended to understand these titles in Eurocentric terms, *Nnabagereka* as queen and *kabaka* as king; contemporary scholars argue that these titles are likely misnomers since both traditionally tended to share in political power. After remaining childless for the first five years of their marriage, Irene Namaganda came to Mama Aate for help. Not long after, she bore two sons, George William Mawanda and Edward Mutesa II. The two women developed a close bond along the way.

The kabaka had many reasons besides gratitude to want to befriend Aate, who was also a priestess in the Yakanye Order, which had been organized as a secret political society in the nineteenth century in opposition to armed raids and the trade in captives. It used sacred water and rituals to bind its members in a single loyal order during times of great social and political upheavals. Central to the ritual was the extract of a daffodil plant, called *kamiojo.* Known as the Water of Yakan, it was "a powerful drug, which causes excitement and elation."[16] The Yakanye Order had come to stand for one central demand: that all foreigners leave the land. It was known to have been active in revolts across the region, in particular the two best-known anticolonial revolts, Maji Maji (1905–1907) in Tanganyika and Lamogi (1911) in northern Uganda.

Kabaka Chwa aspired to be let into the secrets of the Yakanye Order. For Daudi Chwa was a kabaka in all but name, even if he could boast of a proud lineage. After all, he was the son of the famed Kabaka Mwanga, celebrated as the last kabaka to resist British domination. Mwanga had joined the ruler of neighboring Bunyoro-Kitara, Omukama Kabalega, to fight missionaries, who both saw as the front paw of a looming British threat. The British fought both Mwanga and Kabalega, ultimately exiling them to the Indian Ocean island of the Seychelles. In Mwanga's place they installed Daudi Chwa on the Buganda throne as a baby king. For the majority of the forty-two years he occupied the throne, Daudi Chwa had been impotent, physically and politically. The adult Daudi Chwa would often visit Aate's shrine at Bundo in Kidusu, hoping to be initiated into the Yakanye Order and regain his manhood.

Rumors were rife around the time Idi was born that the real father of Aate's expected child was none other than the kabaka, Daudi Chwa. Under this cloud of suspicion and hostility, Aate decided to deliver the baby with her own hands. The circumstances of Idi's birth are recounted by his son, Jaffar, in an unpublished manuscript.[17] Jaffar says that Eidi, or Idi, was born at four o'clock in the early morning of Wednesday, May 30, 1928, at the Shimoni Hill police barracks, near the European-only neighborhood of Nakasero, in the capital city of Kampala. Idi's mother gave him his Kakwa name, Awon'go Alemi—Awon'go meaning "much noise arising from backbiting, rumors and allegations," and Alemi, derived from the Kakwa word *lemi,* meaning "just cause."

The story of Amin's childbirth has taken on the proportions of a family legend.[18] The legend has two parts: the first is that Idi was born during a hailstorm, for the Kakwa an omen signaling the coming of important times. It is said that the baby landed on a pile of hailstones and let off a shriek which resounded through the neighborhood. The second part has it that, overwhelmed by the rumors that questioned the baby's paternity, the father asked clan elders to subject the child to a traditional but potentially deadly paternity test. Rarely practiced, this test involved abandoning a newborn infant for four days if the baby was a male, and three if a female, in a jungle filled with wild animals. The story, says Jaffar, was recounted to him by Amin's uncle, Siri'ba of the Piza clan, one day in 1994 in Kawempe, another Kampala suburb. Furious when accused of adultery, Aisha Aate strode in front of her husband and clan elders, put an old army rifle on the ground, stepped over it and pronounced a curse—that if the child is not born of the husband, let him languish in poverty and misery; but if he is, let him succeed in this world, but let the father not partake of his fortune in any form. The infant Idi was taken to Koboko, the main town of the Kakwa in the northwest, and from there to the jungle around the slopes of Mount Liru. There the baby was left for four days. Aisha was confident that Nakan, the legendary seven-headed snake, to whom the faithful of the powerful Yakanye Order prayed, would save baby Idi. And that, she claimed, is indeed what happened: the snake wrapped itself around the baby as it would around its own eggs, placing its crown on the baby's head, protecting it as it would its own.

These events left the marriage in tatters. The parents separated when *baba* Amin, Idi's father, was transferred from Shimoni-Nakasero to Kololo Hill police barracks, all in Kampala, and retired in the 1930s. Daudi Chwa built a house for Aisha in Kitigulu, which is just before one enters the town of Entebbe from Kampala. To this day, says Jaffar, there are those who say that Idi Amin was a Muganda—that is, one among the Baganda, the people of Buganda—not a Kakwa.

The story of baby Idi's childhood included two very different versions: one mythical and cultural, the other secular and biographical. The cultural thread was conveyed through stories elders told of his early years, to him and his peers, and through them to subsequent generations and to anyone else who would listen. Some of the mythical stories, such as that of the legendary snake Nakan, gave the baby a sense of invulnerability combined with a sense of mission. The historical was limited to what the colonial state and its institutions archived, and what a researcher would cull from archival sources and field interviews.

The young Idi lived with his father in Arua. No sooner had Idi finished grade 4 in Arua Primary School than his mother, Aisha, sent a delegation of Nubi ulema (learned religious leaders) from Bombo, an important Nubi settlement, to convince the father to let Idi be enrolled in a well-known madrassa run by Sheikh Mahmood. The father agreed and the boy studied there for the next several years, staying with his maternal uncle.[19] At least one of his fellow students at the madrassa, Abdul Qadir Aligha, went on to become a renowned sheikh. During the four years that Idi was at the madrassa, he was in the care of sheikhs in Semuto in the region of Luwero which would later be the site of the 1981–1986 civil war between forces loyal to Obote and those to Museveni. Meanwhile, his mother married an ex-serviceman, called Ibrahim, and moved to Lugazi, a company town run by the Mehtas, one of two wealthy Asian families. It is there, at Bundi-Kidusu, in Buyukwe Mukono district, that the family established its roots and created a permanent home.[20]

According to a story recited by Jaffar, young Idi impressed the sheikhs with the quality of his recital of the Qur'an and his ability to memorize it. By the time he was thirteen, his teachers and contemporaries thought the mosque and the madrassa as a possible future for Idi. This, however, was not the only path that beckoned him. The other led to the military barracks of the colonial King's African Rifles, for the Nubi a traditional calling.

If Idi's mother sent him to the Quranic School in Bombo, his father represented the military tradition in the family. Baptized as a Roman Catholic and named Andre, Idi's father converted to Islam in the first few years of the twentieth century under the combined influence and pressure of his patron and employer, Sultan Ali Kenyi. Conscripted as a bugler in the Sultan's army, he took Amin as his Muslim name. Baba Amin joined the colonial police force in 1913 and was conscripted into the King's African Rifles the next year, remaining there until 1921. He joined conscripts from neighboring Tanganyika who in World War I had been forced to fight for the British. At the end of the war, each man was given a plot of land in a village near the town of Arua, named Tanganyika after where most of the retired soldiers had come. Baba Amin retired again at the end of World War I, but then rejoined the police force in 1921. And when he retired for the third time from the police, Baba Amin took a job with the district commissioner's office in Arua township.

During the years of conscription in the army, and settlement in the barracks, from 1913 to 1921, the Amin family became part of the larger Nubi culture.[21] Some Kakwa spoke Kinubi along with Kakwa; others so identified with the Nubi that they came to shed their ethnic language, speaking only Kinubi and identifying exclusively with the Muslim *ummah* (the global community of believers). Among these was Amin's uncle, Amodo Rajab Yangu. Jaffar Amin tells the story of Amodo, who would after ritual ablutions set out in his Friday best every week for the local mosque. If called by his Kakwa name, Yangu, he would exclaim *'astaghfirullah* (May Allah / God forbid), and, considering himself polluted, would turn around to perform ablutions yet again. Eventually, it turned into something of a game whereby some would purposely call him by his Kakwa name, just to see how many times he would actually turn around and perform yet another ablution. But Amin's parents were different. They continued to respond to their Kakwa names and spoke Kakwa alongside Kinubi. Others assimilated into the dominant Kiganda culture, speaking Luganda too, and maybe some other languages. (Baganda are the people of Buganda, Muganda is a person in the singular, Kiganda is their culture, and Luganda their language.) Born into this cosmopolitan heritage, Amin was known to speak at least eight languages with varying degrees of fluency: Kakwa, Kinubi, Luganda, Swahili, English, and the three neighboring languages of Lugbara, Madi, and Luo. According to his commanding officer in the colonial King's African Rifles, Iain Grahame, though Idi was "often ridiculed for his slender knowledge of English, [he] was in fact fluent in at least a dozen African languages."[22]

Amin was on his way to becoming a child soldier in the colonial army. His first job was in 1939, where at the age of eleven he worked as kitchen help in the King's African Rifles mess aboard the naval ship *SS Yoma.* According to Ronny Bai, one of the two recruited with Idi on that day in 1939, the triple-deck ship they worked on was part of the East Africa-Overseas American (Allied) 44th Battalion, 27th Division USA under the Allied Forces. The trio worked until the end of the war in 1945.[23] Amin often regaled his children with names of places where the ship had docked: Mombasa, Cape Town, Madagascar, Djibouti, Aden, Port Sudan, Suez Canal. Among the stories he told the family was one that had Amin being rescued by an American Destroyer when the ship was downed by a U-boat. Jaffar claims to have read the official records and confirmed that *SS Yoma* was indeed sunk on June 17, 1943, between the port of Alexandra and the Libyan coast.

Amin returned to Kampala in 1945–1946, and from age seventeen to eighteen worked as a bell boy at the Imperial Hotel. Around this time he was inducted in the King's African Rifles. As was often the case with Amin, there is more than one version of how this came to be. Two of these can be traced to Jaffar. In the first, Amin encountered a Scottish officer at the Imperial, and communicated his interest in joining the fighting unit of the colonial army in simple and direct Swahili: "Sir, I want to join the KEYA (KAR)." The Scottish commander is said to have taken one look at this youth whose powerful physique and facial scars would have reminded him of youth he had encountered during recruitment exercises in Koboko. "All right, jump in the truck," he is purported to have said. Amin would often tell another version of the story, as a typical Kakwa *adiyo,* an oral narrative, which had him selling a kind of donut-shaped snack called *mandazi* on the streets of Kampala when he was forcefully conscripted by a Scottish officer.[24] A third version of the story was narrated by Judith Listowel, the English aristocrat who came to befriend Amin during his presidency and wrote a book about him. According to her, the King's African Rifles "had had heavy losses in Burma where 1,924 African private soldiers were killed. On its return to East Africa, the 4th Battalion was stationed at the Langata Camp, outside Nairobi. From there a recruiting safari was sent to northern Uganda where it signed up a group of Kakwa, among them Amin."[25] Whatever the circumstances of his recruitment, Amin was conscripted in the Jinja-based B Company of the 4th Battalion, King's African Rifles, as N44428, and taken to Magamaga for training.[26]

Amin became known for two strong qualities early in his army career. He was quick to resort to violence to settle scores, and he had little patience with racial injustice. At age thirteen, when in primary 4, Amin joined a protest against missionary practices that discriminated against Muslim African children. Given the simple fact that schools for African children beyond primary 4 were run by missions, no Muslim child had the possibility of a post-primary 4 schooling unless they first converted to Christianity. The protest failed and Amin went on to join the madrassa in Bombo.

In the army, Amin was sent in 1957 to Nakuru, a town ninety miles west of Nairobi in Kenya, for an *affande* training course—*affande,* meaning officer in Kiswahili, was also the highest rank that could be bestowed on an African officer in the colonial army. Amin's promotion to the rank of *affande* came in 1959. The day of his promotion, Amin walked past the sergeants' mess, where he was expected to go as a Black officer, and instead strode straight into the "Whites Only" officers' mess in the 1st Battalion and ordered a drink. The white bartender reminded him that his place as an African was elsewhere. Grabbing the bartender by the collar, Amin pulled him over the counter and landed a sharp right on the Englishman's chin. The room full of white officers were shocked into hushed silence. In a few days, the authorities scrapped the rule and the officers' mess was desegregated. It was a prelude to yet another desegregation. Already known as a star athlete and a great rugby player, Amin was soon invited to join the exclusively white Rugby Club.[27]

Amin excelled in those sports that required a combination of agility, strength, and stamina. He won the Uganda Light-Heavyweight Championship in 1963, holding the title for nine years.[28] Whether in or out of the ring, Amin's preferred response to a challenge was a knockout so there would be no doubt as to who had won. As president of the country, he would often warn Ugandan boxers of the racism rampant in international sports. Cautioning them of pervasive favoritism by white judges, Amin would warn fellow boxers to discard the illusion that they could win against a white boxer on points. A knockout, he would tell them, was the only sure way for a Black man to win an international boxing contest.

Amin quickly became a success in the colonial army. He specialized in counterinsurgency, a mode of fighting which had few rules. What counted was not the process but the result. So long as he won, his superiors were happy to turn a blind eye to his methods. In Turkana, he was accused of killing three civilians and on the Congo side of the Ruwenzori Mountains he was said to have shot dead another two in the course of setting up training camps. Cruelty and violence had become an integral part of Amin's training kit.[29] Terror, he was taught, was a legitimate weapon so long as you achieved your assigned objective.

Amin mastered these lessons. His career in the colonial army was marked by a meteoric rise. His first promotion was to the rank of Warrant Officer Platoon Commander (WOPC) in 1948. His superior officer, Iain Grahame, gave him a revealing recommendation: "As a Platoon Commander, . . . I found him first class. It is always his unit that had the best esprit, discipline and standards of field training. *In the simple methods by which we operated where the written word was kept to the minimum and where a natural eye for the ground was more important than the calculations of grid references on a map, his low intellect was only a minor handicap*" (italics my emphasis).[30]

A quick resort to violence went along with failure to take responsibility for one's actions. On tours, Amin easily and comfortably integrated into the culture of male soldiers who behaved as sexual predators in their encounters with local women. The practice was to leave behind children born of casual sexual liaisons, with no arrangement for the upkeep and welfare of either child or mother. Amin's son, Jaffar, writes of several siblings that he had heard of but never met, whether in Somalia or Kenya or, as we shall see later, Israel. Fellow soldiers in Somalia talked of a daughter Amin had left behind in Hargeisa to his mistress Mama Amina and a son in Bale-tuen to Mama Howra Allah.[31] During a state visit to Kenya as president of Uganda, Amin asked his listeners of the whereabouts of two kids he had fathered during his Mau Mau sojourn.[32] It was a public boast from the (male) leader of the pack. Jaffar tells of Amin's encounter with an Israeli intelligence officer he had met at Nasser's funeral in Cairo and with whom he fathered twins. According to Jaffar, Mossad would send his dad pictures of the twins every year.

It was in hunting the Mau Mau in Kenya that Amin proved his worth to his British superiors. As a reward, Amin's commander during the Mau Mau campaign, Major A. E. D. Mitchell, tried his utmost to get Amin promoted to sergeant but failed because Amin could not pass the English language exam that was a prerequisite for promotion in the colonial army. Amin would also boast of his cruelty publicly. The story is told of how, during the 1972 OAU summit in Rabat, "almost out of the blue, Amin offered to show OAU members—all heads of state—how to suffocate a man with a handkerchief. 'This is what I used to do to the Mau Mau,' he said with a wry smile, 'that was an excellent exercise to keep one fit for rugger or football.'"[33]

In 1961, just a year before independence, Amin was sent to lead the military operation against cattle raiders in Karamoja. The operation was considered an unqualified success even though he was accused of committing atrocities against civilians. That same year, in 1961, Amin was promoted by the then governor, Sir Frederick Crawford, to the rank of lieutenant, a position hitherto beyond the reach of any African soldier. It was an indication that the times were changing: Sudan had become an independent state in 1956, Ghana became one a year later, and it was evident that Uganda would soon follow suit. An independent Uganda would need African officers.

In 1962, the year of Uganda's independence, Amin was part of a company charged with disarming the Ngwatella section of the Turkana tribe across the Kenya border on the grounds they had been involved in cattle thefts. The commanding officer, Major Rogers, had divided the responsibility between three platoons, appointing Amin as commander of one. The accusations that Amin had murdered three Turkana civilians were taken seriously enough to lead to an inquiry in Lodwar in the Northern Frontier District of Kenya.[34] But that did not stop his British superiors in Uganda from showering accolades on Amin. Once again, what counted were the results and not the conduct. Amin was promoted to the rank of captain during Queen Elizabeth's birthday celebrations in July 1962, three months before independence. As chief of staff under Captain Shaban Opolot, Amin was now second in command of Uganda's armed forces. Coming barely three months before the birth of the independent state of

Uganda, the promotion confirmed Amin's position in the top hierarchy of independent Uganda's armed forces.

The Nubi and the Bayindi (Luganda for Asians or persons of Indian descent) came to Uganda as frontline soldiers for the British empire, at roughly the same time, in the late nineteenth century. The Nubi came first, as part of Emin Pasha's private army, later as the core of Britain's King's African Rifles. Often force marched, and seldom paid enough to keep body and soul together, the Nubi mutinied against their British officers. There were two Nubi mutinies in less than a decade, the first in 1888. Nine years later, when Nubi troops were ordered to march to Central Sudan to forestall a French march to Fashoda on the West Nile, many refused, having just gone through a long march to and from Eldama Ravine in Kenya. Late that year, 1897, a company at Lubwa murdered their British commander, Maj Thurston, and five other European officers. The refusal turned into a mutiny, the second in a decade.[35] The British brought a counterforce of 420 Punjabis—Sikhs and Muslims—from their older colony, India. More followed. Several mutineers were killed before order could be established. This was the first "African-Asian" encounter on Ugandan soil, well before any railway workers, *dukawallas,* or merchants arrived.

Asian and Nubi troops were often part of the same army battalion or police unit, and lived in adjacent quarters. Amin's mother, Aisha Aate, grew up in such a "mixed" quarter. Aisha's closest friend and daily companion was a Baluchi woman, the mother of Colonel Suleiman Bai. Then a region in India, Baluchistan is now a part of Pakistan. Both enterprising women, neither Mama Amin nor Mama Suleiman wanted to be confined to domestic quarters. The two friends would take turns, one going to the market while the other tended to the two babies, offering each a breast. This is how Suleiman Bai and Idi Amin came to share two caregivers—one Asian, the other Nubi.

The last of the Asian troops left Uganda in 1913. In the meantime, there were indentured laborers who came to build the Uganda Railway, though most left when the railway was completed. The lasting Indian presence was that of the small shopkeeper, the *dukawalla,* whose numbers multiplied over the decades with the building of the railway and the spread of British rule. As the British presence expanded, a group of coastal-based Asian financiers and merchants—who had been present for centuries in coastal cities like Zanzibar, Mombasa, Malindi, and others—saw the opportunity to spread their commercial network inland.

They turned to poor caste relations in India, encouraging them to emigrate and take charge of inland shops, often ahead of the arrival of the railway.

The Amin family was no stranger to Asians. Their association went back to the nineteenth century, and included family life. According to Jaffar Amin, the story starts with Amin's great aunt on his father's side, Asungha Yasmin, who had adopted Amin's grandfather, Amin Dada Nyabira Tomuresu. Asungha was married to an Englishman working with the Southern Sudan colonial administration. She returned home to her clan when the marriage ended. There, Asungha married an Indian Sikh working in the colonial police force. Transferred to Nsambya police barracks, the Sikh husband moved to Kampala with his wife and their young adopted son, Amin's grandfather. Upon retirement from the police, this same Sikh husband joined others to establish the Arua Bus Syndicate Company "that plied routes in and around the West Nile region of Uganda and other parts of Uganda."

Amin grew up with the idea that there are two kinds of Indians, the good and the bad: the former intimate, friendly, and worthy of trust; the latter remote, arrogant, and dishonest. The good Asian was a soldier or a policeman in colonial forces; he lived in the same barracks with African soldiers or police, ate the same food, and shared stories. Sometimes, the good Asian married an African woman. The bad Asian was the plantation owner and overseer, socially distant from Africans, a symbol of brute force. Young Idi encountered them even before he was ten. From 1937 to 1940, when he was between nine and eleven years old, Idi worked as a *kasanvu* (semi-forced) sharecropper at the Mehta sugar plantation near Kawolo, Lugazi. From 1941 to 1944, when he lived at the home of Sheikh Mahmood, Idi alternated between working in the sugar plantations and studying at the al-Qadriyah Darrasa (an Islamic school) in Bombo. This was his own experience of childhood poverty, and of working under Indian overseers who specialized in squeezing the last ounce of energy from laborers under their supervision. This, Amin's second "Asian" encounter, left him with a bitter memory.

2

GOOD ASIAN, BAD ASIAN

The in-between world of Asians (*Vasanjee*) unfolded within parameters carefully sculpted by colonial policy makers. Those economically privileged among the Asians, a minority, looked to the high and mighty for protection. When they faced racial discrimination, however, they supported anticolonial mobilizations. For the most part, Asian upper and middle classes lived relatively isolated and sheltered lives in "racially" demarcated spaces. It is the Asian poor who lived on the margins or in "mixed" Asian-African slums like Kisenyi and Bakuli, and who faced racially tinged skirmishes as they negotiated their daily lives.

Asians in rural areas were too few and scattered to be able to live in relatively self-contained ghettos. They lived amid peasant communities, or within walking distance of them. The Asian *dukawalla* (shopkeeper) was an immigrant, not to be confused with the white settler. The difference between them was simple: the white settler could not be found without a gun, while the dukawalla rarely possessed one. In the absence of colonial police who could have provided protection to person and property in the countryside, the dukawalla could not afford to abuse the peasant on whose goodwill he was dependent. He was known more for accommodation than for aggression. Of course, the relationship between the peasant and the dukawalla was unequal: it was a relationship between buyer and seller, between debtor and a creditor. No matter how unequal, the relationship between the dukawalla and surrounding peasants had to be mutually advantageous to endure.

I could find no social history or ethnographic study of the Asian dukawalla or the Nubi soldier. The closest I came to it was Jaffar Amin's family history.

For a glimpse into the lives of the in-between Asians, I turn to my own recollection of our family history.

The dukawalla usually lived in a shack with a tin roof and mud-baked walls—the front of the shack, a shop, or *duka;* and the rear, sleeping quarters, in some cases containing a metal container to gather rainwater in the back. The WC was a short twenty- to thirty-yard walk on the edge of the premises. This description fit our home, some miles from the town of Masaka, in Nyendo, next to the cotton ginnery where my father was manager, from 1951–1952. "Manager" was a fancy title for one who earned a meager salary and managed a staff of two. We called the Kampala-based owner Habib *Mama* (the Gujarati word for uncle), and my mother told us he was a distant cousin of hers. But in the society in which we lived, the poor and the nearly poor tended to claim one rich family or another as a distant relation.

Unlike the dukawalla whose very survival in the countryside depended on maintaining good relations with surrounding peasants, that was not always the case with the ginnery manager and his team, whose relations with peasants were often strained, especially after the cotton harvest. My father sometimes told us stories of peasants who would pack stones in sacks of cottonseed they brought for sale. "And what would you do?" "Well, my staff are not fools. They find ways of tampering with the scales or even tipping the scale with one foot." One day I asked him, "Which came first, the stones or tipping of the scale?" He gave me a long look.

The world of the dukawalla, too, changed in 1958 when Augustine Kamya, a cobbler, organized a Buganda-wide boycott of Asian shops. Politics in Buganda had followed two different trends: there was peasant mobilization against colonial chiefs, leading to two uprisings—one in 1945, the other in 1949—both marked by violence as houses of chiefs were burned down and Nsibirwa, the *katikkiro* (prime minister) of Buganda was assassinated. The other was the Kamya-led "Asian" boycott of 1958. Both issues tapped real grievances, but only one had a national resonance. The peasant mobilization was limited to Buganda since the colonial government's distribution of miles of land to individual agents had been largely limited to Buganda. But not so with the trade boycott. Asians were the primary agents in the formation of a British-controlled market. They bore the brunt of peasant resentment as the expanding market differentiated peasants into the few rich and the many poor. This countrywide process inevitably generated countrywide grievances. The boycott set the stage for postindependence politics.

Asian dukawallas were part of the landscape throughout East Africa. The Asian immigrant was sandwiched between the native and the colonizer in Kenya and Tanganyika, but in Uganda the Asian was different in one way. Here, Asian merchants had competitors—the class of Baganda *mailo* landlords who had given rise to a merchant class. With the end of the war, their ranks were augmented by returning soldiers whose modest savings were more than matched by their life-size aspirations to realize the freedom they had purportedly defended in the war. This development would shape the unique fate of Asians in Uganda.

My family belonged to neither group—neither the "good Indians" (integrative with Black Africans) nor the "bad Indians" (socially or professionally distant from Black Africans). We lived somewhere in between. Much as I have tried, I have been unable to excavate a family history beyond two or three generations. We came from a line of Khoja small traders, who were impoverished during the sleeping sickness epidemic that preceded World War I in India. We had little to do with the big merchants, financiers, or sailors of the precolonial era, including Ahmad ibn Majid, the sailor who guided Vasco da Gama from Mombasa to the West Indian coast, or with the railway workers brought in the nineteenth century as indentured labor to build the Uganda Railway. We were part of a third group, one that came at the cusp of the colonial period, to make our future across the "black waters" (*kala pani*) of the ocean, following the lead of more prosperous members of the community, the best known being Allidina Visram.

Birth and Home

My *ada*'s (grandfather's) family came from the village of Hadiyana in Kathiawad, about twenty miles off Jamnagar Road. *Ada* had originated in Zanzibar in the 1910s, joining the export trade in rubber. An uncle, or *fua,* was an engine driver who plied the Dar-Mwanza route. My father, Yusuf Karmali, was born in Dar es Salaam and my mother, Kulsum Panju, in Kigoma on Lake Tanganyika on the Tanganyika/Congo border. My two uncles married two sisters from Mombasa. But my parents, who had been childhood neighbors, became the talk of the community since theirs was said to be a "love marriage," a rare occurrence in those days. None of the men were educated beyond secondary school, and no women, including my mother, went beyond Primary 4. The men could speak

English with varying degrees of fluency, but the women spoke only Gujarati and Kiswahili, as well as a smattering of Hindustani they picked up from Bollywood films. The women wore only Gujarati clothing, sometimes the *salwar-khameez,* also known as a Punjabi suit, whereas the men combined Western and Asian clothes. *Ada,* for example, had two sets of clothing. He wore the Indian pajama and kurta at home, but when he went out, he would wear a Western shirt and trouser on top of it, taking these off as soon as he returned home.

My father, whom we called "daddy" in Western fashion, had ambitions to go to college, in Mumbai. *Ada* thought he should get married before going to a big city, and so he did. This is how I came to be born in Mumbai, in the Wadia Nursing Home, opposite Chaupati. We lived in a modest tenement in a lower-class Muslim neighborhood called Kurla, in two rooms—one occupied by my parents, and the other by my *mamujaan,* or maternal uncle who shared his bed with me. I was born in 1946, one of India's midnight's children. It was a time of great turmoil.

From the time I became politically conscious, I remember feeling resentful about being born in India. Why could I, too, not be born in Uganda, at least in East Africa, like everyone I knew? I would try and hide this fact, but without lying outright. Whenever someone asked, where were you born, I had a practiced answer: "My parents were born in Tanzania. My grandparents came from India in the late nineteenth century on my mother's side and early twentieth century on my father's. I was five years old when we came to Masaka from Dar." No one was vigilant enough to spot the missing time and ask, But where exactly were you born?

My first opportunity to visit the Gujarat region came in December 2008, when a Mumbai-based photographer friend, Ketaki Sheth, asked me to write an introduction to her photo collection of sidis, or Africans in India, and offered to take me on an extended tour of sidi villages and town settlements.[1] The whole experience was a revelation for me. Sidis had come from Africa and were making a future in India. I was born in an Indian-descended community, intent on making a future in East Africa. The sidis had been in India for hundreds of years, some almost a millennium. I could not count more than three generations in Africa. The sidis in Gujarat spoke Gujarati with grandmothers speaking a smattering of Kiswahili. The Bayindi, or Asians of Uganda, spoke an Indian language at home, and an African language in the marketplace. The dukawalla spoke Luganda, and my family, like many others who did not have a duka, spoke Kiswahili. The only people I knew who spoke Kiswahili as their mother tongue, along with a smattering of an Indian language, always with a Kiswahili accent, were the coastal Bayindi, especially those from Zanzibar, Lamu, Malindi, and smaller towns. The Gujarati we spoke included several Kiswahili words, especially those to do with the kitchen, such as *esowani* (plate), *sufaria* (vessel), *fagio* (broom), and so on. Our cuisine included Kiganda foods, *muhogo* (cassava), *matoke* (plantain), and so on, the latter cooked with Indian spices. And Indian preparations—like samosas, *ganthia* (fried cornflour), and chapati (wheat bread)—were on sale in local markets.

Upwardly Mobile

My parents left Mumbai for Dar es Salaam in 1947. Then, in search of better times, we moved to Masaka, Uganda, in 1950 and from there to Kampala in 1952, well before Kamya's 1958 boycott. My father had convinced our distant uncle, Habib Mama, to bring him to the head office in Kampala. Suddenly, the fancy title of ginnery manager gave way to a mundane one: accounts clerk. The so-called head office was halfway down Nakivubo Road, a block away from a smelly open sewage channel that divided the city in two. On that same road, about a hundred yards from his headquarters, Habib Mama had built a block of flats.

No architect had been hired to design this venture. When the block was built and we moved into a flat on the second floor, we realized its two bedrooms had no access to sunshine. Habib Mama went for another ad hoc fix: a hole from the roof to the ground floor. Now, everyone got sunshine but the problem with the fix was that it also let in water. Whenever it rained we had to close all doors and block the gap between the door and the floor with towels, dish cloths, or just cardboard or paper. While we managed to block out rainwater, most of it made its way to the first floor, where residents would form a human chain, filling buckets with rainwater and emptying them on the street outside. Across the street was the Thief Market, where local authorities guaranteed immunity to anyone selling stolen goods, so long as the sale took place within the premises of the market. Many a story was told of goings on within the Thief Market. My favorite was of a smartly dressed fellow who walked to a stall selling motor parts and told the owner he was looking for two Peugeot 403 front-wheel hub caps, which had just been stolen. The stall owner inquired if it was for the car in front. In no time, the attendant produced two hub caps. Pleased to have saved on the transaction, the car owner paid and left, only to realize later that he had paid for his remaining two hubcaps.

My father only earned three hundred shillings a month (about forty dollars at the current exchange rate of seven shillings to a dollar) from his clerical job. His meager salary could provide the children with minimal "luxuries" like a Sunday slice of cake from a bakery and a 35-cent small-size Coca-Cola, which had been introduced in the mid-fifties. What sustained him was a lifelong devotion to writing poetry and editing a Gujarati-language publication, *Manzil* (destination), as a community service, the community being the East Africa–wide Khoja Ithnaashri jammat.

My father struck "gold," as he would have put it, when he met an Afghani owner of an auction mart. The auction mart had gone broke, and was itself about to be auctioned. The owner was looking for someone with cash to cover the debt in exchange for 50 percent ownership. My father, who had saved eight thousand shillings over the years, jumped at the opportunity. Freed from Habib Mama's tight grip, he was keen to move out of this "mixed-race," lower-class, slum-like accommodation to an officially designated "Asian Only" residential area. That place turned out to be Madras Gardens. It was one of three Asian residential locations of small bungalows with little front gardens—named Madras Gardens, Delhi Gardens, and Bombay Gardens. We could not afford the rent for a bungalow, so we lived in a flat on the ground floor of a block owned by the Yemeni firm of Fazal Abdallah. Next to us, down a slope, was a small shack with two rooms, occupied by a Hindu widow and her two kids. Behind her, on flat ground, was a more spacious bungalow, occupied by a European man. One day it rained heavily for nearly two days. Water flowed from the street to the widow's house, which was at a lower level. As the water level rose, the widow came out, pleading for help. We all heard her but no one responded. All except one. This was the European neighbor who appeared with gumboots, raincoat, hat, and a big spade in hand. He began to shovel bits of earth to create a kind of a levy to stop water from entering her front room. I was almost ten. For a long time I wondered: What kind of a solidarity was this, which was neither racial nor religious? I had not yet learned to think of the "human."

In another year, we changed accommodation yet again, still in Madras Gardens, but this time up the hill, no longer in a flat. We were now proud residents of a bungalow with its own garden. Our landlord was Mwami Kulubya, the former treasurer of the Buganda government. As soon as I moved to Old Kampala Indian Secondary School, next door, my beat changed, from the "Asian Only" Gardens to Nakulabye, Bakuli, and Mengo, the capital of the old Buganda kingdom, all "mixed race" neighborhoods.

When my parents moved back to Uganda in 1952, they left me with my cousins, uncles, and aunts in our joint family home on Morogoro Road in Dar es Salaam. My formal education had begun there, in Dar es Salaam, where I attended a community-run madrassa, which doubled as a nursery school; I then joined grade 1 in the government-run primary school for Indian children. The three of us cousins, all a year apart, enjoyed healthy competition. The eldest, Zehra, and I were in the same class. Hasina, a year younger, was in a lower class. Zehra always came first in exams; I came in second; and Hasina, a year behind, tied with Zehra for first. I grew up thinking girls were smarter than boys. My aunts complained that I was always quarreling with my two cousin sisters, pulling their tied pigtails. The aunts sensed an opportunity when the grandparents went to Hajj. They got the uncles to buy a ticket, take me to the airport, find the most Asian-looking passenger, who turned out to be an Arab, and ask if he would take me, under his wing, to Entebbe Airport and from there to wherever he was staying in Kampala. My parents had a telephone at home, and my uncle shared the number with this Good Samaritan. He called my parents and said he had a parcel for them from Dar. Surprised, they came to pick up the parcel and found their eldest son. No longer in the same class as cousin Zehra, I discovered the joy of being first in my class.

I went to government-run secular schools wherever my family moved, from Dar es Salaam to Masaka to Kampala. Each school reproduced an administratively imposed racial exclusiveness. Each was officially named an "Indian" school. We paid nominal fees, thirty shillings, the equivalent of four dollars, a month. In return, the school provided us with instruction, and reading and writing materials. At the time of independence, the school name changed as the qualification "Indian" was dropped when a few "African" students were enrolled. Nothing else changed. Racism now joined with other forms of discrimination based on caste and religious sects, all rationalized as tradition. Prosperous business groups, whether organized as castes (Patels, Lohanas) or religious sects (Sikhs, Khoja orders such as Ismailis and Ithnaashris) had their own "community" schools. But all observed the race principle as holy grail. There was a comfortable coexistence between official administration and community tradition. At that time, there was no sign of an insurgent tradition.

During these years, we prayed in temples, mosques, and churches. Hindu temples were earmarked for particular castes and were thus de facto segregated. Muslims were proud to be outside the caste system, formally embracing equality of all believers. In practice, though, Asian mosques were also marked by exclusion, both sectarian and racial. The only meaningful racial inclusion was practiced by Goan churches where Asian and African Catholics prayed together. When it came to high holidays, like the two Eids or *maulidi* (the Prophet's birthday), upper-class Asian Muslims prayed with members of the Baganda landed gentry, their class brethren, in one of two national mosques: either the Kibuli mosque, perched on one of Kampala's original seven hills, where prayers were always led by a member of the Buganda royal family; or the Wandegeya mosque, next to the university, led by prime minister Obote's Muslim cousin, Adoko Nekyon, a member of the new independence-bred political elite.

The 1950s were the heyday of anticolonialism. In 1958, the year of the Augustine Kamya–led boycott of Asian dukas, I was preparing to go to secondary school. The epicenter of the mobilization were rallies in the taxi park in Nakivubo, where all itinerants, workers, or hawkers, whether arriving from the countryside or returning to it, would gather to hear Kamya speak. A parallel mobilization of cotton growers, led by Semakula Mulumba and Ignatius Musazi, called for a boycott of Asian-owned ginneries. It was a time when Indians were fearful, of the present and the future. The Brits would surely go back home to Britain, but where would we go? India had just been partitioned—we were from Gujarat, but as Muslims, we had no connection with our ancestral villages since no family member had been left behind. A few had moved to Pakistan, others elsewhere, maybe to Jamnagar or even to Mumbai. The point was that all had scattered. There was no other home for us, not even in the imagination.

As the tempo of the nationalist movement shifted from direct action in the streets to election-oriented mobilization, Asians found a voice. Some on the educated fringe, university graduates from either Makerere or from the United Kingdom, formed the Uganda Action Group and supported the left wing of the Uganda People's Congress (UPC). Others of the older generation joined moderate sections of either the UPC or the more conservative Democratic Party (DP). In a constituency-based election in a racially segregated city, they would be assured a seat from a majority "Asian" constituency. But by and large, Asians were uncertain of what was to come next.

The biographies of Mohandas Karamchand Gandhi have made the world of early twentieth-century Asian entrepreneurs and activists familiar. Sandwiched between Europeans and Africans, they were stung by their exclusion from European society and its privileges. Think of Gandhi being thrown out of the first-class compartment in Pietermaritzburg and his subsequent mobilization of an Indian-only protest against racial discrimination, in the process making sense of their own petty privileges in the racialized pecking order. So long as whites sought to monopolize political power, wealthy Asians looked for a counterweight, and gave financial support to anticolonial movements, which some of the educated middle-class professionals joined. The center of Asian politics in East Africa was in Kenya. The big Asian names in the world of political mobilization were Makhan Singh, who pioneered the formation of trade unions in colonial Kenya and East Africa; and Pio Gama Pinto, who was among the leading mobilizers associated with the Mau Mau. Neither belonged to the shopkeeping class. In Uganda, Asians organized electorally in response to concessions made by the British following the decade of anticolonial protest. There were two notable exceptions. One was Sugra Visram, the only Asian woman politician who joined the Kabaka Yekka Party and became a member of the Buganda Lukiiko (parliament). The other was Rajat Neogy, a different kind of *muyindi,* one with a literary sensibility, which led him, at age twenty-two on the eve of independence, to found a magazine that combined both literary and political commentary. From the outset, *Transition* declared its independence from the government of the day. It would be a costly self-definition.

An American Education

My parents had never thought of any of their children going to the United States for higher education. I had a good friend, Inayat Malik, who was a year ahead of me. He was the brightest person I knew. And I could not understand why he was working as a junior officer in the American Embassy when he had scored a first (top) grade in his O levels. He explained his family was poor, his father was sick, and they needed the money. I did not agree. I said that he could get a scholarship and send half the money home. He smiled good-naturedly. I knew that would be the end of it all unless I did something about it. I walked to the United States Information Service, then on Bombo Road, combed through their higher education catalogues, and jotted down addresses of as many American universities as I could find listed. Then I began writing, the same letter, each time signing on behalf of Inayat. Along the way, I decided to add my name to his, since I, too, had just passed my O levels with a first grade. When the replies began trickling in, they all said the same thing—that they do not give fellowships to overseas undergraduate students, but that the US government has a program for it. They sent the address to write to. I wrote again on behalf of both of us, and the reply came, inviting us to go to USIS on a fixed date to take the required entrance examination. Both of us passed and were shortlisted for an interview. Inayat did not go, I did. One member of the interviewing team asked me the population of Uganda; I guessed one million. It was seven. They all laughed. They passed off my low level of civic knowledge as characteristic of someone wanting to be an electrical engineer.

It was decades later, in 2021, that I learned from an American member of the selection committee that there had been a more serious reservation in the committee about my candidacy. I had returned to Uganda in 2010 as director of Makerere Institute of Social Research. One evening, I was invited to dinner at an Asian home. Among the guests were the Alikers. Dr. Aliker was a dentist, also a well-known politician from Acholi. Mrs. Aliker was an African American academic administrator who had been the representative of the African American Institute on the Selection Committee. As we meandered lazily through the dinner, she told me the reservation had come from a well-known academic, Professor Senteza Kajubi, who would later become vice chancellor of Makerere University. "Why waste one of twenty-three precious fellowships on a student of Asian descent"? asked Professor Kajubi. "What guarantee do we have he will come back?" Mrs. Aliker recalled saying, "Why would you take your view of a group and stick it as a label on one individual?" As the donor representative on the committee, her voice must have carried weight.

The chance to study engineering in the United States turned out to be my opportunity to opt out of the trajectory I had so far been trapped in. Ugandan secondary schools automatically moved bright students into the science stream and only those with mediocre grades could go into nonscience streams. It was an administrative way of steering smarter brains away from social commitment and political curiosity.

The American system required all undergraduates to take a certain number of elective courses before deciding on a major. I did, and in the process discovered a whole new intellectual world, in the social sciences and the humanities. That year, I changed majors, from engineering to political science, combining it with history, economics, and philosophy. It seemed I had been famished. My world was changing fast.

Toward the end of the 1962–1963 academic year, I began to plan what to do during my first academic summer. My sponsors in the Africa-America Institute thought I should get a summer job, but I had other ideas. I wanted to see the country. Upon arrival in the US, all African students on the program were enrolled in a host families program. My hosts were Jo and Ralph Lloyd, a middle-class family of modest means, with four or five kids, living in Butler, Pennsylvania, about fifty miles from Pittsburgh. They were barely making it, but they would register every year to host an international student. Over the years, I met two other foreign students who came to stay with them, one from Saudi Arabia, the other a graduate student from Uganda. I do not know if Jo and Ralph received supplementary funds to cover their hosting expenses, but I do remember that we all lived on a shoestring. Jo was clearly the family head and Ralph, a good-natured dad who did as he was told. Over Labor Day weekend, just before the fall semester began, we would all go camping in Ole Bull State Park. The high point of each day was the evening campfire where we toasted marshmallows, eating them with chocolate, as we learned and sang country songs like "Ring of Fire" and "Oh Susanna."

That summer of 1964, I decided I would duplicate this experience of "host family" living across the country. I bought a season ticket on Continental Trailways, a bus company that offered a novel program called "ninety-nine days for ninety-nine dollars"—in other words, pay ninety-nine dollars and travel anywhere in the country for up to ninety-nine days. I made an itinerary that went from Pittsburgh to Chicago, Salt Lake City, San Francisco, Los Angeles, Las Vegas, Taos, Dallas, New Orleans, Nashville, and back to Pittsburgh. I contacted the host families program headquarters, I think in Chicago, and sent them the proposed itinerary. They introduced me to a host family in each city. And off I went.

I had heard of Las Vegas as the casino capital of the world. I planned to arrive in Las Vegas in the evening, see a show, play the machines the whole night and leave by the early morning bus. I had set aside forty dollars for the show and the machines. This was for me a high point of the trip. The next day, as the bus moved through New Mexico, my eyes feasted on a landscape like nothing I had ever seen before. Around noon, I approached the driver and asked if he could stop the bus so I could pray; it would take only ten minutes. "What kind of religion is that?" "I am a Muslim." At that point, he turned on the microphone in the bus: "Folks, we have a Muslim with us. He wants us to stop for ten minutes so he can pray. All those who think we should stop, raise your hands." The entire bus raised their hands. He pulled the bus to the roadside. I went out, and the whole bus followed. As I started praying, they formed a circle around me, silent but watching. When I finished, everyone filed back into the bus, satisfied that they had just witnessed a prayer. The journey resumed.

My education continued. During my third year at Pitt, in 1965, a friend and I were walking by the student union. There was a sign advertising a talk on the struggle for civil rights in the South by leaders of the Student Non-Violent Coordinating Committee (SNCC). An announcement followed that buses would be leaving for Montgomery, Alabama, in an hour. All those wishing to demonstrate in solidarity with the civil rights struggle in the South were welcome to board buses. I walked out of the hall and straight onto a bus. We learned and practiced civil rights songs as the buses made their way to Montgomery. As we neared the Mason-Dixon line, one of the organizers announced that they would be coming round to distribute a twenty-dollar bill to each of us. They said the law in Alabama considered anyone with less than twenty dollars in their pocket as a vagrant liable for arrest. The money was not to be spent, but to be carefully kept as protection from arrest.

The experience in Alabama was a turning point in my political development. That night, we slept in a Black church, singing one protest song after another. The next day we went to an open ground where big names from the civil rights struggle, including Martin Luther King, talked of the importance of this struggle, and of waging it with prudence. I noticed King was wearing a suit and was chauffeured in a white Cadillac, and spoke in measured tones, all important symbols of class. Then there was James Forman, in more proletarian gear, speaking in a fiery voice. He said something I will never forget: "If you do not let us sit at the table of democracy, we will blow them legs off." We went from one (Black) school to another, singing the same song in every classroom: "My father was a freedom fighter, I am a freedom son. Which side are you on, boys, which side are you on?" Students would stand up, one row after another, and march behind us. Gradually, we marched to the center of the city. We had been taught methods of nonviolent resistance in the bus: if the police charge, do not run, nor use force. Go down on all fours, place your arms on your head, protect your skull. But when the police did come, they came on horses. We ran, forgetting all about the guidelines. The police pushed us into a cul-de-sac with no exits. Motorcycle police rode from each end in opposite directions. Our only option was to run to the walls of the building, and hug these, arms eagle-spread. We were arrested and taken to jail, one by one, and, as the law says, allowed to make one call. I called the Ugandan ambassador in Washington, DC.

"What are you doing interfering in the internal affairs of a foreign country?"

"This is not a foreign matter. Have you forgotten that we got our independence only a few years ago. This is the same struggle, for freedom."

There was silence at the end of the phone line. That evening we were all released.

Roughly a month after returning from Alabama, two FBI agents knocked on my door, wearing beige raincoats, badges in hand. The FBI—I was thrilled. Just like on television, I thought.

After a few preliminaries, they asked what I thought of Marx. I said I had never met him. Not surprisingly, this Ugandan Muyindi had never heard of Karl Marx. "He's dead."

I said, "I'm sorry, what happened?"

"No, he died long ago."

I wondered why, then, the question. "Why, then, are you asking me?"

They said that Marx believed that the money of rich people should be taken away and distributed to poor people.

I said it sounded like a fine idea!

At that point, they seemed to decide there was little point in continuing the conversation, and they left. That, however, was not the end of the story. I went to the library to look up Marx. Later, I would remind myself: the FBI introduced me to Karl Marx! This was 1965. It would mark my entry point into the civil rights movement. There was a student organization at the university called the Hill Education Project. The Hill referred to the area where poor African American families lived. The project brought together college students like me to mentor a secondary school kid from the neighborhood once a week. The presumption was that we would have something to teach these kids. Very soon I realized I didn't have much to teach this particular kid. The best thing I could do was to take him for a nice meal, and talk over the meal about anything he was interested in. So we used to go to a Lebanese restaurant, Umar Khayyam, in an upscale neighborhood, Shadyside, eat pita bread with hummus and barbecued lamb . . . and talk. I don't know how much it helped him, but it certainly did help me.

The 1960s in the US were an amazing decade, especially culturally. There seemed few limits to the risks you could take and the boundaries you could transgress. Everything was provisional, everything was experimental. It began for me a decade of activism, and I moved seamlessly from civil rights to antiwar mobilization.

In the summer of 1966, I worked as an intern, first at the UN Secretariat, then at the Uganda Mission to the UN, both in New York City. At the UN, I had been assigned to the Office of Public Information. My boss, Mr. Romanov, asked that I write reports on two international conferences, the first a Land Reform Conference in Rome, and the second a disarmament conference, also somewhere in Europe. I wrote the first, handed it to Mr. Romanov, watching closely as he placed it in a filing cabinet. A few weeks later, I gave him the second report. He did the same, as if habitually prompted. Every day, I would open the filing cabinet, each time to find the two reports exactly where he had placed them. I soon realized the chances of anyone reading the reports were remote. The next month, I moved to the Uganda Mission. My job there included writing speeches the ambassador gave in committee meetings; I would sit in the gallery and listen to the speech I had written. Week after week, I witnessed the monotony of these meetings. At any time, half the members were missing; the remaining half would either be dozing or distracted. The only ones in the gallery were junior staff like me. It occurred to me that if I were truly successful, I could end up as an ambassador, delivering a speech written by a younger version of myself who would be sitting and listening to what they had written from the very gallery where I now sat.

I concluded that diplomacy was not really my calling. Determined to radically change course, I applied to Shantiniketan, the ashram founded in colonial times by the Bengali poet and philosopher Rabindranath Tagore. I wanted to study the sitar, the only instrument I had practiced during my vacations in Kampala. I bought myself a ticket on the *Queen Elizabeth,* on what was said to be the ship's farewell voyage. The idea was to work that summer at a camp in the Adirondacks and then board the ship.

My life was soon to take another unexpected turn. I finished the internship in the summer of 1966, graduated from college the following year, and then joined the Fletcher School of Law and Diplomacy at Tufts University. My American roommate was going to Africa for the summer and said I could have his car while he was away. So, off I went in his Mustang to the summer camp, with all my worldly belongings packed in the car, on the way stopping in Harlem to see a friend. When I came back after an hour or so, the car had been burgled. Everything I owned was gone. The thieves had left a police flier under one of the windshield wipers: "Thieves in Harlem are very smart. Please do not leave any belongings in the car." I discovered that Harlem thieves were not only smart; they also had a wicked sense of humor.

Among the stolen goods was my passport. When I got in touch with my most recent employers, the Uganda Mission in New York City, requesting a new passport, I received a terse note: "We have been advised by Immigration in Kampala that your case can only be handled in Uganda." I was sure there must have been some mistake, so I wrote again. The response was even more opaque: "We can neither add to nor subtract from this statement." Much as I tried, I could not get them to say anything more.

But now I had no passport and thus no prospect of a new life anytime soon. Then something happened, which seemed to close all but one option. Those days, every foreigner in the United States was required to register as an alien sometime during the month of January at a post office. Without a passport, I could not register. Soon after, I received a notice from the US Army, requiring me to appear at one of their recruitment centers for a physical, as the bodily exam was then called. Terrified at the prospect of being drafted into the army, even if as a prospective American citizen, I flushed the letter down the toilet. Coming to my senses, I realized that this move would not solve my predicament. I needed a less dramatic and more considered solution. My Somali-Tanzanian friend, Hussein Adam, who was then at Brandeis University, came to my rescue. He wrote to his father-in-law, the Somali Republic's new minister of foreign affairs, and made what he thought was a compelling case: Mahmood is a Pakistani (not true) and a good Muslim (hardly true), and in trouble (true) and needs help (the truest of all). Would Somalia help a fellow Muslim in trouble? In one week, application forms for a Somali passport arrived. That same night, however, fate struck again: there was a coup in Somalia and the government was overthrown. The minister was without a job, and I without prospect of a passport.

In the late 1960s, I decided to apply to graduate schools in the United States, hoping I would get admitted to one and be offered a fellowship. I applied to Harvard University and to the University of California, Berkeley, and was offered a full fellowship at both. I decided to go to Harvard, maybe because the fellowship was a little more generous, maybe because the institution was so prestigious—in spite of the fact that I was deeply in love with UC Berkeley. After all, it was the home of the Free Speech Movement and I could recite from memory many speeches of its charismatic student leader, Mario Savio. It was hard to tell my motivation from this distance. In my very first month at Harvard in 1969, I was invited to a cocktail hour where new students were introduced to faculty and city leaders. One of these was the British Consul in Boston. I told him my story. He invited me to the consulate, saying he could get me a passport with the status of a British Protectorate Person; it would allow me to travel anywhere in the world, except to Britain. How bizarre, I thought, but jumped at this possibility: I would be delighted to have the document, I said, since all I wanted was to go home to Uganda and press my case for return of my citizenship. I stayed at Harvard for three years (1969 to 1972), then went to Uganda for doctoral fieldwork, intending to return to Harvard the following year to complete my five-year fellowship.

Years later, I would reflect on my experience at Harvard and at Dar. At Harvard, I thought, I had spent the most time mobilizing as an activist, for civil rights and against the Vietnam War, even joining a Progressive Labor Party study group and distributing leaflets at early-morning factory shifts, joining the building occupation when the United States invaded Cambodia, and finally, being an active member of the Steering Committee of the Graduate Students Strike. As a Graduate Prize Fellow, I was to be a teaching assistant in my third year, so I joined Professor Karl Deutsch's group of teaching assistants (TAs) for his large undergraduate course, but I resented the curriculum I had to teach. I thought students deserved to have an anti-war curriculum. I figured out a way to take charge of the class and change the curriculum. I had come to realize that as a TA, I would be teaching all tutorials and marking all papers. I asked my students to ignore Professor Deutsch's reading list, and distributed my own. I then asked them to ignore Professor Deutsch's exam while I distributed my own based on my reading list. I proceeded to mark the answers and give out grades. I should have realized—but for some reason never gave thought to it—that at least some students would complain to Professor Deutsch. Some did, but the good professor said nothing. Until the day I went to say goodbye when I was leaving for fieldwork in Uganda. You taught a good course, he said with a smile as he shook my hand and bid me farewell.

I learned the importance of political activism, of linking classroom learning with public mobilization, in the United States and in particular at Harvard. But it would be later, during the six years (1973–1979) when I held my first job at the University of Dar es Salaam, that I would deepen my education with a study of ideas and movements that sought to transform the world over the twentieth century.

In 1972, in the six months after Harvard but before Dar, I had little idea what was awaiting me back home. Armed with a new passport, I prepared to leave for Uganda. There had been a coup in Uganda the year before, and the Obote government had been overthrown. In March 1972, Idi Amin ordered all Israelis to vacate the country. I decided to go anyway, convinced that I had no other option. I arrived in Uganda in July 1972. That same month, Amin announced that all persons of Asian descent would be expelled from the country.

PART I

THE AMIN REGIME *and the* BIRTH *of a* BLACK NATION

3

THE BREAK WITH ISRAEL

The years 1971–1972 presented Uganda with a remarkable set of developments. Idi Amin became president with the support of two powers: Britain and Israel. During his first year, Amin toed the British line, especially when it came to South Africa, calling for "reconciliation" with apartheid. A year later, Amin reversed himself, calling for a determined struggle to rid the world of both apartheid and Zionism. In those two years, Amin carried out three expulsions: first the Israelis, then Ugandan Asians, and then the British.

This chain of events raised two questions. The first: Were these events connected in any way? The international media had a ready explanation: Amin's simple and erratic personality was taken advantage of by astute adventurers like Libya's Colonel Muammar Gaddafi. (More on this later.) And the second question: Why was Amin successful in staying in power for another seven years? If anything, this suggested more than simplicity.

The East African Mutinies

In 1962, the independent state of Uganda had an army of roughly one thousand in a country of seven million people. On the morrow of Uganda's independence from the United Kingdom, Amin was to assume command of the First Battalion, and Shaban Opolot, the commander of the army, took charge of the Second.

Amin became a public figure in political circles following his role in managing what became known as the 1964 army mutiny. Beginning in Tanganyika, the colonial territory ruled by the United Kingdom from 1916 to 1961 and which now forms part of Tanzania, mutinous soldiers demanded higher pay and a faster pace of Africanization of officers. A radical coup in Zanzibar on January 12, 1964, triggered the events leading to a chain of mutinies in the three East African armies of Tanganyika, Uganda, and Kenya. Ugandan colonel John Okello then led the mutinous police, who had similar wage demands, in Zanzibar; the sultan fled, and an estimated ten thousand Arabic-speaking civilians were massacred in the events that came to be known as "the Zanzibar Revolution." A chain of mutinies followed on January 20, less than three weeks later. Quickly after this, on January 22, the mutiny spread to Kenya, and then to Uganda. Almost immediately, the mutineers won pay raises; Africanization of senior ranks followed soon after. News of substantial pay increase was widely covered in the Ugandan press. Soldiers demanded to talk to Prime Minister Obote or to one of his ministers. When Ugandan Minister of Defense Felix Onama, said to be an uncle of Idi Amin, appeared with a police escort, mutinous soldiers roughed up the police and detained the minister. Amin was credited with aborting the mutiny and ensuring stability for the new government.

All three East African countries called on British troops to intervene and restore order. The response to Obote's plea for help came within hours: the First Battalion, the Staffordshire Regiment, and two companies of the Scots Guards, all stationed in neighboring Kenya, landed around midnight on January 24. Having identified and arrested thirty "ringleaders," they left. Amin, who previously had been sent up-country on a recruiting mission by his British commanding officer, Colonel Tillett, returned on January 26 to find that politicians had arrived from Kampala, and informal *barazas* (consultations) were being held, though British officers had been excluded from these. When Amin addressed the soldiers, he was careful both to distance himself from British officers and to remind the men that they would likely lose everything they had won if they did not show discipline. By seven o'clock the morning of January 30, Amin had managed to gather all five hundred men in the barracks on the playing field, promising to teach them how to play rugby. This was Amin's first taste of power.[1] Some thought Amin had a hand in inciting the mutiny. Whatever the case, the course of the mutiny demonstrated that Amin enjoyed the support of soldiers.

There was a telling difference in how each of the three East African countries proceeded to consolidate order once British troops had left. In Tanzania, the ruling party dismissed mutinous soldiers and replaced them with recruits from the party Youth League (TYL), creating a politicized army run by political commissars. A party-dominated army turned out to be the first step in setting up a one-party state. Kenya took the opposite course, calling on British support: a full battalion of British soldiers came to restore order and remained as custodians of that order. Only in Uganda did the soldiers get not only everything they demanded, but also a full amnesty. It was clear to the soldiers that politicians were afraid of them. Sensing the prevailing wind, each political faction in the government went on to woo its pick of commanders. The kabaka cemented relations with the commander of the army, Shaban Opolot, who had recently married into the Buganda Royal House. Obote decided to make Amin the new commander of the 1st Battalion of the Uganda Army (Uganda Rifles). The State House, the official residence of the president of Uganda, gifted Amin with a Mercedes-Benz. Henceforth, he would be a regular on the list of invitees to State House functions. Obote topped this up with the offer of a "royal" bride: betrothal to Mama Nora Aloba Enin of the Royal Oyakiri Langi clan—the same clan which had given refuge to Kabalega, the king of Bunyoro, during the Nubi-led colonization of Bunyoro in the late nineteenth century.

Israel, Uganda, and Amin

Soon after the mutiny, all eyes were on Amin. Obote promoted him one more time, to major, and took him to Israel on his maiden state visit, just a month before independence, leaving him there for paratrooper training.[2] Obote was not the only one grooming Amin. Israel and the United Kingdom had similar ideas. In time, all would find out they had badly misjudged Amin.

Official Israel had little knowledge of Uganda at the time of independence. This knowledge was likely limited to a single historical fact: Uganda was the place the British had proposed as a future home for the Jewish people long before the Balfour Declaration. How abysmal their knowledge of contemporary Uganda was became clear in 1960 when the Israeli Foreign Ministry received a telegram from the Foreign Ministry of Austria that Obote was visiting Austria and would like to come to Israel. The Austrians "recommended a favorable response because they thought he would assume an important position in an independent Uganda." The Israelis obliged. Dr. Arye Oded—then an associate lecturer at Makerere University and, later, part of the staff of the Israeli embassy in Kampala—was asked to accompany the presumed Milton Obote. In Oded's words, this person "spent a week in the country, meeting with leading figures who discussed with him possible cooperation with Uganda in several fields." It is only after he had left for Sweden that "the Foreign Ministry received a telegram from there stating that this individual was not really Obote but an impostor." A great embarrassment for Israel. The real Milton Obote visited Israel September 2, 1962, a month before Uganda's independence.[3]

Israel prioritized relations with Uganda immediately after Uganda's independence, and Uganda reciprocated. Labour Minister Yigal Allon represented Israel at independence celebrations and announced the gift of 150 fellowships for Ugandans to study in Israel. Israel was among the first countries to open an embassy in Uganda. Foreign Minister Golda Meir visited Uganda in September 1963, less than a year after independence. Minister Yigal Allon returned that same month to inaugurate a course for youth leaders. A wide range of development projects were launched, including the Kabale-Ntungamo Road, a housing estate at Bugolobi in the Kampala neighborhood, development of water sources in the semi-arid Karamoja region, roads and an airport in Arua, and a pesticide factory to boot. Major Israeli companies, spearheaded by Solel Boneh, a leading Israeli construction company, followed the state initiative.

The relationship between Amin and Israel began with the paratrooper course Amin took in Israel at Obote's behest in August 1962. Amin never finished the course, but Israel is said to have awarded him a certificate anyway. Thus began an extended relationship between Amin and key Israeli officials, right to the 1971 coup, until Amin precipitously broke relations with Israel later that year. On the Israeli side, the relationship was managed by Colonel Bar-Lev, the First Secretary of the Mission, also its military attaché in charge of setting up a paramilitary police force and training the army and the police.[4]

As the Israeli military presence mushroomed, dozens of advisors came to train Uganda's infantry, parachutists, armored corps, and air force. Uganda bought Israeli Fouga jets, and Israelis trained Ugandan pilots. The first course for Ugandan infantry officers concluded in Israel in July 1963. Intelligence courses were held in both Uganda and Israel; other courses followed in Uganda. On the African continent, Israel's military presence in Uganda was second only to that in Ethiopia.[5] Levi Eshkol, the Israeli prime minister, paid a state visit to Uganda from June 12 to 15, 1966. Clearly, Uganda was high priority on Israel's African list.

The depth of Israeli interest in Uganda goes back to the general policy formulated by Prime Minister David Ben-Gurion in the 1950s known as "the periphery doctrine." According to this doctrine, Israel was to seek strategic partnerships with states bordering the Arab world. Prominent among these were Uganda, Kenya, Iran, and Turkey.[6] Israel's core interest in Uganda had to do with its interest in Sudan. When the Foreign Office in London asked its high commissioner in Kampala to explain why Uganda was so important to Israel, the high commissioner spelled out: "The main Israeli objective here is to ensure that the rebellion in southern Sudan keeps on simmering for as long as conditions require the exploitation of any weakness in the Arab world. They do not want the rebels to win. They want them to keep on fighting."[7]

Amin became critical to Israel because of his key role in managing Uganda's Congo policy and, as a result, its policy with Sudan. This involvement expanded with the growing crisis in Congo. Nearly two years before Uganda's independence, on January 17, 1961, former Congolese prime minister Patrice Lumumba was murdered in a CIA-inspired coup and General Joseph Mobutu overthrew Joseph Kasa-Vubu in 1965 and became president. Obote decided to provide Lumumbist rebels with a bridge to the outside world, and chose Amin to lead Uganda's Congo operation. Amin's brief was to broker peace deals between warring rebel factions, to set up training camps for the Lumumbist rebels, and to help facilitate a barter deal whereby gold and other natural resources would be exchanged for arms.[8]

In 1964, Congolese rebels (*Simbas*) were defeated, many fled across borders into Koboko in Uganda and Yei in South Sudan, and their arms ended up with South Sudan rebels (the *Anyanya*). Of great interest to Israel, Amin played a critical role in this operation and developed his own connections with Anyanya rebels in South Sudan. A three-way relationship developed involving Israel, the Anyanya, and Amin's men in the army. As army chief of staff, Amin had access to military helicopters, which he used to deliver arms and ammunition to the Anyanya in remote locations. Among the pilots who ferried Amin in and out of Congo were two operatives closely connected to Israel: Bob Astles and Rolf Steiner.

Israel, Amin, and the Coup

Following a period in India, Bob Astles had been an ex–royal engineer in Kenya in the colonial days. He left the King's African Rifles (KAR) in 1952 and became an employee of the Public Works Department in Uganda. In an interview with Norman S. Mivambo of *Black Star News,* a New York City investigative newspaper, on July 30, 2006, Astles clarified, "In 1964, I was directed by Dr. Apollo Milton Obote's government to be Amin's pilot during the Congo crisis until my position was taken by Israeli pilots in 1966."[9] One of these pilots was Rolf Steiner, a German mercenary working with Israel. Arrested while trying to reenter Uganda in October 1970, Steiner told Ugandan police that Amin had helped him train Anyanya guerrillas in 1964 and after. The growing friendship between Amin and Anyanya rebels was overseen and blessed by Israel until the 1972 Addis Ababa Agreement, which pulled the rug from under Israeli policy, bringing the first Sudan civil war to an end. It would lead to the break between Amin and Israel.

Meanwhile, as relations between Israel and Amin warmed up, Israel began throwing in perks for Amin, first small, then big. Jaffar Amin says that at one point, in 1966, the Israeli mega-contracting company Solel Boneh built three bungalows on Amin's freehold plot 33/35 Sir Daudi Chwa Road on Mbuya Hill, adjacent to the Mbuya Military Hospital.[10] As relations got cozy, Amin's Israeli patrons gave Amin a Hebrew name, Hagai Ne'eman, meaning "reliable helmsman."[11]

Israel's ambitions in Uganda expanded with the building of a gigantic air strip at Nakasongola on the road from Kampala to Gulu. Unlike the early airport constructed in Arua, the capital of Amin's home district, it was designed to enable as many as six Phantom jets to take off simultaneously. It was not until the Egyptian president and prime minister Gamal Abdel Nasser's funeral in Cairo in 1970 that this elephant in the room came up for discussion. Amin had two fateful meetings around the occasion of the funeral, mainly because he was without the shadowy presence of Obote's security. The first, according to his son, Jaffar Amin, was with an Israeli lady intelligence officer (to which we shall return later). The second was with Crown Prince Faisal of Saudi Arabia. After the first formal meeting, the crown prince requested a more discreet meeting where he raised the question of the massive air strip being built by the Israelis, apparently at a frenzied pace, in the Nakasongola Military Air Base in northern Uganda. This is how Jaffar Amin paraphrased the crown prince's concern: "You call yourself a Muslim, Eid al-Amin, when you as army commander let your land be used for Zionist hegemony over the Arab Muslim nations in Africa and the Middle East? Have you ever sat down and asked yourself why Uganda would need a sixteen-capacity simultaneous takeoff runway, for F4 Phantom jets on your land, if not but to be a southern hemisphere rear base to enable the illegitimate Jewish state to attack Arab Muslim countries from the southern hemisphere? Ask yourself sincerely," the crown prince continued.[12] Uganda had no financial clout and only miniscule Israeli Fouga jets and bombers.[13] The mismatch between Uganda's needs and the new facility being constructed by the

Israelis was obvious. Amin listened. The *London Times* asked the same question, but only after Israel's expulsion from Uganda: "What is it needed for? Perhaps for the Phantoms to attack Egypt?"[14] It seems the matter was shelved for later, a year after the coup, when, disappointed with his relations with Israel and Britain, Amin would look for other possibilities.

Relations between Amin and Obote soured after Amin was accused of going into hiding following the 1969 assassination attempt on Obote. When Nasser died the next year, Obote canceled Uganda's independence celebrations, which coincided with the day of Nasser's funeral, October 9. Obote asked Amin to represent him at Nasser's burial in Cairo, which turned out to be an opportunity for both sides—Obote and Israel—to forge new plans. Obote took advantage of Amin's absence to make new appointments to the army high command, appointing Brigadier Suleiman Hussein as army commander and Lieutenant-Colonel David Oyite-Ojok as quartermaster general. But the plan also meant that Amin would be present in Cairo without the shadow of Obote's state security. It was a welcome opportunity for Israeli intelligence to consolidate plans with Amin. Jaffar writes in his unpublished family memoir that after the funeral service, as he strolled to his official hotel residence, Amin was "cordially accosted by an enchanting Mediterranean lady of unspecified origin." She had arrived to cover Nasser's funeral as one of the New York–based press corps. She requested a private meeting, saying she had an urgent message for Amin from Colonel Baruch Bar-Lev. Amin invited her to dinner. She related that Obote was busy rearranging high ranks of the military structure and that Amin should immediately return to Uganda but not through the direct route to Entebbe, for his life was in danger. The agent said Obote was intending to charge Amin with the murder of Brigadier General Pierino Okoya and embezzlement of funds from Ministry of Defense coffers, citing information unearthed by Ugandan economist and politician Aggrey Awori.[15] Colonel Bar-Lev advised that Amin head for the northern Ugandan air base of Gulu, which had the strongest presence of Israeli trainers. The story is no doubt embellished, but in the main it is in accord with other narratives of the events.

An alternative version of this story comes from an American academic, Helen Epstein, in the *New Yorker*. Epstein cites the Israeli military historian, Yehuda Ofer. In this account, there is no "enchanting Mediterranean lady"; instead it is Amin who calls Bar-Lev from Cairo, worried that he would be arrested on return to Uganda.[16] In both stories, Bar-Lev furnishes Amin with a way forward, advising, really commanding, that Amin head for the northern Ugandan air base of Gulu, with its strong presence of Israeli trainers. Amin's DC-4 landed in Gulu and continued from there to Entebbe, but without Amin, who stayed in Gulu to get a briefing from Israeli military instructors. From then on, the Israeli team would guide his every movement in the country.

When the pilot of the DC-4 returned to Entebbe, he was surprised by the heavily armed presence on the tarmac. Amin, he told them, had stayed behind to inspect the facility at the Gulu air base. When Amin did finally touch down at Entebbe, he was welcomed by his loyal assistant, Captain Mustafa Adrisi, and escorted with a heavy convoy to Kampala. Pretending to be suffering from rheumatoid pains, Amin was transported in a wheelchair to the president's office.

Bar-Lev returned to Uganda on December 20 to lead the plot to overthrow Obote, according to Jaffar Amin, but Obote had his own plan, having flown to Singapore on January 24. The head of the General Service Unit, Akena Adoko, flew to London the same day. A series of fumbles undid the Obote plan. Adoko's message to Oyite-Ojok to arrest Amin was intercepted by a Kakwa officer. Around the same time, Amin was tipped off by a woman friend working in the President's Office.[17] The Amin coup was preemptive.

A story in the Israeli paper *Ha'aretz*, published after the 1976 Entebbe raid, threw further light on the subject: "Col. Bar-Lev, who headed the delegation and is still on good terms with Amin, said that Amin had approached him, saying that his loyal supporters were outside Kampala and that the President would be able to arrest and kill him before they could rescue him. Bar-Lev advised Amin to bring to Kampala those soldiers who were from the same tribe as Amin, and to make sure he had paratroopers, tanks and jeeps. So equipped, explained Bar-Lev, 600 men could overpower 5,000. *These forces, which had been trained by the Israelis, played a key role in the defeat of the Obote army*" (my emphasis).[18] So ended Bar-Lev's remarks to *Ha'aretz*.

In the literature there are two versions of the coup. One stresses the internal processes, the other focuses on external involvement. Rather than see them as alternatives, it is better to put them together for a more comprehensive and complete understanding of what happened.

The internal view is gathered from interviews with former soldiers, mainly recorded by the 1986 Uganda Commission of Inquiry into Violations of Human

Rights set up by the incoming Museveni government. Thomas Lowman, now a historian at University of Cambridge, has put together a narrative based on these interviews: Former soldiers have stressed that the coup was initially a mutiny, instigated in response to rumours of Amin's impending arrest, and driven unilaterally by a small group of low-ranking soldiers who feared what would happen to them if Amin was removed.[19] The first to raise the alarm on Idi Amin's impending arrest was Sergeant Major Adan Musa, who then "rallied a small number of officers to his defence at the crucial Malire Mechanised Regiment." Having armed themselves after breaking into the armory and securing "several armoured personnel carriers (APCs)," they overpowered and disarmed their senior officers. The Malire Regiment then proceeded to "capture the key institutions of government overnight in Kampala and Entebbe." Around that same time, other barracks were taken over: the takeover of Jinja barracks was led by Brigadier Charles Arube, and the military police barracks at Makindye were placed under the control of Brigadier Hussein Marella, the newly installed head of Uganda's military police, after its takeover. Isaac Maliyamungu captured Entebbe Airport with an armored personnel carrier (APC).[20] Born in Congo, Maliyamungu had become one of Amin's most trusted officers and was held responsible for large-scale killing of civilians and soldiers during periods of instability.

This "internal" account focuses on individual leaders and locations and says little or nothing of any communication or coordination between mutinous units in these barracks. It says where the mutiny began and where it spread, but there is no mention of a coordinating or command center. It also suggests that it is only after the takeover that "Amin and other senior officers were contacted, presented with a fait accompli, and brought in to help develop a plan of further action."[21]

The Coup and Mass Murders in Barracks

It was widely assumed in East Africa at the time that the coup was conceived, planned, and executed by the British. But that assumption was strongly challenged when British Foreign Office (FO) files were opened after the thirty-year secrecy rule. The files included correspondence between the Foreign Office in London and its high commissioner in Kampala. The correspondence suggested the honor belonged to the Israelis. Based on a study of telegrams between the FO and the high commissioner, Richard Bowden wrote in *The Independent*

(London): "The first telegrams to London from the British High Commissioner in Kampala, Richard Slater, show a man shocked and bewildered by the coup. . . . He found the Israeli colonel with Amin. They had spent the morning of the coup together."

Indeed, the high commissioner appeared to have no clue as to what was going on as the coup unfolded. According to a story in *The Monitor* (Kampala), based on a reading of the same official telegrams, Bar-Lev explained to the British high commissioner that "Amin's plan" had been "to let Obote return and then shoot him at the airport together with a number of those who had gone to meet him. This plan was abandoned [more likely vetoed by the Israelis] because of the difficulty of synchronizing it with the liquidation of pro-Obote elements in the army."[22]

Slater's next telegram, according to Bowden, cites the authority of Colonel Bar-Lev: "In the course of last night General Amin caused to be arrested all officers in the armed forces sympathetic to Obote. . . . Amin is now firmly in control of all elements of [the] army which controls vital points in Uganda. . . . The Israeli defence attaché discounts any possibility of moves against Amin." Slater continued: "The Israelis moved quickly to consolidate the coup. In the following days, Bar-Lev was in constant contact with Amin and giving him advice."[23]

Thomas Lowman has gone through hundreds and hundreds of pages of testimony before the Uganda Commission of Inquiry into Violations of Human Rights to chart the contours of the large-scale massacres that followed over a year: from hundreds of Luo-speaking captives at Ogwec Corner in Lamwo District on the northern border with Sudan (April 17, 1971) to the massacre at Simba battalion in Mbarara, carried out by soldiers transported from other barracks (June 1971); then at Moroto, Jinja, and Magamaga (July 11, 1971); and, finally, the massacres at Mutukula on the Tanzania border following the transport of at least six hundred prisoners from Luzira prison on the outskirts of Kampala (January 1972). These were connected developments, a response to the perception that Luo-speaking soldiers would represent "a potential threat, be that as deserters, informers, or counter-coup plotters. It is often suggested that foreign advisors to Amin in this period cautioned him of exactly this." Who drew these conclusions and made sure the lessons were applied across the board? At the 1986 Commission hearings, a civilian resident in the area, Mr. Machimino Ochen, said he witnessed a helicopter landing by the school bringing "three Africans and one white man."[24] Was the "white man" in this testimony British, Israeli, or otherwise? Whatever his identity, he is unlikely to have been a solitary adventurer.

All this is totally consistent with another hypothesis—that the British were most likely involved in high-level planning of the coup. The FO telegrams make clear that the British strategy was twofold: "Avoid being seen as too close to the Israelis in Uganda while increasing contact in Tel Aviv." Meanwhile, UK Prime Minister Edward Heath sounded clairvoyant at the Commonwealth conference in Singapore, warning some that they were unlikely to return to the comforts of home.

As events unfolded, Bar-Lev took on the role of giver of life and death. In one telegram, Slater says Bar-Lev told him that "the police chief, Erinayo Oryema, was being chased by Amin soldiers and took refuge in Bar-Lev's residence . . . that he persuaded Oryema to surrender and persuaded Amin to forgive him and include him in the new regime." Oryema became the new Minister of Internal Affairs. The FO exulted in London: "We now have a thoroughly pro-Western setup in Uganda of which we should take prompt advantage. Amin needs our help."[25]

The next morning, crowds danced in the streets of Kampala. Prominent among them were traders, both Baganda and Asian, relieved to see the last of Obote, in their eyes a centralizing and nationalizing despot. And behind them were the smiling faces of Israeli and British military officers and diplomats. All would have an opportunity in the not-too-distant future to rethink events and reflect on the part they had played in the changeover.

Amin's first cabinet was made up of professionals, not soldiers. Lowman identifies two strong influences "who put together Amin's first civilian cabinet in February 1971. Some say Wanume Kibedi. Others suggest Israelis had a strong hand in it."[26] It is widely believed that it was put together by the British ambassador. The only exception was Lieutenant-Colonel E. A. T. Obitre-Gama, who was brought in on February 8, two weeks after the coup, to take charge of internal affairs. He was an Israeli appointee.[27] According to Aggrey Awori, the Israeli ambassador sat in on all preliminary cabinet meetings.[28] If so, his presence was never recorded in the official minutes. Uppermost in Amin's mind was the question of regime survival. A large section of the country's army was across its borders, in Tanzania and Sudan, taking orders from Obote. He had, after all, played a key role in realizing Israel's plans in both Uganda and Sudan. That Amin turned to Israel in his hour of need should not be surprising.

Reversing Gears: Peaceful Coexistence with South Africa

Having come to power with the support of Britain and Israel, Amin continued to follow their lead in international affairs. The most important was his support of Britain's efforts to normalize relations with South Africa. In a direct reversal of Obote's militant stance, Amin said he would not withdraw from the Commonwealth if Britain resumed arms sales to South Africa, and that "those vehemently opposed to British policy first address their internal problems and give priority to putting their own house in order." Amin's turnaround faced opposition in the Cabinet, which resolved "that Uganda reject apartheid policy in stronger terms" and "take a firm stand on non-alignment."[29] Amin modified his stand to say that "he would have to study the minutes of the Commonwealth meeting first." He proposed to the Cabinet that "Uganda send a ten-person fact-finding committee composed of members from outside the cabinet" to visit South Africa and submit a report on conditions there.[30]

Amin's first overseas trip was to Israel. According to a European eyewitness, there were so many Israelis to see Amin off at Entebbe when he left for Tel Aviv that hardly any Black faces could be seen. An Israeli officer was then in charge of Amin's personal security.[31] Amin had urgent matters on mind, especially regarding the regime's survival. When he met with Prime Minister Golda Meir, he asked Israel to supply Uganda with a few Phantom jets. After all, he had the airstrip to launch them. Meir asked why. For action against Tanzania, Amin responded. *Why,* persisted Meir. There are multiple constructions of the exchange that followed, most based on recall. *The Economist Intelligence Unit* wrote that Amin wanted an outlet to the sea, in Tanga, northern Tanzania, across the Kenyan border. The Hungarian-born journalist Judith Listowel says Golda Meir advised him to negotiate this with the East African Community. Amin was incredulous. Obote and his military were already gathered in Tanzania and Sudan, ready to remove him from office. Obote had the overt support of President Julius Nyerere of Tanzania; how was Amin to appeal to the same Nyerere, who had refused to recognize his regime? What Amin needed were "aircraft to bring Nyerere to his senses, and he wanted Israel to supply them."[32] Instead, Israel gifted Amin an executive jet and promised to sell the new government arms worth a million dollars.

Humiliated but not humbled, Amin changed his plans and asked the pilot of his Israeli executive jet to fly him to London that July 11, 1971. He meant to put these aircraft demands to the British; surely, they owed him a favor. That Amin was coming to London without prior notice or even an announced agenda came as a surprise to the British. They decided to arrange a reception at Buckingham Palace as the first item on Amin's agenda. The queen was briefed to ask Amin the purpose of his visit, which she did over lunch. Amin responded, without missing a beat, that he had come to London to shop: "A pair of size 14 boots and a Scottish pipe major to teach my chaps to play the bagpipes." Amin could be quick-witted. The queen laughed. The next day, the Foreign Office came to realize that their customer was not as naive as they had presumed. At dinner, Amin let Prime Minister Edward Heath and the foreign secretary, Alec Douglas-Home, know that he wanted Hawker-Harrier and Rapier jets, and armored cars with ground-to-air missiles, but the Brits declined. Instead, the foreign secretary offered to sell Saracen and Saladin armored cars at 1.5 million sterling, and training for fifty officers, along with civil aid of ten million sterling, which would be administered by Britain.[33]

Would this be the end of the road for him? Amin made a third unscheduled stop, in Cairo. Anticipating that the Israelis and the British might not prove receptive to his demands, and recalling his conversation with the Saudi crown prince at Nasser's funeral, Amin had sent his education minister, Abu Mayanja, to Cairo with a message for the Egyptian president, Anwar Sadat. While in London, Amin received a telegram from Egypt asking him to stop in Cairo on the way back.[34] And, in Cairo, Sadat advised him to see Gaddafi in Tripoli. Gaddafi offered him support in return for a favor.

Gaddafi's "favor" was related to the question of South Sudan and the widening rift it had created in the government of Gaafar Nimeiry, leading to a Communist Party–led coup in Sudan in July 1971. Gaddafi had played a key part in foiling that attempt. He now wanted to take a further step to solve the South Sudan conflict. Would Amin play an active role in convincing Anyanya rebels in South Sudan to sign on to a north-south reconciliation in the country, in return for the Sudanese government closing Obote's training camps and dispatching his soldiers out of the country? The agreement was signed at a conference in the Ethiopian capital of Addis Ababa, when Emperor Haile Selassie declared the Israeli advisor to the Anyanya delegation persona non grata. In the resulting agreement, Obote's soldiers were removed from their training camps in Owiny Kibul and moved to a camp at Handeni in Tanzania. The Sudanese also wanted Uganda to host many of the former rebels from the South, and Amin was happy to incorporate them into the Ugandan army, especially given that a significant part of his army had just fled with Obote.

Amin's turnaround came, according to his son, Jaffar, in 1971. Amin was "upset the British can give all arms to South Africa but only Saladin [armored cars], etc. to him." According to Jaffar Amin, the idea to expel, first the Israelis, and then Asians with British passports, was discussed over two days, February 13–14, 1972, in a dual communiqué between Gaddafi and Amin. They discussed both the agenda and Gaddafi's offer of forty million dollars. "Amin and Gaddafi did not talk shop like Nyerere (president of Tanzania) and Kaunda (then president of Zambia), but were about action—Amin stood for nonalignment, he was obsessed with Tito and Sukarno." The ideas were fleshed out in Kampala in an all-night meeting with Athio Lorika (Labor), Naburi (his brother), and Oboth Ofumbi (a member of the Cabinet). "The dream business was metaphysical—but they spent the whole night talking the technicality of expulsion. My uncle (Wanume Kibedi) was very good at explaining."[35]

With the Owiny Kibul camp in Sudan closed, Amin agreed to visit Khartoum. The Israelis were no doubt displeased. At the same time, Sadat wanted Amin to visit Cairo. Amin stopped in Cairo on his way to West Germany, and from Cairo flew to Tripoli for a twenty-four-hour stopover, extending his trip to include a flight to Fort Lamy (in Chad) to negotiate with President François Tombalbaye through an interpreter. It was another small favor for Gaddafi. Amin had turned around his entire foreign policy. Gaddafi and Amin issued a joint communiqué on February 14, 1972: "The two Heads of State undertook to conduct themselves according to the precepts of Islam, and assured their support to the Arab peoples in their struggle against Zionism and imperialism for the liberation of confiscated lands and for the right of the Palestinian people to return to their land and homes by all means." In another foreign policy reversal, the communiqué went on to demand that "Britain should end the white minority rule in Rhodesia to enable the people of Zimbabwe to have a full share in the rule of their own country."[36] Two weeks later, on February 28, Uganda and Libya signed an agreement on economic and cultural cooperation.

Brokered by Gaddafi, the Addis Ababa Agreement was signed on March 17, 1972. It proved to be a turning point in the relationship between Sudan and Uganda on the one hand, and Uganda and Israel on the other. Within a month, all Israeli military instructors were thrown out of Uganda. All arms deals with Israel were canceled, and all civilian construction by Israeli companies, including at Arua Airport, were stopped. On March 23, 1972, Israel announced that it had decided to repatriate all Israeli military experts in Uganda. Amin replied the same day by ordering all Israeli military instructors with his land forces to leave. Charging them with "subversive activities," he told Israeli intelligence personnel to "pack and go back to Israel as soon as possible." There followed a series of quick decisions: all arms orders were canceled on March 25; Israeli personnel and Israeli companies were asked to leave on March 27; the embassy was closed on March 30; and Israeli citizens, all 470 of them, including children and wives, left Uganda on April 8. When a PLO delegation visited Kampala on July 6, Amin housed them in the Israeli ambassador's former residence.[37]

In November 1972, King Faisal, no longer crown prince, paid a state visit to Uganda.[38] It would be his only trip to Africa south of the Sahara. It is during that visit that the king promised to build a grand mosque on Museum Hill, where Frederick Lugard, the soldier-administrator who had pioneered British colonization of Uganda, had built his fort. To make up for the loss of the Israeli executive jet, the king gifted Amin a Gulfstream II. From here on, Israel would look for ways to effect a regime change in Uganda. Amin, meanwhile, seemed bent on executing a mission. Having cut ties with Israel, he turned to Britain, the colonial power, first to Asians, who he considered a vestige of the British presence, and then to Britain itself.

4

THE ASIAN QUESTION

After the fall of the Amin regime in 1979, I returned to Uganda as an intern with the All Africa Conference of Churches, a Nairobi-based ecumenical Christian alliance, and was given an office at the Church of Uganda establishment in Mengo. The following year, I joined Makerere University. At both places, I asked those I met to share their thoughts about the 1972 expulsion. Most were troubled not by the decision to expel the Asians, but by the way it had been carried out. This was the beginning of wisdom for me. Ten years later, I put the same question to my Asian friends, former neighbors and schoolmates, living in Kampala or London. To my surprise, more than 90 percent said they would not want to return to the years before Amin ordered them out: like the "indigenous" Ugandans I'd been questioning since 1980, they too had nothing against the expulsion.

The situation that most Asians, whether Ugandans or not, did not want to return to had its origin in the colonial period. Postcolonial governments seemed content to build on this foundation. Its essentials include both the colonial model of governance and the colonial definition of citizenship. The outlines of this form of governance took clear shape once the colony had been "pacified" in the period after World War I. This system of rule turned on two main forms of discrimination: the first was based on race, the second on tribe. Race discrimination distinguished natives from non-natives, whereas tribal discrimination divided natives in each local authority, distinguishing migrants from those indigenous to each district. Race discrimination was written into civil law, the positive law of the colonial state; ethnic (tribal) discrimination was written into a version of customary law, presumed a time-honored cultural legacy of the land. This version of customary law was transcribed with a strong colonial hand.

Both forms of discrimination were written into the 1962 Constitution, under which the country became independent; and the 1967 Constitution, which was introduced by Obote when he abolished kingdoms. All discrimination was "prohibited" in the opening section of the Constitution which paid allegiance to universal values, including human rights.[1] At the same time, the Constitution permitted both forms of discrimination under particular circumstances and on exceptional grounds.[2] These exceptions were defined as "affirmative action" when it came to race-based legislation, and "customary right" in relations between tribes. Whether under civic law or customary law, indigeneity became the overriding justification of discrimination under colonial law.

The language of "protection" of Africans from Indians had been a part of colonial rhetoric from as early as 1938. The 1938 Trading Ordinance was enacted "with the effect of restricting Indians to urban centers ostensibly to 'protect' Africans from Asian competition in the countryside." "Restricting Indians to urban areas while Africans stayed on their 'ancestral land' ensured the separation of two colonial subjects," writes the Makerere historian Godfrey Asiimwe. He concludes that "this projected undertones of Africans as 'victims' of Indians rather than the colonial system itself"; as a result, "indirect rule constructed Indians as 'aliens' [and] thus laid ground for the Indian citizenship question in Uganda."[3]

The colonial government responded to the 1958 boycott of Bayindi shops with a policy known as "Africanization." It called for a race-based affirmative action program where preference was given to "Africans"—that is, Black Africans—as a race. The alternative to racial justice would have been class-based social justice for all needy persons who had been "subjects" of the British Crown. In both cases, the beneficiaries would have been "Africans," but the impact on public policy would have been radically different.

"Africanization" was based on a couple of assumptions: first, that the colonial government had historically meted out injustice to "Africans"; and, second, it was the Bayindi—and not government—who should make amends for this original injustice. Thus, Article 29 of the 1962 Constitution distinguished two categories of citizens, African and Asian, specifying that only African citizens could own land, property, or business in areas designated "development areas." This would later clear the way for legislation canceling residence permits, trading licenses, and labor permits for "non-Africans," whether citizens or not. In a final move on the eve of colonialism, the British had set up "Asians" for "African" revenge.

The Constitutions of Uganda, 1962 and 1967

Uganda had two different sets of conditions for those who became citizens at independence. Only people of Asian descent who had applied for, and been granted, Ugandan nationality were required to "renounce their previous nationality in the presence of a magistrate and two witnesses within ninety days of applying for Uganda nationality."[4] This made little sense for Asians born in Uganda. For what was their "previous nationality"? After all, there was no Ugandan citizenship before colonialism. All residents of Uganda, regardless of race or ethnicity, were subjects of the British Crown. What then was the rationale for having different sets of regulations for African and Asian residents of the country? Few were aware of this provision; even fewer followed it. According to Judith Listowel, the biographer of Idi Amin, "on the basis of this regulation all Asian members of parliament were not Ugandan citizens."[5]

The Asian response to racially exclusive legislation was to press for citizenship, and to call for equal rights for all citizens. The demand for citizenship came mainly from those who realized that, at a time when citizenship was fast becoming a prerequisite for acquiring trading licenses or work permits, they were unlikely to keep their jobs or their businesses unless they were citizens. The issue of passports became rapidly politicized. As the postindependence decade came to a close, two demands—one for equal rights, the other for racial justice—began to sound more as alternatives than as complementary. Was the Asian demand for citizenship—that is, equal political rights—a way to resist a call for racial justice? Or had the failure to distinguish between social justice and racial justice politicized citizenship, eventually leading to a demand for a racialized citizenship that excluded Asians?

The 1962 Constitution and its successor, the "Republican" Constitution of 1967, specified two possible circumstances for those seeking Ugandan citizenship: birth or registration. These categories really distinguished between two kinds of citizens: "indigenous" and "non-indigenous." Citizenship by birth required proof of "African descent": at least one of your parents had to be born in Uganda.[6] Given that most Asian immigration had occurred in the period after World War I—even after World War II—no more than 5 to 10 percent of Asian residents of Uganda were likely to qualify under this provision. Their only option was to become citizens by "registration." Rather than a right, this was a privilege that the state could grant—and withdraw—at will. Bayindi were advised to exercise this option within two years of independence and renounce their presumed right to British citizenship within that same period. Here was a second unwarranted presumption in law: since all residents of the colony were subjects of the colonial power, why presume that only Asians became "dual citizens" at independence? A similar argument was made by J. B. Kakooza in an article in *Sunday Vision* on the fortieth anniversary of the expulsion.[7]

However, citizenship by registration ceased to be a meaningful path for Asians, for the very reason that it was more a privilege granted by the state than a right conceded by it. For those who had applied for, and been granted Ugandan nationality, there was the additional requirement that they "renounce(d) their previous nationality in the presence of a magistrate and two witnesses within ninety days of applying for Uganda nationality." Though many had applied for citizenship, government officials processed no more than a few applications.

I, too, seemed to belong to this category, which is why when I applied to the Uganda Mission to the UN in New York for a replacement of my passport, in 1966–1967, I was told that I was no longer considered a citizen of Uganda since I had not followed required procedure and renounced my "right" to a British passport. It did not matter that I had been granted a scholarship to the United States on the presumption that I was a citizen of Uganda. I was not given a chance to renounce my presumed right to a British passport on turning twenty-one. As I soon learned, the British did not think I had any such right. As a result, I became a stateless person. When I returned to Uganda in 1979, after the Amin regime, I applied for my citizenship to be reinstated. The Ministry of Internal Affairs informed me that I first needed to follow provisions of the law and renounce my previous nationality "in the presence of a magistrate and two witnesses." (By then, the British Consul in Boston had issued me with a British Protected Person passport.) When I proceeded to renounce it, I was informed by the Immigration Office that to be valid this renunciation had to be at the British High Commission and acknowledged by them. So off I went to the High Commission, who seemed both alarmed and amused by this request. They told me they had plenty of applications from those seeking to become British citizens, but none from anyone seeking to renounce it. We have no forms for that, the secretary declared. She said they would write London for the appropriate forms and get back to me. Eventually the forms arrived. When I did fill and return the appropriate form, the High Commission staff informed me that I would have six months to rescind my renunciation just in case I had not been of sound mind when first making it. Surely, the white secretary seemed to be saying that no one in their right mind would renounce British citizenship! My case illustrated that migrants could not be easily slotted into the binary category, citizen / noncitizen (foreigner), making them easy targets in a two-way contest between two states—in this case, Britain and Uganda.

Asian holders of British passports soon became victims of a pincer movement. On the one hand, newly independent governments of East Africa were reluctant to grant them the right to citizenship. On the other, British legislation began to distinguish between holders of British passports on racial grounds, introducing legislation that would erode constitutional rights of non-white citizens in a step-by-step fashion. The distinction had guided Britain's negotiations with governments of East Africa—the so-called Lancaster House constitutional talks—in which Britain worked out separate deals for Asian citizens of the United Kingdom. Key to this was an arrangement between Duncan Sandys, the then–UK colonial secretary, and Jomo Kenyatta, the president of independent Kenya: Britain acknowledged that "British passport-holding Asians were a British responsibility"; and Kenyatta undertook to "gradually squeeze out non-Kenya Asian citizen[s] instead of expelling them en masse."[8] All involved were moving to identify citizenship with indigeneity or race.

Soon, Britain began introducing legislation, first in 1968 and then in 1971, compromising the liberal notion of a single and equal citizenship and at the same time formalizing ancestral descent as a criterion for full citizenship. The 1968 Commonwealth Immigrant Act specifically targeted non-white British citizens who were not resident or born in Britain. It severed the connection between British nationality and right of entry into Britain. Hitherto presumed to be a right of all British nationals, the right of entry was now qualified on the basis of race, depriving some 1.5 million non-white British citizens from various former colonies around the world—Africa, the Caribbean, South Asia, and Southeast Asia—from an automatic right of entry into Britain.[9]

The law violated several existing legislations considered the hallmark of "civilized" behavior in the post–World War II period. Among these was Article 3(2) of the Fourth Protocol of European Convention on Human Rights, which stipulated that "no one shall be deprived of the right to enter his own country." Similarly, Article 5(d) of the International Convention on Racial Discrimination provided that a person carried the right "to return to his country," and further stipulated that this right should be held "without distinction as to race."[10]

Britain no longer had a single and uniform citizenship after 1968. Though those affected by the 1968 and subsequent legislations remained British nationals, they no longer possessed core rights of British citizenship. In creating race-based citizenship laws that bestowed different categories of British nationals with different rights, it followed earlier precedents set by Nazi Germany, where the Nuremberg laws distinguished between two categories of citizens: Germans and Jews. Earlier, nineteenth-century United States had created separate laws for whites and for different categories of non-whites. In post-1968 Britain, race-based citizenship legislation created a new class of disenfranchised nationals who had legally been rendered stateless, even if described and classified as British subjects, nationals, or citizens. Among these were South Asian citizens of the United Kingdom and colonies resident in Uganda. In their case, expulsion would follow disenfranchisement; the two were part of a single connected process. In response to British legislation, first Kenya, then Uganda, passed two acts; in both cases, the Trade Licensing Act (1968) and then the Immigration Act (1970) targeted South Asian noncitizens. As a result, several thousand Ugandan residents of South Asian descent, previously British citizens, "became in reality stateless, though they continued to be described as British citizens."

Disenfranchising an entire group went alongside individual exceptions. The exceptions came under the voucher system. The UK Home Office created 1,500 "special vouchers" per year for entry into Britain. These could be given to South Asian "heads of household" who were "under the most immediate pressure to leave East Africa." Whether male or female, such a "head of household" had the right to bring their dependents with them. The relationship between the group disenfranchisement and the individualized voucher system was like that between war and the Red Cross; the latter could address only a small percentage of the victims of the former.

To get an idea of the number of Asians affected, we need to look at official Ugandan figures. The Asian Census of October 12, 1971, recorded 26,657 Ugandan citizens of South Asian descent.[11] There were, in addition, an estimated 6,000 residents who were Indian and Pakistani citizens. Though Ian Sanjay Patel writes that the remaining 40,000 or so Ugandan Asians had "a

British status of some sort, either British Protected Persons or British citizens," I am doubtful of this claim.[12] Only those of a certain socioeconomic status and those with a need to travel abroad would have applied for a passport and acquired an official "British status of some sort" in the period before independence. Those lacking a need to travel outside the country had no passport. They were British subjects before independence, who seemed to have no determinate status after independence, and it is difficult to know their numbers. Of these, upwards of 10,000 had applied to become Ugandan citizens by registration after independence. In September 1972, Richard Slater, the British High Commissioner in Kampala, wrote the Foreign Office in London that "from about mid-1965 the Ugandan government [had] approved virtually no applications for Uganda citizenship on behalf of Asians," sometimes refusing even to "take delivery of applications."[13]

"Refugees" vs. "Belongers." After 1968, the British state and bureaucracy began to distinguish between two categories of British nationals resident outside the United Kingdom: whites with an automatic right of entry into the United Kingdom, and non-whites without such a right. The latter, persons of color, were now officially designated United Kingdom passport holders (UKPHs). The bureaucracy developed a terminology to distinguish the UKPHs from their white counterparts in colonies like South Africa or Hong Kong: they were known as "belongers." The Asian expulsion showed that, in a moment of crisis, the position of UKPHs could rapidly deteriorate to that of "refugees" who could hope for little more than charity.

Only three days after Amin's expulsion order, Foreign Secretary Alec Douglas-Home declared in the House of Commons that his government "accept a special obligation for these people" whom he estimated as "some 57,000 British citizens in Uganda."[14] According to Douglas-Home, that responsibility was humanitarian, not legal. The posturing allowed Her Majesty's Government to maintain the moral high ground. Edward Heath, then prime minister, would later write in his memoirs that Ugandan South Asians were "unfortunate people" whom Britain "had a moral duty to accept" as a "civilized nation."[15] The Home Office was more direct. T. Fitzgerald, a Home Office official, wrote to C. P. Scott at the Foreign and Commonwealth Office in August 1972 that "it seems preferable to accept the UKPHs from Uganda on the basis that they are 'refugees,' *whether or not they are technically refugees.*"[16] It is "the framing of Ugandan South

Asians with British nationality as refugees," writes Ian Sanjay Patel, that "allowed Edward Heath's government to set up a Uganda Resettlement Board, designed to ensure the 'orderly' reception of Ugandan South Asians" as refugees, the objective being to disperse them "as widely as possible throughout the country." Based on collaboration between the Home Office, the Department of Environment, and the Ministry of Defense (MoD), the board proceeded to resettle Ugandan Asians in sixteen rural locations, "from Devon to Warwickshire, Kent to Lincolnshire, and Dorset to Gwynedd." According to its final report, these resettlement centers housed 21,987 people, the idea being "to keep the new migrants far away from urban centers, both on arrival and in the future."[17] If British colonial directives in Uganda had sought to keep Indians in urban areas, this same government wanted to limit Asian settlement in urban areas when it came to Britain.

In Uganda, the UK High Commission accorded separate and privileged treatment to white "belongers." Both Amin and the Ugandan authorities understood this. As early as September 17, looking to put pressure on the British government to speed up the evacuation process, Ugandan authorities ordered the detention of eighty white Britons resident in Uganda, calculating that it was the arrest of "belongers"—and not of UKPHs—that would force British authorities to act with speed. They were right. It took no more than five days for the British High Commission to speed up the process, after which all "belongers" were released.

There were an estimated 7,000 white British in Uganda, mostly teachers and "volunteers" financed by the Official Development Assistance (ODA). That same September, British authorities drew up contingency plans for their evacuation. These included the use of military force, should it become necessary.[18] By the time Amin declared in December that some 3,000 British "belongers," too, would have to leave, they had already "been surreptitiously airlifted out of Uganda."[19]

This sharp difference in the official treatment of non-white UKPHs and white "belongers" did not escape the scrutiny of the Uganda Mission to the UN in New York. In a document it circulated to members of the General Assembly, the Mission cited Harold Wilson's Commonwealth Immigrants Act of 1968 as precedent for Amin's 1972 expulsion order. The 1968 Act, it claimed, was "a racist device put in the way of British people of black and brown races," but not "those British citizens whose parents and grandparents were from the British

Isles." "Why," it asked, "should a white Briton from South Africa, Zimbabwe or Hong Kong be able to [go to] Britain any time he wishes while his counterpart from Asia is refused [permission and] frustrated when he tries to gain entry?"[20]

The objective of British policy in the days after the 1972 expulsion was to get the international community, especially the West, to accept that British passport–holding Ugandan Asians were in reality refugees, and Britain should be acknowledged as a "civilized" and benign patron exercising a "humanitarian" obligation. Once successful, Britain was able to get other states, mostly Western ones, to join this "humanitarian" mission. Classified as "stateless persons" under UN protection, British passport–holding Asians were soon settled in a number of countries: Canada (2,160), the United States (1,620), and Sweden (344), among others.[21]

The Homeless

By the time of the 1972 expulsion, thousands of Asians had applied for Ugandan passports, but their applications had not been processed. The government refused to release figures, but estimates ranged from 12,000 to 30,000. Britain too was unwilling to acknowledge any obligation to honor the rights of Asians with British passports. What resulted was a deepening social tragedy. With more and more Asians lacking official permission to work or trade, there was an explosion in the numbers of those unable to afford decent housing. Initially, these Asians began to move into religious sanctuaries—temples, gurdwaras, and mosques—and then overflowed into cheap one-room lodgings in slum communities like Kisenyi. Initially in the hundreds, their numbers grew rapidly over time. Their plight became widely known, to both community leaders and to government officials, both Ugandan and British, charged with overseeing their fate and welfare. A few responded with empathy.

The Lea Kidnapping. By 1970, the numbers of stateless Asians had grown rapidly, and their plight worsened visibly. Three persons in particular were familiar with their predicament and were deeply moved by it. The first was B. A. Lea, first secretary and passport officer at the British High Commission in Kampala, in charge of issuing visas. The second was Bob Astles, who had been in the British Army in India in an earlier life, but had been retired for openly sympathizing with Indian nationalists during the colonial period. He had moved to

Kenya and then to Uganda, married a Muganda woman and become close to Baganda royal circles, reinventing himself as an intelligence officer, first with the Obote and then with the Amin government. Astles wrote his memoirs with the specific instruction that they be published only after his death. They were serialized in the Kampala-based paper *The Monitor.* Both Lea and Astles were intimately familiar with the issue and were deeply sympathetic with the growing plight of Asians. In Astles's words, these people were "frightened." Finally, the third figure was A. G. Patel, the Asian mayor of Kampala.

The political class in Uganda believed that all Asians were unpatriotic, with no more than an opportunistic interest in being Uganda citizens, and were responsible for the dilemma in which they now found themselves. Having looked into the issue in some detail, Astles was convinced otherwise. He wrote in his memoirs: "Immediately after independence, in 1962/3, well over 30,000 Asians and other nationalities submitted papers for citizenship. . . . Nothing, absolutely nothing, was done about those applications except to bundle them up and pile them into cupboards in the immigration department where they stayed until I personally pulled them all out to examine the evidence when the Asian issue erupted again after Amin came to power." Already, in 1970, these Asians "were now living in ghettos often as many as 14 to a room in conditions similar to wartime concentration camps." He summed up their predicament: "not Ugandan citizens because their applications had not been processed; not able to find work of any type because they had no work permit; driven from their shops by Augustine Kamya's boycott years before; without hope since Britain was taking only a few each year by quota." Astles concluded: "There is no question, but that the great majority wanted to remain part of the Uganda they loved. By far the greatest number wanted to stay in Uganda where they had been born and that was their only home."[22] Caught in a cross fire between Britain and Uganda, the Asians' situation was aggravated by the indifference of India (and Pakistan), both claiming that the matter was a British legal responsibility. Meanwhile, they were rapidly becoming impoverished.

The other person familiar with this unfolding tragedy was B. A. Lea. Unlike most British diplomats, whom Astles believed to be racist, Lea was different. In Astles's words, Lea "mixed with the Asians as the officer responsible for operating the British quota system and they must have come to see him as their champion. Whatever the reason, he was drawn into an incident that startled the world when it woke up one morning to see the headlines in the newspapers; 'British Diplomat Kidnapped in Uganda.'"

Astles found himself in charge of investigating the Lea Affair. He had already been in touch with youth at the weekend camp he ran on the beach some miles from Entebbe, and had been informed that fishermen were talking of "a white man stranded on an island and that his canoe had been found wrecked on a beach close to their camp after a storm." Astles then approached Mohammed Hassan, the head of Criminal Investigations Department (CID), also an Asian, to join him in the search for Lea. Together, they located the canoe in which the party had traveled, and then the camp with a well-constructed grass hut, but there was no one in sight. Meanwhile, the British government also initiated independent action. In London, the Secretary of State for Foreign and Commonwealth Affairs told parliament that the prime minister had spoken to the Ugandan president and agreed that Britain would send a security expert from the Foreign and Commonwealth Office to establish continuous liaison between the High Commissioner in Kampala and relevant Ugandan authorities. For their part, the Ugandan government instituted an official inquiry headed by a white judge of British origin—no doubt as a confidence-building measure.

The kidnapping story turned out to be bogus. According to the counsel for the investigators, "the kidnapping had been planned by Mr. Lea to highlight the plight of British Asians in Uganda who could not obtain entry visas to Britain." A detective superintendent, Festus Wauyo, told the six-week official inquiry that the police had received testimony that Mr. Lea had been complicit in the whole affair: the "kidnapping" had been planned by Mr. Lea, with the involvement of three British Asians: B. L. Rao, P. V. Gosai, and Shafique Ahmed. Asians talked of Lea as someone championing their cause. At the same time, "they did not trust the Asian lawyer who had formed a committee to look into the plight of those stranded in Uganda." This person was "found not to be a qualified lawyer, but to have been a police officer in his native India. He had come into Uganda with experience of police law and his deceased uncle's law certificate, cleverly altered, which he had hung on his office wall."

It became clear that the British government was determined to shame and discredit Mr. Lea. Toward this purpose, Britain used the testimony of Lea's wife, Jeanne, who testified that her husband had confessed to her that he was ashamed of his relationship with a Black woman on the island. Mr. Lea corroborated her testimony: "My wife is speaking the truth. There was no sexual intercourse, but it got very near it." Every effort was made to portray Lea as a man of weak character, out to have a good time. Witnesses were produced toward that end. Soon, some fishermen, and others, testified that Lea spent the two days on

Nkunzi Island in Lake Victoria "happy and free" with his "kidnappers." The counsel for the inquiry said that Mr. Lea was "basking in the sun on a lush island on a frolic of his own." According to the *New York Times,* "The inquiry also heard testimony that a party with four Black women took place on the island on Mr. Lea's first visit."[23] Asked to take sick leave in England with his wife and two daughters, Mr. Lea said he would appeal. The British Foreign and Commonwealth Office announced that he had been asked to resign "in the light of certain facts" about his conduct.

Justice Robert Gordon Russell, who headed the official inquiry, pontificated that Mr. Lea's motives were mixed—that he "secretly sympathized with the Asian cause," speculating that it may "also win him some personal reward." The judge went on to cast aspersions on Mr. Lea's character, declaring that he was "a man of a weak and unstable but emotional character who most imprudently became associated with Asians." He concluded thus: "It is difficult to sort out the facts from fiction. The only conclusion I can arrive at is that a plan was conceived by Mr. Rao to stage what would appear to be a spectacular kidnapping with a view to focusing world attention on the plight of the Asians in Uganda with British passports who were aggrieved at being denied entry to Britain." *The Times* of London chimed in: "The real truth behind the Lea affair may never be known. What is virtually certain is that Lea will return from Uganda a broken man."[24] For its part, the British government hoped to have restored discipline among those of its functionaries who may be tempted to go native.

The remarkable thing was that no one was ever tried for the kidnapping, and the matter was quickly dropped. President Obote advised Richard Slater, the British high commissioner, to arrange for Lea to be quietly recalled to London. According to Astles, "behind it all was the appalling situation of the Asians which no one wanted to publicize." The Ugandan authorities had no intention of giving them citizenship, without which they could not obtain permits to work, and the British did not want to expose the Ugandans because it would risk exposing their own hypocrisy. Only Lea, the officer responsible for the issuance of permits for permanent residence in Britain, was "fully aware of their terrible condition and was known to want to do something to help them," in the words of Astles.

The mayor of Kampala, A. G. Patel, a Ugandan-born Asian barrister, sympathized with Lea and described him to Astles as "a hero." "Patel had scrutinized hundreds of those applications for Ugandan citizenship and knew that they were not being processed by the Ugandan government," wrote Astles. "He said to me, 'Bob, all of you are going to be in trouble if you try to solve this case. My Asians are not going to get Ugandan citizenship and Britain does not want the boat rocked and to have them flooding into their country. Keep out of it. Lea is an honest and brave man, but we have to bury him; we shall do so with honours.'"[25] Even with Lea out of the way, the social tragedy he had tried to highlight did not go away; it exploded into a political crisis.

5

PRELUDE TO THE EXPULSION

By the time Amin took power in 1971, the situation in Uganda did not differ substantially from that in the neighboring former British colonies of Kenya and Tanzania. In all three countries, citizenship laws distinguished between "indigenous" and "non-indigenous" residents. Post-1968 British legislation distinguished "belongers" from "UKPHs" and affected Asians in all former British colonies in East Africa. There was at first a trickle, then a flow, of British passport holders (UKPHs) from all three countries to Britain and elsewhere. But only in Uganda—and not Tanzania or Kenya—was there an expulsion of all Asians. The reason was mainly internal.

It was only in Uganda that a native elite grew parallel to and in contention with the Asian business class. The origins of this elite lay in the circumstances of the British colonization of Buganda in the late nineteenth century. By the time Britain entered the region, the kingdom of Buganda had begun to expand, having developed a standing army and a civil administration. As Buganda absorbed adjacent territories, it sought to build alliances against its dominant neighbor, the kingdom of Bunyoro-Kitara. The British would play a key part in shaping the outcome: first they intervened in Buganda in a civil war between three factions—Muslim followers of Kabaka Mwanga, followers of French (Catholic) missionaries, and followers of English (Protestant) missionaries—tipping the scales in favor of the Protestant party. Then the British roped the Protestant party into drafting most of Buganda's adult population into military service and set about subduing Bunyoro-Kitara. When Bunyoro-Kitara was defeated, a third of its territory was transferred to the Buganda monarchy as a reward for collaboration. At the same time, eight thousand square miles of the kingdom's land were distributed as a freehold to Protestant notaries, laying the groundwork for a land aristocracy. With the conquest of Bunyoro-Kitara accomplished, the Baganda were demilitarized; at the same time, agents were posted from the kingdom to newly subjugated territories with orders from the British to organize a Buganda-style hierarchical administration. Following official agreements with Buganda and with other kingdoms in the south, all of which were required to accept British "protection," the country was legally defined as a "protectorate" and not a colony.

Amin and the "Asian Problem"

At the outset of the colonial period, the British had experimented with a plantation model in Uganda, giving large land grants to ex–British soldiers who turned them into rubber plantations. The experiment plummeted into crisis following the crash in rubber prices after World War I, and the plantations were auctioned. The buyers were wealthy Indian merchants, the Mehta and the Madhvani families, who replaced rubber, an export crop, with sugar for domestic consumption. After World War II, they became conglomerates with holdings in engineering and manufacturing in towns like Kakira (also known as Madhvani-nagar or Madhvani town), and Lugazi (under the dominance of the Mehta family). Like American sugar magnates in prerevolutionary Cuba, each town bore a family imprint.

More than in neighboring Kenya or Tanzania, there were two elites in Uganda in contention: one a native landed elite, the other an immigrant merchant elite. When the country became independent, the new government developed political bases outside Buganda, in the north, the east, and the west. To counter power play with a strong Baganda middle class of landlords and bureaucrats, Obote's government built an alliance with the Asian merchant and manufacturing class. Before 1971, there was little to endear Amin to the Baganda, whether the elite or the common people. Amin had led the charge on the kabaka's palace (Lubiri), from both the ground and the air, earning him the title of "Butcher of Lubiri." Two successive events reversed Amin's fortunes. The first was Amin's overthrow of Obote's "northern" government in 1971. The second was his public resolve to "solve" the "Asian problem," which had grown in public significance since the 1958 trade boycott. Both developments cemented his alliance with the Baganda.

Soon after the 1971 coup, Amin began a critical engagement with the leadership of the Asian community in the town of Fort Portal. These were his "bad Indians." Amin accused Asians of deliberately keeping a social distance from the African majority: "In some of the towns where I have addressed rallies, I found Europeans with us but not Indians. And yet the numbers of the Indian community in Uganda is larger than that of any other people. . . . The only feeling—bad feeling—inside all Africa, all Black Africa, to Indians is because you cut your community off completely. You do not cooperate or join together with Africans in social activities either here, or in Nairobi, or in any place. I want you to cooperate in social activities with your African brothers and sisters. My aim is to unite Uganda." Amin claimed that his aim was not to alienate Asians, and certainly not to promote hate toward them: "It is good for you that somebody like me should be as frank with you as I am, as a leader. I tell you, it will help you for your future. I do not want you to take it that I hate you. I do not." He concluded with a warning: "The small minority of Asians cannot be allowed to rule Uganda the way 250,000 whites are ruling five million Africans in Rhodesia."[1]

On October 17, 1971, Amin ordered a special census of all Asians, whatever their nationality.[2] An Asian Only census had been proposed by Obote a year before, in September 1970. During his January 1971 visit to London, Amin continued Obote's discussions with the British, raising the question of British passport–holding Asians. The British response to Amin was the same as to Obote: to hold off on the Asian question.[3] Amin followed by implementing the rudiments of the plan that had earlier been conceived by Obote. Though the Asian residents of Uganda were its immediate target, the plan was to be carried out with minimum injury to them. From Amin's point of view, the plan's targets were more the British than the Asians.

Amin then called two separate meetings in Kampala with leaders of the Indian community. Representation in these meetings was based on residence, and not caste or communal grouping, as had been the colonial custom. The Asian community prepared a separate memorandum for each meeting.

The First Memorandum was presented on December 7. Its framers stated "that the conference would mark a new era in race relations in Uganda."[4] In so saying, they had already accepted the framing of Asian-African relations as relations between two races, not between citizens with different histories. Then followed a list of "Asian" grievances about long delays in processing citizenship applications, and legal discrimination against Asians in trade and employment.

Amin's speech rehearsed every key argument on the "Asian Question," starting with how Asians received preferential treatment during the colonial period. He went on to compliment the Madhvani and Mehta families for their contribution to commercial and industrial life, and on their expansion of educational and medical facilities. He paid tribute to those serving in government, and then stated, "But, and this is a big but, there are several disturbing matters which I now want to put before you frankly as, indeed, is the purpose of the conference."[5] First among these was the practice of social segregation, which Amin claimed had persisted among Asians for generations. The proof lay in one fact: that, even after generations in Uganda, interracial marriage was a rare phenomenon. "It is particularly painful that about seventy years have passed since the first Asians came to Uganda, but, despite the length of time, the Asian community has continued to live in a world of its own to the extent that the Africans in this country have, for example, hardly been able to marry Asian girls. A casual count of African males who are married to Asian girls in Uganda shows only about six such couples. And even then, all the six married these women when they were abroad and not here in Uganda. The matter becomes even more serious when attempts by Africans within Uganda to fall in love and marry Asian girls have in one or two cases even resulted in the Asian girls committing suicide when it was discovered by their parents that they were in love and intended to marry Africans." This meeting of Indian leaders chose to discuss the question of social apartheid in the narrowest of possible ways: was not Amin calling for forced intermarriages, in the fashion of the Abeid Karume–led revolutionary government in Zanzibar? Their understanding was that there were only two options: social apartheid or forced integration. Not surprisingly, they failed to address the challenge.

Amin responded on December 8, shifting focus to political issues, starting with an absence of loyalty to the country: "Between 1962 and 1968, the government sponsored 417 Asians for training as engineers. Today, however, only 20 of the 417 Asians work for the government." He went on to give more statistics. During that same period, the government had sponsored 217 Asians to train as doctors, and 96 as lawyers. But only 15 doctors and 18 lawyers were serving the government. Even those who went into government service were unwilling to serve outside main towns; "those transferred from urban centers—Kampala, Jinja, Entebbe, Mbale—more often than not resigned from government service."

Next on Amin's list of "Asian malpractices" were smuggling, hoarding, renting of front rooms to Africans, unfair competition in trade, evasion of income tax by keeping two sets of books, and bribes to government officials. As the "economic war"—Amin's name for the Asian expulsion of 1972—continued and the results turned out to be different from what had been expected, the regime instituted courts to combat high prices alongside scarcities, which it defined as "economic crimes." There was a growing public acknowledgment that some of these malpractices were characteristic of traders as a class and may have little to do with "Asians" as a race. He then returned to the question of social apartness. "Many Asians refer to Africans who they employ as laborers and servants, or maids, as black monkeys." Amin asked that they embrace their share of responsibility: "It is you yourselves, through your refusal to integrate with the Africans in this country, who have created this feeling toward you by the Africans." He called on these "Asian leaders" to take the initiative and spell out practical steps to address complaints against the community.

Time passed before Asian representatives drafted the memorandum Amin had asked for—a list of concrete steps to improve the situation. The Second Memorandum was delivered at a meeting between Indian leaders and General Amin on January 4, 1972.[6] Its basic premise was that the community was small. It was looking forward to cooperating with the government but the direction of future change in Uganda would have to be defined by government policy: "May we at the outset point out that the small minority of the Asians in Uganda lacks the constitutional authority or organizational resources, by itself to bring about major economic and social changes that appear necessary at the present time. Inevitably the Government with the power and the organization at its disposal must take the initiative and direct the course of changes in Uganda." Ugandan Asians loudly and clearly denied that Asians had any responsibility either in making or solving "the Asian problem."

However, those same Asians were used to taking credit for the "development" of East Africa. Decades later, Vali Jamal would write a self-congratulatory email to (mostly) Ugandan Asians admonishing them for not taking public credit for their contribution to East Africa: "We are a unique community. We built East Africa, but were too engrossed in providing for everyday survival and not too aware that we were doing something unique to keep notes."[7] Even public leaders as farsighted as Manzoor Moghal of Masaka would in his memoirs repeat the same fable about Asian contribution: "The Asians were the first to teach Africans the art of commercial trade."[8] In reality, regional trade, including over the Indian Ocean, had been going on for centuries if not over a millennium; among the major traders were the Wanyamwezi, the Waswahili, and the Baganda. The reason the British were keen to promote Indian trade in their colonies was not because there were no local traders; rather, their strategic purpose was to reorient trade in the new colonies from its traditional routes to empire-based commercial circuits.

Social isolation had been a hallmark of caste-ridden South Asian lives in the Indian subcontinent. Most Asian youths in my secondary school went on to have "arranged" marriages. Families made the choice of partners, within bounds of caste and religion, and undoubtedly race; their progeny followed. Few breached these conventions, which were backed up by social and religious sanctions. Among the few was Akbar Thobani, the only other Asian (beside myself) in the airlift of twenty-six students to the United States at independence. Akbar returned from the United States in 1972 with an African American bride. It was the same year I returned. There was by then a radical difference in our lifestyles. I was living with my family in the upscale neighborhood of Kololo. Akbar and his wife lived with his aging parents in Bakuli, the down-scale, mixed-race neighborhood next to my old secondary school. When Akbar and his wife would take a walk near Bakuli market, hardly any passersby, Asian or African, believed they were a married couple. All assumed theirs was a commercial transaction. Insults were plentiful, including shouts of "malaya!" (prostitute). The marriage could not withstand the strain. The last I heard, they had returned to the United States and, soon after, divorced.

Before he closed the meeting, Amin informed his audience that all applications for citizenship, ranging from 12,000 to 30,0000 were considered as "having been automatically cancelled by lapse of time." He closed with the refrain that was recognizably the key point of his speech: "It is you yourselves, through your refusal to integrate with the Africans in this country, who have created this feeling toward you by the Africans."[9] On January 5, 1972, Amin warned thirteen representatives of the Asian community that "Uganda is not an Indian colony." A week later he said he would like to see Ugandans owning businesses on Kampala's main street. On May 9, he instructed the

Minister of Finance to tell the Bank of Uganda to give available money to Africans and not to Asians.[10]

Following a reading of the two memos and the discussion on May 7 and 8, it is difficult not to conclude that the Asian community was sadly wanting for leadership in a moment of crisis. Amin's speech raised the larger question of historical responsibility. Asians may point to the colonial past as having deliberately fostered the segregation between races. But colonialism was over, yet the Asian response seemed not to have changed. In Amin's words, "I am aware that one of the causes of the continuing distant social relations between Asians and the Africans in this country was the policy of the colonial government which ensured that the Africans, Europeans and Asians had entirely separate schools, hospitals, residential quarters, social and sports clubs, even public toilets, with the facilities reserved for the African being of the poorest quality and hopelessly inadequate. We have, of course, changed all this, but there are Asians who still live in the past and consider, like the former colonial government, that the Africans are below them."

Amin was right on one thing: historical facts alone do not absolve anyone from responsibility for their actions. But the history Amin had recounted was incomplete, and thus misleading. It focused on British policy and Asian responses, but it lacked awareness of how the Asian community was sharply divided between a wealthy minority and a majority caught in a squeeze between two governments, British and Ugandan. Amin was aware he was addressing a minority among the Asians, the rich. What he said was highly performative and radically at odds with his remarks in the cabinet the following year when he claimed that the expulsion had "liberated" the poor majority of Asians.

We have seen that when leaders of the Asian community responded, they said little that was new, even if what they said was true. They split the blame between the colonial government and culture (both African and Asian). When it came to the future, they claimed they had no power to shape it: the capacity and responsibility for change lay exclusively with the government.

A defining characteristic of this period was the failure of Ugandan leadership to appreciate the gravity of the predicament the Asian community faced and to find a way out of it. True, Asians were a rich minority, but as a community they needed to invest a lot of resources into creating a set of institutions to correct the past. Some sections of the community—especially the Ismailis, the Goans, and the Sikhs—Amin's "good Asians," had led the way, consciously moving to shed the legacy of institutional racism, deracializing entrance to community-run schools and medical facilities.

The most far-reaching initiatives came from a few individuals. Some took a political approach, like the Uganda Action Group. All had political ambitions: Gurdial Singh became a mayor of Kampala; Shafique Arain, a member of parliament; and Yash Tandon, a university professor who was widely believed to have been one of the authors of Obote's *Common Man's Charter*. They rubbed shoulders with both the new generation of African politicians, like Obote, and with Asian financial magnates like the Madhvanis. In the public eye, they sought to have their proverbial cake and eat it too. Amin looked at them as "the Asian mafia." Others were more original and took greater risks, like the lone female Asian politician Sugra Visram, who participated in Baganda politics and was elected as a member of the Buganda Lukiiko. All were politicians. They focused on mobilizing Asian constituencies and building alliances, often with African leaders. Only one literary figure took on the daring task of organizing and mobilizing those interested in imagining a different future. This was Rajat Neogy.

Rajat Neogy and *Transition:* Imagining a Decolonial Africa

Rajat Neogy was born in Kampala of immigrant Bengali teachers. In 1961, at the age of twenty-two, Rajat launched a radical monthly, *Transition,* a hybrid between a magazine and a journal. Neogy designed *Transition* as an organ for literary and political commentary by writers and scholars, from within Africa and the broader African world. Its ambition would be to craft the outlines of a decolonial Africa. Ngũgĩ wa Thiong'o wrote nearly two decades after Neogy's death in 1995: "He believed in the multicultural and multifaceted character of ideas, and he wanted to provide a space where different ideas could meet, clash, and mutually illuminate. *Transition* became the intellectual forum of the New East Africa, and indeed Africa, the first publisher of some of the leading intellectuals on the continent."[11]

Transition ran for fifty issues, thirty-seven published from Kampala (1961–68) and thirteen published from Accra, Ghana (1971–1974). After Neogy's resignation, the final issues were edited by Wole Soyinka, the first sub-Saharan African Nobel laureate in literature; 10,000 copies were printed each quarter, half read across Africa, the rest outside. By the mid-1960s, *Transition* came to enjoy immense prestige for both its roster of literary figures and its willingness to defy convention. In 1968, the *New York Times* applauded Neogy's initiative: "A questing irreverence breathes out of every issue."[12] Contributors included budding scholars from around the Black world: James Baldwin and Langston Hughes from the United States; Chinua Achebe and Wole Soyinka from Nigeria; Ngũgĩ wa Thiong'o from Kenya; a group of South African writers who were wrestling with apartheid, among them Nadine Gordimer, Ezekiel Mphahlele, Dennis Brutus, and Lewis Nkosi.[13] From the outset, *Transition* also commissioned work from political figures: Julius Nyerere of Tanzania, Tom Mboya of Kenya, and Kenneth Kaunda of Zambia. And it went on to feature remarkable essays—among them Ali Mazrui's "Nkrumah: The Leninist Czar" and "Tanzaphilia," and Paul Theroux's "Tarzan Is an Expatriate" and "Hating the Asians."

A young Kenyan-born scholar, Ali Mazrui had been catapulted from the position of a lecturer to that of a professor a few years after independence. This unusually speedy ascent was a response to two facts. Just as a newly independent country had to have its own flag and national anthem, an African university in a newly independent African country had to have an African professor. That Mazrui was chosen to be that professor pointed to a second fact: he was the best of homegrown timber. Though a beneficiary of nationalism, Mazrui was not dazzled by it. He was, indeed, among the first to recognize the Janus-faced power of nationalism—in particular, its tendency to ride roughshod not only over ethnic and religious minorities, but also over dissidents in the majority.

Mazrui's essay "Nkrumah: The Leninist Czar" did not just aim at far-off targets from a safe distance. He spoke just as critically of the growth of nationalist power and autocracy at home. On the morrow of Idi Amin's 1972 Asian expulsion, Mazrui distributed a signed pamphlet at Makerere University entitled "When Spain Expelled Jews." He did not wait to register his opposition after the event, but voiced it when the risk of doing so was immense.

Mazrui's favorite pastime was to target icons on the intellectual left. The result was a set of debates between Ali Mazrui and Walter Rodney, the Guyanese scholar and political activist, on the role of imperialism in the era of independence and the relationship of intellectuals to nationalism in power. Walter Rodney was best known for *How Europe Underdeveloped Africa,* a book that summed up the past five hundred years of the relationship between Africa and the rising West as an era that laid the foundation of formal colonialism and informal *dependency.* Written in the tradition of the Latin American school of underdevelopment, it presented external constraints on nationalist power. Ali, in contrast, highlighted the internal face of nationalism and its tendency to erode *democracy.*

Mazrui elaborated on this in his essay in *Transition,* entitled "Tanzaphilia: A Diagnosis," in which he defined Tanzaphilia as a disease that afflicted leftist intellectuals, liberal or socialist, expatriate or local. Seduced by the language of socialism, they had come to treat nationalism with soft hands and were invariably caught in the drift to single party rule. "Many of the most prosaic Western pragmatists have been known to acquire that dreamy look under the spell of Tanzania."

Mazrui was not just taking a polemical swipe at his ideological opponents. He distinguished between "ideological conversion" and "intellectual acculturation," and thus between the political and the conceptual: "No amount of radicalism in a Western-trained person can eliminate the Western style of analysis which he acquires. After all, French Marxists are still French in their intellectual style. Ideologically, they may have a lot in common with communist Chinese or communist North Koreans. But in style of reasoning and the idiom of his thought, a French Marxist has more in common with a French liberal than with fellow communists in China and Korea. And that is why a French intellectual who is a Marxist can more easily cease to be a Marxist than he can cease to be a French intellectual." Mazrui brought the point home by focusing on Nyerere: "Applying this to Julius Nyerere, we find that someone like him can more easily cease to be 'pro-Western' than he can cease to be 'Westernized' in his basic intellectual style and mental processes. And it is the latter quality which has often captivated Afrophile Western intellectuals."

This was the background to a series of memorable debates held, first at Makerere and then at Dar es Salaam, between Walter Rodney of the University of Dar es Salaam and Ali Mazrui of Makerere University. Rodney called on intellectuals to join the struggle to consolidate national independence by joining the anti-imperialist struggle. In contrast to Rodney's preoccupation with the external—big power domination—Mazrui called for a focus on the internal, on the struggle for democracy within the newly independent country in an era when a new form of power was consolidating. If Rodney called on intellectuals to rally around the need to consolidate national independence, and thereby realize the unfinished agenda of anti-colonialism, Mazrui called attention to the authoritarian tendencies of nationalism in power. If Rodney focused on the outside of nationalism—how imperial powers tended to constrain national autonomy—Mazrui called attention to the inside: how national powers were beginning to restrict democratic space within newly independent countries. In East Africa, Mazrui emerged as the first critic of nationalism from the standpoint of democracy.

A close second, published in the pages of *Transition,* was Paul Theroux, who wrote the essays "Tarzan Is an Expatriate" and "Hating the Asians." Both were influential essays on the question of race in a post-colony. "Tarzan" was a political reading of comic book characters, Tarzan and Jane, as prototype expatriates: "Tarzan may be gone from the comics; I have no way of knowing. But I do know that he is here, in Africa, in the flesh. I see him every day." Theroux identified white privilege as the defining characteristic of the expatriate: "His color alone makes him distinct. He does not have to lift a finger. . . . The realization that he is white in a black country, and is respected for it, is the turning point in the expatriate's career. He can either forget it or capitalize on it. Most choose the latter." The expatriate is soon ardently dealing in skin and this, "with the death of the mind and the conscious assertion of colour, is the beginning of the true Tarzan Complex." For the expatriate liberal, skin privilege goes alongside a good conscience. "He can hold leftist opinions in a lovely climate. Sub-Saharan Africa is one of these paradises: the old order does not alter, the revolutions change nothing and still to be white is to be right; being British is an added bonus."[14]

With "Hating the Asians," Theroux joined the ongoing public discussion on how politicians were prone to promote the hatred of the Asian minority: "In East Africa nearly everyone hates the Asians. . . . and when the pressure of fashion attracts Asians themselves to slander each other, I begin to worry and think it may be too late to do anything about it except talk."[15] "I also think that the position of the Asian in East Africa today is the result of a collaboration, between outsiders and insiders; almost a conspiracy of Africans and their European apologists, who would very much like to see Africa succeed, even at the expense of a pogrom, a thorough purge of these immigrant peoples."

East African Asians were often compared to Jews in Europe. Theroux argued that the comparison was stretched, but did not entirely dismiss it: "In one respect only do the Asians resemble Jews. Their humor is what is popularly held as Jewish; their self-parody is Jewish, and sometimes their English accents have a vaguely Semitic intonation. But in another sense the humor is that of any minority, Negro, Puerto Rican, West Indian, any group which finds itself at the mercy 'of a prejudiced government.'"

The years after independence, when *Transition* flourished, were times of great optimism, especially among literary and scholarly circles. There was one notable exception, V. S. Naipaul, who spent a year at Makerere University in the late 1960s. Paul Theroux wrote in his obituary note for Rajat: "We all assumed that Uganda would just get better. Naipaul disagreed. The politicians were clearly opportunists and crooks, he said: 'This country will turn back into jungle.'"[16]

Neogy was able to build enduring relationships with leading writers in postindependence Uganda and beyond. In the 32nd issue of *Transition,* there was an article by Uganda's most celebrated literary writer, Okot p'Bitek, author of a Luo-language epic poem *Song of Lawino,* which he had translated into English. He wrote, "The most striking and frightening characteristic of all African governments is this, that without exception all of them are dictatorships." Soon after, p'Bitek was relieved of his duties as director of Uganda's National Cultural Centre. The writing was on the wall.

By opening the pages of *Transition* to opposition figures, Neogy became an official target. This followed government proposals for a third Constitution. *Transition* 32 (1967) also included an article by Abu Mayanja, Member of Parliament (MP) and advocate, warning against the Detention Act—which would allow the government powers to detain individuals based on suspicion rather than evidence presented to the courts—as adding to unchecked concentration of power in the presidency. The government position was defended in the next issue by Akena Adoko, head of State Security, secretary to the Cabinet, and chief advisor to the president. Mayanja then responded with a letter in *Transition* 37 in 1968.[17] President Obote spoke on the matter on October 4 and identified two dangers against the nation—one tribal, the other imperial. The President seemed to be pointing to Mayanja as the tribal danger and Neogy as the imperial danger. Abu Mayanja was arrested at gunpoint on October 8th, and Neogy was arrested on charges of sedition and placed in solitary confinement in Luzira prison by noon time the same day in October.

Four days later, he was stripped of his Ugandan citizenship, on a ruse that could be used—and sometimes was—against dissident Uganda Asians: that he had failed to renounce his "right" to a British passport on becoming a Ugandan citizen.

Neogy and Mayanja were taken to court and charged with sedition. Both the prosecutor, Mr. Hassan, head of the of the Criminal Investigations Directorate (CID), and the chief magistrate, Mohammed Saied, were Asians. The chief magistrate ruled that the passages in question were "not seditious" and acquitted the accused.[18] As soon as they were released, both Neogy and Mayanja were rearrested, and returned to their cells, measuring 5 × 7.5 feet, to continue their already four-month-long detention.

Neogy was released from detention only after Amin's coup in 1971. By then, he was a broken man. He left Uganda for Accra, and then for the United States. On return to Uganda after the overthrow of Obote, Rajat went to see Ali Mazrui and declared his intention to convert to Islam in 1995. Mazrui recounted in his eulogy for Neogy:

> It was a Friday morning when Rajat [Neogy] walked into my office on Makerere Hill. In the course of the conversation he asked if I was "coming to Kibuli mosque" for Friday prayers. I was startled. Rajat's childhood might have been Hindu, and his adulthood was totally secular. Where did the mosque come into it? He abruptly said he would see me at the mosque. And as he was walking out of my office, he said, "It is a submission, not a conversion." It was then that it dawned upon me, almost with a shock, that he planned to join the Islamic faith that day! I was even more shocked when I detected a compelling desire in me to stop him. I of all people—descended from a long line of devout Muslim Ulema, son of the late chief Kadhi of Kenya. Why did I want to close the doors of Islam against Neogy as a new supplicant?[19]

"Rajat did convert to Islam, though under circumstances not known to me," Wole Soyinka reminisced in his eulogy for Neogy:

> And the image of him that continues to linger in my mind? Rajat rolling out his rolled-up goat-skin prayer mat acquired during his encounter with Islam, soon after his release from prison. He had brought it with him from Uganda, the hide of the very ram that was sacrificed

> during his conversion ceremony by the Chief Imam of Kampala, no less. It was a phase I never truly understood, especially as he would impishly remind me that he belonged to the Brahmin caste whenever I asked him what a glass of whisky was doing in the hands of a devout Muslim. Was it not El Amin that he adopted as his Muslim name?[20]

Apparently, Neogy remained a Muslim until the end of his life. His last wife, Djamila Anne McNutt, an American artist who had been a fashion model, reminisced in her obituary note, "I met Rajat Neogy in 1979. I fell in love and became a Muslim. I took the name Djamila. We had two children together, Kamal, 17, and Ayesha, 15."[21]

After Neogy took *Transition* to Accra in Ghana for two years, he resigned and Wole Soyinka became editor in 1973. About three years later, in 1976, it folded for financial reasons. Neogy moved to the United States with his wife at the time. In 1991, *Transition* was revived by Henry Louis Gates, Jr., who brought it to the W. E. B. Du Bois Institute for African and African-American Research at Harvard University, where it continues to be based. For years it was cared for like a hothouse plant, its vision blurred and tamed over time. Deprived of those original challenges that come in the open with fresh air, wind, and storm, it lost originality, and wilted, petal by petal. Neogy moved to San Francisco where he lived in a small hotel. He died alone.

After his death, one of his daughters, Tayu, asked his colleagues and friends from his *Transition* years to pen their reminiscences of Neogy. She shared these with me after her visit to Makerere Institute of Social Research (MISR). Wole Soyinka wrote, "He was a special breed, a budding literary editor—or, more accurately, a literary innovator—and he was engaged in piecing together a unique journal that would both nurture and serve African literature, art and politics."[22]

MISR held a symposium in Neogy's honor in 2019. His daughter Tayu and her two sons traveled from California to represent the family. They carried his ashes in an urn. They said their father's wish was that his ashes be taken to Uganda. Following a solemn ceremony on the grounds of MISR, where the speakers included Norbert Mao, a well-known politician; Robert Kabushenga, the editor of the daily paper *New Vision;* and me as the director of the institute,

Neogy's ashes were scattered in the wind from MISR grounds, to go forth into the wider world. The *New Vision* editor promised to put up a plaque commemorating the occasion, some time in the future, said Robert with a smile.

The Asian Question had reached an impasse. The British government had no intention of taking responsibility for its colonial history, in Uganda or elsewhere. Britain's response to Obote, as to Amin, was to ask each to mark time in the waiting room: as if the mere passage of time would solve the problem. Following the refusal of Israel first, and then Britain, to help rescue him from the danger that Tanzania's support of Obote's forces presented to his own regime, Amin had no choice but to rethink his overall predicament. His solution to the Asian Question would be part of that larger consideration, leading to a triple expulsion—of the Israelis, the Asians, and then the British. The expulsion would consolidate Amin's support in the political and commercial heart of the country, Buganda, among both its people and its commercial and political elite. With their literary son, Neogy, in jail, then in exile, the Asians remained without a voice. They remained captive to a self-aggrandizing business elite, as if awaiting a predestined fate.

6

THE EXPULSION

Time passed and the leaders of the Asian community continued to slumber, calling on the government to take action, which it did, even if the action was not what they had hoped for. Amin's threats to Ugandan Asians had in fact escalated quickly into action. On August 4, 1972, Amin told troops in Tororo, "I am going to ask Britain to take over responsibility for all Asians in Uganda who are holding British passports because they are sabotaging the economy of the country. I want the economy to be in the hands of Ugandan citizens, especially Black Ugandans; I want you troops to help me protect the country from saboteurs. There is no room in Uganda for people who have decided not to take up local citizenship, especially people who are encouraging corruption." The next day, August 5, in a speech on radio commemorating Cooperative Day, Amin gave the British government an ultimatum to remove all Ugandan Asians entitled to British passports—that is, all 80,000 Asians—within three months, by November 8. The British Under-Secretary at the Home Office in London, David Lane, dismissed this possibility in an angry retort: "We are already a crowded island, and immigration must, and will, remain strictly controlled." Uganda's Foreign Minister Wanume Kibedi, Amin's brother-in-law, then in London, told the British press: "Asians must go." Kibedi meant especially those who were not Ugandans, who had decided not to take Ugandan citizenship, but had hoped to stay on year after year; he named them as those who were "making a good living, sending money abroad and preventing our Ugandans—especially Black Africans—from getting ahead in commerce and industry."[1]

Amin kept returning to the theme over the next few weeks, each time bolder and more threatening. In his August 8 pronouncement, he proclaimed, "I am determined to teach Britain a lesson over the Asians." Claiming "divine guidance," he went on: "I had a direction in which God told me to effect the expulsions. Responsibility for the situation rests only with the British government." Meanwhile, the British government began looking for ways of dealing with this unexpected calamity. Among the first proposals was one conveyed by A. A. Ackland of the Foreign and Commonwealth Office to the Prime Minister's Office on December 13, 1972: "Our colleagues have expressed interest in the possibility of settling Asians on a suitable island in the dependent territories. Various possibilities have been examined."[2] Meanwhile, Amin stuck to his guns, telling the Sudanese foreign minister at a luncheon in his honor, "I am willing to sacrifice my life—all I have, all I am, for the good of Uganda."[3]

The British continued to ignore Amin, hoping the unfortunate episode would pass; after all, they had groomed Amin and surely knew him better than he knew himself. Their next move was to send as envoys those who had personally known Amin, to talk to him privately. The first, Lord Rippon, flew to Kampala on December 9, without an appointment, and met a quick rebuff. He was told by officials that Amin had a very tight program and could only give him an appointment a week later, on December 15.[4] Then followed Iain Grahame, Amin's superior officer in the colonial King's African Rifles. Grahame had lived seventeen years in Uganda and spoke fluent Swahili. Amin told Grahame that "his conversation with Geoffrey Rippon had been awful for he had not understood one word of what Rippon had said." No doubt Rippon spoke the Queen's English. According to Grahame, Amin then repeated his firm stand in fluent Swahili.[5] One wonders why Rippon had not had the good sense to come with a Swahili interpreter.

Having already targeted British citizens, Amin now went on to spread the net wider. On August 17, Amin canceled all exemptions for professionals. Next on his list were all noncitizen Asians, even Asian citizens of Tanzania, Kenya, and Uganda. Amin went so far as to ask Kenya and Uganda to send only Black citizens to work in East African Community institutions based in Uganda. On August 19, Amin declared that *all* Asians must leave, asking them to follow a set of requirements: all departing Asians must be flown out by East African Airways; any Asian who receives an exit permit must leave the country within forty-eight hours of their papers being processed; and, finally, departing Asians could leave with fifty British pounds, but no more.[6] First disenfranchised, then expelled, the departing Bayindi were being pauperized step-by-step.

The Cabinet and the Asian Question

Amin's dream was a politician's dream: God is always on our side. But Cabinet minutes show otherwise. The Asian Question was on the agenda of the Cabinet from its very first meeting in 1971, when Amin advised government ministers to avoid seeing Asians informally: "His Excellency the President advised the Minister to avoid, as far as possible, having any private associations with Asians, be they citizens or not, because apart from the fact that Asians, through their traditional practice of social isolationism and tendency to corruption, had partly let down the previous government. He said that if it was necessary that Asians should see a Minister, they should do so at an official level and during official hours. He observed that, by following that advice the new government would live up to its declared policy of leading the country with 'clean hands.'" The Minister of Commerce, Industry, and Tourism, said "the proposal by the previous government to grant citizenship automatically to all those Asians who had applied for it in 1964, but whose applications had not processed through no fault of their own, would be reviewed by the Government of the 2nd Republic of Uganda."[7]

The discussion continued in the second meeting of the Cabinet. One minister proposed that "a careful check be made on those Indians who applied for Ugandan citizenship only to protect their property."[8] Another suggested, "Some of the big Indians should in fact be detained like Ugandan Africans were being detained to make the Indians begin to respect the government."[9] The Cabinet "directed the Minister of Education to ensure even more strictly that in future the number of Indian students entering Makerere was drastically reduced."[10] At the third meeting of the Cabinet on the question of citizenship, a minister said it was "time to undo the dominance of Asians in trade—but [it] should be done carefully to avoid sabotage."[11] In that same meeting, the Cabinet decided to conduct an Asian population census. The Cabinet minutes noted: "It was observed that obtaining Uganda citizenship did not necessarily mean that those who received it had the interest of Uganda at heart. . . . The continued social and economic isolation of the Asian community in Uganda was noted with concern. . . . It should be made publicly known that while the government of the 2nd Republic was in the process of reviewing their citizenship applications the

Asian community should show itself to be ready to blend with the Ugandan African community by e.g., intermarriage and carrying out mutual social and economic activities." That same meeting, the Cabinet decided "that one of the subjects that the proposed Committee should deal with should be that of finding out the up to date figures of the Asians in Uganda."[12] All the while the debate in the Cabinet had been between two points of views: those calling for a phased reduction of Asians in trade, and those claiming that the gradual approach had failed over decades and the only way forward would be a radical approach.

The balance tipped in favor of the "radical" approach at the Cabinet meeting of September 2, 1971, a year before the expulsion was announced. The discussion on "Promotions of Africans in Trade" began with the minister calling for more aggressive action under the Trade Licensing Act of 1969 imposing "restrictions on trading by noncitizens in certain areas."

Although pronounced as a decree, the expulsion order was the outcome of a Cabinet debate for over a year. Cabinet minutes show that both sides, proponents and opponents of radical action, were free to voice their points of view. Critics said that "such action would appear discriminative and racialist. . . . With the present standard of African businessmen," would not "turning out Asians all at once in order to replace them with Africans cause a lot of hardship in the country?" Supporters "stressed that it was high time Uganda took very strong action in introducing and establishing Ugandan Africans in trade. . . . The proposal of the Minister under discussion should be treated as though Uganda were declaring war on Asians in trade . . . that in war some people were prepared to suffer or even to die but then effort must be made and devotion shown toward the cause so as to win the war. . . . For many years Uganda Government had been making laws which were aimed at introducing Africans in towns and in trade but hitherto the Nation had had no success. . . . Now was the time for action, unpopular as that action might prove to some people."

Critics called for a phased implementation of proposals. The proponents of what would later come to be called "the economic war" responded that "a revolutionary proposal" could not be implemented "in phases . . . there was no other way by which Ugandan Africans could be established to take charge of the country's economy except by drastic steps which might be unpopular." The Cabinet went on to adopt the proposal, and appointed a Cabinet Committee "to go into the terms and methods of implementing the policy adopted." Finally, the

Cabinet "directed that the Memorandum should be marked 'Top Secret' and 'Restricted' and be available to Ministers only and those who needed to handle them." The minutes recorded that H. E. General Idi Amin Dada, President of Uganda and head of the military government had been away "on duty" and that the Cabinet meeting had been chaired by the Attorney General.[13] Preparations for what would come to be known as the "economic war" began fully a year before it was publicly declared by Amin.

The Cabinet meeting of August 6, 1972, discussed implementation.[14] Amin opened the meeting. After noting the consensus in the Cabinet around his decision to expel all noncitizen Asians, Amin proposed a few questions: How to proceed? Should the Asians to be expelled be gathered in one place? Should their assets be seized? Should all assets be frozen? What if the United Kingdom refused to accept Asians, shuttlecocking them back to Uganda as had happened to individual deportees in previous years? After noting that these alternatives were meant "to guide the Cabinet discussion," he "appointed the Minister of Power and Communications to chair the meeting while he went for another engagement." As soon as the discussion began, a counterview began to emerge on all options identified by Amin. The counterview held that Asians be left to find their own way to leave. Uganda should not become a "breeding ground for Asians." Should there be exemptions?

Next on the agenda were questions of compensation. Should Asian properties be sold or compensated? After a long discussion, the Cabinet decided (1) "that all Asians who were not Uganda citizens, including students and minors, should be declared *personae-non-gratae* and be given three months notice within which to leave the country"; (2) "that those who failed, for one reason or another, to get out by the expiry of the period of notice would be rounded up by the Ministry of Defence and Internal Affairs and dealt with under the law of the land"; (3) "that non-citizens should not be rounded up and assembled in one place pending their removal but that they should continue to reside in the areas where they had been hitherto"; . . . (7) "that there was no need for compensation to be paid to Asians since Government was not taking over their property, and that Asians who were leaving would make arrangements to sell their premises within the limited period given to them while those who would not have sold their premises by the time of their departure would make their own arrangements with their own lawyers to take over their premises"; (8) that "the Minister of Defence and Internal Affairs [should] verify the citizenship of those Asians who claimed to be Ugandans"; . . . and (10) "that the bank accounts of Asians were frozen to allow the Minister to work out a secure way of preventing the outflow of currency from Uganda by Asians."[15] Meanwhile, the Departed Asians Property Custodian Board (DAPCB) was established as trustee over expropriated properties.

After appropriation came redistribution. There were three sets of contenders: the Baganda economic elite, military officers, and ordinary people. The last group was the first to be ruled out. There would be no free-for-all. The army kept theft of Asian property to a minimum during the expulsion period. The redistribution of expropriated properties was done by committees appointed by the Cabinet or nominated by Amin.[16] Amin laid down minimum guidelines: expulsion should be orderly and humane; a minimum of women public officers should be appointed in committees; and properties in the capital city should be distributed to all—meaning that the list of beneficiaries should reflect the ethnic and religious composition of the country, Kampala being a national asset.

All kinds of committees were created: a central committee to transfer economic power, another to reorganize Uganda, committees to transfer businesses. And there was a plethora of forms: departing Asians had to fill out forms to declare businesses, aspiring African businesspersons had to fill out forms to apply for businesses.[17] Army officers came to dominate committees. The brigadier-commander of the 2nd Infantry Brigade, Major Maliyamungu, was put in charge of "abandoned shops" in Masaka to "ensure the fair distribution of business." Thirty army and air force officers were to work with committees "in checking and distributing to Ugandan businesses which were left by the British Asians."

As the expulsion gathered momentum, new issues arose, and the Cabinet began discussing "Asian malpractices."[18] Some Asians were selling property privately; others were transferring assets to Africans, bypassing the official process. There were illegal takeovers.[19] The Cabinet decided to evict illegal occupants and there were further delays, including reports of "African saboteurs" and Senegalese smugglers.[20] Some in the Cabinet began to voice doubt that the new owners were competent.

There followed shortages of commodities and of services. As early as 1972, the government began discussing a shortage of doctors and approved a call to bring in doctors from India and Scandinavia, and then considered bringing in African Americans on expatriate terms.[21] By 1974, the Cabinet was told that the country needed more expatriates. Amin explained to the country why it was all right to turn to India, Pakistan, and Bangladesh for expatriates so soon after he had expelled people of Asian origin. He gave three reasons: Asians were cheaper than Europeans; they understood Ugandan problems better since their own conditions were closer to conditions in Uganda; and finally, unlike the pre-1972 Asians, the new ones were unlikely to think that this was their home.

Undermining an existing system proved easier than devising a new one and putting it in place. There were shortages of milk and meat to begin with. The Cabinet hoped these scarcities would prove temporary. With shortages was born the notion of "essential commodities." When shortages persisted, the regime responded by passing a Prevention of Hoarding decree in 1974. Other decrees followed, such as a petrol decree in 1976. The next year, it was acknowledged that there was a general fuel shortage.

In 1975, there was a full-blown discussion on hoarding, punishment, and law. What are the requirements for a good law? What are the main causes of shortage? What is the definition of hoarding? What should be just payment terms? What is an act of overcharging?[22] What should be the philosophy behind penalties? The outcome was the 1975 Economic Crimes Act. Next was a debate on the death penalty, with both those for and against having a say, followed by the proposal for a new act, on a death penalty for hoarders. With the economic crisis of 1976, the discussion broadened to cover "economic crimes": Cabinet members talked of "people becoming lazy"; of government parastatals—government-owned or established bodies with autonomy like private businesses—and rich individuals "refusing to pay tax"; and of the Custodian Board failing to perform to expectations.[23] There were suggestions that residential properties be transferred to the Ministry of Housing, which would "eventually sell them to allocatees."[24]

The British-Tanzania Supported Invasion of Exiles

Once the expulsion became reality, Britain decided to join the effort to reinstall the Obote regime, the very government it had done everything to remove. The British and Tanzanian governments, and forces allied to former President Obote came together to take advantage of what they thought was an opportunity to effect a regime change. Radio Uganda announced on September 6, 1972, the day the Asian expulsion was to begin officially, that Tanzanian troops had invaded Uganda and captured the three towns of Kyotera, Kukuto, and Kalisizo. The invaders had crossed the border at Mutukula and were already within a hundred miles of Kampala. Amin ordered tanks into the streets of Kampala and arrested fifty-two British citizens, men, women, and children, all "belongers," together with journalists of various European countries.[25] That same day, Radio Uganda announced that the British military team would leave the country by September 17.[26]

The invasion was a disaster, mainly because its planners had totally failed to grasp the popularity of the Asian expulsion within the country. The only vocal protest to the expulsion announcement came from leaders of organized student associations, the National Union of Students of Uganda (NUSU) and the Makerere Student Guild. Both had been closely linked to the leadership of the Obote regime. In a letter to Amin, Kisimba Masiko, the president of National Union of Students of Uganda (NUSU), registered his opposition to the order expelling all Asians, whether or not citizens, as racist.[27] In a move that some thought was a brave expression of principle and others dismissed as a reckless gesture, Tumusiime Mutebile, the president of Makerere Student Guild, used his speech at City Square, with Amin standing next to him, to convey the same message: Amin should target all the rich, regardless of race, not just those restricted to one racial group. I was among the few thousand listening to Mutebile that day, and I could feel the ripple—a mixture of excitement, disapproval, and bewilderment—that seemed to run through the crowd.

The next day, I went to my office. There was a knock at the door, which was ajar. Mutebile stepped in. His clothes were dirty, he looked haggard, his eyes red from lack of sleep. He said he had been running from the military police and was preparing a quick exit from the country. A global student body with its headquarters in Prague had agreed to fly him out of Entebbe to Brussels and then to Prague. "They are looking for me. I must leave the country. They have sent me a ticket," he told me. I asked Mutebile if he needed to pick up his belongings. "No, they will be looking for me to do just that. Take me to the Sabena office in town. I will take the passenger bus from there to the airport. [Ahmed] Mohiddin's wife has arranged a ticket for me." Ahmed Mohiddin was a lecturer in the Political Science Department. His English wife worked for Sabena Airlines.

Mutebile had been a student in Ali Mazrui's lecture course, and I had been Mutebile's tutor in a seminar with twenty students. I said yes and got in my Mazda, taking a couple of precautions: the first was to ask Bob Lubetsky, a fellow leftie who was also a teaching assistant in the department, to drive ahead of us and be on the lookout for military police until we could take the turn to Old Kampala; the second was to take a circuitous route, away from the main roads which would surely be under military observation. I decided to go out of the Western gate of the university to Naakulabye, then Bakuli, both lower middle-class Asian suburbs in which I had grown up and which I knew well, to the adjoining slum, Kisenyi, where there was a small Somali community numbering in the thousands. The Somalis had come just after World War II and were then known as Ugandan Somalis, a people differentiated from all subsequent Somali immigrants to Uganda. We negotiated those narrow streets, which I would normally avoid, and then cut across Kampala Road, which used to divide the European and Asian parts of the colonial city but was now the city's chief artery. We turned left by the new post office, and finally, after a short one hundred yards, took a right to Airways House and the Sabena office. Both of us heaved a sigh of relief on arrival. I waited until the bus left.

The next time I saw Mutebile was four years later in Dar es Salaam. He had gone to Prague, then to London, and to Oxford on a fellowship. There, he completed his doctorate in economics, joining the faculty at University of Dar es Salaam. He was now a colleague. When Amin was removed in 1979, both Mutebile and I returned to Kampala. I was an intern ("frontier-interne-in-Mission") with the World Council of Churches, attached to the Church of Uganda as a research assistant; and Mutebile was a presidential advisor. Our paths seldom crossed, except on the day the Military Commission overthrew the fifth president, Godfrey Binaisa in 1979. Unlike in 1972, I had no car and I was walking everywhere. Mutebile had a car, saw me through his side-view mirror, hastily making my way to the university. In a reversal of roles, he stopped the car and took me to my destination. I asked him what was going on. "Too much!" It was clear he was in the know. But it was also clear that he would not talk, at least not to me. From a Marxist student militant, Mutebile had grown into a discreet professional. He rose higher with each subsequent regime, eventually becoming the governor of the country's central bank, the Bank of Uganda. By then, he had made an ideological turnaround, becoming, under Museveni, the leading voice of free enterprise and the International Monetary Fund's man in town. He would become the architect of Uganda's neoliberal program under Museveni.

Asians as Undifferentiated Victims

Neither the British nor the Ugandan authorities could be relied on for definitive figures on the legal status of different categories of Asian residents in Uganda. When the expulsion was announced, the foreign secretary told parliament that there were 54,000 estimated holders of British passports in Uganda. The actual number turned out to be much less, close to 25,000, with another 15,000 Ugandan citizens.[28]

Since 1972, a global industry portraying Ugandan Asians as victims has developed. Few of us in the first generation of those expelled wrote of our experiences. We were not chroniclers and we were not given to reflecting critically on our experiences. It is the children of refugees—the second generation—whose hand-me-down stories have gradually homogenized into victim narratives.

The flip side of Asian victim narratives was another chorus, one that demonized Amin as an uncivilized brute responsible for countless crimes. How Amin, once regarded by the British as a noble savage who had delivered the country from the erratic dictatorship of President Obote, was suddenly transformed from a well-meaning jolly giant—as in a *Sunday Times* magazine article—into a monster is a long and fascinating story with several narrators: British politicians, the British media, and Ugandan public figures like Henry Kyemba, who spun tales of Amin as a cannibal and a voracious killer of one and all, including his own wives and children. UK Prime Minister James Callaghan's foreign secretary, David Owen, compared Amin to Pol Pot; he also looked into the possibility of having Amin assassinated.[29]

Expulsion stories are replete with accounts of widespread thievery. Most are difficult to believe since the expulsion was itself a large-scale expropriation of property. My own experience during the three months of the expulsion was rather different: there were hardly any cases of Kondoism (armed robbery) in the well-heeled, low-density suburbs of Kampala. I knew because my family lived in Kololo, probably Kampala's wealthiest suburb, on 15 Baskerville Avenue, albeit in a rented flat. Amin's police and army had orders to ensure the sanctity of property for one reason: the Asian property they were safeguarding would soon be theirs. Ordinary soldiers, not so sure of being among the beneficiaries, would look for opportunities to partake in the loot, but they could only do so where there was no oversight—for example, at roadblocks on the road to the airport, or at the border where the train to Mombasa had to stop.

Even then, there were cases of kindness mixed with greed, the good with the bad. Manzoor Moghal narrates the story of his family as they arrived at the airport. The airline attendant gave him three extra tickets to make sure the family would not be tragically split. But, in another part of the same building, a customs official relieved his wife of her jewelry.[30] My mother, too, worried about how she would carry the family jewelry. Over years, probably decades, she had painstakingly gathered different items of jewelry, three sets for the wedding of each of her children. It was an ancestral custom to use savings to buy family jewels and pass them from generation to generation, mother to daughter and daughter-in-law. Transportation of jewelry was a big issue for almost every departing family. Some chose to bury their jewels in the ground, hoping to retrieve them one day in the future. Others looked for ways to transport them. My father said he knew someone in customs who had assured him that he had a way of getting things through, a box at a time. We carefully packed family belongings into five boxes. We decided to send the first as a trial balloon, packing in it the least valuable items, from clothing to kitchen utensils. Only on confirmation that the box had reached its destination would we pack more valuable items in remaining boxes. My mother waited to pack all her jewelry in the second box. It turned out the customs official was not stupid; he seemed to have read our mind. He let the first box through but not the remaining four. My mother was inconsolable for the next few months.

Naming and Shaming

The literature on the Asian expulsion shares a pair of tropes: Indians as victims and Amin as the master perpetrator. It suffers from a couple of delusions.

There was no one uniform Asian experience. At one extreme were the expropriated. These were a numerical minority. At the other were those who had already lost their sources of livelihood, whether a job or a trading license, and had nearly exhausted the charity of neighbors and community. They had little or nothing to lose. They experienced the expulsion as some kind of liberation from a purgatory. This group included stateless persons.

Several years after the expulsion, I remember visiting a friend in his family's council flat (public housing apartment) in East London. Let's call him Mahesh. Mahesh showed me around the flat. We came to the prayer room, the smallest of all rooms. Among the portraits of gods and goddesses was a photo of Amin. "Why?" I asked. "Where would we be without him?" responded Mahesh's mother. We had become penniless in Uganda, with no jobs and no right to travel. Amin opened the door to Britain, to work, to council housing, public education, health care, and transport. I could not disagree. Later in 2022, my wife, Mira, and I were having lunch with a family friend, Sarita, at the popular Lugogo restaurant, Café Javas. We were discussing different responses to the expulsion. Sarita recalled going to at least seven or eight homes in London where she found Amin's portrait alongside those of gods and goddesses in family puja or prayer rooms. In the middle were those who lost small fortunes, like Moghal's wife or my mother.

Then there were merchant families. Their position is the subject of a novel, *Kololo Hill,* by Neema Shah.[31] Her portrayal of the upper middle-class Indian family is drawn with rare candor through the eyes of Asha, the daughter-in-law. The step-by-step discovery of half-truths and silences common to her shopkeeper husband, Pran, leads to a larger exposure, of lies and deceptions that had become so much a part of the lives of Asian business families that they seemed normal and no longer cause for concern. The more Asha realizes this, the more her world unravels, layer by layer. In the process, the novel raises many questions about the standard depiction of Ugandan Asians as victims of theft, rape, violence—all of these now commonplace in the genre of expulsion literature. These are the second-generation stories, but since none or few of their authors could have been more than ten years old in 1972, these tales are part of a mythology around a larger tale of Amin's Hitlerite African presence whose victims were rescued by the leaders of the "civilized" world, led by Great Britain.

At the heart of the experience of "the Asian expulsion" was a sense of shared loss of home, of community, of continuity. Every immigrant knows that a sense of belonging develops over generations. Those who were expelled went on to live as "strangers," *musafir* in Hindustani; wherever they ended up, they had a sense that it was provisional and that they might have to uproot again at short notice. Every place we lived in after the expulsion, we lived as if we were guests, our houses or rooms stamped with the feeling of being transients in our own homes. Years after we married, Mira remarked on how our family homes, whether in Wembley or Dar or back in Kampala, always seemed like guesthouses and we, their occupants, seemed ready to leave at a moment's notice. With the loss of Uganda, we lost a sense of belonging, and of rootedness. This was our greatest loss.

As we neared the last week of October, my parents prepared to leave. I was the eldest and decided I would leave last. My sister, Masuma, had secured a scholarship to Wellesley College. She left for New York City. My father had a car that he decided to leave behind. My brother, Anis, an aspiring businessman, who had been born in Dar es Salaam and held a Tanzanian passport, sold his assets and bought a secondhand Mercedes-Benz and drove it across the border to Kenya, then to Tanzania. "Customs have strict orders to stop any smuggling.

How will you get the car across?" I queried. "I will go with only my personal belongings. They will not know. They will be looking for goods I may be carrying across. They will not realize that I am really taking the car." He was right. The next time we met, which was in London, Anis told me that soldiers had stripped the floor mats, etc. looking for hidden goods. But the car, the elephant in the room, went unnoticed.

I left on the last official day of expulsion. The evening before, I was taking a final look around the house. All our belongings, everything too heavy to be moved or removed, were there. There was a knock at the door. I recognized a senior professor of history from the university. He did not recognize me, an ordinary teaching assistant. "Do you have anything to sell?" he asked. "No, nothing, but you can come in and take whatever you want." He came in. There was furniture, accumulated by my parents over decades of married life, but it would have required muscle to load and a lorry to transport it. It was already evening and it was getting dark. As I took him around the rooms, he spotted a box under the staircase that led to the upstairs gallery. "What is this?" I opened it. It was a carton of whiskey, Johnny Walker Red. "Can I take this?" "Sure." "How much?" "Just take it. I have no use for it." A few days later, reunited with my parents in the transit camp on Kensington Church Street, London, I asked my father, "What was a case of whiskey doing in our home?" We were a Muslim family. There was never alcohol in the home. My parents did not drink. We, the kids, did, but never at home. My father responded, "That was not whiskey. It was cooking oil." It was my turn to be surprised. "Someone had brought it to the auction. We sold it but the client returned it, saying it was counterfeit, cooking oil, packed and sealed in whiskey bottles. So I brought it home." I could imagine the scene: this professor had probably gone home and called his friends to a party, opened one of the twelve bottles of whiskey as part of a celebration, toasting Amin or the Asians or both, only to find that it was cooking oil. Most likely, I thought, the experience confirmed his hunch that Asians are born crooks.

The process we know as the expulsion lasted for three months. Those who left could only take out fifty pounds sterling per person. For those who had any money left, the option was to spend it in the time one had left in the country. For us, the last three months felt like a big party. Its quintessential representation was a dinner and dance event at the Imperial Hotel. The guests were almost exclusively Asian, and we wined, dined, and then danced as the all-African band played in multiple languages. The favorite song to which the crowd danced joyously with abandon was an Indian film hit: "*Zindagi ek safar hai suhana, yahan kal kya ho kisney jana*" (Life is a beautiful journey, who knows what will happen here tomorrow?). We danced with abandon, laced with sadness. This atmosphere, the bonhomie, the feeling of community, continued in the refugee camp. After the camp came loneliness, anxiety, depression. My parents lived in Wembley, in the United Kingdom, for several years before returning to Dar es Salaam to join my brother and me. One day, when they were back in Dar es Salaam, I asked Ammy and Daddy what their favorite pastime had been in Wembley. They said it was going to Gatwick Airport to receive the weekly flight from Entebbe, on the off chance they might recognize one of the disembarking passengers. That night, I cried.

Most literature on expulsion portrays Amin as a sadistic brute who killed without discrimination and took delight in the murder of vast numbers of victims. The estimate of the numbers killed catapulted, from thousands to even a million. The growing numbers reflected the changing sensibilities of those making the estimates. You can see it in the estimate of rape cases in Congo, or of killings in Darfur. In the latter, which I had investigated in detail, the procedure was challenged by none other than the Office of Public Accountability, an office set up by the US government to ensure the honesty of its own agencies.[32] But it had no effect. One scholarly work, by Mark Leopold, shows how the narrative on Amin changed as the tide turned in his relations with Western powers.[33] This literature begins with Henry Kyemba's *State of Blood,* a chilling account from Amin's private secretary, and continues with steady contributions from a string of self-interested characters. The exception, Leopold points out, has been the Ugandan academic and scholarly community.

There was neither large-scale loss of life in 1972 nor sporadic massacres for which Uganda has become notorious. Massacres, and indeed genocide, have been the fate of minorities who have vied for power, such as the Tutsi in Rwanda. For minorities, such as the Asians, whose ambitions have been confined to the marketplace, expulsion has been their fate. In Uganda in 1972, there was not much in the way of large-scale robbery or looting, for one reason: the expulsion itself was one big, well-organized collective theft.

7

THE REGIME STABILIZES

There is scant literature on the inner political life of the Amin regime, especially during the half dozen years that followed the triple expulsion in 1972. We have little knowledge of how differences were resolved internally and how the regime responded to public disaffection. The main focus has been on attempted assassinations and coups. Missing from this literature is any acknowledgment and evaluation of public policy formulation under Amin. Among those who turned to the Amin regime with fresh public policy initiatives was Reverend John Mbiti, professor and head of the Department of Religious Studies and Philosophy at Makerere University. Professor Mbiti had been a distinguished scholar of religion in Uganda and the East African region. Like Amin's early Cabinet ministers, Wanume Kibedi, Edward Rugumayo, and Dani Wadada Nabudere, Mbiti also seemed to have reached the conclusion that the new regime lacked clear direction and could be guided, or taken advantage of, depending on one's point of view. Mbiti wrote Amin in 1971, proposing that the government establish a Ministry of Religious Affairs.[1] The events that followed the submission of Mbiti's letter in just the second month of the regime's life provide a glimpse into the consultative process that guided Amin's nonmilitary approach. Mbiti argued that the government needed to give serious consideration to Uganda's "history of religious wars and conflicts," for "where religion has such a major role to play in the entire population of the country, it seems clearly necessary for the government to have formal interest in the religions of the people."[2] This proposed ministry, the good professor advised, would promote a religious dialogue, as well as cooperation and coordination of development projects and welfare schemes between different religions; facilitate the government's communication with the people; and help churches with worldly challenges, such as "bookkeeping," "embezzlement," and "failure to pay pastors on time."[3] Mbiti asserted that, in Uganda, religion and government need each other: "The government is fundamentally an institution for the physical welfare of man; religion aims at both the physical and spiritual welfare of man . . . they need each other in order to serve the whole man adequately." The ministry would carry forward an African philosophical tradition: "African traditional life does not have a division between 'secular' and 'sacred,' between what is religious and what is not. African people experience the whole of life as a religious phenomenon, and as a matter of fact there are no African words for 'religion' as such."[4] Professor Mbiti's proposal, however, came to naught the more Amin realized that the proposed Ministry of Religion was likely to become a theater for political contest among religions with institutionalized hierarchies.

Amin faced serious challenges to power from the outset. The army had been drastically reduced in size: there were soldiers who had run with Obote immediately after the coup, and more soldiers followed after massacres in the barracks. Speculation grew both within the country and in the region that the ancien régime may be restored before the first anniversary of the coup.

Amin turned to Britain and Israel for military support. When it was not forthcoming, he sent his Education Minister Abu Mayanja to Egypt. On Anwar el-Sadat's advice, Amin met Muammar Gaddafi and, through Gaddafi, President Gaafar Nimeiry of Sudan. The result of the tripartite consultation was the Addis Ababa Agreement of 1972, which brought an end to the Israeli presence in southern Sudan, as well as Israeli links with the southern Sudanese rebels, known as the Anyanya. Nimeiry suggested that Amin absorb close to half of the Anyanya forces, which Amin was eager to do since it would replenish his troops after the loss of practically half the army in the aftermath of the coup. Nimeiry reciprocated by closing Obote's bases in South Sudan.

The political geography of the region was now changed, first by Amin's expulsion of the Israelis, then later that same year by the expulsion of Asians resident in Uganda. Amin saw the Asian expulsion as a challenge to Britain's position in Uganda, as did the British. It was this that brought three unlikely forces—Britain, Nyerere's Tanzania, and the armed Ugandan opposition in Tanzania—into an opportunistic alliance. The armed Ugandan opposition based in Tanzania invaded Uganda on September 17, 1972, in an attempt to overthrow Amin. Opposition troops included Obote's *Kikosi Maalum* (Special Battalion) alongside a parallel infiltration by rebels of the Front for National Salvation (FRONASA), formed that same year by Yoweri Museveni, who had openly declared his desire to be independent of Obote. The invasion ended up a farce, and the infiltration turned out to be a fiasco. Without support from the Tanzanian army, neither Kikosi Maalum nor FRONASA would have survived. The rebels had expected to be welcomed by a popular uprising against Amin. Instead, most of the population was happy to hand the rebels over to Amin's security forces. What neither Obote, nor Museveni nor Nyerere had realized was that the Asian expulsion had triggered a transformative social change in Uganda, especially in the more developed southern part of the country. Humiliated by their failure, Nyerere had no choice but to sign a peace agreement in Mogadishu, agreeing not to interfere in the internal affairs of Uganda.

The main source of danger for Amin was no longer Obote's forces in neighboring Tanzania, but Israeli attempts to link up with dissenting factions inside his own army. On the surface, Amin's armed forces had been bolstered by the integration of a large number of South Sudanese (Anyanya) troops into the army. With their numbers estimated at up to twenty thousand, the ex-Anyanya posed a competitive threat to Amin's core supporters, who had been with him since the 1971 coup. His supporters from the West Nile, in particular, sensed a threat to their leading positions in the army. Their initial response was to resolve their differences with Amin in a peaceful yet persuasive manner. In a doctoral dissertation on institutional violence under Amin, Thomas Lowman has traced this initiative to a group of senior Kakwa, Christian officers—Lieutenant-Colonel Ali Musa, Isaac Maliyamungu, and Brigadier Charles Arube—who, in mid-1973, attempted to convince Amin to step down as president.[5]

Amin believed that these officers had the backing of Israel. Unlike Britain, Israel had been a player in factional struggles inside the Ugandan military. It had intimate knowledge of those who had taken a leading part in the 1971 coup, particularly those from Amin's region, West Nile.[6] When it came to this internal military opposition, Amin responded separately to each of its leaders, sending Charles Arube to Russia on a six-month course, and retiring Lieutenant-Colonel Musa, who had rapidly risen to prominence after the coup.[7] In contrast, he wooed Isaac Maliyamungu, moving him from his command position in Masaka to take charge of the main ordinance depot at Magamaga. It was evident that Amin continued to trust Maliyamungu.[8]

On his return from the Soviet Union, Charles Arube stepped up his efforts to replace Amin. He sought out Kakwa officers whose positions had been undermined by two groups of South Sudanese, former rebels (Anyanya) and Uganda-based refugees, both recruited into the Ugandan army following the Addis Ababa Agreement. The plot against Amin was led by senior officers in top leadership positions who had been replaced by leading Anyanya officers. Arube had been supplanted by Lieutenant-Colonel Hussein Marella while in Russia. Among the new high-ranking officers were Ali Towelli and Isaac Maliyamungu. They shared a common resentment over the cutting of ties with Israel. Amin accused three senior army officers—Charles Arube, Elly Aseni (Amin's uncle), and Isaac Lumago—as well as Justice Opu, of leading the attempted coup on January 23–24, 1974, with Israeli support, but Amin's response to the attempted mutiny was conciliatory. He ordered Lieutenant-Colonel Hussein Marella, then commanding officer of the military police in the Makindye Barracks, to return to Sudan; according to Jaffar Amin, Marella did so in a large convoy of cars and trucks.[9] Then Amin appointed Mustapha Adrisi, "a former KAR [King's African Rifles] soldier like himself, and particularly popular with the Lugbara soldiery," as his new chief of staff.

Of the reforms the Amin regime is known to have implemented, three were notable. The first was the return of the kabaka's body and its burial, alongside what Amin called "the burial of the kingdoms." The matter had been at the heart of Uganda's postindependence constitutional crisis. Britain had bequeathed Uganda a mix of centrally ruled districts and autonomous kingdoms in a semi-federal setup at independence. During the 1966 crisis that pitted the central government against the government of Buganda, and led to the replacement of a semi-federal setup with a centralized unitary government, Amin had led the forces of the center against the kabaka's government and its police. Following the Amin coup of 1971 that overthrew Obote, the Mengo establishment wanted a return of the monarchy, and not just the body of the dead monarch.

The second key issue concerned the question of land tenure. Like the system of governance, the country's system of land tenure at independence was also a patchwork arrangement. Its two extremes were marked by clan land—dubbed "customary tenure"—in the North and landlord-dominated *mailo* lands in Buganda. The 1975 Land Reform Decree abolished *mailo* lands and assured tillers security of tenure and the right to work the land. It also created a system of uniform land tenure throughout the country.

The third reform was the 1974–1975 Commission of Inquiry into "disappearances." This was a bold attempt by the Amin government to check military excesses, restore the confidence and the autonomy of the police in relation to the army, and assure a modicum of rule of law in civilian life, thereby strengthening its own legal foundation.

In 1971, Amin set up a committee chaired by Abu Mayanja and charged it with preparing the return and ceremonial burial of the kabaka's body. Amin was determined to keep the question of the restoration of the monarchy separate from that of the return of the kabaka's body. Captain Ronald Owen (guardian and godfather of Prince Mutebi) and Major Richard Carr-Gomm (a close friend whose flat kabaka had stayed in London in 1969), the British guardians of the kabaka while he was alive, claimed to be custodians of his body after his death. They further maintained that they had been instructed by the royal family and the Baganda elders that the body of the kabaka remain in London until the kabakaship was restored.

The kabaka's family had been split on the question of how to proceed. The high commissioner in London referred to General Amin's public declaration following the coup, known as the Thirteen Points, "the twelfth of which laid down that there would be no restoration of the monarchies." On March 12, two of the four members of the royal family and the elders of Buganda signed "a statement that it was their wish that the body of Sir Edward Mutesa be returned home for burial in accordance with the arrangements being made by the government of Uganda." The kabaka's widow applied to the Home Secretary for just that. But the kabaka's sister, Princess Mpologoma, and her brother, Prince Henry Kimera, remained adamantly opposed to the arrangement. They conveyed their joint opposition to the Bishop of London and said arrangements were being made to apply for a court injunction. Both the British government and the Church of England seemed keen to take advantage of the return of the kabaka's body and its royal burial to press the case for a return of monarchies as part of the restoration of the 1962 "independence" constitution. Amin took firm steps to forestall this possibility. According to Judith Listowel, Amin invited the people of Buganda to restore Kasubi, the twenty-eight-hectare traditional royal burial site in Kampala for Buganda's kings. To underline his determination,

Amin announced at Uganda's independence celebrations on October 9, 1971, that "Uganda would remain a Republic and that none of the kingships would be restored."[10]

Amin wanted the burial to take place before the Organisation of African Unity (OAU) conference in Kampala in June 1975. The OAU conference would be a fitting occasion to celebrate his government's internal achievements. Amin's major achievement on domestic policy was the rapprochement with Buganda. He told the Cabinet that "Obote's mistake" was "not to abolish kingdoms but to treat kings as enemies." No leader, Amin told his Cabinet, is wholly good or bad, and there should be a central burial place for all past presidents. Following a countrywide consultation on the restoration of monarchy, Amin told the Cabinet that several districts were opposed to the idea. Not surprisingly, these were districts without a history of kingdoms, and thus without a constitutional basis for autonomy in the "independence" constitution. The burial of Mutesa, he told the Cabinet, should also be a burial of kabakaship. It should mark the end of kabakaship in Buganda.[11]

After laying to rest the institution of kingship, alongside the body of the kabaka, Amin's next project was to put an end to the institution of *mailo* land. This was the goal of the 1975 Land Reform Decree. Amin gave the following guidelines to Cabinet: There would be a single uniform land tenure policy, along lines of the land reform in Ethiopia following the 1974 Derg revolution, the coup d'état that overthrew Emperor Haile Selassie. The reform abolished landlordism and introduced a land reform that guaranteed the tiller full rights over land while leaving legal ownership in the hands of the government. With the 1975 decree, all land in Uganda became public land. *Mailo* land was converted to a ninety-nine-year lease. All unused land was nationalized, the idea being to protect tenants from extortion or eviction.[12]

Amin's most ambitious initiative was the appointment of the Commission of Inquiry into Disappearances of People in Uganda since the 25th of January, 1971. The Commission was a response to mounting pressure from different sectors of society. The seriousness of concern was evident when a delegation of senior police officers visited Amin in April 1974 to voice concerns over growing militarization. Amin promised a full inquiry into the matter. Two months later, he appointed a commission of inquiry to look into "disappearances" under his rule.

"Disappearances" were a direct consequence of militarization of the regime. Its main victims were civilians and the police that had traditionally been trained to maintain civic order. If the police lost their autonomy, civilians lost both life and property. Amin's response to the general breakdown of law and order was to set up a Commission of Inquiry into growing numbers of civilian "disappearances." It was chaired by a British Asian (Pakistani), Justice Mohammed Saied, the same judge who had presided over the trial of Rajat Neogy and Abu Mayanja during the Obote regime. That he had the courage and foresight to declare both of those men innocent of official charges had boosted the judge's public reputation for autonomy and integrity. The other members of the Commission were S. M. Kyafulumya and A. Esau (commissioners of police), as well as Captain Haruna (Uganda Armed Forces). The Commission's charge was, in brief, to establish the identity of missing persons, whether dead or alive; reasons for leaving the country, if they did; for those who died, the circumstances of death; and the criminal responsibility of individuals or organizations. The Commission was also asked to recommend steps the government should take to wind up the victims' affairs and to assure justice for families, as well as "what [the] government [should] do to put an end to the criminal disappearances of people in Uganda." In addition, the Commission was advised to stay away from politically sensitive issues: "We were directed to give due consideration to the logical and natural events of the Military takeover as well as the events pertaining and ancillary to the defence of Uganda when the nation was invaded on the 17th day of September, 1972." Finally, the Commission was advised that "the inquiry [shall not] extend to persons of Asian origin or extraction."[13] The Commission began its work on July 1, 1974, and the report was signed and submitted on June 13, 1975.[14]

The Commission on "disappearances" was unusual for a number of reasons. It was among the first truth commissions in the world; the Latin American commissions followed later, and then came the South African Truth and Reconciliation Commission (TRC). One significant fact distinguished Amin's commission from those that followed. The scope of the latter was limited to unearthing the truth of injustice meted out by previous regimes, whereas the 1974 Commission's mandate was particularly to unearth the truth of the regime in power.

What made the 1974 truth commission possible? Thomas Lowman of the University of Cambridge, the only scholar to treat the work of the Commission with any degree of seriousness, argued that the few scholars who bothered to look at the Commission's report tended to dismiss or downplay it, either as a hoodwinking exercise that "failed to meet its mandate or uncover any truth" (Quinn), or as just a formal and token response to a damning report from the International Commission of Jurists (ICJ) about rights abuses in the country. From this point of view, the Commission's report was no more than "a fine performance of political theatre" (Decker).[15] Lowman suggested that though international pressure was doubtless important, internal disaffection with growing "disappearances" among both the public and the police were likely the main driving force behind the establishment of the Commission.[16] Two further developments, the failed mutiny just months before and a more recent serious attempt on Amin's life, suggested evidence of a deep split within the regime.

The 1974 Commission began in Kampala, but its reach extended up-country to include Kitgum, Lira, Gulu, Mbarara, and Fort Portal. In Lowman's words, the investigations "elicited a degree of genuine popular engagement from the moment they began." Public hearings organized by the Commission were the first opportunity for ordinary people to confront members of the armed forces and security units directly about their behavior. As the public seemed skeptical that the Commission would be open to receiving complaints about the regime's own armed forces, the Commission was slow to start. But, gradually, as the first witnesses described their experience with the Commission, more and more family and friends of the "disappeared" came forward to tell their own stories. Justice Saied was entirely convinced as to the integrity of these civilian testimonies: "We believe the evidence given by the simple, straight forward and unsophisticated civilian witnesses, women and young men, whose husbands and fathers disappeared, some in front of their eyes and they could do nothing to keep them back. We are of the opinion that such witnesses, knowing that their kith and kin were snatched from them forever and are not going to come back, no matter what they say or do, will speak the truth and only the truth."[17]

The Commission documented cases of victims regularly affronted on the road or in neighborhoods, bundled in the boot of army or civilian vehicles, and taken to unknown destinations; in the words of relatives and neighbors, they had "disappeared." The Commission was Amin's response to growing concern, among the larger public and the police. Its chair was well known for having upheld the independence of the judiciary and championed the rule of law under Obote; its other members represented the police and the army. Though the Commission's report was never published, Amin sent it to the United Nations—which seems to have ignored it—and the international media seemed blissfully unaware of it.

The Commission confirmed that most victims had been "unlawfully disposed." Most of these were state personnel—army men (154), police officers (34), chiefs (19), prison officers (12), and magistrates (2)—221 in all. These incidents were spread over large parts of the country. Victims were either killed during the days of the military coup or were targeted as suspects given their regional or ethnic origin (Acholi, Langi) or institutional affiliation (police, prisons, chiefs). Then there were "disappearances" motivated by individual considerations, such as revenge, greed, or "trouble over a girl," meaning that the perpetrator had aimed to take possession of the victim's female partner. Finally, there were cases where soldiers took it upon themselves to lend their uniform or gun or land rover as a favor to a kinsperson or a friend for purposes of revenge.[18] In only two individual cases did the Commission register "no finding" and recommend further investigation, since the culprits were likely known. In both cases, the kidnappers were thought to be imposters, either looking for material gain or motivated by "trouble over a girl."[19]

Why would soldiers kill fellow soldiers? According to the Commission, barring few exceptions, they were an outcome of the army takeover of January 25, 1971: those killed had either been arrested, or were opposed to the change, or died in the armed conflict.[20] Personnel of Acholi and Langi ethnicity had been under suspicion from the day of the January 1971 coup. Interviewed by the Commission, Deputy Superintendent Kidega said "he was arrested by some soldiers from his home on 29th January, 1971" and "taken to the barracks and beaten up on the allegations that the Acholi people are the people who were intending to break the government."[21]

The problem went beyond targeting individual officers on the basis of their ethnic identity; the entire police force had been relegated by the army to an inferior position, exposed to ridicule, even humiliation. These actions went beyond violating the rights of individual officers to undermining the integrity of the police as an institution. The Commission pointed fingers at two of the four main security institutions of the state: the Public Service Unit (PSU) and the military intelligence. At the same time, Amin's first substantive Minister of Internal Affairs, Lieutenant-Colonel Obitre Gama testified that the government itself had to bear some responsibility for setting this process in motion: "The tribulations of the Police started with the promulgation of a decree which gave powers of arrest to the soldiers." He was referring to the Armed Forces

(Powers of Arrest) Decree No. 13 of 1971: "Section 2(1) of the Decree read, 'A soldier or a prison officer may, without an order from court and without a warrant, arrest any person whom he suspects on reasonable grounds of having committed or being about to commit any of the following offences: (a) an offence against public order; (b) an offense against the person; an offence relating to property.' When it expired in twelve months, the Decree was replaced by Decree No. 26 of 1972, a verbatim reproduction of the previous Decree."[22] The decree gave soldiers powers of arrest that normally belonged to the courts.

The state agency that stepped in to take full advantage of Decree No. 13 was the Public Service Unit (PSU), established in 1972 as an "anti-kondo" unit (Kondoism refers to armed theft). Under the leadership of Towelli, the third person to take its command, the PSU began to give itself the power to decide who to arrest and when, even going so far as to arrest senior police officers. In the words of the Commission, "rather than staying a friend of the public who needed it most in times of distress and emergency, it earned itself a notoriety of an oppressor who was to be dreaded."[23] Next in notoriety to the PSU was the military police under Brigadier Marella.[24] Often, the two institutions worked arm in arm, often "using false number plates obviously to camouflage their identity."[25]

The destruction of the police force led to the militarization of relations between state and society: "Soldiers who were required to enforce the provisions of these Decrees, were themselves the worst offenders. . . . Such soldiers became pinchbeck dictators in their own right where they abused these powers and obligations and, in so doing, ridiculed the provisions of these Decrees."[26] Referring to the disappearances of the District Commissioner of Bukedi, Mulekezi (subject no. 16), and the manager of Rock Hotel in Tororo, Nahekanabe (subject no. 17), the Commission noted: "There was in fact no possible reason or excuse for the arrest of these two citizens who, for all intents and purposes, had committed no crime."[27]

The police tended to freeze when faced with army personnel: the very knowledge that the case might involve army personnel was enough to bring a police investigation to an abrupt end, sometimes even before it had started.[28] Soldiers were prone to taking anybody they arrested to their barracks instead of to the nearest police station.[29] All the while, the Ministry of Internal Affairs and the Ministry of Defense, the two ministries in charge of providing oversight to security services, did nothing, even when abuses were reported to them.[30] The result was predictable; excesses of some soldiers had adversely effected the entire police force.[31] The Commission noted that "considerable" numbers of people disappeared and "the inhuman practice of taking away people in boots of cars" soon became "public knowledge." As "the police became ineffective," the result was both "complete loss of confidence" and an overall "breakdown of law and order."[32] The Commission held both heads of security institutions like the PSU and military police, and key ministries, like Internal Affairs and Defense, responsible for this sorry state of affairs.

The downside of the Commission's report was that it absolved President Idi Amin of any responsibility, both criminal and political, even when it acknowledged that prominent members of society had "disappeared." The best known of these was Benedicto Kiwanuka, the chief justice of Uganda, kidnapped on September 21, 1972, from his chambers by "three men in civilian dress" and murdered soon after; the disappearance occurred only four days after the rebel invasion from Tanzania. The Commission concluded that the chief justice was probably murdered by his kidnappers. Yet, the report concluded: "When dealing with the case of the former Chief Justice . . . there was no evidence where there was even the remotest suggestion that Your Excellency had directed the disappearance of any person or the annihilation of any ethnic group of persons."[33] Similar disclaimers followed reports of the disappearance of other senior public figures, such as William Wilberforce Kalema (subject no. 35), who had been a Cabinet minister in Obote's government; then George Kamba (subject no. 36), Uganda's high commissioner, first in India and, at another time, in Germany. Then there was Amin's own Minister of Foreign Affairs, Lieutenant-Colonel Michael Ondoga, an early beneficiary of the "economic war" who had been allotted Anguruma Company, a mill producing soap, oil, and maize meal in the Kampala suburb of Kawempe. The report said he was "murdered" by unknown kidnappers who threw his body in the Nile.[34]

It is understandable that the Commission would only trace criminal accountability to those whose hands were actually blood-stained. But what about political responsibility of those who presided over this rapidly ongoing breakdown in public order year after year? Let us note that Amin's Commission was not isolated in focusing on criminal responsibility and at the same time obscuring the question of political responsibility; the South African TRC, whose report would be published two decades later, would take the same route.[35]

In spite of allegations made by several foreign writers, the Commission was not just an empty public relations exercise; it had significant consequences for the internal life of the country. The Commission called on the government to "reorganize the police force with special emphasis on restoring morale and confidence."[36] It also called for a drastic reform of the PSU, which "should be restricted in its activities . . . (and) be made to function under the umbrella of the Police . . . and come under the supervision and control of the Commissioner of Police."[37] The government replaced heads of both the PSU and the military police. Efforts were made to restore the autonomy of the police. The submission of its report could have been a moment of significant reform, signaling a possible turning point in the life of the regime. But that moment disappeared as the regime moved on to another crisis.

The unusual fact that the Commission's terms of reference included only the existing regime—none before—made for both its strength and weakness. The Commission's report is a remarkable document in the breadth of its coverage, the depth of its analysis, and the boldness of its findings. But as the Commission's Report was not published, few could access it. Amin sent a copy of the Saied Commission's final report to the United Nations, a fact noted by the ICJ. The ICJ had in fact been pushing for an inquiry since 1974.[38] It is not clear to me whether most academics who dismissed the work of the Commission had actually read its report. For my part, it took me over a year to track down the report. I found sections of it in the library at the Parliament (with the help of a colleague at the Makerere University School of Law), and other sections with the help of the director of the Centre for Basic Research in Kampala. Even then, large sections were not fully readable because they were copies of copies. I eventually found the full report with Amnesty International in New York City, but even then some sections were difficult to read and decipher. It was only when I had completed the first draft of this manuscript that a colleague at the Makerere University School of Law sent me a fully legible report.

As the regime stabilized over the next year, the United States seriously considered whether or not to reopen its embassy in Kampala. Ambassador Anthony D. Marshall argued in 1975: "Amin appears, according to diplomatic observers in Kampala as well as senior Kenya government officials, to be learning arts of statecraft rather more rapidly and effectively than one might have expected on basis of his earlier behaviour. . . . Informed observers appear convinced that he can and does learn from experience and that his understanding of foreign affairs has definitely improved and will continue to improve."[39]

By any standards, Amin was a fast learner. He faced an all-round challenge in both foreign and domestic policy following the triple expulsions of 1972. Amin's foreign policy initiatives were ridiculed by the Western press as evidence of a crazy personality at the helm of a government. But the rapprochement with the government of Nimiery of Sudan successfully undercut Obote's efforts to organize an invasion simultaneously from two fronts (Tanzania and Sudan). It bought Amin another half decade before the same alliance of forces—Tanzania, Britain, and the armed Ugandan exiled opposition—came together to oust him.

On the domestic front, Amin was able to secure widespread popular support in Buganda, at the same time driving a wedge between the people and the establishment there. When he lost the Kagera War (otherwise known as the Uganda-Tanzania War) in 1978–1979, it was not because he had lost popular support in Uganda. It was more a consequence of the growing rift between two wings of the army—his original base of support among the West Nile officer corps and the Anyanya officer corps that joined him after the Addis Ababa Agreement of 1972.

8

THE REGIME IMPLODES

During its first year, 1971–1972, the Amin regime was preoccupied with survival. After the coup, nearly half of the former regime's army, supporters of ex–President Obote, were lodged in military camps in Tanzania and Sudan. And, as we have seen, Israel had made attempts to link up with dissenting officers in the army, those it had trained in the past, to effect regime change. Amin's way of breaking out of a hostage-type situation was the Asian expulsion. The expulsion won him a civilian social base, most of which remained loyal to him until the end of the regime. It also won him new friends in the region. Thus, given this support, we ask, how specifically did Amin's regime fail? What ultimately led to its downfall? And what can we identify as Amin's personal and institutional legacy?

Amin's response to opposition from within the regime was a combination of reform and repression. He offered carrots to his supporters when it came to distributing the spoils of the "economic war" in 1972–1973, but also sought to reform the military structure by appointing the Commission of Inquiry into "disappearances" and implementing its far-reaching recommendations. The change was noticed by many of those engaged with the regime. As we have seen, among them was US Ambassador Anthony D. Marshall, whose views were only aired in private. In public, however, the anti-Amin propaganda machinery, wielded by Britain, continued in high gear. At the same time, several prominent East Africans began to rethink their own participation in this propaganda drive.

Among these were two East African–Asian photographers, Mohinder Dhillon and Mohamed Amin (both nicknamed "Mo"), as well as the scholar Ali Mazrui.

Ali Mazrui's public break came in February 1978 in his testimony before the subcommittee on Africa of the US House of Representatives. Mazrui distinguished between dictatorship and anarchy in his testimony.[1] He attributed the murders of Chief Justice Benedicto Kiwanuka and Vice Chancellor Frank Kalimuzo in 1972, as well as the 1977 murders of Archbishop Janani Luwum and two Cabinet ministers, to the prevailing anarchy. Many civilian deaths, Mazrui argued, may not all be at the hands of Idi Amin, as there were many cases of "decentralized brutality—of individual soldiers 'executing' a man behind a dance hall in order to 'inherit' his girlfriend for the night, or of civilian criminals wearing army uniforms on loan from real soldiers as a strategy of extorting money." He also questioned "the reliability of the news coming out of Uganda." As an example, Mazrui focused on the report filed by the British journalist David Martin in *The Observer* (London) on the massacre and mutilation of women students at Makerere University:

> In August 1976 it was reported that a massacre of students had taken place on the campus of Makerere University in Uganda. The report was detailed. It included the precise place where the massacre took place (on Freedom Square in front of the Main Administration Building), the approximate number of casualties (at least one hundred and conceivably up to eight hundred), the details of other brutal atrocities (mutilation of breasts of girl students), the usual sexual assaults (soldiers raping girl students), etc. etc.... Since then, I have checked out the story meticulously.... I am now completely satisfied that there was no "massacre" on Makerere campus in the first week of August 1976.... The soldiers did get out of hand and started beating up students, kicking them, injuring them with rifle butts. But nobody was killed. And apparently no girls were raped, let alone mutilated.... On balance, many more people must have died, or been mutilated in Uganda as a result of decentralized violence than in response to purposeful brutality by the regime. (3–4)

Mazrui had returned to the larger argument and concluded that the problem was "not just Amin but general normative collapse" (13).

Mazrui was not the only one wary of being misinformed by a powerful and ubiquitous propaganda machine. In a widely circulated email on the death of Mo Dhillon in March 2020, the Ugandan Asian academic Vali Jamal recalled Dhillon confessing how he had in the past been fooled by the anti-Amin machinery and its key architect, the British journalist David Martin. He particularly regretted taking the bait about the infamous de-breasting of seventy-seven girl students at Makerere University and the murder of tens, all published in *The Observer* (London). Mo Dhillon had gone to Kampala, likely on assignment there, after the fall of Amin. He recalled the vice chancellor of Makerere University telling him and other journalists as he welcomed them to the university, "Gentlemen, sorry, but I have no girl students to produce for you with scars." He added that only one Makerere University student had been killed during the life of the regime and that that had happened off campus.

Mo Amin, the other photojournalist from Kenya, had covered Idi Amin "from very up close," in Vali's words. Fond of Mo, Idi Amin used to call him "Junior"; Mo went to Jeddah in Saudi Arabia to interview Idi Amin after his fall. Vali suggests that Mo Amin likely met Idi Amin in Jeddah to atone for the innumerable stories he had put out on Amin, including those testifying to "the president's taste in flesh." When Mo Amin asked about Idi's son, Moses, who reportedly had been killed by his own father, Idi "did reluctantly bring out Moses and allowed Mo Amin to take a photograph."[2]

In his testimony to the Africa subcommittee of the US House of Representatives, Ali Mazrui noted "a widespread consensus that at least a hundred thousand people have been killed in Uganda since Amin captured power on January 25, 1971." What Mazrui did not say was that the largest massacres had taken place in barracks in the aftermath of the coup, and that both the British and the Israelis were complicit in these. The estimates of those killed continued to rise over the years. The ICJ estimated the numbers annihilated by the Amin regime to be between 20,000 and 200,000, a remarkable range to be broadcast by an international agency in a public report.[3] It stood alongside another widely bandied figure of 300,000 to 500,000 killed during Amin's eight-year rule[4]. By 1979, the Labour Foreign Secretary Dr. David Owen (now Lord Owen) proposed that MI6 be ordered to assassinate Idi Amin. David Hebditch and Ken Connor suggest in their book on coup making that "perhaps David Owen was influenced by the fact that, ten years earlier, MI6 had actively planned for the assassination of President Milton Obote as an alternative to the coup plot." Interviewed on BBC radio shortly after Amin's death in 2003, David Owen admitted that many saw his proposal as "outrageous." At the same time, Mr. Owen insisted: "I'm not ashamed of [having considered] it, because his regime goes down in the scale of Pol Pot as one of the worst of all African regimes."[5]

In its Saturday broadcast announcing the death of Idi Amin on August 16, 2003, the BBC "reported that he kept the heads of seven victims in a fridge in his kitchen." These stories made their rounds. In the 1981 film *The Rise and Fall of Idi Amin,* the character of Idi Amin opens a fridge and calmly shows his visitors two heads of his former victims. In another scene, Amin dismisses a coroner doing an autopsy, picks up a scalpel, and cuts and eats a piece of his victim's flesh as he mumbles some incomprehensible words. Amin then seeks the counsel of a witch doctor on how to retain power. He is told to sacrifice his three-year-old son, Moses. The same son, Moses, had greeted Mo Amin when he went to visit Amin in Saudi Arabia after he was overthrown. According to Fred Guweddeko, a PhD student at the Makerere Institute of Social Research, Moses received a university degree in France, and was by his father's bedside at his death.[6]

Mark Leopold's doctoral thesis focuses on Idi Amin in official and journalistic writing, mainly from the West, which is made up of memoirs written by those who commanded Amin or worked with or under him. All wrote book-length memoirs describing their encounter with the monster. Notable among these are his British military superior (Iain Grahame), political allies (Henry Kyemba, who was a member of Amin's Cabinet, until he fled and wrote a "sensational" memoir titled *A State of Blood*), journalists (David Martin), civil servants (Kato), Western diplomats (Brian Smith, Thomas Melady, and Margaret Melady), and teachers and lecturers (Heather Benson and Denis Hills).[7]

According to Leopold, Henry Kyemba "seems to have been the first to claim that Amin was an enthusiastic cannibal." Like others who wrote of Amin, Kyemba resorted to Amin's cultural background to explain his otherwise bizarre behavior. Kyemba argued that Amin's wild conduct had to do with "his own aberrant personality" and "his tribal background." In Kyemba's words, "like many other warrior societies, the Kakwa, Amin's tribe, are known to have practised blood rituals on slain enemies."[8] Others, such as the journalist David Martin, attributed Amin's cruelties to "the sadistic brutality" characteristic of the Nubi.[9]

Kyemba acted as an advisor on the 1981 movie *The Rise and Fall of Idi Amin* and, along with Iain Grahame, remains to date an important source for TV documentaries and other accounts of Amin's life and times. Decades later, I was asked to be a consultant on the 2021 Netflix documentary *How to Become a Tyrant.* I obliged, spending an entire morning at the Netflix-rented studio in Brooklyn, only to realize months later that Netflix had used but one sentence from what had been at least a one-hour, face-to-face interview. The reason was not difficult to guess: nothing I said or narrated fit their preconceived notions of Amin.

Among those who understood that the figure of Amin had been racialized by the media was the actor Forest Whitaker. When he was making *The Last King of Scotland* (2006), he asked Mira, my wife, if he could come and talk to me about Amin. I said yes. Whitaker and I sat in the garden of our home for several hours. He was agitated, and disturbed, by the picture of Amin he had gathered from the filmmakers and from those they suggested he talk to about Amin. He was looking for a credible, believable picture of Amin. The endeavor took us several hours.

Few Ugandan writers shared this widely held caricature of Amin. A leading Ugandan journalist, Daniel Kalinaki, wrote that "apart from the myths (the human head in the refrigerator, a taste for human flesh, et cetera), other important questions, such as the exact number of people killed under his hand and regime, remain answered inconclusively. Even basics, such as whether compensation was paid to departing Asians for their properties remains unsettled."[10] The only Westerner to depart from the chorus of Western writers was Bob Astles, the British officer who had become a close associate of Amin's, and who in a memoir published after his death, wrote, "Over the years, Amin's antics have made good copy to sell newspapers. . . . [Amin] was human enough to know that by 'putting his foot in it,' he was giving them a good story but they rarely acknowledged that he had helped their careers. Much has been written about him both in praise and execration. We should forget stories about keeping heads in refrigerators and eating human flesh. They are accusations without evidence, which is not surprising, as they never happened."[11] None of the Ugandan scholars who have written extensively on the Amin years—Amii Omara-Otunnu, Phares Mutibwa, Abdou Kasozi, George W. Kanyeihamba, Kiddu Makubuya, and others—mention cannibalism. Otunnu "dismiss(es) it" outrightly.[12] Mark Leopold could have used this literature as a springboard to write an alternative account of the Amin years. But he did not.

Reassessing Amin

For nearly a decade, Amin was able to outwit Israel and Britain. Portrayed as a buffoon and a racist, Amin deliberately and persistently played to the racism of his adversaries, inviting them to underestimate him, leading them to think of him as no different from the caricature they had painted of him for their own people and for the rest of the world to swallow. It resembled in broad contours the time-tested racist caricature of a Black person: childlike, but capable of abundant brutality.

Amin paid back in kind. Tongue in cheek, he would respond in the very language they used to depict him. Asked whether he had "eaten" his enemies, he would respond metaphorically, "I ate them before they could eat me."[13] And when asked about the lack of freedom of speech in the country, he would respond, "In Uganda, we have freedom of speech. What we cannot guarantee is freedom after speech." Amin's wordplay made for a sensational press, and guaranteed publishers soaring sales.

Amin made constant fun of his adversaries. His birthday telegram to Queen Elizabeth II of England was addressed to Mr. and Mrs. Queen. And his telegram to President Richard Nixon wished the president a speedy recovery from Watergate. Sometimes, he resorted to ridiculing white authority, as in 1972 when organizing a public fundraiser to help Britain in its hour of financial crisis. I remember witnessing the public rally where Amin had asked ordinary folk—*wananchi*—to donate anything they could afford, however small or modest, to help Britain. And so they came to the Old Air Strip in Kololo, humble folk in the thousands, carrying anything from a goat, to chickens, to a bundle of *matoke* (plantain) to a sack of maize flour or beans or groundnuts. In December 1973, the British High Commission staff in Kampala telegrammed London to pass on an offer from General Idi Amin Dada to save the United Kingdom from financial ruin. In his telegram to the British government, Amin wrote, "In the past months the people of Uganda have been following with sorrow the alarming economic crisis befalling Britain. The sad fact is that it is the ordinary British citizen who is suffering the most. I am today appealing to all the people of Uganda who have all along been traditional friends of the British people to come forward and help their former colonial masters." Toward that end, Amin launched a Save Britain Fund, offering 10,000 Ugandan shillings as a personal donation.

A month later, Amin announced that "the response from ordinary folk had been overwhelming," informing Whitehall, "today, 21 January 1974, the people of Kigezi donated one lorry load of vegetables and wheat. I am now requesting you to send an aircraft to collect this donation before it goes bad. I hope you will react quickly so as not to discourage Ugandans from donating more." When there was no response from Whitehall, Amin offered his diplomatic skills, "suggest(ing) he could broker peace in Northern Ireland": "This serious and regrettable development calls for Britain's best and sincere friends to come to her assistance. Consequently, I avail my good offices at the disposal of the opposing sides in Northern Ireland."[14] Amin went on to declare himself the King of Scotland, wearing a kilt on ceremonial occasions.[15] Amin's title, toward the end of his presidency, was "President for Life, Field-Marshal al-Hadj, Doctor Idi Amin Dada, VC, DSO, MC, Lord of All the Beasts of the Earth and Fishes of the Sea, Last King of Scotland, Conqueror of the British Empire in Africa in General and Uganda in Particular."

Clearly, Amin did not expect a response from Whitehall. His real audience, though, was not the authority in Whitehall but the people of Uganda, and all those around the world who had historically felt aggrieved by British imperial practices. When the Swiss filmmaker Barbet Schroeder made his 1974 documentary on Amin, *General Idi Amin Dada: A Self-Portrait,* Amin made sure the film showed him "largely as he wished to be seen." Mark Leopold writes, "According to some sources, 'Amin and his subordinates worked to direct the camera, staging scenes and generating scenarios for the dictator to pursue,' while the president himself contributed the musical score on his accordion. There remained a few scenes Amin himself did not like and, when Schroeder refused to remove them, Amin threatened to detain all French citizens in Uganda until they were cut. Schroeder conceded and thereafter subtitled the film *A Self Portrait,* declaring Amin was its real director, as he had 'the final cut.'"[16] Amin was a master of theater.

At other times, Amin dished out humiliation. To the great amusement of heads of state at the 1975 Organization of African Unity (OAU) conference in Kampala, he arranged for a group of white men to carry him shoulder high in a sedan chair in an image reversing Kipling's "White Man's Burden."[17] During the saga of Denis Hills, the British author who was imprisoned for writing of Amin as a "village tyrant," Amin said he would spare Hills's life only if the Queen intervened as head of state of the United Kingdom and apologized on behalf of Hills to Amin as head of the Ugandan state. Britain agreed to send a letter from the Queen, carried by Amin's former commander, Iain Grahame; when that did not work, Whitehall sent Foreign Secretary James Callaghan, with seven senior officials: "Callaghan had to 'bow' to enter a 'hut' with a low entrance, a gesture Amin had televised and broadcast." Hills was then "released to Callaghan after 102 days in captivity."[18]

Amin left behind a twofold legacy, both personal and institutional. The popular image of Amin in Uganda is that of a man of the people—a populist—a less elitist version of Julius Nyerere. If Nyerere had a driver take him around in a modest car, observing all traffic lights like any other motorist, Amin often drove his own military jeep. When the president of Rwanda, Juvénal Habyarimana, arrived in the country at a time of acute oil shortage, Amin rode a bicycle to the airport to welcome him and his thirty-six-person entourage in April 1976. At the same time, Amin used the occasion to appeal to the Ugandan people, urging them to follow his example and ride bicycles to work so long as the fuel shortage lasted in the country.[19]

Amin always spoke of Africa for Africans, echoing the sentiments, if not the exact words, of his mother. Bob Astles, who had known Amin ever since the 1960s, when he used to fly him to South Sudan, wrote that no other woman had a greater impact on Amin than his mother, Ama Aate. His mother taught him that Africa is a continent of Black people. Amin shaped Uganda as a Black nation and his conviction, that an African is a Black person, remains the dominant understanding of African identity in today's Uganda—among both ordinary people and the regimes that followed Amin. Many see Amin as having upheld the dignity of Africa. I have lost count of the number of times I have seen a poster on the back of a *matatu* (public taxi) in Kampala, with photos of Malcolm X, Muhammad Ali, Bob Marley, and Idi Amin, and no caption, because none seemed necessary.

During the Asian expulsion, Amin invited ambassadors and selected leaders of the Asian community to his official residence, speaking to them informally and freely about how he wished the expulsion to be remembered. The conversation was filmed and broadcast by the London-based Independent Television channel, ITV. That clip continues to circulate on social media in Uganda. Amin claimed that the expulsion had ushered in true independence for ordinary people. When asked what he would do should some Asians choose not to leave, he replied without hesitation, "They will find themselves sitting on fire."

Amin was not all about symbolism, or bravado. He also left behind an active legacy, partly building on the colonial legacy and partly attempting to find an alternative to it. The day-to-day business of colonial governance was summed up in the notion of customary law. We can see this at three levels. Laying the foundation of colonial rule involved nothing less than spectacular violence, leading to the mass murder of a substantial part of the population of Bunyoro during the Buganda-Bunyoro war.[20] A different kind of violence emerged, not spectacular but more or less continuous, steady and perpetual, when it came to disciplining pastoral populations like those in Karamoja, where the British continuously attempted to fix a mobile population to a particular territory, but never succeeded, driving home the lesson that violence must be integral to day-to-day governance. This lesson was written into what was defined as "customary law" under colonialism.

As defined under colonial law, a measure of force was integral to define the relationship between native officials (chiefs) and native subjects. Part of colonial wisdom was the claim that whereas a civilized population could be kept in order through judicious dispensation of civil law, only direct administration of force would keep savages in line. Native chiefs were encouraged to use corporal punishment (the lash of the hippopotamus hide) routinely on erring native subjects, rather than resort to fines and confinement, which were reserved for errant civil subjects. Amin was nurtured in the colonial army in the arts of counterinsurgency, which shaped his instrumental outlook on violence: if it works, it is right.

The colonial legacy involved both official violence and institutionalized corruption, meaning the use of political power to get privileged access to resources, over and above one's entitlement under a law and order regime. Here, too, there were both spectacular and routine manifestations of privilege. In the realm of spectacular corruption, we can identify at least two instances: one, the transfer of a third of Bunyoro's territory ("the Lost Counties") to Buganda as acknowledgement of its role in the conquest of Buyoro; and two, the declaration of square miles of land in Buganda as the exclusive preserve of individual chiefs, now landlords with a right to extract rent from their tenants. The routine manifestation of colonial privilege was written into the regime of race privilege. Racially defined privilege was written into the administration of day-to-day life: membership of the master race (whites) or of immigrant races (brown) was enough to give one regular access to privilege, with regard to every aspect of day-to-day life, from residence to employment to recreation or leisure.

Amin tried to turn the world of institutionalized corruption upside down. The appropriation of Asian wealth in the aftermath of the expulsion was his attempt to restructure the world in line with the principle that the weak shall inherit the world. In doing so, he also drove home a more general lesson: that political power is the key to worldly goods. It is a lesson that would be unfailingly learned by subsequent regimes. Though he turned the world upside down, he could not change it. After Amin, the notion that political power was the assured way to acquire prosperity and wealth became common sense.

Where Amin tried to transform the world was in the very notion of who we are. When it came to public representation, colonial power recognized its subjects as belonging to "tribes." In place of the colonial claim that natives belong to tribes and have no wider identity, Amin proudly and boldly proclaimed a national and racial identity for natives—as Africans. As we shall see later, Museveni would draw a sharp contrast with Amin here: returning to the colonial legacy, he would proclaim the African identity as an ethnic being and reconfigure the political sphere as a constellation of different tribal territorial spaces.

State Violence

The Amin regime was born in an orgy of blood. The coup set in motion a civil war within the army. The two factions, one side pro-Obote and the other pro-Amin, often identified each other in tribal terms. Significant sections of Luo-speaking Obote supporters fled to Tanzania and Sudan. Probably an equal number were physically eliminated in the barracks. But many remained, an easily identifiable internal enemy who would be targeted during successive crises.

The rift in the army did not end with the flight of Obote sympathizers who had served in it. A new fissure opened with the integration of an estimated 20,000 ex-Anyanya rebels (and refugees) into the army. Once again, numbers are not reliable but can be taken as an indicator of the scale of the problem. Amin sent many of the ex-Anyanya outside the country for training, and promoted several on their return.

The regime was now riddled with two forms of internal tensions: institutional tensions between different sections of the armed forces (police and the military), and an even more explosive rift between two sections of the officer corps—the original creators of the 1971 coup from the West Nile, and growing numbers who had come from South Sudan in the period following the 1972 Addis Ababa Agreement. Among those of South Sudanese origin was Lieutenant-Colonel Godwin Sule. South Sudanese in origin and Christian by faith, Sule had held several important commands in the Ugandan army under Amin, including commanding the Malire Mechanised Battalion and the Paratroopers Military School.

Who were the Anyanya? Were they mercenaries who had come from across the borders of colonial Uganda? Or were they members of communities that had been partitioned by colonial borders and made political strangers overnight?

Historian Thomas Lowman cites several examples.[21] Was Isaac Maliyamungu a "Congolese," or was he "a former casual laborer who had become a gatekeeper at Nyanza Textiles in Eastern Uganda"? Was Ali Waris Fadhul a "Sudanese" or "a Nubian speaker from the Basoga ethnic group in Eastern Uganda"? The same with Hussein Marella, the former Ugandan head of the military police, recruited into the army in 1954 in Hoima, in the Western region of Uganda: "When later exiled from Uganda in the wake of the 1974 mutiny, Amin praised him for twenty-one years of military service in the country. Onama told the 1986 Commission that Marella's relatives had come to Hoima from Sudan to work in the cotton ginnery and in sawmills and whereever else work was available. Marella was recruited in 1954 in Hoima." In his testimony to the 1986 Commission set by Museveni, Moses Ali pointed out that "a Black person in Uganda is often assumed to be Anyanya as is often a person from the North."[22]

Should we understand Marella, and many others like him, as "mercenaries" or as labor migrants that provided human fuel to the colonial economy? Labor migration was central to the colonial economy. Probably for that same reason, colonial notions disenfranchised migrants when they limited (customary) rights only to persons defined as indigenous under colonial law, which limited the designation "indigenous" to those born in the country before colonial conquest.

Nubian-speaking communities often moved between urban communities within the East African region such as Juba, Khartoum, Nairobi, Kampala, Bombo, and many other locations: "Ugandan officers like Isaac Maliyamungu had kin relations with the Kakwa in Jaki county in Congo, as did Taban Lupayi with the Pojulu, and Moses Ali with the Bari, both in Sudan."[23] The same could be said of the Tutsi, who had come to live for generations in refugee camps since the 1959 Hutu Revolution. These migrants without an officially acknowledged homeland became ready-made fodder for any army, whether government or rebel, looking for fresh new recruits in large numbers. For the Nubians (and many border communities), as for the Tutsi and the Asians, the entire East African region had come to be home.

State Corruption

I have seen no evidence to suggest that Amin was individually corrupt, except for an undocumented allegation in Wanume Kibedi's 1973 letter of resignation as foreign minister. Amin had been directly implicated, along with Obote, in the first Congo crisis in 1964; he had been accused by Daudi Ochieng, a leading opposition member of Parliament (MP), of corruption in the Congo affair. Obote appointed a Judicial Commission, drawn from the three East African high courts and headed by a white judge of the East African High Court, one of the institutions of the East African Community. Though the Commission's report came out after Obote's overthrow, it found Obote, Amin, and others not guilty of charges made by the MP Daudi Ochieng.

Though there is little evidence pointing to Amin as a corrupt person, there is abundant evidence to suggest that he built on the British legacy of institutionalized corruption. Expropriation and corruption are parts of a single but connected process. You can expropriate a group in response to a public demand for justice, but the act is given its final meaning by what follows, how and to whom proceeds are distributed. Are the resources turned into public property or into new sources of private wealth? Does expropriation lead to nationalization or privatization?

There have been two instances of state-driven, large-scale expropriation in Uganda, and both had led to privatization. In each case, the beneficiary has not been society, but an old elite restored or one newly created. The first expropriation was carried out by the colonial state, in the interest of stabilizing colonial rule at its outset. Following the end of the battle between religious factions in Buganda, the British decided to award land grants to the Protestant faction, lesser grants to the Catholic faction, and the least to the Muslim faction. These grants in square miles of land (*mailo)* were codified in the 1900 Buganda Agreement; in return, chiefs pledged loyalty to Britain. Similar agreements with the other kingdoms followed in the South, though on a smaller scale. The land grants radically altered agrarian relations in Buganda. When a chief received a grant, he was expected to move with "his" peasants to "his" land. He now became the lord, or *mwami,* of the land and they his *bakopi* (peasants). In the pre-British system, the chief was not the lord of the land, for he did not own it. The land was regulated separately from the formal power system, by the clan heads, or *bataka,* as trustees and not as owners of land. The 1900 Agreement was a forced appropriation of the *bakopi* that ended with the redistribution of the loot to the British-connected gentry. The *mailo* landowners have since safeguarded the loot as a historical birthright, *ebyaffe* ("our things"). The 1900 Agreement also left the losing (Catholic and Muslim) sections of chiefs with a dual grievance. They had been denied an equal share in the pie on religious grounds.

The second large-scale expropriation in the contemporary history of Uganda was the Asian expulsion of 1972. Amin promised UN Secretary-General

Kurt Waldheim in 1972 that Asian-owned property will not be nationalized but will remain in private hands. Indeed, by and large, it did. The expropriation was followed by privatization, leading to a neoliberal jamboree. Expropriated properties were designated as abandoned properties, with the state as trustee, with powers to allocate and reallocate abandoned properties, usually for political reasons.[24] How many Asian properties were confiscated? A Makerere University research study estimated the number at a total of 7,000.[25] If we assume that each was a family property, with an average family numbering five, that gives us 35,000 family proprietors. This would be a half of the 75,000 Asians usually estimated as then resident in Uganda.

Those expropriated properties were divided into three groups: citizens of India, UK citizens, and stateless persons. The Amin regime compensated two of these groups. The first were Indian citizens. According to the Parliamentary Committee (2021), "In 1976, Ushs 13,415,414/16 to Indian government, being compensation to Indian citizens for their assets left in Uganda." This amounted to US $1,627,114.60 at the prevailing 1976 exchange rate of one dollar to 8.3 shillings.[26] A year later, in 1977, Uganda signed "an agreement with UNHCR to pay a total of Ushs 40,409,995/51 being compensations to persons of undetermined nationality for assets left in Uganda." The payment was to be made in several annual installments. The committee noted that "after payment of only three installments, the government was overthrown." According to the *Daily Monitor,* the compensation through the United Nations High Commissioner for Refugees included 344 properties. In addition to that, there was compensation of a further 116 properties for British Asians.[27] Amin wanted the United Kingdom to regularize relations with his regime before its citizens could be compensated.

The appropriation of Asian properties opened up mega opportunities for corruption and enrichment. This happened at several points. Distribution took place in two phases. The first was direct distribution to individuals by committees set up by the Cabinet. I was unable to find a list of those who received Asian properties through direct distribution. The second was distribution through the Departed Asian Property Custodian Board (DAPCB). These properties were often allocated, and then reallocated, sometimes to more than one individual.

According to Joe Oloka-Onyango, professor of law at Makerere University, who spoke at the public discussion organized by the Asian African Association (AAA) in August 2013, the Departed Asian Property Custodian Board (DAPCB) was by then "the largest owner of property in the country." Under the 1972 law, "the DAPCB was designated as a trustee/caretaker over the expropriated Asian property," a provision reproduced in the 1982 Expropriated Properties Act. This is how Professor Onyango summed up his research on the subject: "My finding illustrates that the DAPCB has been riddled by problems of gross management, legal shenanigans, and outright fraud and embezzlement." According to the Ugandan auditor general's report of May 15, 2009, "the DAPCB does not have an assets register. Since 1999 no financial statement has been prepared preventing the Auditor General from carrying out a statutory audit." The auditor general's report revealed other malpractices, including "illegal disposal of properties under the influence of high-ranking government officials," "lack of verification of payments by Government of Uganda to several Indian nationals, stateless Indians and Indians of British nationality," and "improper property valuations and insider purchases."[28]

The Board both allocated and sold individual properties, and then resold them. Each action provided an opportunity for further corruption. A glimpse into this process is provided by the handover report of the Divestiture Committee, set up by parliament to wind up the DAPCB by December 31, 2005.[29] The Committee's report "to the Minister of State for Finance, Planning and Economic Development revealed that a total of 1524 [enterprises] had been sold [by the Board] and fully paid for as at 31st December 2005, realizing a total of Ushs 15,378,872,388 in proceeds from . . . cumulative sales since 1993." The 2021 Parliamentary Committee noted that "the Board stated that monies collected from sales would be utilized for compensation claims and the daily operations of the Board." Between them, statutory bodies like the Auditor General's Office and Parliamentary Committees provided snippets of information, but none of it was sufficient to establish any measure of accountability. The DAPCB remained beyond the reach of legal accountability.

Over the years, there was no proper accountability on file for these funds. The Committee concluded: "At no material time did this figure ever get reflected on any account of DAPCB as a lump sum." The 2021 Parliamentary Committee noted that corruption had been a continuing practice by the Board: "DAPCB continues to allocate same properties to different individuals as revealed by the Auditor General's special audits." Every round of distribution led to forced evictions and a fresh round of violence: DAPCB properties had become part of a circuit whereby "some formerly compensated [for] properties by [the] government had ended up in the hands of unscrupulous individuals" only to be later transferred to "bona fide purchasers for value without notice." Along the way, fertile partnerships mushroomed between government bureaucrats or politicians on the one hand, and businesspersons (mostly Asian) on the other: "The Committee noted that some Asians had gotten their property back but they had also been compensated."[30]

After Amin, the return of properties under Museveni's National Resistance Movement government provided another set of opportunities for private corruption by individual businesspersons, mostly Asian, but also Africans, including individual members of the Board. These individuals secured powers of attorney to represent owners from 1972 and before, especially those cases involving one or a few proprietors who had little interest in returning to Uganda and going through the process of repossession, which included pledging that they would be personally responsible for the upkeep and maintenance of the property. These individuals usually handed over powers of attorney to individual estate agents or lawyers from the pre-1972 era. Though they signed agreements that stipulated fees for representation, either as a percentage of the proceeds acquired through the sale of property, or as a percentage of the value of the property, former owners were seldom in a position to have knowledge of the amounts involved.

The 2021 parliamentary report named those claiming to represent the largest number of former proprietors. Prominent among these were six businesspersons: Mohammed Alibhai, "a beneficiary of 1,200 properties (appendix 2)"; Unia Ssebaggala (235 properties), Praful Chandra (66), Praful Patel (50), Mumtaz Kassam (58), and Minnex Karia (46). The Committee pointed to rampant malpractices by these persons: 997 properties "had only letters of repossession without certificates of repossession" and "were without any supporting documents, POA or Certificates." These 1,200 would be a quarter of the 5,000 properties estimated by the Makerere University–based research team as confiscated by the government in 1972. Their owners fought tooth and nail to keep their possessions and prevent official inquiries from being concluded and their reports from being made public. The Committee went on to deplore the way in which many in this group "continually fought the committee"—including public campaigns and "attempts to use the judicial system to muzzle the committee and prevent it from conducting the inquiry"—and concluded that "such conduct constitutes contempt of Parliament."

State Reform

The crisis of the Amin regime was both economic and military. In the aftermath of the Asian expulsion, Amin's government allocated thirty-eight large properties—plantations, factories, mills, printing presses—to cooperatives. And

Amin was said to have personally distributed five hundred businesses to individual friends and supporters.[31] Two groups vied for this property: the Baganda land and commercial elite on the one hand, and army officers on the other. The outcome was foreclosed in favor of the latter group. Its members came to chair "distribution committees," even though they lacked any experience in business or economic management. This single development opened the floodgates to a deepening economic crisis.

The military crisis was an outcome of the recruitment of South Sudanese soldiers, mainly following the Addis Ababa Peace Agreement of 1972. Their absorption in the official army bolstered its ranks with Amin's supporters, and, as mentioned earlier, Amin sent a number of them for training courses overseas. The effect would introduce a slow poison in the system, particularly in the army, spreading discontent among Amin's earlier military allies and supporters. For those who saw the army as a national institution, this change was akin to an expanding mercenary influence within its ranks. But for those who traced the genealogy of the army to its Nubi precedents, this was seen as a natural development, akin to building on an established tradition.

The internal conflict between soldiers of Ugandan and South Sudanese origin came to a head during the 1978–1979 Uganda-Tanzania War. The final counteroffensive during this war, one that culminated in the Battle of Lukaya, March 10–11, 1979, was led by Lieutenant-Colonel Godwin Sule, acknowledged as one of the most talented soldiers in the Amin army. The highest-ranking South Sudanese and Christian officer in Amin's army, Lieutenant-Colonel Sule was killed on March 11, 1979, some say by "friendly fire." His death was followed by the collapse of the Ugandan offensive. This is the moment the army imploded. The military defeat of the Amin regime followed.

One question remains unanswered: Why did Amin decide to launch a war against Tanzania in 1978–1979? The question has never been satisfactorily answered, though speculation has been rife on the subject. Many think it was Amin's way of resolving the ongoing and growing contention in the national army between the West Nile and South Sudanese factions. Others think the motivation could lie in the growing threat from anti-regime forces inside Tanzania, mainly organized around former Prime Minster Milton Obote. Whatever the case, the outcome delivered a final blow to the regime in Kampala.

PART II

THE TRANSITION

9

NAMING THE WAR

At the heart of the political mythology crafted by the Ugandan National Resistance Movement and its architect, Yoweri Museveni, since their rise to power in 1986, is the story of a guerrilla war that overthrew an African regime without any significant external support. "Mamdani, I overthrew an African dictator," Museveni told me in April 1986 as Winnie Byanyima, then his companion and now a political opponent, served us tea in his living room at the Kilimanjaro Hotel in Dar es Salaam. I was struck by the use of "I" as the subject of this deed, but I let the conversation continue to other subjects.

After the Amin coup in 1971, the Ugandan opposition divided into several groups. The main opposition cohered around the ousted president, Milton Obote. The rest organized as three groups, their leadership drawn from the educated strata. One, led by Dani Wadada Nabudere who, along with Wanume Kibedi and Edward Rugumayo, had joined the Amin regime after the coup, argued that the regime had no clear direction and could be influenced and pushed to the left. As a reward, Kibedi and Rugumayo won ministerial posts in the Amin Cabinet, and Nabudere was appointed head of the East African Railways and Harbours Corporation. A second group, led by Yoweri Museveni, had refused to follow their lead or to join the Amin regime. Once in Dar es Salaam, they separated from Obote and formed the Front for National Salvation (FRONASA). A third group, led by the UPC Youth leader of the early 1970s, Raiti Omongin of Karamoja, argued against both going into exile and joining the regime, and called on progressives to stay and organize in the country. Raiti and eight others, including Wabwire Kwoba (of whom we will learn more later), went to China for political and military training. On return, they formed the Communist Party of Uganda. Soon after, Raiti was murdered, the circumstances of which are still unclear, and the nascent party disintegrated.

Was the war that raged over five years in the Luwero Triangle a guerrilla war waged by a mainly peasant army led by Museveni against a government army supporting Obote, or was it a civil war between two factions of a fractured government army—one faction, Kikosi Maalum, supporting Obote and the other, the Front for National Salvation (FRONASA), supporting Museveni? Each side in this war had its genesis in a different history. Kikosi Maalum was created from the thousands of soldiers who fled from Uganda to Tanzania and Sudan in the aftermath of the 1971 coup. FRONASA, wrote Museveni in *Sowing the Mustard Seed,* was formed "in 1971 of those not willing to work with Obote." It started out small; by the second half of 1972, when Ugandan exiles launched an invasion with the support of Tanzania, FRONASA had no more than "50 trained cadres."[1] But what they could not make up in numbers and level of training, they did so in high hopes. In a version of the then–popular "foco theory" of Che Guevara, they expected that just the sight of armed rebels would set the population in motion, if not on fire, and they would be determined to rise up and remove the dictator. But precisely the opposite happened. In those days, when the Asian exodus was just beginning, and Amin's popularity was unassailable, the population identified the rebels as so many worms in grain silos, which they were happy to isolate and hand over to the army.[2]

Museveni writes of building an "alliance" with Tanzania, of sending Tanzanian president Julius Nyerere a telegram outlining options.[3] One option was a Tanzanian-led invasion of Uganda by neighboring countries; the other, an internal struggle supported by Tanzania. When the invasion came, these plans collapsed like a house of cards. Museveni noted that Tanzanian bureaucrats were hoping for quick results; Prime Minister Edward Sokoine informed Museveni on September 14, 1972, that the invasion would take place the same evening.[4] The main force of the invasion would be the 1,300 Obote people who had been training in the Sudan, and FRONASA's platoon of forty men would be expected "to go along."[5] When the expected popular revolt did not materialize, Nyerere was humiliated and forced to send diplomats to the Somali capital of Mogadishu to sign an accord pledging not to intervene in the internal affairs of Uganda. Museveni took a job teaching at the Cooperative College in Moshi.[6]

I first met Museveni in 1973 during his regular visits to the University of Dar es Salaam. I had joined an exile group of ten or twelve Ugandan progressives. We used to meet every Sunday morning at fellow progressive Augustine Ruzindana's house in the working-class suburb of Chango'mbe, and soon came to be known as the Chango'mbe group. Over time, members in the group coalesced around two political factions. On one side were Nabudere and Yash Tandon, and later Omwony Ojwok, all university professors; on the other were Augustine Ruzindana, Wafula Oguttu, Henry Akankwasa, (and occasionally Yoga Adhola) and me. Except for me, all were members of the non-university salariat; four students—Sam Magara, Augustine Kayonga, Charles Beyisa, and Sam Katabarwa—occupied the middle ground.

Ruzindana, who had been part of FRONASA in the pre-1972 days, landed a job as an accountant with a Tanzania government parastatal when the rebellion collapsed. Oguttu had finished his literature degree at Tsinghua University in Beijing, returned to Dar just after the coup, and worked as an editor at the government-owned Tanzania Publishing House. Adhola worked at the East African Railways and Harbours Corporation. He, too, had been in FRONASA; unlike others, however, he had retained his ties with Obote. Adhola, Oguttu, Ruzindana, and I would sometimes go to my parents' flat on Morogoro Road. My mother would cook us tea and kebabs, and we would discuss the latest developments around the continent. Museveni would come to the Chango'mbe group about once a month. He would mostly listen, quietly. Issues like history or theory were not of immediate concern to him.

One day in 1975, Museveni invited me to his apartment for dinner. Museveni's wife, Janet, cooked us a meal as the children played in the living room. "Mamdani, we need intellectuals in FRONASA," Museveni said at one point during the dinner. It sounded more like a job offer than an invitation to a common struggle. I stayed quiet. Maybe this had been the point of the dinner, I later thought.

Another close friend was Saki Mafatshe, who had been with the Black Consciousness Movement in South Africa. He had fled to Dar after the uprising in Soweto (South West township), a suburb in Johannesburg, and joined the Pan-African Congress (PAC). He and his buddies seemed to be in endless meetings, as if perpetually on vacation, their monthly expenses paid as allowances by the Tanzanian state. Somewhat ungenerously, I used to call them "revolutionaries on stipend." One day, Saki came to see me. He said the PAC needed my assistance. Their commander, known by his initials, TM, had gone to the front, then in Manzini, the capital of Swaziland just off the South African border, but had not been heard from for several weeks. Would I go to Manzini and look for him, discretely? Why me? "As an Indian person, you would be less suspect," Saki said. I could not disagree. It was not difficult to put together a credible plan. Just a few months ago, Nathan Shamuyarira, a colleague from Zimbabwe, had been asked by his organization, Zimbabwe African National Union (ZANU), to move to Maputo, which had become the frontline with the independence of Mozambique. Shamuyarira had asked me to finish teaching his course and I had agreed. Now that the semester was over and students had finished writing exams, I told Shamuyarira I would be coming to Maputo to give him student papers so he could mark them while I take the opportunity to see the country. I took the bus to Manzini.

The PAC comrades had told me to avoid hotels, which they said were South African intelligence beehives. I met an Indian-looking person on the bus. We got to talking. He said he was a tailor in Manzini; on learning that I was stopping there overnight, he invited me to stay with him. I happily accepted. I had been told that I would be able to find TM through the local Coca-Cola manager, whose garden had the distinction of having the tallest Coca-Cola bottle in town. All I had to do was to survey the horizon, find the bottle, and walk in its direction, which is what I did; I had no problem finding TM. We talked and I took his reply back to Dar.

In the 1970s, Dar es Salaam was the headquarters of the Liberation Committee formed by the Organization of African Unity (OAU). The government of Tanzania hosted a dizzying array of "liberation" movements. There were the OAU-recognized, anti-apartheid "revolutionary" groups from Southern Africa: South Africa, Rhodesia, Southwest Africa (now Namibia), Mozambique, and Angola. Then, there were those not officially recognized by the OAU as "liberation" groups, such as the variety of anti-Amin groups from Uganda.

Those officially acknowledged considered themselves "professional" revolutionaries, in the Leninist fashion. More than likely, they were paid a stipend by the Liberation Committee. The unofficial revolutionaries, like those of us from Uganda, had no such stipend, unless of course it was provided by the Tanzanian state. We thus divided between those who earned a living from a job, and those who were on official stipend. Among the latter were the Obote and Museveni cadres. This fact could not escape the discerning eye of Philip Ochieng, the unfailingly humorous Kenyan journalist, himself in exile. Ochieng wrote in the Dar-based *Daily News:* "Dar es Salaam is full of counterrevolutionaries, those who drink at the counter and talk revolution."

People like me, who earned their keep "on the hill," which is how the university was known, received no government subsidy. Life on the Hill was punctuated by multiple study groups. I had seven in a week: a group on Marx's *Capital* every Monday night, several on a variety of themes, from internal struggles in the international socialist movement, to the Agrarian Question, the Russian Revolution, and the Chinese Revolution. On Sunday morning there would be a large gathering of between seventy and two hundred progressive students and academic staff, known as the Ideological Class. The name marked it as an alternative to church gatherings on Sunday mornings. The week would be capped with the meeting of the Sunday afternoon Chango'mbe group.

After the 1972–1973 invasion of Uganda, FRONASA wilted; with few activities to breathe life into it, it became a more or less a paper organization. Museveni acknowledges that it was treated by Tanzania as an auxiliary group, to be attached to Obote's forces whenever action was called for. Meanwhile, Museveni would liaise with Ugandan activists, whether at the university or in town, so long as they were not affiliated with Obote. The last time Museveni joined us in Chango'mbe, he asked us to nominate a comrade from among us to join the "armed struggle." We suggested Sam Katabarwa, a law student who went on to become a leading commander in Museveni's National Resistance Army. Years later, one day in 1984, as I returned to 2 Livingstone Terrace, home during my Makerere years, my mother said someone had left a note for me. The note was signed by Katabarwa. It said they were just twenty or so miles outside town and added that the bearer of the note, who worked in the main administration of the university, would be happy to bring me along the next time he came. I flushed the note down the toilet and told my mother that should the person come back, to tell him I would not be traveling. Some months later, I heard that Katabarwa had set out for Kampala to meet with the Prime Minister Paulo Muwanga, who ruled briefly in August 1985, in secret NRA-government talks; along the way, he had been betrayed, ambushed, tortured, and killed. I wondered what would have been my fate had state security found Katabarwa's note on me at a checkpoint outside the city.

In late 1978, we prepared for the consequences of the Kagera War, Kagera being the river that marked the Tanzania-Uganda border. The Tanzanian government announced that it would host a conference of anti-Amin groups in the town of Moshi. Every exiled anti-Amin group was to be represented by two delegates, no matter the size of its membership. No one, of course, talked of anti-Amin forces within Uganda. Ruzindana and I had gone to Moshi to represent the Chango'mbe Group but were not allowed in. This is when we realized that our group had broken into two factions. Unknown to us, Nabudere and Tandon had been among the organizers of the Moshi conference and were now part of the Credentials Committee, which decided on the groups that would be represented by delegates. Claiming to be the legitimate representatives of the Chango'mbe Group (known formally as the Ad Hoc Committee for the Promotion of Unity Among Ugandans), they had locked us out.

Through part of the conference, Museveni, too, had been marginalized. When the conference ended, Museveni said he had use of a VW Combie and invited me to join him for the ride to Dar. Inside the Combie, he complained that he was doing all the hard work at the front but had been left out of the leadership of the Military Commission of the Uganda National Liberation Front (UNLF). "Should I write Mwalimu?" he asked me. "Sounds right," I replied. He asked the driver for a sheet of paper and began to write an appeal to President Nyerere, otherwise known as *Mwalimu* (the teacher). It was short and straightforward. Museveni wrote that he had spent all these years training military cadres and had now been left out of the leadership of the Military Council. He passed the sheet to the driver: "*Mpe Mwalimu*" (Give this to Mwalimu). I understood that we were likely in a security vehicle, and the driver a member of state security. The next day the government radio announced the new leadership of the UNLF. The Military Commission had been reconstituted, with Paulo Muwanga as its chair, and Museveni its vice chair. Museveni wrote in *Sowing the Mustard Seed,* "Paulo Muwanga was elected Chairman instead of myself. Even for me to be elected Vice Chairman was at the intervention of President Nyerere after the conference."[7]

The turning point in the Kagera War came after the Moshi conference. Once the opposition had driven Amin forces out of Tanzanian territory, Nyerere called on his army to pursue them into Ugandan territory. This required crossing the Kagera River, which was not possible without significant support from outside sources. For this, Nyerere turned to the United Kingdom. It was a fateful decision that would have a lasting impact on both Uganda and Tanzania.

FRONASA came back to life with the Kagera War as Ugandan fighters in exile joined the Tanzanian army as auxiliaries. The armies in exile resembled their colonial predecessor in at least one respect; all had been put together using tribal building blocks. Kagera was adjacent to western Uganda, ethnically home to Museveni and most of FRONASA. They recruited rapidly and in large numbers. Museveni wrote in *Sowing the Mustard Seed,* "By the time Amin's regime collapsed on 11 April, the Fronasa force had grown to 9,000. . . . In my sector, I immediately started a massive recruitment exercise, taking in every available youth who cared to volunteer. On the Masaka side, however, there was no recruitment because Obote's group did not want to recruit from the 'wrong' tribes who lived in that part of the country." Kikosi Maalum had by then roughly 1,500. They, too, began recruiting, but in the northern part of the country, Obote's ethnic home. Museveni would grumble about how "later on, Oyite Ojok [senior military officer in Kikosi Maalum] started recruiting illegal militias from the north of the country."[8] The Uganda National Liberation Army (UNLA) was less a national army than a coalition of tribal militias. Their political leadership was known as the Uganda National Liberation Front (UNLF).

Signs of the forthcoming civil war were evident in the aftermath of the Moshi conference. Competitive recruitment had swollen the numbers of all factions. Museveni writes of receiving an official letter from Yusufu Lule, the first president in the post-Amin government, asking him to disband those he had just recruited, saying Uganda needed "a small but professional army" of about "7,000 officers and men." According to Museveni, "Of the 9,000 fighters we had recruited, only about 4,000 were eventually integrated into the UNLA and trained at Kabamba, Mubende, Nakasongola, Masindi," soon after the overthrow of Amin in 1979, wrote Museveni in *The Mustard Seed.* FRONASA also developed its own corps of trainers: "Some of the trainers were from the original group of trainees from Mozambique, but we had also trained many people with the Tanzanians between 1979 and 1981, including 300 officer cadets whom we sent to Monduli Military Academy in Tanzania." Among those trained as officer cadets was Pecos Kutesa, who had attended that academy in 1979–1980 and went on to write about his experience. Kutesa had by March 1981 left his post at Nakasongola to become part of the Luwero bush war against the second Obote regime.[9] But FRONASA seemed to lack administrative control over its own fighting cadre. They were under the national army command, led by officers close to Obote. Museveni would later complain, "Our young men had been deliberately deployed in very remote areas—for example, Karamoja and northeastern Uganda—and it was very difficult to contact them. We therefore had to adopt a strategy that would allow us to marshal our forces slowly, using people from the old army (the UNLA) and the civilian population."[10]

If the core of Obote's Kikosi Maalum were the part of the Ugandan army that left with Obote in 1971, the same could not be said of Museveni's FRONASA, which began from no more than a handful of individuals who had run to Tanzania in 1971. Once its claim to have an underground rebel network in Uganda was exposed as a sham in 1972, FRONASA was left to shelter under Tanzanian protection until 1978. It was during the Kagera War of 1978–1979 that FRONASA recruited thousands, feverishly, as Museveni said—this, too, under the protective umbrella of the Tanzanian army. This phase would come to an end when the Luwero war began in 1981.

The Luwero war was Museveni's response to the 1980 general elections, whose results, he believed, were rigged. Throughout the election campaign, Museveni had publicly warned that FRONASA would not hesitate to "go to the bush" should the results of the election be rigged. The Luwero war officially began with an assault on a Ugandan army post at Kabamba on February 6, 1981. Kabamba was the heart of what came to be known as the Luwero Triangle, part of Buganda. Since it was the one region in the country bitterly and consistently opposed to Obote since independence in 1962, Museveni concluded that it was ideally suited to be the site where to begin an armed campaign against the Obote government. The thirty-four (of whom only twenty-seven were armed) who mounted an assault on Kabamba were not an embryonic guerrilla group. They were part of a much larger group, all belonging to Museveni's FRO-

NASA, numbering in the thousands, led by trained officers. At the same time, they were scattered, deployed in remote areas. After Kabamba, each was no doubt under close watch. Nonetheless, most were over time absorbed into the rebel force, as if drop by drop, sometimes at a trickle. The Kagera War marked a period of dramatic growth for Museveni's army: "The number of our soldiers had grown to about 4,000 by early 1983," wrote Museveni.[11]

The assault by the FRONASA detach on Kabamba had been fended off by a single Tanzanian soldier. Three days later, on February 9, 1981, Tanzanians disbursed the FRONASA detach. Over 11,000 Tanzanian soldiers were stationed in Uganda in 1981.[12] The war unfolded in two phases. Until July 1981, when Tanzanian forces withdrew from Uganda, the war had been between FRONASA and the Tanzanian army. Keeping a fighting force of over 11,000 in a neighboring country was costly. Given that the Ugandan Treasury was already depleted, the cost of the war was likely borne by Tanzania, at a time when the country was already in debt to Britain for the military supplies it had bought on loan (more on this later). Once Tanzania withdrew its soldiers from Uganda, a civil war in Uganda began between the two armed factions that had been cobbled together as a national army under the watchful eye of the Tanzanians.

There is no agreement on how many of the 9,000 Museveni claimed to have recruited in western Uganda went into the bush. According to Charles Onyango-Obbo of *The Monitor*, and *The East African*, who had done extensive interviews during the last stages of the war, the estimates of those who trained in Tanzanian military academies were upwards of 2,000.[13] We have seen that one of the officer trainees, Pecos Kutesa, had been trained in Monduli, Tanzania.[14] When the NRA came out of the bush in 1986, its fighters were estimated at 16,000, of whom 4,000 were said to be Banyarwanda, many being post-1959 Rwandan refugees who had been housed across the Rwandan border in UN-administered camps in western Uganda, from where many fled to join Museveni's army. A second group were peasants from the Luwero Triangle who had volunteered in the name of the kabaka, but the NRA seemed to have little capacity to train them.

For many of the smaller groups, the NRA was a powerful magnet. The most significant of these smaller groups was the Nabudere faction. According to Ugandan journalist Charles Onyango-Obbo, who had covered the Luwero War (1981–1986) at close quarters, "the UNLF-AD (Anti Dictatorship) had sent educated progressive individuals, like David Tinyefuza (who led the NRA assault in the North after 1986), into the bush." Nabudere claimed they had an edge over Museveni's group in that their cadres had benefited from sustained political work: "People in Ruwenzori (Chef Ali, Kayunga, former students who had been young recruits in the anti-Obote struggle) . . . had done patient political work which was not in Museveni's constitution to do." Onyango-Obbo said Nabudere claimed that the primary reason the NRA moved to the West under pressure from the UNLA during the final phase of the war was because they were already in contact with Chef Ali who had promised them protection.

I asked Onyango-Obbo how many of the 16,000 fighters who came out of the bush at the end of the war were peasants from Luwero. "Many peasants joined, mainly because the Musevenis would go and tell peasants, the kabaka has sent us, this is his fight, any help you want to give, put it under this muvule tree, including any persons—they would find sacks of food and dozens of young men seated there, waiting." Onyango-Obbo said, "They never had a way of training these people—there was a very high casualty rate among the peasants." He concluded, "At the core of it, the NRA had a FRONASA infrastructure—it did not germinate from the soil organically on Feb 6."[15]

We have two versions of relations between peasants and the NRA in the Luwero Triangle, the arena of the bush war. One is from the American journalist Helen Epstein, who states that the NRA often staged "false flag" attacks "made to look as though they were committed by the government army, but were really the work of the NRA." Epstein marshals several reports, one from *The Monitor* of "a villager who lost his entire family"; another from John Kazoora, a senior NRA officer, who in his memoirs writes of NRA revenge attacks against Alur villagers (migrants from the North) said to be Obote supporters; and freelance journalist reports published in *The Observer* (London) and other papers.[16]

Onyango-Obbo offered another version, skeptical of those who believe that the NRA went around in UNLA uniforms killing peasants to discredit the UNLA. He said that the claim has two problems. First, "when we went to the bush after 1985 when Obote fell, we could see that their [i.e., the NRA's] state was such that it would be easy to identify them as rebels in UNLA uniforms"—meaning that their general state set them apart from better nourished government soldiers. Second, "in those early years it would be easy to see that [the soldiers] were not UNLA—even in ethnic terms. [The] NRA would have had a hard time finding Northern soldiers to disguise as UNLA."[17]

The NRA did carry out punishing raids against peasants, but under specific circumstances, especially when peasants were seen as having collaborated with government forces. Onyango-Obbo described one such case: "In the early years, senior officers could bring spouses and girlfriends into the camp—until late 1982–1983 when there was a UNLA attack on one of the camps. Some of the soldiers had left for an operation so the camp was easily and comprehensively overrun. The UNLA killed virtually everyone, [the] majority of whom were partners of senior officers. When these [NRA officers] returned, they concluded that without extensive collaboration of peasants, the UNLA could not have come undetected so far into a remote camp. The surviving soldiers, led by [Fred] Rwigyema [a Rwandese officer who later became the first commander of the Rwanda Patriotic Army], went on a punishing mission carrying out extensive killings."[18]

According to Onyango-Obbo, the question of bringing women companions to camps was not easy to solve: "The NRA had position papers on various issues (women, dealing with civilians)" and had "develop[ed] a series of rules" based on these papers—"one of these said you could not bring female partners into camps, particularly operational camps—they had learned a lesson: it causes disarray and also anger among others. The rule against bringing partners into camps was observed for some time. Then [Museveni's brother] Salim Saleh brought a partner, then David Sejusa and Pecos Kutesa also brought partners." There were a "lot of emotions," and a meeting was held. The dominant "view [was] that there was a disaster last time and we had a new rule, but a small group [was] violating it. For the first time people like Matiya Kyaligonza, who would never speak up to Museveni, spoke up and said, *Effande* [Sir], this is just not on. Museveni's response focused on Salim Saleh: Why do you focus on him when he is a good fighter? Is it because he is my brother? And for the first time he mentioned anti-Bahima sentiment and moved to the issue of 'sectarianism' and invited those who were objecting and claiming that the NRA had moved away from its original objectives to feel free to leave and form their own movement. People listening were surprised that Museveni would go so far as to defend his brother." Many thought that Museveni carried a special sense of responsibility—even guilt—for the brother he had pulled out of school to care for his family, so that his son may have a father figure, and his kids a guardian, at home, while he was away "in the struggle."

Onyango-Obbo continued, "Within FRONASA, Museveni's view was always a minority view." He gave another example, from the last executive meeting of the Uganda Patriotic Movement (UPM), a coalition of progressive intellectual groups, at the home of Kintu Musoke, considered a leading member of the Buganda section of their party, the UPM. The discussion focused on what to do following the rigged 1980 election: "They divided the country into regions, Mukwana Maumbe in the east, Bidandi Ssali and others in Buganda [both leading members of the party from their respective regions, east and Buganda]. The meeting ended 5:00 A.M. or so, . . . most of the night Museveni had been quiet . . . he reaches the bottom of the stairs and says: 'All this stuff you guys said, it is well and fine, you can do what you want, but me, I will go to the bush.' The rest were amazed; he had chaired the meeting and never let them know he was not on board."[19] Onyango-Obbo's account provides a valuable insight into Museveni's leadership style: let all voices chime in, no matter how discordant, but Museveni makes the final decision.

The relations between FRONASA (renamed National Resistance Army after it brought the Yusufu Lule–led Baganda monarchists into its ranks) and Tanzania changed once again after Obote's overthrow by a section of his own army in July 1985. I was then in Dar, having been declared persona non grata by the Obote government. One morning, I had gone to the Embassy Hotel to meet a friend who worked there as a secretary. As I left her office, which was on the lobby floor, I saw Museveni and Adam Marwa, chief of Tanzanian security, waiting by the elevator.

Marwa pulled me over: "Mahmood, come with us for a few minutes." We got out of the elevator and entered an empty room; I assumed it was a security room.

Marwa turned to me and said, "What is your assessment of the situation?"

I said, "Now that Amin's forces have entered the country from the north, everything has changed. Everyone must reassess all previous alignments and oppositions in this new situation."

Marwa and Museveni looked at one another, meaningfully, I thought.

"Thank you, Mahmood," Marwa said as he led me out.

As I walked to the door, Museveni said, "Mamdani, I am at Hotel Kilimanjaro. Come and see me in the afternoon." He gave me his room number.

In the afternoon, I went to Museveni's room. Winnie Byanyima served us tea as we talked. This is the conversation that had begun with Museveni's claim, "Mamdani, I overthrew an African dictator." I chose to ignore it.

"Museveni," I asked—since he was not yet president, I continued calling him, as before, by his last name—"what is going to be your main project as president?"

"The land question. Without a resolution of *mailo* land [referring to square miles of land granted in 1900 by the conquering British to their Protestant Baganda allies], we will not be able to tackle the question of development in the country."

"And how do you propose to do this?"

"Well," Museveni replied, "we have to learn from South Korea. The *mailo* landlords are too powerful for us to confiscate their land. We will have to compensate them, in other words, to buy the land."

Even after thirty-six years in office, Museveni has been unable to realize these ambitions.

We return to the two questions with which I began this chapter: How should we name this war between forces led by Obote and Museveni? And what was Tanzania's role in the war? Museveni wrote that because FRONASA forces had been scattered by an army administratively not under their own control, "we had to opt for a protracted people's war."[20] He was right that as opposed to being a positional war where the concentrated forces of two armies face one another in armed combat over a short period, this war stretched out over time. But this was not a guerrilla war fought in the main by armed peasants, following the 1981 attack on Kabamba. It was a war fought mainly by those recruited—and subsequently trained—in Western Uganda, and by smaller groups that joined them after the Tanzanian army moved into Uganda.

From the time of Amin's 1971 coup, Nyerere made certain strategic decisions that together would lay the ground for the coming civil war in Uganda. Nyerere's hospitality extended to the section of the army that had fled into exile with Obote. He offered them more than political asylum and housed them in camps where they would continue training for a future return to power. He also consistently pursued a strategy of regime change in Uganda, flouting fundamental rules of Pan-African unity as embodied in the charter of the Organization of African Unity—in particular, noninterference in the internal affairs of fellow African states. Over time, Nyerere permitted the formation of two separate and competitive armed groupings: one, Kikosi Maalum, under Obote; and the other, FRONASA, under Museveni. When Tanzanian forces pursued Amin's army into Ugandan territory, both Kikosi Maalum and FRONASA followed. Each recruited competitively under separate command. *Forward,* the magazine of the Chango'mbe group, which had moved with us from Dar es Salaam to Kampala, editorialized in April 1979: "The main forces which are active in southern Uganda have so far been disunited, and there existed a real danger of warlordism developing. . . . The parties concerned have realized the danger of a civil war that this posed."[21] Following Amin's invasion of the Kagera Triangle on October 30, 1978, Nyerere switched from pursuing a defensive war limited to pushing back Amin's troops across the border to an offensive charge, an invasion, aimed at taking the capital city of Kampala and then the whole country. Museveni confirms that at first "seven battalions, then nine, entered Uganda on the march to Mbarara."[22] Issa Shivji, one of Nyerere's three Tanzanian biographers, writes: "At the peak of the war, about 45,000 Tanzanian troops entered Uganda."[23] Museveni later recalled, "When we were fighting Idi Amin, we had a bad experience of depending on outside bases (in Tanzania). If you have to depend on a foreign country, even if it is friendly, you are hostage to that government."[24]

Finally, the switch from a defensive to an offensive war provoked a debate, inside Tanzania as well as in the OAU. According to Shivji, several in the Tanzanian leadership disagreed with Nyerere. Mrisho Sarakikya, the first Tanzanian chief of defense forces, "believed that it was unnecessary to enter Uganda once Amin's forces had been driven out." When faced with opposition from leading members of the OAU (Nigeria, Sudan, Senegal, Kenya, Libya), Nyerere denounced the OAU as a "trade union of heads of state." When the OAU sent emissaries, Nyerere "rebuffed" them "several times by keeping them waiting in hotel lobbies while attending to other matters." There was no mistaking that Nyerere was not interested in consulting with dissenting African heads of states; he had made up his mind. Shivji confirmed that in the face of strong opposition in the OAU, and at home, Nyerere "hesitated." Then, Amin-style, he claimed divine inspiration. Pius Msekwa, the party's secretary-general, recalled Nyerere telling him at the Sunday Mass at St. Peter's Church in Dar, that he had "heard a voice, a revelation that he should not retreat."[25]

But he now needed to find resources before he could march into Uganda. For these, Nyerere turned to Britain, the second time in a decade, the first being in 1971–1972, when he had sought diplomatic support. Shivji writes, "On 8 November, Sokoine submitted a list of military equipment to the British High

Commission that included communication and river-crossing equipment as well as anti-tank and anti-aircraft missiles costing millions of pounds. A floating bridge costing some 1.5 million pounds was most crucial for the Tanzanians to transport heavy tanks and artillery across the Kagera River. When the High Commissioner intimated that some of the equipment could be supplied if paid for, Sokoine was disappointed and Nyerere was angry. They had assumed that the requested equipment would be supplied, possibly as a gift. . . . Eventually some equipment was given as a gift but much of it on credit."[26] The UK Cabinet Minutes of November 9, 1978, noted: "Cabinet expresses pleasure that Nyerere turned to the UK for (military) assistance." It added that the UK prime minister hopes the Cabinet will approve the sending of "modest supplies of military equipment to Tanzania."[27] Wittingly or not, Nyerere had become an accomplice in the British project to replace Amin.

For the British, this was an opportunity to extract more than just the proverbial pound of flesh. They were now in a strong position both to name the new leadership of post-Amin Uganda and to bring to a close the era of the Arusha Declaration—a declaration of self-reliance that led to nationalization at home and nonalignment in foreign policy—by dictating a change of course in Tanzania's internal and external economic policy. At Moshi, the exiles formed the Uganda National Liberation Front with Nyerere's blessing. Professor Yusufu Lule, Britain's preferred nominee for the presidency of Uganda, was flown in from London and "stayed in Dar-es-Salaam for several days as a guest of the British High Commission, before flying to Moshi."[28] Though he did not represent any Ugandan organization, Lule was elected the chairperson of the UNLF. At home, Nyerere had to bend to the Washington consensus if he was to get British assistance for the war. This included adopting conditionalities spelled out in the Bretton Woods structural adjustment package. Nyerere resisted at first, and then gave in to British demands, eventually blaming the outcome on neoliberals in the country's leadership. The fact is that Tanzania's choices were limited by concessions Nyerere had to make to the British before he could launch the offensive war against the Amin regime and Uganda. And the sad fact is that Nyerere never had the moral courage to take responsibility for the pact he had signed with the devil.

The story of Uganda is also one of Julius Nyerere. The first president of Tanzania from 1964 and a key player in postindependence Uganda for the decade that brought Amin to power in 1971, Nyerere may be thought of as the link between Amin and Museveni. This untold story should shed new light on Nyerere's known story. During the last decade of his rule, Nyerere seemed possessed by one obsession: regime change in Uganda, to dislodge Amin and restore Obote. It is a project he embraced from 1971 to the end of his own tenure as president of Tanzania in 1985, without regard to cost, either to himself or his people, or to the people of Uganda, whom he claimed to have liberated. Nyerere pursued his ambition "by all means necessary" (as Malcolm X had put in a different context), even if this meant forging an alliance with the United Kingdom, not once but twice, in 1972, at the time of the Asian expulsion and then again in 1978–1979, during the Kagera War. As Nyerere pursued his ambition, of ridding the African continent of Idi Amin, he also undid the lifeline of a "self-reliant" Tanzania, which he left mired in debt. Given that the debt could only be repaid through multiple loans from the International Monetary Fund (IMF), Tanzania had little choice but to accept its "conditionalities," which would involve tight budgetary control along with far-reaching restraints on overall spending. Unwilling to take responsibility for his mistakes and own up to the consequences, Nyerere resigned as president in a seemingly noble gesture, leaving to his successors the difficult and unpleasant work of picking up the pieces and paying the tab. At the same time, Nyerere blamed them for the national humiliation and hardship that followed.

But the consequences for Uganda were far worse. From 1971, Nyerere had sheltered two rival armed factions, Obote's Kikosi Maalum and Museveni's FRONASA, each with its own tribal political following. After the fiasco of the 1972 invasion, Nyerere muzzled both factions, while keeping each going on a slow burn, to be brought to full fire if and when necessary. That day would come with the Kagera War of 1978–1979. As the Tanzanian army moved into Uganda, it ravaged Mbarara and Masaka, two of Uganda's largest towns after its capital, Kampala, announcing its arrival in acts that left behind the stench of vendetta and revenge. Meanwhile, the two militias—Kikosi Maalum and FRONASA—tagged along. Museveni and FRONASA recruited feverishly in western Uganda, the part of the country the Tanzanian army entered, while Obote and Kikosi Maalum awaited their turn, which came the day the Tanzanian army reached the North. By the 1980 elections, the new Ugandan army comprised two major factions of thousands of soldiers. Like its colonial predecessor, this army, too, was a collection of "tribal" militias identified by two protagonists—Obote against Museveni, North against West, or Luo against Bantu.

The day Museveni and his group of twenty-six attacked an army barracks in Kabamba on February 6, 1981, has been mythologized as the start of a guerrilla war in the Luwero Triangle. In reality, it was the beginning of a civil war between two tribal militias, each numbering in the thousands. Both sides had been trained mainly by Tanzania. The people had become so fed up with the notion of "liberation" that the word acquired a perverse meaning. If you met a friend after the "liberation" of Kampala and asked what had happened to their wristwatch, the answer would likely be, "It was liberated." If someone talked of a "liberator," they meant a soldier, whether Tanzanian or Ugandan. When Tanzanian troops finally withdrew from Uganda a few years later, the people of Kajjansi on Kampala-Entebbe Road came out to bid them an enthusiastic farewell, jeering, not so politely, "*Kwaherini, waizi*" ("Goodbye, thieves"). Ugandans continue to live the consequences of the British/Nyerere war to remove Amin. To deal with the aftermath, Ugandans will have to turn to their own internal resources.

10

RETURN HOME

Working above Ground

I returned to Kampala in 1979, after Idi Amin had been ousted. Museveni had five rooms at the Imperial Hotel in the middle of the city, likely meant for the leadership of the Front for National Salvation. Museveni gave one of the rooms to John Ruzindana (who had not yet reverted to his birth name, Augustine), who invited me to share his room. I had known the city of Kampala like the back of my hand. I was familiar with just about every street, especially in the old part of the city center. Now, however, I no longer knew anyone living on those streets. There was a total disconnect between places and people. The utterly racialized colonial geography of pre-1972 urban Uganda had come to an end.

I have had two different coming-of-age experiences in Kampala: one pre-1972, the other post-1979. The pre-1972 experience was testimony to how completely the racial architecture of the city—its residential areas, schools, playing fields, and places of worship—had come to dominate and define our individual lives. The full-time residents of what Amin called "Bombay in Africa" had been mainly Asian. As the sun set, most Black workers would leave town and move to adjoining bedroom communities of the poor. From Katwe to Bwaise, these communities had become home to expanding nationalism in the postwar period. Katwe had a long tradition of metalworking from before colonial times, when the adjacent town of Mengo (77,000) had been the capital of the Buganda kingdom. Bwaise was more of a commercial hub. In 1972, they buzzed with new possibilities.

After 1979, the only place in the city where I felt at home was Makerere. It was a sanctuary for me, and I would leave during the day and return as the sun set. Throughout the day, I went to different places in the city, my main haunts being Sapoba Press in Katwe, a printing press with a long history of being home to anti-colonial and nationalist publications; Uganda House on Kampala Road, constructed and owned by the Uganda People's Congress (UPC), the ruling party at independence; the two Ugandan bookshops, both owned by the Church of Uganda, with their coffeehouses in the central part of the city; Namirembe Cathedral of the Church of Uganda on Mengo Hill—the home of Anglican and Baganda power ever since the British colonized Buganda; and the Sikh gurdwara in Old Kampala, where the Sunday lunchtime community meal (*lunger*) was served to a conspicuously deracialized group. Then came friendship societies and study groups scattered throughout the city, in the railway club, the factories, and a range of secondary schools. I had no car. As I walked the city, day after day, I grew up in it, as it were, for a second time.

At some point, Godfrey Binaisa, then the country's president, left on a state visit. Museveni, then defense minister, became the acting president while Binaisa was away. One morning, he sent a car to the Imperial Hotel to pick up our group and bring us to his ministerial home. I was away that particular day. "Comrades, we have state power for these days. What shall we do with it?" Museveni asked. Wafula Oguttu told me that all through the interaction a young woman sat on the floor washing Museveni's feet.

As long as I lived at the Imperial Hotel, or any other place in the city, I had no one to visit in the evening. All other exiles had returned home; but for me, home was nowhere in sight. Others would go out in the evening, visit relatives, friends, even some they had just met. I would park myself in the open-air *baraza* of the hotel, chatting with the only other person who seemed not to know anyone in the city. Just for that reason we became regular companions. He was Laurent Kabila, the Congolese revolutionary who would later become president of the Democratic Republic of the Congo. We would drink beer, procured at the official factory price, which was a quarter of the market price, and talk about the possibility of "revolution" in the region. He was then a wiry fellow, the very opposite of the substantial figure I would meet in the Congolese town of Goma a decade and a half later, in 1996.

At that time, I was teaching at the University of Cape Town and writing an occasional column for the South African *Mail & Guardian.* In 1996 I flew into Kigali Airport, where I was picked up on the tarmac by James Kabarebe, head of the Rwandan army, who had promised to introduce me to Kabila. James had been a student in my final-year seminar at Makerere University, "Marxism and the Third World," by then a signature course for graduating students of radical views. At least three students who had enrolled in my class went on to become army commanders in the region: James Kabarebe himself (Rwanda), as well as Mugisha Muntu and Aronda Nyakairima (heads of the Ugandan army). At least half of the students ended up in the bush with Museveni's National Resistance Army. I realized later that the course had left a divided legacy among its graduates. All seemed to have come out with a magic potion, "armed struggle," in which the old order could not be inherited but, in Lenin's words, had to be "smashed." One group became flag bearers of a growing militarism in the region; another, its critics. That differentiation of views would take place over the 1980s and would inform successive developments, from the civil war (1981–1986), to the consolidation of Museveni's Front for National Salvation (FRONASA) as it morphed into the National Resistance Army (NRA) before its takeover, to the growth of several splinter movements, one of these headed by Mugisha Muntu, who would go on to chair the main opposition party, Forum for Democratic Change (FDC), and then to found a new party, Alliance for National Transformation (ANT) in 2018. That day in 1996, when James drove me to the border town of Goma to meet Kabila, then supported by Uganda and Rwanda, Kabila himself was about to begin his march to Kinshasa in the Congo to oust Mobutu Sese Seko, who had been president of Congo from 1965.

The University as a Sanctuary

Makerere University was a privileged sanctuary in those times. The army stayed outside the campus. The only armed men on campus were individual policemen assigned to guard expatriate academics sponsored and funded by either Western missions or UN agencies. My neighbor was a Scotsman in the Faculty of Science. As a UN-sponsored consultant, he had been assigned a guard. The guard would drink at night, usually in moderation, but not always. Once in a while, he would carelessly press the trigger and fire a bullet. Most nights, though, we slept peacefully, at least once we had got used to the ululation coming from one of the neighborhood slums, Makerere Kivulu, Wandegeya, Bwaise, or even from the residential communities of Nakulabye, Bakuli, and Mengo, among others. Like doctors tending to the victims of a war or an epidemic, we cultivated the degree of insensitivity necessary to sleep, eat, and survive, so life might go on.

Our lives took form within the bounds of the campus. Over time, we assembled in small groups, which met during evenings to drink and talk. The most popular of these country drinks were *malwa, mwenge bigere,* and *waragi. Malwa* and *mwenge* were akin to beer and wine; *malwa* was a drink from the eastern region, a beer made by mixing fermented millet in warm water in a pot. A group would sit around the pot, with each person holding a hollow reed through which he (I never saw a she) would draw in *malwa,* a breath at a time. Those with personal reeds would often adorn these with ornamental beads. *Mwenge* (also known as foot wine) was a drink from the Buganda region, made from "beer bananas" (*mabidde*) used for this express purpose, as distinct from other types of bananas, including plantains. Once fermented, the banana would be placed inside a grave-size hole, with young people singing and jumping on it for as long as it would take to smash and liquify the banana. Thus the name: *mwenge bigere,* or foot wine.

Waragi, also made from *mabidde* was Uganda's version of hard liquor. The double distilling method had been introduced by Ottoman army soldiers in the late nineteenth century. Until then, alcohol was single-distilled and relatively benign in its effect. Double-distilling came with colonization and was then introduced from Egypt and Sudan in the nineteenth century. Known as *arak* in Egypt and Sudan, it arrived in Uganda with Nubi soldiers and became known as *araki* or *waragi.* The colonial state banned home-brewed alcohol, both because it was unsupervised and because it was seen as a tax evasion. The more illegal the brewing process, the greater the chances of alcohol poisoning.

Once the sun set, the campus became both our sanctuary and our enclosure. We, a group of four, would meet at the house of John Katuramu, a senior university official. John and his wife supplemented his salary with income from secondary activities, one of these the domestic production and sale of the local drink, *waragi.* Three of us—John Busingye, Manzoor Mehdi, and I—would meet at John's place once or twice a week for a *waragi* session. Our talk would meander over a whole host of topics, from the university to the country to the world, and flowed as easily as the drink. We disregarded all government media. Katuramu brought news from Radio Katwe, the name given to street stories which often provided alternative versions of official news. Katwe was the artisanal suburb of Kampala, home of the nationalist movement in the 1950s and ever since considered an opposition hub. Mehdi, a left-wing exile from Pakistan (more later) was a devotee of Radio Tirana (Albania) and its version of the world. Busingye's version of the news had an African American twist (more later on this too), though it never came from a single source. When Busingye shared a story, he seldom gave emphasis to its origin.

John Busingye was born John Marshall Branion to one of the leading Black families in Chicago. In his younger days, he was known to have had a flair for high life, complete with riding horses, racing cars, and a home gun collection. John told us his wife had been murdered with a gun from his own collection and the police framed him for the murder. At the time, he was having an affair with Shirley Hudson, whom he would marry nine months later.

Branion had been one of Martin Luther King, Jr.'s personal doctors. A common practice of King lieutenants was to line up physicians and nurses to march with King. The idea made sense: should anything happen to King, help would be immediately at hand.[1] Though not a member of the Black Panther Party, the police knew of Branion as a close ally of the party, and as one of five doctors in Chicago, men and women, Black and white, who in 1966 were willing to treat gunshot wounds without reporting the case to the police. In no time, "John began to receive telephone calls . . . purporting to come from the state's attorney's office and threatening him with reprisals if he didn't stop treating Panthers."[2]

Was it, as the police were then fond of saying, time to teach "the nigger" a lesson? After all, this Panther Party–loving Black man was a Swiss-trained gynecologist whose average annual earning was six to seven times that of an ordinary Chicago cop. Things reached a climax in Chicago during the long, hot summer of 1968, after Dr. Martin Luther King, Jr., had been assassinated and the Chicago riots followed. That same summer, John Branion was charged with and then convicted of the murder of his wife, Donna Branion, in a case where all the evidence was circumstantial and where the police and the judge (who was later convicted of racketeering and extortion, and accused of taking a bribe from Branion's attorneys to convict Branion) were all white.[3]

Branion was given twenty to thirty years for his wife's murder. In 1971, while on bail and shortly after an appeal that upheld his conviction, Branion fled to

Algiers. At the end of the second week, he went to Black Panther headquarters, also in Algiers, looking for help. Cold-shouldered by Eldridge Cleaver, he decided to visit multiple African countries, including Sudan and Tanzania, eventually finding asylum in Uganda.[4] Branion told us he met Amin in the Congolese capital of Kinshasa when attending to Muhammad Ali as his doctor at the Ali–Joe Frazier fight, and Amin invited him to Uganda. Barbara D'Amato writes in her book *The Doctor, the Murder, the Mystery* of Branion that he was introduced to Idi Amin in Kampala by Roy Innis of the Congress of Racial Equality (CORE). He took a hospital job in Kampala and changed his name to John Busingye. Busingye was immediately appointed consultant gynecologist for the Ugandan Ministry of Health, first assigned to Mbarara, and later promoted to senior civil servant status in the Amin government.

Newspaper and media coverage on Busingye after his death in 1991 describe him as "occasionally" being Idi Amin's personal doctor. Amin gave him Ugandan citizenship without Busingye renouncing his US citizenship (the United States would not allow him to renounce it without appearing at the embassy in Kenya). Then, in 1979, Busingye had been recovering from a heart attack in Kenya, where he had gone after a double bypass surgery in Switzerland, when Amin was overthrown. Busingye subsequently returned to Uganda as a lecturer at the university hospital at Makerere. When I met him, he lived in a nice university-owned bungalow opposite Mary Stuart Hall, one of two women's residences on the Makerere campus known as the Box, the other being Africa Hall, nicknamed the "Suitcase" by male students since, in contrast to the vertical reach of the Box, it stretched horizontally.

That is where I met Busingye in 1981, and where I would later meet his wife, Shirley, and their son, Jeff, when they visited in 1982. Busingye could no longer afford to buy and drink Scotch whiskey. Instead, he took to home-brewed Ugandan *waragi*. I talked to him about my encounters with Black America during my ten years in the United States, from the time of the civil rights marches in the South, to the summer of 1968 when I worked as a volunteer with literacy centers—known as street academies—in Black communities of Trenton and Newark, New Jersey.

The third member of our inner circle was Manzoor Mehdi, who had been a left-wing organizer in Pakistan in the early 1970s. He had climbed the ranks to the position of the vice chair of the Mazdoor Kisan Party (Workers and Peasants

Party). Hounded by the police, he took to an underground life, and eventually responded to a local announcement inviting applications for contractual posting in Uganda. A trained lawyer, Mehdi *saab,* as we used to call him, was appointed district magistrate in the town of Kabale in Western Uganda. Mehdi became known as the Asian Magistrate, who had the gall to arrest a local landlord for beating one of his laborers and then to bring him to court presuming that the court would reinforce the original punishment. When Mehdi released the laborer and arrested the landlord for having tortured him, the crowd carried him in a ceremonial procession; he became an instant household legend in the district. At the time Amin was ousted, Mehdi was transferred to Kampala and took on the post of a magistrate in one of the city's courts. He lived with expatriate Pakistani families on the university campus and met Busingye at the Senior Staff Club before the three of us formed our own drinking circle.

Neither Mehdi nor Busingye long survived the Amin years. Mehdi's contract came to an end in 1982 and was never renewed. He took a job at the University of Dar es Salaam but was unable to make a transition from practicing law to teaching it. A year later, he returned to Pakistan. The Busingye saga in Uganda came to an end in 1983 when Obote's Minister of Internal Affairs canceled his passport, put him in detention, and then turned him over to Interpol, which put him on a plane and on that very plane handed him on to Cook County Sherriff's Department, whose officers escorted him to Chicago.[5] In prison, he worked as the librarian, serving seven years before being released on health grounds. He died of a brain tumor and heart ailment in 1990 at age sixty-four.[6]

Once established at the university, I began moving to different parts of the country as an academic researcher. I started in Kitende in central Buganda, along the Kampala-Entebbe Road, close to home, and then moved to Amwoma in Lango in the North, and next to the Rwenzori region in the West, then Kisoro in the Southwest, and finally Busia in the East.[7] Every time I arrived in a village, I would settle down, and begin putting questions to peasants. It was clear they, too, had questions of their own, even if they were too prudent or polite to ask directly: Who was I and what was I doing there? I realized I would not be able to interview anyone until I had dispelled all doubts. Inevitably, I would have to write off the first week. Villagers assumed at the outset that I was either a government agent, or a missionary, or some sort of an entrepreneur. I made two modifications in my research strategy: I limited myself to villages from which

I had taught students, and then to students from middling peasant families, as opposed to the rich or poor. Finally, I had my story: I was a university professor, and one of my students was a son of the village. How radically this had changed my position became clear only after George, one of my students, and I had returned to Kampala from Amwoma in late 1984. A few months later, when George returned from his trip to the village, I inquired after his family and neighbors, in particular a neighbor who had been pregnant:

"She must have delivered. A girl or a boy?"
"A girl."
"What did they name her?"
"They named her after you."
"Really, so what did they call her?"
"Professor!"

Back on campus, I began work among both students and academic staff. I joined John Musinguzi, a political science student, to organize student study groups, at the same time initiating research with individual staff members. I joined Phares Mutibwa, a history colleague, to restart *Mawazo,* the old journal of the Faculty of Arts and Social Sciences. We received external funding from the Canadian International Development Research Centre (IDRC). The journal came out twice a year. Each issue was preceded by a conference to which we would invite well-known scholars from around the region, first from Kenya and Tanzania, then also Sudan. At one of these conferences, I gave a paper on Karamoja, arguing that the district had been so transformed during the colonial period that it had literally been turned into the site of an ecological crisis, ravaged by famine during the dry season. It was during that session that I met the great Ugandan poet Okot p'Bitek, the author of the Acholi-language epic poem *Song of Lawino* (which he later translated into English). Okot stood up during question time and turned to the audience: "Who is not a Karamojong here?" The silence was marked; everyone realized that Karamoja was a metaphor for the colonial experience. In other words, "Who is not a victim of colonialism?" In the evening we went to the Faculty Club for drinks. After a few, I suggested we go eat something. "What, eat on an empty stomach?" was Okot's hard-to-forget response. The more I worked in the countryside and in the city of Kampala, the more I began to think of how to organize in these varied regions. Back at Makerere, I would discuss my half-baked ideas with several comrades, gradually gathering the courage to implement one idea after another.

Civil War: Obote's Army versus FRONASA, 1980

The second Obote period was marked by a civil war. It hearkened back to fighting within the Ugandan army triggered by the Amin coup of 1971. But with the Amin regime now defeated and its army fragmenting, the new power set about creating a new army, the Uganda National Liberation Army (UNLA), its nuclei none other than the Kikosi Maalum of Obote and FRONASA, led by Museveni. Both had separate training camps in Tanzania before 1979. Both received support from the Tanzanian government but continued to operate not only as separate but as competitive and, at times, even hostile groups. At the same time, both answered separately to the same piper, Tanzania. Western Uganda, the part of the country through which the Tanzanian army entered Uganda in 1978, favored FRONASA, whose recruits were mainly Banyankole from the western part of the country. As soon as they entered home turf, the Museveni group started recruiting, its numbers soaring from a few hundred to around 7,000 by the time Amin was overthrown.

Competition soon turned to hostility. The war between the two army factions, which began in the city of Kampala in 1979, broke out into open warfare after the rigged election of 1980. Soon, the FRONASA faction withdrew into the Luwero Triangle following the raid on military barracks in Kabamba on February 6, 1981. The official army, now mainly an Obote preserve, continued to occupy Kampala. Soldiers set up roadblocks, arbitrarily and at will, stripping civilians of property—anything from a watch or the contents of one's pocket to a backpack or shoulder bag. Often drunk on *waragi* or high on marijuana, many officers resembled thugs more than official peacekeepers. The city would empty as darkness fell, and soldiers regrouped to target one of the poor slums in the neighborhood of Kampala. As soon as they sighted soldiers, residents would start banging pots and pans, ululating as loudly as possible, to raise an alarm. The alarm made little difference since there was hardly anyone to respond to it. But it was not entirely useless since the noise assured one and all that they were not alone, and reminded the rogue soldiers that they could not go about their business unnoticed. I lived on campus, and there was not a night we did not hear the banging of utensils along with ululating voices, calling for help. At first, we would listen to it, sad that there seemed no way to respond. But as the weeks passed and the sounds became a "normal" nightly affair, we learned to sleep through the night.

The university was an early version of what would be called green zones in worldly capitals, like Baghdad and Beirut and Tripoli, engulfed by civil wars. As this process gathered momentum, I became a witness to the tragedy experienced by several friends who did not have the good fortune to live on the university campus. The saddest of these was the experience of a friend I will call Festo. I had met Festo through the friendship society we had formed, and then drew him into our literary activities and study groups. Festo lived in a flat on Bombo Road, along a stretch that connected Makerere with the center of the city. I would go every week to his flat, greet his wife, and play with his four young children—two boys and two girls, all below seven or eight—before going into their living room for a study group meeting that would last two to three hours. Some weeks I would be there twice. This went on for several years, almost like clockwork. Then one day, as I was to turn the corner and go up the stairs to Festo's flat, his neighbor stopped me, speaking in a whispered tone, "There is no one in the house." Soldiers had come a couple of days back. Both Festo and his wife were out. But the children were in. Soldiers broke into the flat, and the children ran to take cover, under the bed or behind a sofa. Whether or not they called the children to come out, the soldiers shot the children, dead, in repeated rounds of fire. It was all mayhem when the parents returned. The children's bodies had to be carried to the village for mourning and burial. The next week we heard that Festo's wife had "gone mad" and run away. Festo, too, was nowhere to be found. Neither I nor other members of the study group ever heard of him, or from him, again. The civil war had struck home, with full force.

Just before FRONASA mounted its attack on the Kabamba barracks in the first week of February 1981, Eriya Kategaya, then Museveni's top assistant, suggested we meet for coffee at Uganda Bookshop off Kampala Road. Kategaya used to visit the University of Dar es Salaam irregularly in the 1970s. He was a good friend of Ruzindana, and we had met several times. After the coffee, Kategaya suggested a walk. He said they planned "to go to the bush" during the next few days.

"Will you join us?"

Taken by surprise, I pointed to my brown skin.

"Have you looked at me? How do you expect to convince peasants that I am part of a liberation force?"

"I think it is best I work above ground, in Kampala."

Kategaya nodded.

Over the next four years, from 1981 to 1984, the Obote regime tightened its grip over the capital. Meanwhile, the armed forces split into two, returning to their original designations: Kikosi Maalum and FRONASA. An armed conflict raged in the part of Buganda known as the Luwero Triangle. Meanwhile, our small group, its core being those of us returned from Dar es Salaam, crisscrossed the country from one end to another. As we worked above ground, our group expanded, mobilizing around a range of activities, of which four were key: a magazine, a literacy group, a friendship society, and a health cooperative.

Literary Efforts

At the heart of our political work during the second Obote regime was the aforementioned magazine called *Forward*, the magazine we had begun publishing in Dar es Salaam. It was the initiative of our faction of the Chang'ombe group in Dar es Salaam. The first few issues were printed in London, brought to Dar es Salaam, and distributed throughout East Africa. The first issue arrived in Dar in January of 1978 and was reviewed in the government paper, *Daily News,* on January 27, 1979; *Forward* would move to Kampala the next year and be printed there until 1987.

John Ruzindana, Wafula Oguttu, and I were the founding editors of the magazine. We regrouped in Kampala at the end of 1979. John, as mentioned earlier, had dropped his FRONASA name and returned to his birth name, Augustine. We expanded the editorial board as we began to find comrades who shared our convictions. The new members were rooted in mobilizations in the Amin period. George Ochwa, a law student, served as legal secretary; and Emmy Baingana, national coordinator of the trade unions, joined the board in 1981. The chair rotated from one meeting to another.

The *Forward* Educational Trust was registered in Kampala on November 12, 1981, and began a journey combining educational with organizational work. Aware of its roots in exile in Dar es Salaam, *Forward* was keen to build relations with those who had continued to do political work in the country during the Amin period. Key to this was the Sapoba Group, whose members had been beneficiaries of scholarships to India and Pakistan during the Obote period and had returned to Uganda in the early Amin period. I met their lead member, Bidandi Ssali, in 1979. I had applied to Makerere University for a position in the Department of Political Science and was told there was no vacancy. Yoga

Adhola, a member of our Dar group, introduced me to Bidandi Ssali, who asked *Weekly Topic* to write a story exposing the absurdity of Makerere's rejection of applications from qualified staff returning from exile when, all the while, the university complained in its press conferences of being understaffed. The following week, Makerere offered me a job.

Oguttu took a job with *Weekly Topic.* Through Bidandi Ssali, I met two other members of the group: Kirunda Kiveginja, who was in charge of finances; and Kintu Musoke, who was responsible for external relations. Oguttu and I negotiated with Musoke and Ssali and got Sapoba to print *Forward* at their Katwe press on a regular basis. Apart from this generous subsidy, *Forward* was funded from sales and fundraising. Bookshops were the main outlet, but individual sales agents were key to providing access to new readers. Averse to the corruption we associated with the market, we resisted advertising revenue. Our sales were modest: 1,430 copies by August 1987. Not surprisingly, finance continued to be a challenge.

Ssali was fiercely independent and remained so. Because he had been secretary-general of the party Museveni had chaired, the Uganda Patriotic Movement (UPM), the Uganda's People's Congress (UPC) government jailed Ssali without trial for over a year. Determined to avoid exile, he was constantly busy negotiating to safeguard his political freedom. Ssali had declined a ministerial position in two successive regimes—first Amin's, then Obote's. Turning to sports, he became manager of the Kampala City Council, a football club with "nationalist" credentials because it shunned affiliation with any particular tribe. He joined the National Resistance Movement (NRM) government after 1986, when he was offered a Cabinet position, but then parted ways to run as a presidential candidate against Museveni.

Decades later, the three founders of Sapoba wrote about their experience in a book, *The Sapoba Legacy,* recording their individual and collective journeys.[8] The book was launched at the Africana Hotel in Kampala on January 27, 2014. Kirunda Kivejinja explained that the idea of establishing a press was inspired by Prime Minister Jawaharlal Nehru, who used to have meetings with African students in Delhi once every few months in the late 1950s. He advised them to form an association and publish a magazine when they returned home. The "Sapoba Three"—as the directors were called—set up what became known as the Sapoba Press. The first set of printing machines were a Chinese donation in the spirit of Bandung, the anti-imperialist, tri-continental congress which took place in the Indonesian town of Bandung in 1956. Sapoba

Press birthed its flagship magazine, *Weekly Topic,* and incubated the journalists who years later would break away to form *Daily Monitor,* today the main independent paper in the country. It also provided a home to *Forward* for nearly ten years.

I wrote a regular weekly column for *Weekly Topic* called "Over the Fence." The column featured a public intellectual, with the name of a bird, *Ssekanyolya,* given to looking across neighboring gardens and pontificating on community affairs. I patterned the human Ssekanyolya character after a well-known scholar activist, Chango Machyo, who used to comment freely on public affairs as he moved in and out of government. When I returned from the University of Michigan, where I had been a visiting professor during the first half of 1986, and rejoined the university that same year, Machyo was Minister of Water. He stayed with me at 2 Livingstone Terrace, awaiting the allocation of a government house—but even when he was allocated one, Machyo seemed to show no sign of wanting to move out. I asked why. "Because if I go to live in this large official house, I know the whole village will come to stay with me." Realizing that this state of affairs was unlikely to change soon, I told him I would gladly do a swap, move to his official residence and let him continue to occupy my two-bedroom university flat. Machyo moved to his government residence the following week.

Our readership expanded the more we focused on local politics. At the same time, the more we got known, the more risks we faced from centers of wealth and power. Once in a while, lawyers acting on behalf of well-heeled clients would sue us for defamation, as happened in May 1984. That same month, John Musinguzi, our coordinator in western Uganda, was arrested in Mbarara for distributing *Forward,* which the police contended was a seditious publication, however he was soon after released. Gradually, we found lawyers who would defend us pro bono, but these encounters taught us that our best defense was to expand our readership beyond the narrow confines of an English-reading public. In 1984, John Musinguzi proposed launching versions of *Forward* in regional languages, so that each issue could also be read aloud to audiences not literate in English. We began preparations to launch four regional issues, starting with a Luganda edition, then expanding to three other regional languages: Runyankole-Rukiga (Western region), Luo (Northern region), and Ateso (Eastern region).[9] To expand the network in different languages, we turned to radio translators and primary school teachers.

The editorial meeting of July 26, 1986, noted that the victory of the NRM called on us to rethink our content and redefine our core audience. The first challenge to our practice of working alongside the NRM came with a report from the eastern region coordinator, Charles Ocan, on July 24, 1987: "I saw *Forward.* It seems it is slightly watering down. . . . If the paper is wary of mentioning NRA / NRM massacres of peasants and school children in the North / East . . . there is no need still trying to justify a movement which clearly in its practice is Bantuist [oriented to the Bantu peoples in the south] and therefore sectarian. You just need to visit Soroti and see how many homes have been burnt down in the villages, how many peasants have been killed and how much property has been looted. The crime is being Northerners. . . . If half a million died in Luwero, one million may die in three years in the North and East." It took us months to realize how prescient Ocan's letter had been.

The editorial board meeting of October 1, 1987, chaired by Wafula Oguttu, resolved that our relationship to the NRM should be defined by "critical support." It was agreed that the editorial board would remain "sympathetic to the ten-point program" and at the same time "maintain our critical independence." But that balancing act would present its own challenge, and the paper ceased publication that same year. It had lasted nine years, from 1978 to 1987.

Civic Efforts

We had founded *Forward* in exile, in Dar, and then brought it home. Our first activity after returning home in 1979 was the foundation of a literacy society, called the Society for the Advancement of Literacy in Uganda (SALU). Registered as a voluntary association in 1980, SALU had several chapters. It was a modest affair. Except for the choice of reading material, the working of each chapter was highly decentralized. Those who ran literacy groups made their own decisions and kept their own records. Among the most active was Okot Nyormoi, a pathology professor at Makerere's university hospital. Nyormoi ran literacy groups in factories and educational institutions, both in Kampala and in Kitgum in Acholi, his home district. I worked closely with Michael Werelunalo and Edward Rubanga, both railway workers. Our work was concentrated at the Nsambya Railway Workers Quarters, and the Blanket Factory in Kampala's Industrial Area. Both Rubanga and Werelunalo were active trade unionists involved in writing and circulating leaflets clandestinely at their places of work. Both used

SALU branches at their workplaces to recruit fellow workers into study groups run mainly by university students.

SALU had a loose curriculum that teachers were free to alter in response to student needs. I had compiled the outline curriculum drawing on my experience in running literacy classes at the Friendship Textile Mills in the Dar es Salaam neighborhood of Ubungo when I was at the University of Dar es Salaam in the 1970s. We would begin with reading and describing pictures: of places, events, personalities, whether local or African or international. Readings ranged from literature (Maxim Gorky's *Mother;* Ousmane Sembène's *God's Bits of Wood;* Howard Fast's *Spartacus*) to history (Eduardo Galeano's *Open Veins of Latin America*) to autobiography (Ngũgĩ wa Thiong'o's *Detained)* and biography (on Mao Zedong and the Chinese Revolution). These notes covered most of the twentieth century: colonialism, anti-colonialism, and after. I later put them together as chapters of a book published by the All Africa Conference of Churches in Nairobi.[10]

Classes met once a week, Sunday mornings or Wednesday late afternoons for workers. Most students were men. Expected to look after children and prepare food, women workers had little free time. SALU's primary focus was workers, in Kampala and up-country. Those enrolled in literacy classes would often get involved in other activities run by our group, such as a study group, a chapter of the friendship society, a *Forward* group to discuss and distribute each new issue, or the health club. Over time, they got to know one another. Some even became friends.

The more the war in the Luwero Triangle heated up, the more we could feel its consequences in the capital city. One could still write, and so *Forward* kept on coming out on a more or less regular basis. But the space was clearly beginning to shrink when it came to holding meetings and creating associations.

The challenge was how to organize in the open. That was why in 1981 we came up with the idea of creating a friendship society linking Uganda and North Korea. The choice of North Korea was driven by its strategic importance to the Obote regime, especially in the military sphere: North Koreans were training a special brigade, at Nakasongola, the former Israeli base. We decided that top positions should be filled with relatively nonpolitical figures friendly to the regime, and preferably with a high public profile. This seemed the best way to assure political protection for Uganda Korea Friendship Society (UKFS). That was the rationale behind choosing General Tito Okello, the head of the army, as patron of the society.

I had met Tito Okello once, in early 1980, through his nephew, Olara Otunnu, whom I had come across in the mid-1970s during a tour of the United States. Then, I used to arrange each trip around several talks and underwrite it by putting together the honoraria, usually $300 to $500 for each talk. I was then at the University of Dar es Salaam, and my plan then was to meet and network with prominent Ugandan students in the United States. The three individuals key to my organizing efforts were Olara Otunnu, then at Harvard Law School, and later a Ugandan UPC candidate for president; Ruhakana Rugunda, a medical student in Philadelphia, who would later become prime minister in the NRM government; and Sebowa Kiboigo, a student at the University of Washington in Seattle. I would stay with them during the course of my visit, and we would spend evenings discussing the situation at home. When I returned to Kampala in 1979, I looked up Otunnu, who invited me home to Gulu in northwestern Uganda. We traveled together to a massive public rally; it was a homecoming for Otunnu, who was to be the main speaker. Otunnu was considered both a "son of the soil" and a likely future candidate for president of Uganda. After the rally, there was a meal on the grounds and I found myself seated next to a kind and gentle elderly man. He introduced himself as Tito Okello and proceeded to also introduce me to Acholi cuisine. There was a dish that I found particularly tasty, and I had several helpings of it before he asked me if I knew what I was eating. I shook my head, no. "That is a paste made of white ants." My imagination so overwhelmed my senses that I could not bring myself to eat any more of it.

The other prominent UPC figures we recruited into the leadership of the friendship society were Chota Vuru as chair and Kagenda Atwooki as vice chair. Vuru was from Arua, Amin's hometown, and he had a big frame that evoked Amin. Ironically, *chota* means "little" in Hindustani. I once asked him how he got his name. Vuru said that he was so big as a baby that a neighbor, an Asian *dukawalla,* named him "chota."

The Uganda-Korea Friendship Society (UKFS) was officially founded on July 21, 1981. The patron held a reception on September 10 that same year to mark the launch, and by September 1, 1983, there were forty-one functioning chapters, spread over all provinces with a thousand members enrolled.[11] As the society grew in members and activities, we began to have closer relations with the North Korean embassy. Though the embassy gave financial donations to the society from time to time, at no point did these constitute the main source of our funds. For example, the funds for the first national delegates' conference in 1983 were raised from three major sources: the chair, 38,330 shillings ($345); the embassy, 15,000 shillings ($135); and membership fees, 6,200 shillings ($56).[12]

The embassy also seemed to assume that it could give directions to individual officers of the Friendship Society, causing relations to sour. The minutes of the Central Executive Committee of the society pointedly noted this. As relations with the embassy deteriorated, we realized we needed to minimize our reliance on its contributions. This called for a degree of self-reliance. Every branch functioned as a study group, then as a health cooperative. In addition, each branch was to identify an income-earning activity. Most of our branches were in factories and schools, particularly in rural areas, where they worked on farms as their income-earning activity. The revenue was divided three ways: 60 percent went to individual members, 30 percent to the chapter, and 10 percent to the National Executive Committee (NEC).

As the number of chapters increased, the NEC appointed coordinators for different regions. The main responsibility of coordinators was to provide oversight for each chapter and to organize regional conferences.[13] The first national delegates conference was held on May 20–21, 1983, at Makerere University in Kampala, and the thirty-eight chapters outside Kampala sent sixty delegates. A set of four keynote speeches were followed by regional discussion groups, where each chapter gave a report on its work. Then the plenary was reconstituted for a general discussion and passage of key resolutions. These resolutions focused on activities. "The focus on Uganda is absolutely necessary because unless we know our problems we shall not know what to learn from the experiences of others."[14] The conference was a modest affair. Out-of-town delegates stayed with society members in Kampala, and costs for attendance were kept to a minimum.[15]

As the work of the Friendship Society expanded, we were able to identify the most energetic members and mark them for recruitment in other activities, starting with a study group. One such member—I shall call him John Namiti—lived in a village midway between Jinja, Uganda's main industrial town on the shores of Lake Victoria; and Iganga, a market town on the main road to Kampala. Both are in the Busoga region. Namiti lived in a village a few miles away from the main road. Our coordinating committee agreed that we use part of our group funds to purchase a bicycle. Since I was one of two in the leadership with a car, I was asked to deliver the bicycle in my small Suzuki pickup, which I did one Sunday. What I did not know was that Namiti and his wife had resorted to a disciplinary technique, threatening their three-year-old that a white man (*muzungu*) would come and eat him up should he continue misbehaving. So long as the child believed the story, it worked, and it turned out that I was the man with a skin more pale than any the child had ever laid eyes on. The minute I parked my Suzuki pickup on the side of their hut and stepped out of it, the child bailed out a terrified cry. Surely, the *muzungu* had come. The plan had been for me to spend the night with the family and return to Kampala the next day. Much as the parents tried to convince the child that I was a family friend, he would not stop crying. When this went on for several hours, we began to worry about the health of the child should the crying continue for much longer. Each of us separately reached the same conclusion: the only solution was for me to leave for Kampala, the sooner the better. It remained for me to voice this, which I did, and then hurriedly left for the sanctuary that was Makerere.

The next month we were on semester break at the university. I decided it was time for me to leave Kampala and visit my parents, brother, and sister in Dar es Salaam. As the month was drawing to a close, I received a call from one of my neighbors, a lecturer in the Science Faculty at Makerere. One of the first sentences out of his mouth was, "Please do not come back now."

"Why not?" I asked. "What has happened?"

"An army lorry came by yesterday. License plate 004 LA 008. Soldiers came out and surrounded your place. They were looking for you."

I delayed my return to Kampala until the next week. But that, surely, could not be a solution. I decided I would go back, but not to my apartment. I would stay incognito in town. Where could a *muhindi* stay incognito in an African city policed by the military, however? It would have to be at a friend's house. One by one, we ruled out each possibility. Finally, Oguttu struck on an unorthodox idea: Manzur Mehdi was staying in a government-paid accommodation in the International Hotel, which had turned into an abode for South Asian expatriates. Mehdi and his wife agreed, and I went to stay with them. This went on for several weeks. Every other day, I would go back to my place at Makerere to get things I needed and to find out if the soldiers had returned. When it was clear they had not for weeks, I felt the danger had cleared. It was time to return home.

The national delegates conference was deemed a great success by all who attended and participated. A few months later, the Friendship Society was invited to send a delegation of three members to attend the thirty-fifth anniversary of the founding of the Democratic People's Republic of Korea (DPRK). Chota Vuru, John Musinguzi, and I represented the society.

The report we wrote on our return was marked by the great contrast we felt between Uganda and DPRK. When it came to social organization, Uganda and North Korea seemed at opposite ends of a continuum: North Korea was highly regimented, Uganda was chaotic. The report began:

> What struck us from the beginning was the immense mobilisation of the population. School children going to or coming from school march in orderly groups singing songs. The groups range from ten to forty members and they are of the same sex. As early as 6 AM the people go on the streets and around their living apartments to do communal cleaning. Up-country, we found schoolchildren cleaning roads in the evening as they go home. The army trucks help peasants with transporting themselves, their crops and their building materials. About fifty kilometers from Pyongyang, we passed a spoilt patch of the road around 11 AM. On our return, we found the patch being repaired by soldiers and peasants including women around 6 PM.

During the daytime, large-scale initiatives were in evidence at various levels: there was "massive construction going on throughout the country" and, in the evening, "acrobatic games, including very young children." Roads were lined with "trees and flowers" and hills "covered with either orchards or forests."[16]

We were taken on a grand tour of three locations: the capital, a representative village, and the demilitarized zone (Panmunjom). The capital tour began with the Tower of Juche, which seemed to resemble the Washington Monument in the US capital. At the base of the tower were a whole set of marble tiles, each said to be a gift of a friendship society around the world. As we scanned this impressive collection, I saw a tile with the lettering "gift of Uganda-Korea Friendship Society." I could not remember any such gift given by our society. I asked Chota if he was aware of this. No, he said with a bemused smile. The next monument was a replica of another Western structure, the Arc de Triomphe in Paris. We began to wonder about the depth of self-reliance (*juche*) that our hosts claimed was the core of the Korean experience. There seemed little evidence to connect the monuments we were seeing to the Korean historical imagination. The next day we were taken to a national site with a grand statue of Kim Il-Sung and asked to lay a wreath of flowers at the feet of a massive statue of the Great Leader. "In our culture, we do not bow before any living human," said Chota. Nonetheless, the evening news, which we saw at our hotel, showed us bowing. We had clearly been photoshopped. At the hotel we encountered an official Ugandan delegation, led by the Minister of Education, Professor Isaac Newton Ojok, who in the Museveni period would become known for joining Alice Lakwena's Christian rebel group Holy Spirit Movement. As soon as Ojok saw me, he said, "Well, just saw you fellows on the TV bowing before the monument of the Great Leader." We assured him that what he had seen on TV was not an accurate portrayal of what had really transpired. He smiled.

Among the highlights of our tour of the capital was a play at the Mansudae Art Theatre and the February 8 House of Culture (later renamed the April 25 House of Culture), commemorating the struggle for independence. The play was in Korean with English- and French-language supertitles on each side of the stage. We were impressed. Next came a tour of the museum marking the victory against US imperialism and the founding of DPRK. We had read of the war and knew of the participation of China in it. But this part of history was totally erased from the commemoration film at the museum. We toured a mechanized library, where a mechanical pulley system relayed books from the stalls to the front desk in record time, as if in a factory; and Wasan Girls' Middle School in Pyongyang where, like in all North Korean schools, students studied in two shifts, day and evening, making sure the facilities were used for a full day. On our way to the demilitarized zone, we were taken to a "typical" peasant home with what they said were key utilities to be found in over 80 percent of peasant homes: electricity and running water, a TV and a fridge, and a guitar along with other traditional instruments. Workers were said to work six days and rest on the seventh; peasants worked nine days with the tenth a day of rest. For Ugandan eyes used to feeding on ravages of an ongoing civil war, these were indeed impressive achievements.

Our senses seemed dulled until we arrived at the town of Panmunjom in the demilitarized zone. The American / South Korean zone was separated from the DPRK zone by less than a hundred yards. Led by a DPRK military officer, we were taken to the terrace of a building. Across the street, within hearing distance, we could see an American soldier on top of a house. "Here you shout, Yankee go home!" said the officer to me. "No, I will shout that in Kampala, my home." My spontaneous outburst confirmed I was getting wary of being taken for a ride.

I was deprived of my Ugandan citizenship for a second time in late 1984 by Obote's Minister of Internal Affairs, just four months before Obote and his government were evicted from power. I went to Dar es Salaam, and from there to the University of Michigan as a visiting professor for one semester, the spring of 1986. Obote had been overthrown in a military coup in July 1985, and the Okello junta survived for a few months, until January 1986. UKFS continued, but without its links with the embassy. A Second National Delegates Conference was held in April 1985. My report as treasurer was given by Okot Nyormoi, the Uganda-Korea Friendship Society's national secretary.

Back home, our most original initiative was setting up a health cooperative in villages around Busia in eastern Uganda. Key to this initiative was a comrade from the village, Wabwire Kwoba, also a member of the core group. We had met Kwoba in late 1979 through Oguttu. Both belonged to the Samia ethnic group, and both came from around Busia. Kwoba, like Raiti Omongin, the youth leader of the ruling party (UPC) in the late 1960s, had supported the Chinese in the ideological rift with the Soviet Union, and had been a founding member of the Communist Party of Uganda. The group of seven, which comprised the founding members of the party, had been invited to China for training in guerrilla warfare in the early 1970s.

Kwoba was the cofounder of the health club that developed in several steps. The first was to identify a suitable location, ideally a village which was home to one of us, so we would not be seen as outsiders. Next was to identify key health challenges in the village. We did a survey of the main ailments suffered by villages in the region: malaria, venereal diseases, and stomach viruses accounted for more than 80 percent of health problems. We then formed a paramedical team; this phase took a year. We began by organizing a study group of six secondary school students. Those running the health club had to combine literacy with political commitment; they would meet once a week as a study circle. Five of the six were assigned a core task: three focused on diagnosis and prescription, one kept stock, and another accounts. The sixth was available to stand in for anyone if and when needed. We agreed that a professional doctor should visit the village every Sunday to attend to hard cases. This doctor would also need to be politically committed.

The first health cooperative was set up in Kwoba's village, where every peasant paid a nominal membership fee to join and the money was used to purchase drugs where they were cheapest, usually in Kenya across the border. All services were voluntary. The cooperative went through several stages as we identified problems, drew lessons, and reformed our work.[17] At its height, the cooperative embraced six to seven neighboring villages. We bought Kwoba a motorcycle so he could move between different villages and, at the same time, attend the once-a-week study group in each village. After many months, Kwoba's wife reported that her husband was often drunk when he came home in the evenings, then stopped coming home, and started living with a barmaid in a rented room. We asked Oguttu to replace Kwoba, but he was too involved in Kampala, and no member of the study group seemed right. There was no other alternative but to wind up work in Busia. And so we did.

Unlike the military mobilization favored by the Museveni and Nabudere groups, we were at this stage devoted exclusively to building civic groups. The response of the Museveni and Nabudere groups reflected the political common sense of the time, and especially of educated youth coming out of the University of Dar es Salaam. Our response was different. And this difference stemmed from our understanding of our limitations: that most of us had spent nearly a decade in exile and needed to reconnect with the land and the people. Otherwise, we would end up reliving the fiasco of 1972 when FRONASA cadres had been handed over to the army. Each of the civic groups we created aimed to combine general education with a particular service (literacy, social welfare, health) and political education. We aimed over time to create a single country-wide political organization whose members were anchored in—and thus accountable to—at least one ground-level group. As it turned out, none of the activities we initiated lasted more than a decade. But many of our members went on to play an active, even a leading, role in civil and political life for more than a generation.

Exile and Return

It was not long before I had to once again return to exile. The International Red Cross decided to organize a series of Disaster Preparedness Conferences across Africa in the aftermath of the devastating Ethiopian famine of 1984. The first was held in Uganda, and I was asked to give the keynote address. I had just returned from Lango, President Obote's home district, where I had been doing research in two villages. I used the occasion to share the conclusions of my work: that whereas adverse climate may bring drought, famine is the result of adverse government policies. Chris Rwakasisi, the intelligence minister and the patron of the Uganda Red Cross, was sitting in the front row. And he was livid.

The next day, I left for Dakar, Senegal, to attend a conference organized by the Council for the Development of Social Research in Africa (CODESRIA). A couple of days later, a police officer came to the Department of Political Science, asked for my office, and slipped a letter under the door. The letter informed me that I was not a citizen of Uganda and should immediately register as a noncitizen and regularize my employment at the university on expatriate terms. My loss of citizenship echoed an earlier denationalization of Rajat Neogy, the editor of *Transition,* in 1968, by the same president, Obote, during his first term.

I decided not to return to Kampala, since that would require that I surrender my Ugandan passport. I flew back to Nairobi, where the immigration officer looked at the passport and then into my eyes: "Is this passport valid?" He clearly had read the morning papers. "You decide," I said. He stamped the passport and returned it to me. I took a flight to Dar. The next day, the attorney general, Joseph S. Warioba, came to see me.

"*Karibu nyumbani*" (welcome home), said Mr. Warioba. He seemed to be in the know that both my parents had been born in colonial Tanganyika.

"*Asante*" (thank you), I said.

"Do you need a passport?"

"Yes, but Ugandan," I responded.

He smiled.

No sooner had I arrived in Ann Arbor, Michigan, in 1986 than I received a call from Colonel Kahinda Otafiire, a senior army officer, saying that President Museveni wanted me to come to Kampala and see him. I said I had no ticket. He said that should not concern me; they would send me one. I said I was teaching and would come during the weeklong spring break. When the plane landed at the airport, and as the doors opened, I could hear the sound of drums and wondered who was coming. When I got outside I realized drums were beating for me; students had come to receive me in a Makerere University bus. There was a celebratory feeling in the air. Ruzindana, too, had come in his car. I told him that I would return with the students in the bus and see him at the university. I stayed a week that time but could not meet the president who was in the North commanding an operation against remnants of the previous regime. After a week, I said it was time for me to leave. The president's staff asked me to stay on, saying the president would be back within the week, but I had to leave since classes were starting in a few days.

The next week, I had a call from Ruzindana.

"The president wants you to take a position in the Cabinet."

"As what?"

"As inspector-general of government."

"And what is that?"

"It is the person whose job is to provide oversight on all government institutions to keep them honest."

I was skeptical that such a position could work.

"There have been ombudsmen in several countries. Some have been totally ineffectual, others have been murdered, and others have joined the ranks of the corrupt. I am not interested in joining any of those."

I said corruption could not be checked by one person. It would require a whole range of reforms to activate important sections of society. Ruzindana said he would call the president and get back in touch. He did, the next day.

"The president says who does he think he is, the President?"

Next I heard, Ruzindana had been appointed the inspector-general of government. He did not last long.

A few days after this phone call in spring 1986, when I was back in Michigan, I received a call from Kahinda Otafiire in Kampala. He was at the time major-general in the NRA and Minister of State for Internal Affairs. From the moment I answered the phone, Otafiire began hurling abuse at me: "We know who you are. We can deal with the likes of you." I was clueless as to the reason for all this. Otafiire said he knew I was not coming back to Uganda and that I had decided to join the opposition. I said I had already bought the ticket to Kampala and gave him my date of arrival. That day, as the plane landed and the doors opened, I could see the figure of Otafiire behind a window on the top floor of the airport. He came to my university apartment that evening, uninvited, and it seemed every evening thereafter, usually without prior notice. I realized that part of Otafiire's job now was to keep track of me, almost on a daily basis—which he did.

Over time, I came to know the reason behind Otafiire's initial hostility. After my first trip at the president's invitation, I had returned to Michigan and written a letter to my friend Wamba-dia-Wamba, a historian at the University of Dar es Salaam, telling him how disappointed I had been with my trip to Kampala. Our new rulers had only an army, the NRA, and there seemed to be no political organization. The NRM, the formal political movement, was in reality just a building in Kampala, the location of a headquarters, I wrote. The letter was intercepted by Tanzanian Security, who shared its contents with their Ugandan counterparts. Wamba eventually received the letter in the mail, resealed, and stamped: "Opened for Inspection: Post Office." The Ugandan authorities had concluded that my attitude was hostile and that I did not intend to return.

Another person who visited my university apartment during those days was Hope Kivengere, one of the daughters of the anti-Amin clergy, Bishop Kivengere. She was then the president's principal press secretary. She said the president wanted me to write a speech for him. I said I will, but then added that I did not want to be rude, but I did think that the president's speechwriter should be someone whose thinking was politically in line with that of the president. She never returned. Otafiire, however, did keep coming, each time taking the opportunity to discuss a range of issues, from the university to the country, to Africa and the world. He was now the Deputy Minister of Local Government. The next time he came he asked me if I would accept to be a part of the National Commission of Inquiry into the Local Government System. It would be the new government's first national commission. I said yes. He asked me if I would be its chair. I was surprised and wondered why they would not appoint one of their own people to that position. He said the position was very sensitive. There were many claimants to it, all fronting their tribal identity. The appointment was sure to be closely scrutinized. I asked him why, then, offer the position to me. He gave two reasons: first, I no longer had a tribe in Uganda, so no one was likely to think my appointment would give an added advantage to any particular group. And second, for that same reason, I would be seen as independent. I said I would like to nominate two members to the nine-person commission. He agreed. I nominated Margaret Odeke and George Ochwa, one from the East and the other from the North, both friends of mine at the Makerere University School of Law.

When the commission's report was ready, the draft was taken to Museveni for an initial read. I was told he was particularly unhappy that we had voted against the recommendation that representatives at each level be elected by an electoral college of lower-level officials, and not by the people themselves. Many of us had come to think of direct elections as the ABCs of democracy. Museveni thought this was a recipe for his armed movement to be held hostage by local elites. When the time came to present the report to Parliament, contrary to practice, I, though the chair, was not invited to present a summary of recommendations and a justification for each.

One recommendation of our Commission was that elected local resistance committees be introduced throughout the country. As soon as "resistance committees" were introduced at Makerere University, I ran for the position of chair of the Resistance Committee for my street, the lowest organ of popular representation, known as RC1. Once successful, I ran for the position of chair at each higher level, ultimately becoming chair of the University-wide Resistance Committee, thus its representative on the Kampala Municipal Council. A confrontation between the Resistance Committee and the university administration was inevitable since our powers overlapped. The university's vice chancellor complained to the district administrator (DA) for Kampala that the Resistance Committee, and particularly its chair, was challenging his authority. The DA called both the vice chancellor and me for a meeting in his office. The vice chancellor wanted to know the role of the Resistance Committee when the university already had an administrative authority. I said our job was not to govern but to hold governors accountable.

"Who are you going to hold accountable?" the vice chancellor asked.

"You," I responded, perhaps a little undiplomatically.

He was stunned. The DA refused to intervene. The vice chancellor had little idea that my boldness arose partly from the fact that the DA had been my student in the Political Science Department only the year before.

11

THE WORLD BANK ENTERS THE UNIVERSITY

When the National Resistance Movement (NRM) took over the reins of government in 1986, the country was in dire financial straits and the university coffers, too, were running dry. The NRM government tried every available avenue to access money, but none worked. The response seemed coordinated—likely by the Americans. It seemed as if the country had been placed under a financial quarantine, which would only be lifted if Uganda first came to an agreement with the International Monetary Fund (IMF). And, that is indeed what happened.

The university was among the first institutions to feel the impact of the structural adjustment program when in 1987 the World Bank laid out its overall plan to improve education in developing countries, declaring that its aim was to reform Uganda's education system, which the World Bank said was still colonial. The university was an exclusive preserve of the children of the elite. Students in primary and secondary schools were paying tuition that families could ill afford, while university students were on state scholarships that included fees, living costs, and an annual supplement. And yet, observed the Bank, the university students almost invariably came from elite, well-off families. The Bank's declared aim was to turn this world upside down in the name of social justice: the country needed to reverse its educational priorities to serve the interests of the vast majority of students, who were either in primary or secondary schools. The Bank held that it was only fair that university students from elite families should meet as much of the market cost of higher education as their families could afford. To this bold preamble, the Bank tagged a neoliberal prescription that fees should cover the market cost of education. Like public health and public infrastructure, public education, too, was to be paid for as a private good, based on market principles. To calculate the market cost of educating one university student, the Bank divided the total cost by the number of students. The logic was to do away with the notion of public education as a social good. In a world where all goods were private, there was no room for any subsidized social good—not even education.

The World Bank set about transforming the university system: day classes were augmented by evening classes, and the number of students doubled and eventually even quadrupled. The university admission—2,186 students in 1992–1993—soared to 10,666 in 2003–2004.[1] And the new students paid fees, 80 percent of which were remitted directly to individual faculties, with only 20 percent allocated to the central administration; faculty salaries were doubled (paid from private student fees) to compensate for a doubled teaching load. This may seem like a lot, but not against devaluation, which had reduced the value of the shilling to a seventh of its previous official value. Each of us had to find a way to meet the shortfall. Those with families in the countryside looked to bring food from villages.

I had a two-door mini Suzuki, and began using it as a taxi, at first an hour a day, transporting a single shift from the Wandegeya stage near the university to the Taxi Park in Nakivubo—enough money for me to buy a kilo of meat, a loaf of bread, and a packet of cigarettes. But prices kept rising. Soon, I had to do two trips, and then even more, to afford the same basket of goods. I realized this solution was a mirage. If I kept it up, I was likely to become a full-time *matatu*, or taxi driver. My dear friend Joe Carasco did homeschooling for students. A Goan Ugandan, he had found himself teaching in northeast Brazil during the Amin period. We had been together in Dar in the 1970s and in correspondence after that. I went to Rio de Janeiro for a political science conference and Joe invited me to visit him in the northeast. He said he wanted to return home. His situation was remarkably similar to mine: his parents had been born in Uganda but he had been born in Goa and had no right to a Ugandan passport. I returned from Brazil with his papers and couriered him his passport six months later. When I was rendered stateless by Obote, Joe kept my university apartment and my Suzuki, and made homecoming easy for me.

There was also collateral damage since lecturers had no more time for research, and no one seemed to be responsible for planning for larger facilities (such as classrooms) to accommodate increased student numbers. There was also a sharp decline in resources for central coordination and growth. Certainly, no one was tasked with finding the money to pay for it. The staff union demanded to be consulted. But the Bank's program was not open to consultation. Not even the administration had been consulted, nor even likely the government ministry. The staff began to plan a strike, and I was a leading and vocal member of the Strike Steering Committee. We decided to lead a march of staff and students into town. But, before we could start marching, President Museveni called me and inquired about our plans. He said we needed to think through the implications of university staff and students marching through the city center. I consulted my colleagues on the Strike Steering Committee, and we agreed on a compromise: the march will go on as planned, but we would restrict ourselves to the campus. In exchange, Museveni agreed to withdraw the police to outside campus.

As structural adjustment and devaluation cut into our livelihoods, every one of us was forced to look for a supplementary source of income. In 1986, I redirected my energies to writing a research proposal for the Canadian International Development Research Centre "small grant." I was successful, but that did not help my eight graduate students, who had the same problem. Funds for research were drying up everywhere. We held several brainstorming sessions and, at the end of those, we decided to set up Uganda's first independent nonprofit research institute: the Centre for Basic Research (CBR). I became its first part-time executive director. I now combined work at CBR with that at the university.

I approached Yusuf Karmali, the younger brother of Amir Mukwano, then Uganda's richest Asian capitalist. I explained the importance of a research center whose focus would be public policy and which had a vision longer than the life of any one government. Yusuf offered us use of a fenced bungalow, along with its premises on Mawanda Road, a mainly lower middle–class residential area. He said he had rented it from one of the families in the community for a year. We were delighted. CBR went from strength to strength, its roster of researchers growing from eight to over forty in a matter of years. But it still had no permanent home.

Then, in 1988, well after Amin's rule and when the government began returning previously seized properties to their rightful owners, Mr. Ponda, my family's landlord, came back to Kampala. The building in which we had lived had been given to the Soviet embassy during the Amin period. Ponda and I took a stroll to 15 Baskerville Avenue, where his family had occupied the ground floor and he had rented the first floor to us. Mr. Ponda said that the Americans wanted to buy it. The Amin years had been difficult for Ponda. I heard he had been taken ill, moved to India, and was staying in a public guesthouse in Anand, a small town. I had taken advantage of a conference in Delhi to go and visit him in the Indian state of Gujarat. I found Ponda on a floor where he had one of ten or so beds. Ponda has had a soft spot for me since then. Upon his return to Kampala, I asked him how much the United States was willing to pay for the building; he said $300,000. I told him that eight of my graduate students at Makerere and I had started a research institute. These were times when research was not easy, since all incomes had been eroded by the devaluation dictated by the IMF. I mentioned that Yusuf, an Asian business friend of mine, had offered us the use of a bungalow on Mawanda Road in Kamwokya, a middle-income Kampala suburb, and was willing to pay rent for twelve months, but the research institute needed a permanent home. We had a $100,000 grant from Sweden. Researchers had contributed a combined amount of $50,000, each fellow paying a 20 percent development levy on his or her monthly income, and I thought we could raise another $50,000. "Tell me," I asked Ponda, "when you come back here twenty years from now to show your grandchildren where you lived before Amin, would you rather point to an extension of the US embassy or to Uganda's first independent research institute?" Since then, for the past thirty-five years, 15 Baskerville Avenue has been home to the Centre for Basic Research.

I was soon rewarded with attention from the newly established intelligence services. A youthful intelligence officer, who only two years before had been in my class, confronted me: "You have set up a private research foundation with CIA funds." (He was referring to the Swedish International Development Cooperation Agency grant to the Centre for Basic Research.) "You can't have it both ways," he said. "Either leave the university or close CBR." Eventually, I would choose to leave both, going into voluntary exile for what I hoped would be a temporary period. I had learned a lesson. When I returned, I resolved to make CBR part of the country's public university, Makerere, not an NGO with small numbers and no capacity to engage public authorities. But matters evolved differently over the next decade.

The African university began as part of the European colonial mission, a precursor of the one-size-fits-all initiatives that we today associate with the World Bank and the IMF. Universities were established in the nineteenth century in South and North Africa and in the twentieth century in Africa between the Sahara and the Limpopo. At the southern end, universities like Stellenbosch, Cape Town, Witwatersrand, were started from scratch. In the north, existing institutions such as Al-Azhar in Cairo, were "modernized" and new disciplines introduced. The model aimed to produce universal scholars in the colonies, men and women who intended to serve as a native vanguard of "civilization" without reservation or remorse, who believed they stood for excellence.

Established in 1922, Makerere University in Uganda was the first university in colonial East Africa and was part of the University of London until 1963. Founded at independence, in 1961, the University of Dar es Salaam in Tanzania was also linked to the University of London. In October 1966, just five years after the institution's establishment, students at the University of Dar es Salaam mobilized against a state ruling that all university graduates undergo a fixed period of national service in the countryside. When the student marchers reached the president's house, President Julius Nyerere addressed them and withdrew fellowships from all 334 enrolled students and sent them home. The university responded with a conference in March 1967 about its role in "development." Isolated disciplines had been failing to think about development holistically. The conference ended with an appeal for "relevance" and recommended "continuous curriculum review," hoping to balance relevance with a commitment to excellence. The University of Dar es Salaam would become home to the discipline of political economy, the new science of nationalism.

The contrast between the University of Dar es Salaam and Makerere University could not have been greater. At Dar, aside from the relevance of the curriculum being called into question, there was also a growing demand for interdisciplinary scholarship, especially from faculty who thought disciplinary nationalism was to blame for the growing irrelevance of higher education to the wider discussion of the country's social and political ills.[2] At Makerere, the reformers were concerned less about the content of curriculum than about who was teaching it. Their demand focused on deracializing the teaching body, whose leading lights were predominantly white. Newly qualified young academics like Ali Mazrui were promoted under pressure from government-appointed senior administrators.

I was hired in 1973 to teach the first year of the core curriculum in the newly consolidated Faculty of Arts and Social Sciences at the University of Dar es Salaam. Called "East African Society and Environment," the course was a concession to the demand that education be relevant to the needs of the country. It was the demand of the radical faculty—that is, militant adherents of the "dependency" school of thought, convinced that newly independent countries continued to be dependencies of former colonial masters. Leading this group was Walter Rodney, a militant Guyanese historian of Africa whose book *How Europe Underdeveloped Africa* became the holy grail of the militant left with its theory that poor nations continue to be in the grip of their former masters for whom they provide cheap labor and natural resources.

Debates at the University of Dar es Salaam during the six years I was there (1973–1979) took place within the parameters of development studies. The first gentle critique of dependency theorists was by Issa Shivji, in a book titled *The Class Struggle Continues.* Shivji argued that the Nyerere regime's anti-capitalist rhetoric and call for an egalitarian society (*Ujamaa*) was an ideological fig leaf for a new type of capital accumulation by a new class of high-level state bureaucrats. He called them the "bureaucratic bourgeoisie." Shivji had aimed a salvo at Nyerere's blameless reputation among progressive intelligentsia. The Ugandan lawyer Dani Wadada Nabudere wrote a blistering critique of what he thought was Shivji's distracting preoccupation with internal developments and class struggle. He said it covered up the main story, the continued exploitation of the country by "the international bourgeoisie."[3] My colleagues and I were not sure that the matter was so simple: that either the bourgeoisie was external (international) or local. Shivji's main point was the development of a local bourgeoisie under the umbrella of international capital, in a renegotiated partnership between the two.

The key achievement of the University of Dar es Salaam can be summed up in one word: decolonization.[4] At the superficial level, as a code word for Africanizing staff, decolonization became the rage not only at Dar but also at Makerere, and indeed in every independent African country. At a deeper level, decolonization aimed to transform curriculum through the introduction of a core curriculum called "development studies."

But there were also problems. Though critics of the colonial period, scholars of development studies came to share its timeline. Studies in political economy became narrowly preoccupied with market formations. By development, they meant economic development. The presumption was that every society must go through the same stages of development—which is why everything that gave a society its historical character, like politics and culture, were considered secondary to the economic study of society. The three-year program at Dar ended with a blueprint on "development" in the final year. Like any off-the-shelf manual, it claimed validity for every newly independent country.

There was also little room for discussion of governance in the developmentalist university. The general assumption was that the state would be the sole funder of the university and the university would be run as a parastatal, an apparatus of the state. Governance and funding provided entry points for the World Bank to restructure higher education in Africa, starting with Makerere.

Uganda's colonial model was the target of two critiques: nationalist and neoliberal. Nationalists called for higher education to be relevant to the needs of a newly independent country. The World Bank agreed that higher education had to be relevant. But the Bank defined relevance narrowly, as would corporations, with reference to the market, and not society. Market-based demand, shaped by profit considerations, would displace social needs. This, in a nutshell, was the neoliberal vision, from which the Bank derived its policy framework. In joining the nationalist call to decolonize higher education, the Bank presented students with a range of narrow career alternatives, without raising larger issues, such as citizenship in the political domain, the direction of economic development, and the cultural diversity of society.

The Bank's critique had three policy implications: First, that the colonial education system had been elitist and could not keep going without a constant inflow of state subsidies. Second, that higher education is a business, and just as with any business, the consumer (the student's family in the case) must pay for the product. And, third, the way to do this is to open the gates of the university to fee-paying students, so that additional revenue from fees can alleviate the financial burden on government. The first assumption was right, but the remaining two made for the disaster the Bank created.

If higher education is indeed a business, the Bank reasoned, then investment in higher education has to be justified, as in any other business. By dividing total investment with the number of students admitted, the Bank arrived at the cost of training a student at each educational level—primary, secondary, and tertiary.

The inevitable conclusion was that returns on investment are highest in primary education but lowest in university education. The Bank concluded this was reason enough for the state to prioritize primary over all forms of tertiary education.

The cash-strapped postcolonial university was the entry point for the World Bank. Starved of financial resources, the National Resistance Movement was willing to swallow "the bitter pill," which is how everyone described the core of the Bank's agenda. The World Bank put Makerere through the grind of a market-oriented reform, in no time overwhelming the undergraduate program with numbers, and destroying the quality of teaching and undermining existing research capacity in the arts (humanities) and the social sciences. At the same time, the government followed the Bank's advice and drastically reduced the flow of public funds to the higher education sector.[5]

The World Bank took over the policy-making apparatus at Makerere in the late 1980s, though it took the Bank fifteen years to implement its reform. The Bank called for an increased intake of fee-paying students in all faculties. The number of students admitted to Makerere exploded roughly fivefold over the course of a decade: from 2,186 in 1992–1993 to 10,666 in 2003–2004. As the humanities and social sciences turned into teaching factories and consultancy units, they ceased to be sites for research.

The Bank needed the active collaboration of the teaching faculty to implement its reforms. Whereas the then–vice chancellor and dean of Arts were faithful disciples of the World Bank, the dean of the Faculty of Sciences was not. He insisted that science education could not proceed without laboratory space, which was limited. As admission increased in Arts and the Social Sciences, classes ballooned in size. More and more classes were held at the same time, requiring students to somehow attend two classes simultaneously; students began by sharing notes with fellow students, then demanding that lecturers hand out typed notes as a substitute for attending lectures. Standards plummeted.

From the time I left Makerere in 1994, I made it a practice to return to Kampala every academic summer. Two issues preoccupied me during those years: that of political belonging (based on two versions of colonial law—modern and customary) and neoliberal reforms introduced by the World Bank in 1987 in the higher education sector. I had long been looking for an opportunity to discuss these two issues with the president. I approached Ruhakana Rugunda in 1999, whom I had known from my visits to US universities in the 1970s. Rugunda, who would be prime minister in Museveni's government from 2014 to 2021, was already an influential minister. I finally got an appointment to see the president several months later, and when I walked into the Nakasero State House, I was admitted to the meeting room where on one side of the conference table were Ruhakana Rugunda (a minister), Eriya Kategaya (first deputy prime minister), James Wapakhabulo (the NRM secretary-general), and Moses Karuhanga (the president's personal private secretary). I was asked to sit on the other side of the table as we waited for the president.

When the president walked in, he turned to me, "Professor, you are always talking, always talking, what is wrong with you?" I said, "Mr. President, professors are paid to talk." His approach was that of a prizefighter, beginning by sizing up the opponent before a knockout punch. Only if the opponent survived would he earn the president's respect and a right to engage him in a conversation. So we talked, about Makerere and Congo. He listened to my views on both and then suggested I chair a commission of inquiry on Makerere. I agreed. He asked Wapakhabulo to liaise with me. After the long vacation of 2003, I returned to Columbia University, where I had been teaching since 1999, and waited, for months. When there was still no word, I concluded that I had been taken for a ride. I wrote Wapakhabulo, who responded, "The president is very busy with the elections. Just wait." I decided I had no choice but to wait and, if necessary, take my own initiative.

In 2004, I was due for a sabbatical from Columbia. I decided to go to Kampala with our son, Zohran, who was by then in primary school in New York City. Mira agreed to revise her plans so she could join us in Kampala for half the year. Zohran settled down with the study of issues such as "zero grazing." I started working diligently with a research assistant, Morris Nsamba, to understand the impact of World Bank reforms on Makerere. We started by looking for a blueprint that had guided the World Bank reform but soon realized that no such document existed and that we would have to reconstruct the Bank's agenda by studying the consequences of its actions. We conducted hundreds of interviews, gathered and read endless minutes of departmental, faculty, council, and executive committee meetings, and went through piles of administrative reports generated by different committees as evidence of "work." At the end, I wrote a book titled *Scholars in the Marketplace: The Dilemmas of Neoliberal Reform at Makerere University, 1989–2005* which was published locally with the Centre for Basic Research, and then republished in a series of locations around the continent.[6]

My sabbatical had confirmed my earlier experience: that the old model does not work, and it is always better to train postgraduate students in the very institutions in which we expect them to work. The next generation of African scholars needed to be trained at home. This would require tackling the question of institutional reform alongside rethinking curricular content. Teaching, research, and institution building would have to be part of a single, coordinated effort.

I bid my time waiting to return to Makerere, in a role that would give me room to make institutional reforms. When the position of director of MISR was advertised in 2010, I applied and was shortlisted. I knew that when the colonial government had set up the East African Institute of Social Research (EAISR)—the predecessor of MISR—in 1949, its stated purpose was to study "the native question" as it looked for an antidote to nationalism in the post–World War II period. The anthropologists brought to study "tribal societies" came from the United Kingdom and North America. For them, Ugandans were to be subjects for study, with a few working as "native informants" for Western researchers. After independence in 1962, MISR turned into a den of consultants.

When I arrived at Makerere in 2010, intellectual life at the university had been reduced to a bare-bones classroom activity. Extracurricular seminars and workshops had migrated to hotels. Workshop attendance went alongside transport allowances and per diem. All this was part of a larger process, the NGO-ization of the university. Academic papers had turned into corporate-style PowerPoint presentations. Academics read less and less. A chorus of buzzwords had taken the place of lively debates.

In 2010, there was no postgraduate program at MISR. There were seven researchers, including myself. We began by meeting weekly for an hour to discuss what research we had done since arriving at MISR. The answers were a revelation: everyone seemed to be studying everything, and anything—primary education, public health, transportation and roads, HIV and AIDS. This was the first manifestation of a consultancy culture where the consultant has no particular expertise. His or her claim involves gathering data and writing reports. Also, consultants seldom read, since consultancies do not require you to read anything more than field data, notes, and official reports. The library was not a priority. I noticed that the MISR library had hardly grown since independence in 1962; in fact, it had shrunk since about 2000. MISR's ten-year strategic plan called for purchasing a mere hundred books.

The little research that was done at MISR was externally driven, the result of a European donor requirement that European universities conducting research on Africa must partner with African universities. Rather than produce institutional partnerships between equals, it led to the incorporation of individual African researchers into many externally driven projects, the result of a donor outreach. I had little patience for this kind of tutelage. I began by canceling two collaborations in which MISR seemed to have played no part in designing the research proposal: one with Sciences Po in Paris, and the other with the University of Oxford in the United Kingdom. As the exercise continued, I had a growing sense that we were not getting anywhere. Experience seemed to have taught my colleagues to be patient: if the director is naive and demanding, you only have to wait for the end of his contract.

In 2010, every research fellow at MISR was a consultant with a comfortable lifestyle. When we asked each of them to divide time between research and teaching, they resisted. They said we must vote. I told them MISR had a national mandate and that mandate was research. Only those who conduct research can have the right to vote on questions relating to research. A handful of people do not have the right to redefine the mandate. I was forcing change from above—a method not likely to be sustainable in the long run—but I was convinced that waiting until you persuade everyone will never bring change.

It was around this time that Professor Holger Hansen, a European scholar working on Uganda, visited MISR. He asked me what I expected to achieve. I explained that my goal was to create a multidisciplinary, coursework-based PhD program to train a generation of researchers. He looked at me, then said with a straight face, "If you are serious about it, you have to clean the stables." His advice struck like a bolt of lightning.

I began to look for collaborators dissatisfied with the culture of consultancy. There were two at that early stage: Okello Ogwang, a colleague and friend since our time together at the Centre for Basic Research in the 1990s; and Adam Branch, who had been my student at Columbia University and had done his doctoral research in Northern Uganda.

Assisted by Ogwang and Branch, I put together a detailed curriculum for an interdisciplinary MPhil/PhD program and shepherded it through the university hierarchy: the College, Senate, the University Council, and then the National Council of Higher Education. I have often wondered why it took little time to jump these hurdles given that our future experience turned out to be very different. For one, the new vice chancellor was determined to move the sluggish bureaucracy and we were also lucky in that our proposal was a purely intellectual document with no finances mentioned, and no apparent questioning of power hierarchies. In short, the program was not a direct challenge to anyone.

As soon as the program was approved, we began cleaning the stables. The core of consultants had been used to signing individual contracts and giving MISR 15 percent of their earnings as a rental fee. We required all academic staff to divide their time evenly between research and teaching. I told them their contracts had been modified by the doctoral program passed by university bodies, including the Senate and Council—the same bodies that had issued the contract. And that those who did not teach would have to forsake their offices and conduct their research in the library. The result was the biggest crisis the program had faced since it was established.

The vice chancellor's niece, a research fellow at MISR, the only one whose appointment I had pushed as director, decided on a public protest in the nude, which she said was an ancient African tradition, now deployed for a nontraditional cause. The fellow, Stella Nyanzi, called the media to come to MISR to witness the protest, which they did, in the process mobilizing their audiences. Since Nyanzi was not only a human rights advocate, but a queer rights advocate and scholar of sexuality, I invited her to teach a course on internal debates in LGBTQ studies, but she declined. Stella received important support from Sylvia Tamale, Makerere's first woman law professor, whose inaugural lecture as professor of law celebrated Stella Nyanzi's rebellion as an act of feminist courage—continuing where anti-colonial feminism had left off, turning women's bodies into a battlefield for liberation. But not all feminists agreed. One of them was Lyn Ossome, newly hired at MISR as a senior research fellow, who defended the decision to move from consultancy to research, as part of a larger project to combine teaching and research so as to develop local research capacity.

The *MISR Review* decided to publish a set of symposium papers in response to Professor Tamale's inaugural address.[7]

Once the program began, questions were on the table. First, What do we teach? Two trends had been dominant in 2010 when we began our deliberations: one was universalist or Westernist; the other, particularist or Africanist. We looked for a middle way as MISR rejected the division between theory-based disciplines and place-based area studies nurtured in Western universities. We agreed that the interdisciplinary program would have a dual orientation: global excellence and African relevance. The big question was: How do we straddle the universal and the particular, how do we introduce students to different intellectual traditions by broadening the range of texts they would be required to read, from pagan (Greek and Roman, for example), to Christian (Saint Augustine) and Islamic (Ibn Khaldun). We also developed a homegrown offering, "Major Debates in the Study of Africa," that became a required core course for students in their first year. Rather than treat each book as an isolated item to be consumed separately in a conventional history of ideas, we insisted that students study texts in their historical contexts, both social and intellectual, so as to read each text as a response to two sets of questions: one posed by their intellectual predecessors, and the other by the larger society.

Our second question was, How should we teach? Key at MISR was the definition of knowledge not as orthodoxy but as a set of debates that change over time, each the outcome of collective deliberation. The definition of a research problem should stem from a dual engagement, with the society at large and with key debates in one's discipline. The point is to rethink old questions and formulate new ones.

So far we had created a model that risked stillbirth if we did not address a third question: Who will teach? It was clear that MISR could not compete with other institutions globally, especially when it came to salaries we paid our academic staff. Expatriate teachers would, in some cases, start looking for other jobs the day they arrived and then leave, sometimes without any notice. The three groups who were likely to stay were Ugandans, East Africans, and those with a commitment to the field of study and the innovative nature of the program. The core faculty had to be local or regional. For now, there would be little alternative to growing our own timber. With these three questions—exploring what, how, and who will teach—we managed to rethink the World Bank's assumptions.

As we have seen, three assumptions had driven the World Bank's agenda. First, the Bank thought of education as a business enterprise. But it is not just physical commodities—goods and services—that bring sustenance and advancement, and feed people. Education is a very special commodity. Ideas nourish, ideas build. Horizons broaden, previously isolated regions are integrated, and established views are challenged. The biggest returns are in the realm of ideas and the innovation of practices. With it, notions of self, of community and the world, change.

Second, the World Bank lost sight of the big picture and looked at primary, secondary and higher education as isolated islands competing against each other. Such a fragmented approach failed to ask questions like, Who will train teachers? Who will produce a curriculum responding to the needs of society, the demands for citizenship, and the need to think of alternative futures in a rapidly changing world?

Third, the World Bank abstracted education from its social and political context. The issue was brought home during the discussion on fees. According to a study by the University Senate, private student fees covered less than 50 percent of the cost of educating a student—no matter the program. This is why a larger intake of students generated not just more revenue but also a larger deficit, simply because fees do not cover the full cost of educating a student. I know of no educational institution, whether public or private, where fees cover the full cost of education. Increasing fees is not a feasible option in a public university. Fees need to be set with two considerations in mind: the cost of education, and the capacity of parents to pay fees. If not for reasons of equity, then for political reasons, no government would be able to endlessly lift the ceiling on fees.

The doctoral program at MISR had clearly been set up as an antidote to World Bank reforms of the late 1980s. It was interdisciplinary and focused on small numbers, barely ten students a year. We hoped to integrate research, teaching, and social inquiry, so that learning would not just introduce a student to a fixed pool of knowledge, but would open new questions for social inquiry. Students studied themes with a view to understand its historical development and future possibilities: migrant labor; land tenure; chiefdom and local bureaucracies;

and precolonial histories of state formation. The plan was not only to see Africa as part of the world, but also to see the world from an ever-changing African vantage point. Research would be the central focus of MISR. Instead of being a landing site for "international" researchers, we would cultivate a generation of African researchers, women and men, reflecting the diversity of Africa as much as possible. Higher education, we agreed, is where a society comes to understand itself through studied reflection. It is where we develop the range of choices that make democracy meaningful in different spheres of life. In an era of rapidly expanding higher education, we hoped that MISR graduates, though few in number, would have the caliber to provide leadership in individual institutions of higher learning.

But the university is not an island. It functions as part of society. And it is to the business of society, how the new power governed, that we now turn.

PART III

THE NATIONAL RESISTANCE MOVEMENT

Tribalizing the Nation

12

HOW THE NATIONAL RESISTANCE MOVEMENT GOVERNED

The National Resistance Movement (NRM) claimed control of the capital city of Kampala on January 29, 1986. From governing a population of about 150,000 in the Luwero Triangle, as recorded in the 1980 census, the NRM now had to expand its governance to cover nearly half the country, whose total population was recorded as 15.07 million persons that year. The NRM began by replacing the colonial-era system of governance through chiefs with the system it had evolved in the Luwero Triangle—by setting up Resistance Councils and Committees wherever it took over the local administration. Yoweri Museveni claimed that rather than "a mere change of guards," the NRM would usher in "fundamental change" in the country. There would no longer be administration through state-appointed chiefs. Every village was to be organized as a Resistance Council. All adult residents, regardless of gender or ethnic origin, were recognized as its members, who then elected a nine-person committee, called a Resistance Committee, to govern the village. After the Village Resistance Committee (RC1) came RC2, equivalent to the colonial parish, a number of which constituted the colonial sub-county, with RC4 the county, and RC5 the colonial council. The key question was that of accountability: To whom would each resistance committee be accountable?

To systematize the new system, the NRM set up a National Commission of Inquiry into Local Government System in 1987. I was appointed its chairperson. We will return to the work of the Commission later in this chapter, but the Commission issued its report in 1989. When it came to the question of local democracy, the Commission's central recommendation contradicted the NRM's practice. In the Commission's words, are the Resistance Committees organs of the people, of the NRM, or of the state?[1] The Commission had questioned the practice of indirect elections central to the Resistance Committee pyramid of representation. Unable to formulate a clear alternative, the NRM froze the elections at the primary village level (RC1).

Having started with a call for direct democracy (Resistance Committees), the NRM proceeded to divide the population into three separate groups: indigenous citizens, women, and non-indigenous minorities. Each group was subjected to a different governance, a practice that hollowed out the notion of citizenship. Groups defined as indigenous became "tribal" citizens, and women became "protected" citizens. Groups branded non-indigenous were subjected to colonial-type rule, becoming "minorities"; unless they were rebranded as indigenous by the authorities, they turned into "permanent minorities."

President Museveni likes to give one of two lectures on governing Uganda. He is fond of giving the first lecture, on class and modernity, to heads of states in international conferences, to visiting delegations, and to academic audiences. This lecture is about how markets develop common interests across ethnic divides, so that his cattle-owning father in Ankole is as interested in the price of milk as any cowherd in the north of the country. Both want a government that will address their interests as cattle keepers.

The second lecture, on democracy and modernity, is for broader audiences. The president is fond of telling them that multiparty democracy can only take root in a modern society where the market predominates and people join parties based on their "objective" (i.e., economic or class) *interest.* In a premodern (or quasi-modern) society like Uganda, people will join a party based on their *identity,* not interest. Where identity guides political choices, it does not make much sense to expect voters to choose between parties based on interest. People need to be guided, not represented. The president ends his lecture with a brief account of the damage done by identity-based political parties driving "sectarian" politics in Uganda.

The president's overarching view highlights the contradictory character of modern politics, both unifying and fragmenting. While expanding markets bring more and more people under a common roof, identity-based politics provide limitless possibilities to fragment these same people. But the idea was not original. It was the essence of the colonial era's indirect rule. The more opposition the president faced, the more he looked for ways to fragment constituencies, whether through creating new districts or new offices, seeking to fragment centers of opposition by first politicizing and then promising the liberation of minorities.

What follows is my reading of politics as organized by the NRA, first in Luwero, then, after a transitional decade, in the country as a whole. It is an alternative explanation of Ugandan politics, different from that of the president's lectures. My account contrasts NRM politics in two different contexts: in opposition and in power. The decade between the two contexts (1986 to 1995) was a period of transition; learning from it, the NRM revised its strategy of governance and summed it up in the 1995 Constitution.

In opposition, the NRA had sought to highlight common grievances in order to build a majority from below. After ten years in power, they concluded that the way to maintain power was to reverse this process: disrupt the development of an interest-bound majority by mobilizing identity-based minorities inside these same majorities. The logic was that continued fragmentation would diffuse oppositional challenges and stabilize power. Identity politics is not necessarily a feature of premodern or modern society. It can be practiced in either context. In Uganda, identity politics developed as a feature of "indirect rule" politics, introduced by the colonial government in response to popular demands for democratic reform.

The NRM had come to power in 1986 with Museveni's promise to effect "fundamental change"; nearly a decade later, with the adoption of the new Constitution in 1995, the same president turned around to promise "no change" as the new Constitution returned the country to a system of multiparty elections. On its own admission, the NRM had reached the end of the road; its vision no longer transformative, its promise was limited to the realization of security. In a phrase that could be heard from every official lip, the president down, was the slogan "at least we can now sleep." Its energies would henceforth be invested in preventing change—never mind that no one in history has ever succeeded to achieve this objective.

The 1981–1986 war between two factions of the state army, FRONASA (renamed NRA) and the UNLA, took place in the Luwero Triangle in Buganda, where over 50 percent of the population was made up of migrants. From a political point of view, the NRM faced a difficult question: how do we define "the people"? Colonial law considered only those with a local ancestry as having customary rights. Any attempt to observe customary rights as defined under colonialism would divide the population in Luwero down the middle: natives on the one side, and migrants on the other. No matter which side one chose, one would only serve to divide the population into two warring halves, lose the other, and thus likely the war. To avoid this dilemma, the NRM based political rights on residence, and not descent, setting up village-based Resistance Councils, run by elected executives known as Resistance Committees. When rebels captured a village from governmental authority and reorganized a new power, they faced two questions: Who can vote? And who can run for office? To neutralize the native-and-migrant divide, which would otherwise have paralyzed the NRM politically, the movement arrived at a new solution. It displaced the colonial legacy that based a person's rights on origin, with a new dictum: one's rights depend on residence (where one lives). All adults who lived in the village would have the right to vote in the village and to run for office as a part of the village committee—regardless of their origin.[2]

It is this practice that the NRM generalized as the basis for a broad notion of citizenship when it assumed governmental power in 1986. The government's new law based citizenship on five years of residence. If passed, the law would confer the right of citizenship on Rwandese refugees who had joined Museveni's army in the bush. Museveni's Rwandese would then become the equivalent of the ex-Anyanya (South Sudanese rebels) who had joined Amin's army in 1972. The initiative met stiff resistance from local elites, particularly in Buganda. President Museveni was forced to call an emergency parliament, and rapidly retreated. Not for the last time, he reversed his position, calling for ancestry as the requirement for citizenship. The outcome eroded the coalition the NRM had built. Nearly a quarter of its army, the Banyarwanda, were disenfranchised. Among them were some of Museveni's top commanders, including Fred Rugyema and Paul Kagame. To minimize the fallout, which would likely be a catastrophic implosion, they agreed on a fallback option with Museveni's support: the new Ugandan government would support Rwandan refugees based in Uganda and organized as the Rwandan Patriotic Army (RPA) to fight their way back home as a right. This is why we need to see the Rwandan Patriotic Front's invasion of Rwanda as at the same time as its armed expulsion from Uganda. In 1978–1979, Julius Nyerere had asked the Tanzanian army to cross the border, remove Amin's government, and install a Tanzania-backed government. Then, a decade later, Museveni would attempt a similar feat—but with much more tragic consequences. I have discussed these events in a book, *When Victims Become Killers,* that explores the background to the Rwanda genocide.[3]

After a decade in power, the movement confirmed this reversal in the mid-1990s, making ethnicity the means to define rights and power. Codified as the citizenship law in the 1995 Constitution, citizenship was no longer an individual right as in the previous constitutions, of 1962 and 1966. It was now a right of "indigenous" tribes, listed in Schedule 3 of the 1995 Constitution. Schedule 3 was subject to revision, and has indeed been revised several times.

"Indigenous" was defined by the Uganda Constitutional Commission (1993) as "able to trace origins to the third or fourth generation of grandparents in Uganda and who can indicate ancestral burial grounds and land within Uganda." Originally the number of indigenous tribes was taken from the list of fifty "indigenous groups" determined by Britain as the colonial power in 1959. The list was revised at least twice, with fifty-six indigenous groups noted in 1995, expanded to sixty-five by the Constitutional Review Commission of 2005–2006. Joe Oloka-Onyango concludes, "The idea of indigenous . . . was essentially a political intervention . . . the concept is indeterminate, highly selective and irrational."[4] Politics reigned supreme. The primary victims of this shift were those of Rwandese descent who had shed their blood in the "bush war" on the promise of citizenship. Yesterday's friends became tomorrow's enemies as the two armies, the NRA of Uganda and the RPA of Rwanda, having removed Joseph Mobutu and installed Laurent Kabila as the new president of Congo, came to loggerheads over who would control the diamond capital of Kisangani. The resulting Battle of Kisangani, the city at *A Bend in the River* (the title of V. S. Naipaul's novel), in June 2000 is also known as the Six-Day War.

Instead of using citizenship as a way to unify a political community, the government wielded it as a device to slice up the country into pieces, each piece a separate district dividing its residents into indigenous and migrants. Every time a new district was created, there emerged a new group of majorities and minorities. With each revision, the government refined the population afresh into "migrants" (or "settlers") and "natives." The 1995 Constitution (with its appended list of "indigenous" tribes) left it to those in power to decide who was indigenous and who was not. Each time, as the new power resorted to ethnicizing/tribalizing, genderizing, and "othering," their decision reflected their ever-changing political considerations.[5]

In 2009, President Museveni went on to clarify the implications of his new policy for local government. He proposed to "ring-fence" elective political office in one part of the Western Region of Uganda from immigrants. Invited to deliver the Abu Mayanja annual lecture at the Kampala International Conference Centre on August 7, 2009, I voiced a public critique. I said the president's use of the familiar anti-colonial language—indigenous and non-indigenous, native and settler—should not blind us to the fact that his proposal indicates "a dramatic narrowing of political vision. . . . To understand the full magnitude of the proposed change, we need to grasp how this proposal defines the settler, and thus, the native."

"During the nationalist struggle, the settler was identified with the colonial power. In the Amin period, the settler was identified with Asians, whether Ugandans or not. Now, the settler is every Ugandan who does not come from a particular district," I said. The implications would be far-reaching and were bound to grow with time: "Given that the market economy tends to move people—and not just products—from one place to another, a growing number of Ugandans, indeed a majority, if not now then soon, will find themselves branded settlers where they live."

Ugandans, I said, needed to be alert to the shift in the definition of citizenship as proposed by the president. "Nationalists defined citizenship as Ugandan, regardless of origin; Amin defined it as Black Ugandan. But, today, it is proposed that the core rights of citizenship—the right to political representation—be defined on a tribal basis. The NRM is the first government in the history of independent Uganda to propose a dilution of national citizenship in favor of a tribal citizenship." I warned that "if we adopt this proposal, we shall be returning to an arrangement resembling colonial rule." This is why it would be misleading to "reduc[e] the question to one of individual leadership." I then concluded: "Every government in Uganda's postcolonial history has had to face the colonial legacy. In moments of crisis, every government has been tempted to adopt measures from the colonial playbook, but none has dared to suggest as wholesale a return to colonial methods of rule as does the NRM leadership today. This is why I intend to focus not on the personality of those who have governed us, but on the techniques they have employed to govern."

During the anti-colonial struggle, the settler was identified as the colonial power. In the Amin period, the settler was identified as the Asian, whether or not Ugandan. Museveni now proposed to designate political office as the exclusive birthright of its "indigenous" residents, thus identifying the rest of the population as immigrants (*bafuruki*) prohibited from this right. Every Ugandan not indigenous to a particular district became a local settler. The implications were grave: if you moved outside the district of your birth, you risked being branded a "settler" in your own country. If implemented, the proposal would be a major boost to identity politics in every corner of the country. Every newly engineered "minority," and every group hoping to be a "majority" as the result of political engineering, would turn to identity politics to secure local power.

The NRM's move politicized the narrowest cultural identities, even subtribes and clans, so as to fragment the population to the maximum, administratively and politically, seeking to make the lines of division seem culturally meaningful and politically credible as a premodern carryover. And this allowed the very power that drove this project to present itself as the only force capable of unifying an ever-fragmenting society. The president stopped talking of "natives" and *bafuruki* in different parts of the country, but his agenda unfolded with a program of district creation. Even the district service committees charged with recruiting staff for local governments often disqualify aspirants from neighboring districts, even when they are of the same ethnicity—the consequence being to lower the standard of local government administration.

District Creation

The first step in this project of ethnicization was marked by a program of district creation, which has been implemented at a galloping rate. The number of districts more than tripled in three decades, from 33 in 1990, to 44 in 1997, 78 in 2006, 80 in June 2009, and 112 in 2022.[6] Museveni gave three reasons for creating 36 new districts in his March 16, 2015, letter to the Minister of Local Government, Adolf Mwesige. One of Museveni's reasons was "the need to separate various ethnic groups."[7] Like the colonial power in a previous era, the NRM claims to protect minorities by offering each a district as its "homeland." However, if new districts created new majorities, they also created new minorities, fueling the demand for new and additional districts. Where historically there had been kingdoms, as in Western Uganda (e.g., the Rwenzururu), the NRM promised to partition the kingdom so each minority may have its own kingdom, with each represented by its own cultural leader ("king").

Every time a new district (or kingdom) was carved out of an older one, the residents of both were reclassified as "native" and "non-native." The consequences were life-defining, for only natives had the customary right to land and to high political and administrative offices. Take, for example, Bukedea, formerly part of Teso (in the East), which was turned into a district, for the Kumam, who had previously been a minority in the former Teso district. The consequence of defining Bukedea as a district is that the Iteso were denied political leadership in Bukedea.[8] Access to land affected the rural population, and limits on political and administrative appointments were a key concern for the educated strata, particularly in the urban population. The NRM's rationale was of course always political. If the existing unit was no longer pliable, the presidency called for its further division and fragmentation.[9]

There was one glaring exception: Ankole, the president's home area, which stayed amalgamated as a single political unit ("tribe"). Ankole's population comprises two caste-like groups, the historically cattle-rearing Bahima and the cultivators, Bairu. Their history predates colonialism, as in Rwanda and Burundi. When Major General Pecos Kutesa proposed in 1994 during the constitution-making process that the pastoral Bahima be listed as a distinct community, President Museveni immediately summoned assembly delegates from Ankole to his country home in Rwakitura and explained why the Bahima should not be listed as a tribe. In the case of Buganda, however, Banyala, Baruuli, and Baganda were listed as separate communities (tribes). Opposition politicians pointed out the inconsistency in dividing one region (Buganda) while keeping another (Ankole) amalgamated.[10] Museveni arrived at a different solution for Ankole: the two districts when Museveni came to power (West and East Ankole) are now twelve districts. Politically, the districts of Kazo and Kiruhara are treated as reserved for Bahima elites.

The colonial period had divided the country between urban and rural areas, with residents of urban areas considered "citizens" with "national" and guaranteed rights, and rural residents identified as members of different "tribes" and guaranteed "customary rights" said to define the essence of life in their respective rural areas. In the Museveni period, the tendency was to fully "tribalize" each area, both rural and urban. The exception was the capital, Kampala, said to be a national and not a tribal territory. More than any other part of the country, it looked like an occupied territory, pockmarked with tanks and artillery. Chopping up the country into ever smaller administrative and political districts worked, except where local elites were strong enough to resist fragmentation. The biggest exception was Buganda; there, the population rallied behind the king to preserve the territorial integrity of Buganda in defiance of the central power. Baganda elites were able to resist extreme fragmentation of Buganda. The seven districts of Buganda (including Kampala) are now 226 districts (excluding Kampala). Certain districts—Sembabule, Lyantonde, and Kyankwanzi—are reserved for non-Baganda elites.

Demonizing Buganda

Whenever postindependence governments have faltered in building majority support around their political project, their tendency has been to demonize a minority as a national threat. This tactic has served as a warning to the rest of the population. In Uganda, the postindependence period can be divided into two. The first period begins with the demonization of the Baganda in the post-1964 period; the first generation of "nationalist" intellectuals were fond of writing of the Baganda as "sub-imperialists" who clearly could not be part of a national anti-imperialist alliance. The second period begins with the demonization of "the North" after 1986. Indications are that we may be returning to the era of officially framing Buganda as a national problem.

The 1966 crisis, when Obote sent in troops to depose the kabaka and undermine the autonomy of the Buganda kingdom, was a harsh reminder that Buganda is irrevocably a part of Uganda. The remarkable thing is that Buganda—which was the target of an Idi Amin–led brutal assault on its king and his palace, Lubiri, the symbolic site of the kingdom—was able to rally behind the same Amin following the 1971 coup and the 1972 Asian expulsion.

Yusufu Lule was the British-nominated president of Uganda after the fall of Idi Amin in 1979. He lasted a mere few months. When Lule attempted to impose a new leadership on the army, he was removed by the nascent Parliament backed by the Tanzanian occupation army. The population in and around the capital responded with peaceful but proactive demonstrations. The "Twagala

Lule" ("We want Lule") demonstrations of 1979 demonstrated—Gandhi-style—that it is possible to mobilize peacefully in the face of armed force, and that such a mobilization could generate a great political and moral force. However, the demonstrators were unable to move from resistance to leadership. Just when the demonstrations needed a political leadership that could see across the ethnic divide, those who came forward to make a claim for leadership turned out to be resolutely ethnic in their conviction.

The battle zones of the Luwero Triangle in the 1980s showed one way out of this dilemma. The lesson was all the more dramatic since the Luwero Triangle was a small part of the country, with a minority population, but it attracted support from large parts of the country. In Luwero, the NRM was able to weld together a multiethnic movement, thereby assuring the population that a movement limited to one part of the country would not necessarily translate into narrow ethnic domination in the country as a whole. The basis of this assurance was the system of resistance councils and committees that replaced the colonial notion of customary rights with an inclusive notion of residents' rights, with villagers organized in resistance councils and committees, without regard to ethnic origin.

Buganda came out of its post-1964 years both steeled and scarred. On the positive side, Buganda seemed determined to safeguard its unity and integrity against all odds. As a result, Buganda is today the only part of the country with the capacity to resist central government–led fragmentation into so many mini kingdoms and mini districts. In Buganda, popular support for the monarchy as the institutional axis for unity had strengthened. On the negative side, Buganda embraced a political psychology not only oppositional but also isolationist. The more Buganda succumbed to isolation, the more its capacity for leadership diminished. Increasingly, it was left to "react" to central government initiatives.

Having experienced demonization, can Buganda provide an antidote to demonization, other than revenge or withdrawing into its own corner? Can Buganda learn from the experience of the Luwero Triangle in 1981–1986, during which the NRM successfully built unity in a multiethnic population, or the earlier 1966 crisis, or the "Twagala Lule" demonstrations of 1979, when the Baganda rolled into the streets of Kampala to register support for Yusufu Lule as "their" president? Now that the NRM has forgotten, if not betrayed, that Luwero experience, can Buganda pick up the standard and be its bearer? In other words, can Buganda move beyond always thinking of itself as a potential victim, incorporating its own specific grievance into a broad demand, exercising leadership by drawing a general lesson from particular experiences, thereby representing all victims? In short, is it possible to unite people without having to create an enemy, an artificial political demon?

Buganda is the most multiethnic of all parts of Uganda. If you go back far enough, most Baganda are immigrants. Baganda are said to have begun as three clans in the thirteenth century, growing over several centuries into more than forty clans through the absorption of immigrants and conquered peoples. The historical tradition of Buganda, like that of most African groups, has been to assimilate, in sharp contrast to the colonial tradition, which tends to segregate. Many of the new Baganda—an extreme example being someone of Asian descent like myself—do not have a historical connection with Buganda. The challenge for historical Baganda is to broaden membership to include nonhistorical Baganda on the basis of equal rights. Should the Baganda be tempted to proclaim native rights at the expense of immigrants, the movement called Buganda will end up repudiating its own history, at the core of which is this incredible capacity for absorption and openness. A divided house will face a dim future.

Contemporary Buganda is firmly committed to realizing a meaningful autonomy within Uganda. Within this larger commitment, there is a lively debate on the nature of cultural (ethnic) and political (territorial) autonomy. The cultural project is known as *federo,* the political project as *federation.* The former accents ethnic identity, the latter territorial location. The challenge is how to reconcile cultural identity with political belonging, and a common past with a shared future. Not all who share a common past necessarily share a common future: some may migrate and become part of a diaspora. At the same time, people with different pasts can commit themselves to building a common future in the same place. This is why those who wish to build a future under a single political roof—no matter how different their pasts—belong to the same political community and thus deserve the same political rights.

The challenge is to combine historical sensitivity with a forward-looking consciousness. To be sensitive to history is to acknowledge that you can never just start afresh, an arrogance that sometimes affects both colonizers and revolutionaries. Buganda's history is testimony that to acknowledge the past does not mean closing the door on migrants as newcomers. Buganda's future, like that of any living community, needs a dual recognition—one of common cultural identity of residents alongside one of equal political rights. All must be committed to forging a common future for Buganda.

Ruling Women Indirectly

Women are a political minority in Uganda, even though they may be a demographic majority. If the NRM seeks to create districts and kingdoms as its local strategy, its national strategy is aimed at politicizing women as a minority that can simultaneously be incorporated into its own support base and neutralized, if not disempowered.

In March 2016, the Centre for Basic Research (CBR), a nongovernmental Ugandan organization (NGO), organized a discussion on "democracy in public life." Armanzan Madanda presented a paper on various ways in which women are disadvantaged: in terms of unpaid domestic work; gender violence; the proverbial glass ceiling (how the patriarchal nature of Uganda society blocks trained and capable women from realizing their full potential); or fear of competing with men and why many women prefer to compete against fellow women. In an otherwise informative paper, I thought Madanda had failed to ask a key question.

We know how women are represented in the NRM and how the NRM has consistently and successfully cultivated women as a constituency. But how does the NRM govern women? For a start, the state governs women differently from how it governs men. It identifies women as a special category—alongside other "minorities," such as workers, the disabled, and youth—to be guaranteed separate representation in parliament. Discriminated against historically, women are said to be entitled to "positive discrimination," or affirmative action. Whether or not it is intended, the consequence of giving women reserved seats is to leave adult men as generic citizens to be represented through open competition for open seats.

This system has a number of consequences. Is the purpose of the reform to lessen gender difference or to build on it, by politicizing and making it permanent? Does it risk turning a historical disadvantage into a permanent disability and attribute, making women representatives seem as if they need permanent care and protection? Most male voters think of open seats as men's seats. Unlike with reserved seats for other constitutionally defined "minorities," seats for women vary over time. Every district has a reserved seat for women, and as districts continue to grow in number, the number of reserved seats for women continues to increase.

There are many unanswered questions about the NRM and women. Has affirmative action in the political domain benefited women as a group or only certain women? Has identification as a "protected" group, a permanent beneficiary of a state-exercised Responsibility to Protect (R2P), led to the disenfranchisement of women as citizens? If the strategic objective is to increase the number of women in parliament, then what is the best way to do it? By increasing the number of reserved seats for women in parliament or by strengthening the participation of women in open competition for open seats? Surely, both the women's movement and the larger democratic movement need to encourage a debate on modes of affirmative action in the political sphere, and evaluate the merits of each. It is also worth asking why there is no affirmative action in the political sphere for women or for any other minority in countries where parliamentary democracy has been a fruit of democratic struggles. Is it because affirmative action in the political domain would likely undermine the principle of equal citizenship rights for all? Is the lesson to limit the scope of affirmative action to civil society—where the rule is difference—and not political society, where equality is the general aspiration? Would permanent affirmative action permanently dilute and erode equal citizenship, leading to permanent protected minorities and entrenched majorities? Would not permanent affirmative action for historically unprivileged minorities in reality turn into a continuation of the colonial legacy of indirect rule, which functioned by permanently fragmenting the population into multiple groups, thereby acting as a permanent barrier to a common citizenship?[11]

Changing Notions of Political Belonging

Notions of political belonging in the East African region have been shaped by colonial governance, especially the division of the residential population into groups of indigenous and migrants. The question of who belongs and who does not was at the heart of the citizenship crisis, which surfaced dramatically with the Asian expulsion in 1972, and then with the Rwandan genocide of the Tutsi in 1994, which ripped eastern Congo apart. The notion that "indigeneity" is the heart of citizenship was formalized by Museveni and the NRM. Uganda's 1995 Constitution literally inscribed colonial notions of "tribe" and "tribal homeland" (ancestral grounds) as central to African lives, never mind that movement and migration had been central to those same lives over millennia. Anyone paying attention to this history would acknowledge that the "homeland" had never been fixed and "tribe" had not been a closed social identity.

The colonial period was marked by a state-planned insertion of migrants both from within the colony (and the adjacent region) and from outside it. They were defined as migrants of two types: tribal (native, African) and racial (Asians, Arabs). While migrant labor fed the sinews of the colonial economy, only those who could establish a connection with the territory before colonialism were considered "indigenous"; those who could not were classified as "non-indigenous." Both Obote's and Amin's regimes called on two groups of colonial migrants—first the Luo (Obote) and then the Asians (Amin)—to return "home." But where was home? Was home neighboring Kenya or Sudan for the Luo migrants? For the Asians, was it their colonial home (UK) or their precolonial ancestral homeland (South Asia)? For the Tutsi of Rwanda and eastern Congo, was "home" their imputed ancestral home (Ethiopia) or their precolonial abode (Rwanda)? At the heart of this question is a larger question: What does decolonization mean? Based on a wholesale rejection of the colonial as a contamination, some called for a return to the precolonial (as the "customary"). Others championed just as wholesale an embrace of the colonial (as "civilization"). Those who cast their lot with the new nation looked for a third way.

When Museveni embraced Washington's neoliberal package in 1987, he restored property ownership, but not citizenship, to Ugandan Asians, welcoming them back as "investors," but not as fellow citizens. Only those with substantial property holdings returned to claim their assets. The rest were to continue with their post-expulsion lives where they had settled after 1972. But the NRM also opened the gates to a new wave of Asians—whether or not they had a historical connection with Uganda—to come into the country as visitors or "investors."

The Second Asian Migration: Post-1972 "Rockets"

Today, the numbers of residents of Asian descent in Uganda are estimated to be between 35,000 and 40,000. The numbers are comparable to persons of Chinese descent who came in as contract workers with big Chinese firms or as small businesses catering to these firms and their workers. Most of the 35,000 or so Asians are new to the country. The Museveni government has been receptive to this inflow of migrants; as investors, the new Asian immigrants could own property but make no claim to political rights. Many came hoping Uganda would be a transit stop in a longer journey to the West. They were known as "rockets"—meaning they could go only one way; they had neither plans nor provisions for a return journey.

Very few have been able to realize this dream of a westward migration. Most came in as earlier waves of Asians had done, using family connections, often starting with work offered by wealthy relatives, learning the ropes of day-to-day life in a new country where they did not speak a local language, then striking out on their own. Some set up *dukas* up-country, others moved into the electronic and IT sector in urban areas. But there were other differences with colonial migrants. Their children have grown up in a post-1972 Uganda where institutions like schools and neighborhoods have been deracialized. As a result, they are often fluent in the language of the locality where they live, and they are able to negotiate the region comfortably. Over time, the depth and reach of their experience has yielded new answers to old questions. The most original of these has been the initiative to establish the Asian African Association (AAA) of Uganda in 2013, a testimony to an ongoing search for a new political identity.

The formation of AAA was the outcome of a protracted learning process, in which we can identify a few steps. The first of these was the Mabira crisis of 2007–2013. Mabira is a revered forest on the road from Kampala to the industrial town of Jinja on the shores of Lake Victoria, also said to be the source of the White Nile. Between Lugazi and Mabira are sugar plantations owned by the Mehta Corporation. In 2013, when the Mehta family planned to extend the cultivation of sugar, they turned to the adjoining forest, and the government said it would happily grant the land in the interest of "development." Thus followed public protests in favor of preserving the forest, leading to violence, which took an anti-Asian turn; one Asian was killed. Panic spread through the Asian minority. The government insisted the project go ahead as planned. The kabaka's government offered to assign land outside Mabira for the Mehta Corporation's purpose. The central government remained adamant.

The same year, 2013, a dissident group of Asians drafted a simple petition declaring support for those calling for the integrity of the forest. The petition was not submitted to any authority, but was published as a paid advertisement in the daily paper. It stated, in bold:

> **SAVE MABIRA!**
> **OPPOSE GREED!**
> **ADVANCE COMMUNITY AND COUNTRY!**

Published in *The New Vision,* the petition was signed by 102 people. Its impact was explosive. The standard Asian public engagement in Uganda had been philanthropic, and mobilization was inevitably initiated by either rich families like the Madhvanis or the Mehtas, or by religious groups with a philanthropic tradition, like the Ismaili or Sikh communities. This time, though, the signatories could not be identified with a particular community, nor with the wealthy and the well connected. Instead, the signatories were openly distancing themselves from the Asian rich in a public protest.

That same year, 2013, several members of this group founded the Asian African Association (AAA) of Uganda, dedicated to forging a different notion of home in a changing world. AAA's founding statement, issued on July 2, 2013, began with a self-reflection: "Whether citizen or not, whether in the country for generations or fresh off the plane, all persons of South Asian descent in Uganda are identified as Bayindi. The strange thing is not just others, but we too call ourselves Bayindi. For someone who thinks of Uganda and Africa as home, to be called a *Muyindi* (sing. an Indian person; pl. *Bayindi*) is to live in the past, to ignore our present, and to be blind to the future. It is to live in this land as if one were a visitor. You cannot be a permanent visitor: that is a ticket to permanent insecurity and permanent irresponsibility. This mindset is at the source of our continuing social and political isolation. We are complicit in our own dilemma."

The next step in the formation of the AAA was to learn from others: "Take a few lessons from around the world. The people of African origin who migrate to the U.S. are known as African Americans, not Africans. Those who go to Britain are known as Black British. But it is a peculiarity of East Africa that we who emigrated from South Asia continue to be known as Indian, Pakistani and Bangladeshi, even after generations of living in Africa." I was the founding chairperson of the AAA and authored its declaration.[12]

"The birth of the AAA," in the words of the organization's founding declaration, "marks a new era in the development of the Asian African community in Uganda. It is an acknowledgement that, like every community, the Asian African community, too, is constantly in the process of formation." Who, then, are we, and "what is our relationship to Africa and African society?" The declaration called for a rethinking of homeland. "We are *not* South Asians (Indians, Pakistani or Bangladeshi), for South Asians live in South Asia and are committed to making a future there. *Nor* are we overseas South Asians, who are part of a South Asian Diaspora whose members aim to return home to South Asia after a temporary sojourn overseas. True, our origin is South Asia, but our present is African. Many of us hope to make a future in Africa. We are Africans of Asian Origin, Asian Africans."

The new organization shifted its activities from philanthropy to public engagement, beginning with a public discussion on the anniversary of the 1972 expulsion. Anywhere from two hundred to three hundred people, the majority Black Ugandans, attended each event. *New Vision* donated free space for advance publicity; its television channel, *Urban TV*, covered the entire event. The event rekindled a public discussion on the role of Asians in Uganda that often sounded like an informal referendum on the justification of the expulsion. Could the expulsion be discussed as if it had been an isolated event in Uganda's history? The point was made with particular forcefulness during the forty-fifth anniversary commemoration by two speakers from the podium: Robert Kabushenga, the editor of *New Vision;* and Augustine Ruzindana, former inspector general of government (IGG). Other Ugandans have been meted out a worse fate, they pointed out: not just expulsion, but elimination, in some cases. Why can Ugandan Asians not locate themselves as part of this wider tragedy rather than speak from a distance?

The next step was to reflect on the citizenship question and, in that context, the minority question in the country. The 1995 Constitution had highlighted citizenship as a group attribute rather than an individual one. All groups resident in the country had been divided into "indigenous" and "not indigenous." Even if one had been born in the country, the latter could only register as a citizen at the behest of the state. The list of indigenous groups (or tribes), published as Schedule 3 of the 1995 Constitution, had included fifty-six groups, expanded to sixty-five in 2005. That time, as well, responses from Ugandan Asians were differentiated.

The mainstream association of Asian residents of Uganda, the Indian Association, appealed to the government to recognize Ugandan Asians as an "indigenous" Ugandan "tribe." AAA disagreed, presenting a memo to parliament questioning the very rationale for preparing a list of "indigenous" tribes, from which to exclude immigrants as "non-indigenous." The choice was between two notions of citizenship: one historical and inclusive; the other nonhistorical, closed, and exclusive.

AAA took the lead in calling for a public discussion on the subject. Among those invited were representatives of the largest minority groups in the country. The discussion on "citizenship in the Uganda constitution" was held on Saturday, July 18, 2015.[13] Representatives of several minority groups participated. Among the speakers were Makerere University academics: Joe Oloka-Onyango at the School of Law and Sarah Ssali at the School of Women and Gender. In a paper titled "From Expulsion to Exclusion: Revisiting the Citizenship Conundrum for Migrant Communities in Uganda," Oloka-Onyango argued, "There is no objective basis on which Schedule 3 was constructed. . . . It undermines social pluralism and diversity." Dr. Sarah Ssali noted "the crucial role played by minorities" who are being "sidelined in the political process." Augustine Ruzindana, the former IGG, told the meeting that ethnicity is a political question that needs to be answered by convening a national conference. My presentation was based on the citizenship memorandum submitted to parliament by AAA on July 15. Participants called for "the deletion of Schedule 3 in the Constitution which lists the 65 indigenous communities and ethnic groups recognized as citizens of Uganda."

The workshop set up a committee to address minority grievances. It brought together key scholars on the subject and representatives of key groups, including the chair of Uganda Banyarwanda Cultural Development Association, a representative of Uganda Somali Association, Augustine Ruzindana, and Joe Oloka-Onyango, as prominent public persons. I was asked to chair the committee.

With the formation of a minority organization, each minority member was learning to participate in the wider public square. We were bound to dirty our hands in the process. We had mobilized various groups as so many "minorities" to demand equal citizenship. Did we now risk falling in line with the regime's strategy of creating as many minorities as possible? Did we need to think of an alternative strategy, one that would distinguish between two kinds of minorities—cultural and political—the former designated outside the democratic process, and thus seemingly permanent, but the latter, a product of the democratic process, temporary and transient? If minorities are the result of a political process, like an election, they can cease to be a minority as a consequence of the same process. The minority mobilization had driven home an important lesson. Unlike minority elites, which naturally seemed to gravitate to the government of the day, ordinary members were becoming conscious of the need to develop an autonomous voice. Instead of a strategy that looked exclusively to government for protection, we had come to a conscious realization of the need to develop a productive rapport with other communities. It meant a shift in how one looked to building strength—less in financial than in organizational unity that highlighted shared concerns.

Imaginative Politics: "Walk to Work"

Opposition parties in Uganda remain legal on paper but are effectively crippled between presidential elections. The NRM has completely banished the opposition from rural areas. Even in urban areas, it has become difficult for the opposition to hold meetings, sponsor candidates for office, or raise funds. The electorate has been repeatedly reminded of the cost of voting for the opposition. Museveni has distinguished between the "development cake" and the "political cake": the "development cake" is for all, but the "political cake" can only be for supporters of the ruling party. It was a new name for the old pork barrel politics that distributed public resources only to one's supporters. This is how the opposition came up with a remarkably imaginative and brilliant mobilization technique, one sure to blur the political distinction between supporters and opponents of the regime by highlighting a dilemma in daily life shared equally by all.

Following the electoral scandals of 2001 and 2006, the government refused to issue permissions for peaceful assembly to protest any aspect of its policy. The one exception was a permit for the Pan-African Movement to march in solidarity with Colonel Muammar Gaddafi and in opposition to NATO bombardment of Libya. The march was to end up as a rally to be addressed by an army commander. But even that permission was rescinded at the last minute for fear that opposition supporters might join the demonstration and subvert it. The opposition announced plans to initiate a new form of protest, whose object would be to direct attention to a domestic issue, rising prices. They called it "Walk to Work."[14]

Walk to Work, the opposition said, was not an assembly and would thus require no police permit. Opposition politicians, who usually drive to work, would instead walk in solidarity with more and more ordinary people forced to walk because of rising fuel prices. This would happen twice a week, every Monday and Thursday. The result was a true theater of the absurd as police looked for legal provisions that would authorize them to stop opposition politicians from walking to work.

Salaamu Musumba, a high opposition official, was walking with one other person, and was stopped by a policeman. "Have you no car?" asked the policeman. Musumba answered, "Yes, I have." "Then why are you walking?"[15] Musumba was arrested. When asked what was wrong with walking, Information Minister Kabakumba Masiko explained that "instead of going to the streets," the opposition should "come up with proposals on how we are going to handle the challenges . . . but we are instead hearing them saying 'let us walk to work.'"[16] Third Deputy Prime Minister, also Minister of Internal Affairs, Kirunda Kivejinja, said the problem was more sinister. Since the motive behind Walk to Work was really political, the organizers should have sought police guidance. But, he said, "the organisers of the walk-to-work demonstrations of last Monday did not follow these guidelines. Police were not notified, the organisers did not identify themselves, the routes were not agreed to," he said. When asked why the police had sprayed schools and health centers with tear gas, he said that "some of them, when engaged by the Police, decided to run into schools and health centres to use children and patients as human shields."[17] Faced with public outrage, the minister beat a retreat the following week, to the point of sounding ridiculous: "If you want to demonstrate, you do not need permission. But it is right to consult with the police first to avoid any future fallacy," Mr. Kirunda said.[18] No one asked if "consultations" with the police are legally mandatory.

Asan Kasingye, chief political commissar of the police, insisted that the "walk-to-work" demo, which the opposition were trying to portray as an ordinary peaceful walk, was bound to turn into a procession, which is why the organizers were law-bound to notify the police. "I have no quarrel with anybody who wants to walk but it must be in accordance with the law by notifying the Police and agreeing on the routes and maintenance of order." Realizing the absurdity of calling on people to get a police permit specifying when and where to walk, he added: "Many people walk but this has turned into a political matter."[19] The chief magistrate in Makindye issued Kampala's lord mayor–elect with a criminal summons for failure to show up in court over Walk to Work charges.[20]

The Inspector General of Police Major General Kale Kayihura tied himself up in knots as he explained the distinction between ordinary walking and political walking. Referring to the leading opposition leader, Kizza Besigye, he said, "Besigye can walk. There is no problem and he does not have to notify the Police. However, when he wants to use walking or running as a demonstration, then he has to notify us."[21] Pressed to explain what was wrong with political walking, the inspector general of police said the opposition's real intention was to create a Ugandan version of Egypt's Tahrir Square.[22]

The image of Tahrir Square fed opposition hopes and fueled government fears. Both the opposition that took to walking and the government that was determined to stop them from walking were driven by the memory of this single event. For many in the opposition, Egypt came to signify the promised land around the proverbial corner. For many in government, Egypt had been the site of a fundamental challenge to power; it had to be resisted, whatever the cost. Matters reached a point where even the hint of protest evoked maximum reaction from the government.

As military resources were deployed to maintain civil order in the streets, the line between civil and military was blurred. Those in power insisted on treating even the simplest civil protest as if it were a precursor to an armed rebellion. Government began drafting soldiers into the police, each identified by wearing a different beret. Previously demoralized by a stolen election, the opposition gathered courage and gained coherence as these protests escalated; in contrast, the government seemed to lose direction. The same opposition whose ranks had been dispersed by offers of bribes, each a passport to patronage or a license to pillage, was beginning to muster resolve and moral courage, even though there was no election in sight and the times continued to be hard.

As the sense of impunity grew over the years, officialdom became shamelessly oblivious to public opinion, whether domestic or international. On February 3, 2023, the foreign ministry wrote the Office of the UN High Commissioner for Human Rights (OHCHR) in Uganda that it would not renew the host country agreement it signed with the OHCHR, which in 2005 established its initial mandate in the country. The letter was a response to OHCHR's acknowledgment of a continuing regime of torture and other forms of abuse by security forces in Uganda.[23]

In the face of growing opposition, the National Resistance Movement turned to the colonial playbook, combining outright repression with techniques of fragmentation based on an ever fine-tuned identity politics, all the while blaming the politicization of cultural difference on the premodern character of society. To be successful, a new politics needed to offer an antidote, an alternative practice that united those divided by prevailing modes of governance. In Egypt, where the army government had wielded religious identity as a weapon to fragment the opposition, Tahrir Square offered an antidote. It shed the language of religion in politics, but it did so without embracing a militant secularism that would outlaw religion in the public sphere. It called for a broader tolerance of cultural identities in the public sphere—one that would include both secular and religious tendencies. The challenge was how to participate in the public sphere—either without inscribing religious identity into politics or by banishing religion from politics.

In Uganda, where the government had chosen to politicize ethnic difference when faced with a growing opposition, the motto of governance was one tribe, one district, with citizenship reserved for only "indigenous" tribes. There was no fixed limit to the number of "tribes" in the country; the government reserved the right to acknowledge which tribes were indigenous, and to declare a subtribe or even a clan as a tribe. The remarkable thing about the events we know as "Walk to Work" is that they followed on the heels of a national election whose results, if we go by the official tally, were anything if not decisive, yet—according to the highest court in the land—had been subverted. Cynicism spread from rulers to the ruled; more and more of the population think of elections not as the time to make meaningful choices but as a time to extract dues from politicians who like seasonal birds are unlikely to be seen until the next election season. At the same time, more and more in the political class are coming to think of an election as a managed exercise where the outcome is decided not by who votes but by who counts the votes. What does it say about contemporary democracy in which even an election where those in power can demonstrate support of a vast majority of people—over 90 percent in Egypt and nearly two thirds in Uganda—does not give you any idea of the level of dissatisfaction among the electorate?

No matter the numbers involved in the activities we know as "Walk to Work," there is no denying the sheer brilliance of the vision that guided it. That brilliance lay in its ability to confer on the simplest of human activities, walking, a major political significance: the capacity to say no. And also the capacity to say yes by inviting the vast majority of the working and student population to walk. The irony is that many in government, and more than a few in the opposition, thought of "Walk to Work" as a shortcut to power, which it could not be. The real significance of "Walk to Work" was that it broke the hold of routine. In doing so, it presented its participants with a challenge. That challenge was to come up with a new language of politics, reflecting a new mode of organization and promising a new mode of governance.

The challenge lay in recovering the moral force of politics through possibilities of reform that seemed unimaginable only yesterday. To rethink the challenge before us is not necessarily to close ranks for a final struggle, as many a radical intellectual is prone to doing, but to build new associations based on new imaginations, so as to transform daily practices and make them more inclusive.

13

REVENGE IN THE NORTH

For its first decade in power, the National Resistance Movement (NRM) ran a civil administration largely restricted to the southern half of the country. The northern part was by and large run by a military administration, as a complement to the war fought by the National Resistance Army (later, the Uganda Peoples' Defence Forces, UPDF). The war in northern Uganda lasted nearly twenty years, from 1986 to 2006. It began like an ordinary counterinsurgency operation aiming to isolate rebels from the population. During the Chinese communists' Long March (1934–1935), Mao Zedong had summed up the logic of guerrilla insurgency as a relationship between fish and water, with guerrillas as fish and the population as water. In the 1960s, during the Vietnam War, Samuel Huntington, the Harvard professor–turned counterinsurgency specialist, turned Mao's dictum inside out: drain the water, expose the fish, and isolate rebels from the population, making them vulnerable. In practice, this meant interning the population on a mass scale. First introduced by the British in the Anglo-Boer War of 1898 in South Africa, the technique of counterinsurgency was perfected in one colonial campaign after another: Bunyoro in late nineteenth century; Malaya and then Kenya in the 1950s; and the Indo-China War in the 1960s.

The war in northern Uganda took on the character of a colonial-type counterinsurgency, whose objective was not only to defeat soldiers of the previous regime, in addition to any new sprung rebels, but also to bring the population to its knees. The objective of the northern war changed after 1995: the aim was no longer to win, but to keep the war going. Unless the rebels were alive and fighting, there would be little reason to continue to intern and punish the population. At the same time, the war in the North was critical to canvassing for global support from international agencies and Western states, the former in support of a noble "humanitarian" objective and the latter eager to wage "the war on terror" on a global scale.

There are a couple of remarkable things about the government's war for more than two decades. First, more than a war against the perpetrators of terror (the rebels), it became a war against the victims of terror (the population). This war was the darkest hour of the Museveni government and may be compared to the violence with which Amin's soldiers had targeted pro-Obote Acholi and Langi soldiers in the barracks in 1971, and the gratuitous violence the Obote army (under Amin) had rained on Mengo, the Buganda capital, in 1966. Indeed, the war in the North has been independent Uganda's darkest hour. Also remarkable is that the "international community" and its "humanitarian agencies" knew about it and even supported it. The government sold the war to the people in the South as a preventive measure, to prevent a Nilotic "northern" government from returning to power and unleashing revenge on the people of the South. It presented the war to the "international community" as its contribution to the global "war on terror." It was thus able to gather support from both Western governments and "humanitarian" agencies. The complicity of silence was broken in December 23, 2003, when the UN's Under Secretary-General for Humanitarian Affairs, Jan Egeland, described the camps in which the vast majority of the population of Acholi had been interned as "one of the worst humanitarian situations in the world . . . worse than Iraq." We will revisit the camp life later in the chapter.

If the bloodshed carried out by Amin soldiers in the barracks in 1971 could be called "massacres," the wholesale targeting of the Acholi people by Museveni's soldiers could more accurately be termed a creeping genocide unfolding over nearly two decades. Genocide, indeed, was the charge leveled against the Museveni government by Olara Otunnu, former special representative of the UN Secretary-General for Children in Armed Conflict (1997–2005) and, before that, foreign minister of Tito Okello's government (1985) in Uganda.[1] Unlike the Amin period, when violence was mainly confined to army barracks, and then to the "disappearance" of individuals in the society at large, state violence in the Museveni period began by targeting entire civilian sectors of the population in northern and northeastern Uganda. After Museveni was elected to a second term in 2001, the poison spread south to the capital.

In 1986, when the NRA took Kampala, its political base was limited to no more than a third of the country. Its first challenge was to broaden the base. To all those who had not been part of the previous regime, including in the North, the NRA offered a handshake of peace, welcoming more into the "broad base" the army was trying to build. All were welcome to a share of the spoils, including participation in the new government, and positions in the Cabinet, on one condition: that they give up those objectives that contradicted the program of the NRA and that they accept to work under the political leadership of the National Resistance Movement. The "broad base" government included the entire range of political formations in Uganda, from monarchists in Buganda to remnants from Amin's government, such as rebels in West Nile (UNRF II), led by Moses Ali, Amin's former Minister of Finance, as late as 1996.

But this strategy did not extend to any part of the Obote II regime. In 1996, when he welcomed the faction led by Moses Ali, Amin's finance minister, into the "broad base," President Museveni ruled against negotiations with movements in northern Uganda, from the Holy Spirit Movement of Alice Lakwena to the Lord's Resistance Army (LRA) of the warlord Joseph Kony. Though their leaders had not been part of the previous regime, both had a social base among the Acholi people from whom the bulk of Obote's army had been recruited. The president said negotiations with "bandits" were out of the question, justifying the excess violence unleashed by government forces—the National Resistance Army (NRA), later renamed Uganda Peoples' Defence Forces (UPDF), aiming to shed its rebel roots in name and adopt a "national" title—on the Acholi at first, and later the Langi and Iteso (people of Teso) populations of northern and northeastern Uganda. These three neighboring communities had been the main source of recruitment for both the colonial army and the army of all pre-Museveni governments. This war continued for nearly two decades, because the government's primary target was not the LRA but the population itself. That is why once it had interned the population, the regime lost all interest either in defeating the LRA militarily or in a political process that would accommodate them. Official interest was henceforth limited to justifying the war in the North as a necessary and legitimate part of the global "war on terror" deserving of vigorous Western support.[2]

The Lord's Resistance Army

At its height, the numbers of the LRA were estimated at roughly 3,000. The United Nations High Commission for Refugees (UNHCR) estimated rebel numbers at 1,000–1,100 (April 19, 2001); the US Department of State (2002) gave an estimate of 2,000; and according to the UN's Office in charge of Coordinating Humanitarian Agencies (UNOCHA), the LRA was composed of 2,000–3,000 fighters, accompanied by a further 2,000 wives and children.[3] How did the Uganda Peoples' Defence Forces (UPDF), numbering 20,000, fail to defeat LRA's 3,000 at its height? The media painted the picture of LRA as an army of abducted women and children, led by a self-appointed messiah devoid of human reason. The BBC reported that "more than 14,000 children are estimated to have been abducted . . . since 1986 . . . and taken to southern Sudan to fight or serve as sex slaves." According to the same report, "nearly 90% of LRA fighters are enslaved children—nearly 6,000 are still missing and it is not known whether they are dead or alive."[4] If the LRA was indeed an army of abducted children, how could it stand for nineteen years against a vastly better resourced and larger government army?

Reports from humanitarian and UN agencies on the ground, however, gave a very different picture. In 2001, UNICEF published its findings stating that roughly two-thirds of the 20,000 abductees were, in fact, adults and that some of the core leadership had received training in Israel, the United States, and Germany before joining the LRA. Furthermore, 77.7 percent of the 10,000 abducted children (as estimated by UNICEF) had been returned within a year and a further 15.9 percent the following year, calling into question media claims that 90 percent of the LRA's fighters were enslaved children. Scholar Chris Dolan estimated that the number of children in captivity was in the hundreds rather than the thousands. Similarly, according to UNICEF, the number of women and girls was much lower than projected by the media. From 1986 to 2001, that number was estimated at not more than 20.8 percent of those abducted in Kitgum district, and 16.7 percent in Gulu.[5] Even if we acknowledge that the LRA was mainly an army of adults, numbers on both sides were totally out of proportion: 3,000 rebels against 20,000 government troops, the latter vastly better armed.

What explains the never-ending nature of this war is a question for which the literature on the LRA, both academic and journalistic, offers several answers. The main culprit is said to be corruption, starting with the phenomenon of "ghost soldiers," soldiers who were on the pay roster but did not exist on the ground, either because they had died, or because they had never really entered the battlefield. Meanwhile, someone else would be collecting their salary. So the official number, 20,000, was inflated because it included those who were paid but were never present on the ground.

Among the first to report on the phenomenon of ghost soldiers was Sergeant Gitta Musoke, a child soldier abducted in 1983 at the age of fourteen. He had fought in the war against Kony in the North; Musoke was then deployed in Rwanda and finally retrained as an auditor. He started reporting ghost soldiers on the payroll and ended up in military jail; even when he was redeployed in Congo, Musoke continued to submit reports on ghost soldiers, right up to the president.[6]

President Museveni appointed a committee of three people to investigate the ghost soldier phenomenon in 2003: Amama Mbabazi, former prime minister; David Tinyefuuza, member of the high command of UPDF; and Salim Saleh, the president's brother and senior presidential advisor. Their report led to the prosecution of dozens of officers, but only Major General James Kazini, Museveni's nephew and former commander of the Land Forces, a colonel in the 4th Division, was found guilty in 2008 for the loss of $35.5 million as a result of the creation of ghost soldiers.[7] Noble Mayombo, the chief of Military Intelligence, admitted that over half of the 4th Division operating in the North were ghost soldiers. Charged with leading Operation Iron Fist—claimed to be the army's biggest and final assault in a bid to wipe out the LRA—in March 2002, this same unit turned out to be a ghost division, the reason why the army had to deploy an additional 4,000 troops to support the operation. Following donor pressure, Kazini was suspended in 2003 as army commander and sent to Nigeria for training at a war college. The 2008 general court-martial charged Kazini with allegedly maintaining 24,000 ghost soldiers on the payroll, costing the army $37.4 million.[8] Andrew Mwenda, another well-known journalist, suggested that Kazini was singled out because he had claimed that the ghost soldier scheme was sanctioned by the president to pay off Congolese soldiers.[9] He was jailed for three years in March 2009, but released on bail.[10] Kazini was believed to have built up a semiautonomous army unit, the 409 Brigade in West Nile, and some thought he was plotting a coup.[11] In 2009, Kazini was killed, reportedly in a lovers' quarrel.

Another person charged with the creation and maintenance of ghost soldiers and misappropriation of funds for personal gain was Henry Tumukunde, who had headed the Internal Security Organisation (ISO) and who Aili Tripp, political scientist at the University of Wisconsin, claims masterminded Museveni's 2001 electoral victory, but who also opposed removing term limits and open voting in parliament on constitutional issues.[12] He was forced to leave politics.

Complementary to the ghost soldiers phenomenon was that of officers selling arms to the LRA. Lieutenant-Colonel Noble Mayombo, who headed a commission of inquiry into the matter, revealed that "the 4th Division Commanders had sold arms to the LRA."[13] For soldiers, war also presented other opportunities for self-enrichment, especially land grabbing, which became so common that even the president felt compelled to take note of it in a public speech.[14] Finally, there was rape and disease, especially HIV/AIDS.

But wholesale corruption, including the ghost soldier phenomenon, was characteristic of Uganda's other wars in Somalia, South Sudan, eastern Congo, and the Central African Republic. They do not explain the distinctive outcome in northern Uganda, an ongoing stalemate. To throw light on the outcome, it is crucial to look at the war in the North as a long learning curve. From the official point of view, the war developed over three phases, each under a different leadership.

Phase 1: Relying on "Undisciplined" Allies. The first phase, 1986–1988, was led by the Federal Democratic Movement (FEDEMU) and the Uganda Federal Movement (UFM), part of the NRA's undisciplined "broad base." FEDEMU and UFM were both limited to Buganda in their recruitment, organization, and leadership, and were committed to a military approach. In contrast to the NRA's focus on organizing peasants in Resistance Committees during the Luwero period, they had lacked a political strategy on how to organize peasants.

The government blamed its allies, FEDEMU and UFM, lacking in discipline and fired by the impulse for revenge against a longtime enemy, for the brutality of the counterinsurgency in the North. Like the NRA, FEDEMU and UFM had fought battles in the pre-1986 period against government soldiers recruited from the northern region, particularly from among the Acholi. They spearheaded the brutal government-directed counterinsurgency that began in 1986 and evolved into Operation North, the first big operation that people talk about as massively destructive of civilians and responsible for creating the conditions that gave rise to the Holy Spirit Movement of Alice Lakwena and, after it, the Lord's Resistance Army (LRA) of Joseph Kony.

Like the Holy Spirit Movement, the LRA began as a spirit-led cleansing movement, one opposed to all soldiers, whether of the new government (NRA) or of the Okellos it had displaced. The population's response to renewed war was to distance itself from both sides. The LRA interpreted reduced popular support as evidence that the Acholi had come to support the government. In response, rebels turned their guns against suspected government supporters and collaborators, determined to punish them and set an example for others. From then on, LRA became a byword for killing, maiming, and torture—cutting lips and defacing captives—followed by forced recruitment, including of children. The NRA also trained its guns on suspected rebel supporters in the civilian population.

Government violence did not subside once its "undisciplined" allies left the battlefields of the North; instead it began as early as 1989 and reached a peak in its war of revenge during Operation North in 1991, when the NRA carried out its first campaign of mass displacement alongside a series of massacres and other atrocities. One distinctive atrocity in this war was the practice of male rape, a violent message of revenge. Many respondents, interviewed by Dolan, "recalled 1989 as the year in which . . . the army's second division used to do this male rape, known as *Tek Gungu* [bend over], on any men who were arrested in the rural villages, over a period of six or seven months. To be victim of *Tek Gungu* was regarded as worse than being killed. Many subsequently committed suicide. There was a period when these events even entered into the songs people sang."[15] When knowledge of these atrocities entered the public domain and became part of official record, the government claimed to have acted swiftly, removing the battalion made up of former FEDEMU and UFM soldiers from the war. But Operation North had not been carried out by a non-NRA battalion; it had been an NRA operation under the command of the then–Minister of State for Defense, Major-General David Tinyefuza, its object being "to aggressively hunt down alleged rebel supporters and cut off support to the LRA."

Justice and Reconciliation, a group dedicated to exposing the nature of counterinsurgency published an illuminating account of the 22nd Battalion over four days, from April 14 to 18, 1991, in the village of Burcoro. Many were killed, but those who survived, both women and men, were subjected to repeated rape. They began with women:

> The women had been separated from the men earlier during the day and just before the sunset they were supposed to gather around two

> bonfires. It would not be too long before they would be selected by the soldiers, taken to their tents, and raped. One group of women was set aside for the higher ranking soldiers and forced into a classroom where they would be raped until the end of the operation. . . . The soldiers set up small tents within the school and it was within these tents and classrooms that the women were gang-raped.

Survivors told researchers, "All the while they said that what we were going to witness right now is what had happened in Luwero."[16]

But it wasn't just women that the NRA targeted; men were not spared either: "While some of the men were forced to dig, others sang funeral songs. When the pit had reached about one meter in depth, they were ordered to stop and to begin gathering logs and grass to cover it." The pit was covered and sealed, and a small hole left for the 35 rebel suspects to enter. "They spent an agonizing night in the pit. . . . Beaten repeatedly and bled . . . when no one recanted, the soldiers ordered them back into pit, gathered dry grass, and tied red pepper to it, then set it alight at the edge of the small opening, blowing the air into the pit. The next day, the last one, they allowed the survivors to come out of the pit, took several into the bush where they were asked to 'bend again,' and sodomized [them]." "*Mzee, gung agunga.*" ("Old man, bend over for me.")

Operation North's stated motto was vengeance. According to a male survivor, "Once in the school the soldiers began to ask us whether we knew what happened in the Luwero Triangle. We said we didn't. They then said they would do to us what the rebels had done in Luwero."[17]

In 1992, the government launched a two-pronged program to support its war aims: incite local people to form militias; and invite donors to contribute resources for development programs for the northern regions. The 4th Division Commander hosted 890 elders to a meal at the Viva Rest House in Gulu. The elders passed a resolution that the population should contribute to its own protection. Tribal militias were formed in Lango (Amuka), Kitgum districts (Frontier Guards), and Teso (Arrow Boys), with the government providing both arms and minimal training. But there was "no separate militia group in Acholi because the LRA itself was perceived as an Acholi militia fighting an Acholi war against the state and extending to neighbouring 'tribes.'"[18] At least 25,000 men were brought under arms in the space of a little over six months. The government followed with an invitation to donors to contribute to the first Northern Uganda Reconstruction Program (NURP I), launched in 1992, targeting fourteen districts in total.[19] Seventeen years later, the *Daily Mail* of London reported that President Museveni had in 2009 spent $50 million of a UK government grant intended for the reconstruction of war-torn northern Uganda to purchase a new private jet, described by its manufacturers as "the world's most versatile and stylish."[20]

Phase 2: Night Commuters: The People Take Their Own Initiative. With the formation of local militias, the cycle of atrocities swung back from the government to the rebels, who meted out punishment to the population in quick succession: the Attiak massacre of April 22, 1995; the ambush of the Karuma and Pakwach convoy of March 8, 1996; the Acholpi refugee camp massacre of July 1996; St. Mary's College (the "Aboke Girls") abductions in October 1996; and the Lokung and Palabek massacre of some 412 people in January 1997.[21] To villagers, this ongoing cycle of atrocities was confirmation that the government was either unable or unwilling to provide effective protection to the local population. As insecurity increased, and more people lost faith in the possibility of official protection, they began to walk to the safety of urban areas.

Thousands began leaving their homes and villages for shelter in churches or schools, or anywhere in and around Gulu Town they thought might serve as a shield from the violence. Lacor Hospital and the surrounding schools overflowed with people sleeping wherever there was space. People left their villages as evening darkness descended, returning to their homes at the break of dawn to attend to their farms and cattle. This was 1997, and these were the "night commuters" who attracted global attention from the media and NGOs.[22] Night commuting was a civilian response to a combination of factors, including government indifference to rebel atrocities.

Phase 3: "Protected Villages" or Internment Camps: The Official Solution. The UPDF responded in September 1996 with a policy of long-term displacement and eventually, internment, of more and more of the population: "The UPDF drove hundreds of thousands of Acholi peasants out of their villages and into camps through a campaign of murder, intimidation, and the bombing and burning of entire villages. After the formation of the camps, the UPDF announced that anyone found outside of the camps would be considered a rebel and killed." The government named the camps "protected villages," but in reality they were places where people were forcibly concentrated and interned. They also became sites of official violence necessary to keep civilians from leaving. A few hundred thousand by the end of 1996, the population of the internment camps ballooned into around a million by the mid-2000s, encompassing nearly the entire rural population of the Acholi subregion.[23]

Young adults recall the time from the mid-1990s when over 80 percent of the total population of three Acholi districts was forcibly interned in camps. The government claimed that it would be easier to "protect" villagers from the LRA once they were concentrated in settlements. Local authorities claimed that people had spontaneously gathered together for their own protection, though it turned out that "displaced people interviewed in Gulu, however, report that UPDF soldiers told them that they would be regarded as rebels if they stayed in their home villages. Leading politicians and soldiers are on record as saying that protected villages will be an important part of their strategy to isolate rebels and deny them food, freedom of movement and the ability to re-group." The internment camps were less a result of design, as in a blueprint, but more of an afterthought, a product of learning from experience concentrated over two months, September–October 1996. Little official thought seems to have gone into what it would mean to intern several hundred thousand people without "providing them food, water, medicine, shelter, or protection." Left without any way of acquiring food or supplies, people were told to build their own shelters within demarcated areas. An article in *The Monitor* revealed that Gulu district was "losing more lives through secondary effects of the war than [from] the war itself," most of those effects proceeding directly from displacement.[24] Force could drive people away from their homes, to internment camps, but, without the provision of basic necessities, force alone would not be enough to keep them confined to internment camps. Once this became clear, the government began to look to the outside world for "food aid." The World Food Programme (WFP) reported in November 1996 that the Ugandan government had asked that it help feed up to 200,000 displaced people.[25]

Internment Camps. Rather than provide people with security where they lived, the government forced people to move to concentrated locations with the promise that they would be protected by the army. These were the "protected villages." Those who resisted were met with force. In Awere, for example, the people were given four days' notice to move to the camp, but in reality the UPDF did not wait for four days; they waited only hours after distributing the notice before shelling areas they wanted cleared.[26]

By 2005, the camp population grew from a few hundred thousand to more than 1.8 million in the entire region—which included Teso and Lango—with over a million from the three Acholi districts. They comprised practically the entire rural population of the three Acholi districts. All were expected to live on handouts from relief agencies.[27] Meanwhile, the government kept changing its target, which expanded from the LRA, to the Acholi population, and then also to the people in Lango and Teso. All faced a total assault on their persons and possessions. Herded into camps, they were reduced to a subhuman level of existence.

Camp Life: Hell on Earth. The government plan to move the population forcibly from villages to camps unfolded in a calculated fashion starting in October 1996. That was the same month as the LRA's notorious abduction of 139 female secondary students from St. Mary's College Secondary School in Aboke, part of Apac District, on October 10, 1996. The deputy head mistress of the college, Sister Rachele Fassera of Italy, pursued the rebels and successfully negotiated the release of 109 of the girls. The Aboke abductions and Fassera's dramatic actions drew unprecedented international attention to the insurgency in northern Uganda. It was part of the backdrop that informed the transition to camps. "Protected villages" were located in centers of administrative and commercial activity, hitherto known as "trading centers" to which the military would send a small unit for "protection." Previously living in scattered villages, people were now concentrated in larger numbers, from a few thousand to tens of thousands. Some moved into the camps voluntarily; others were forced by the army.[28] Thus, the government began its own version of the LRA's "abduction."

In the camps, there were virtually no sanitation facilities—for example, the village at Pabbo had one pit latrine for every 168 people in June 1998. UPDF soldiers in Gulu were said to earn money hiring guns out to thugs who in turn used these to rob civilians. Researchers wrote that those in "protected villages" often claimed "they were raided by government soldiers in rebel disguise." The press in Kampala ran articles, at first occasionally and then frequently, giving substance to these reports. *The Monitor,* for example, ran an article on February 28, 1998, about an ambush that took place only three hundred meters from the location of a major UPDF military unit when the lead "UPDF, not LRA rebels ambushed [a] Gulu bus."[29]

Once the government enlisted humanitarian organizations to provide amenities in the camp, it was able to use the provision of services as a way to control the interned population. Thus, the government politicized the distribution of services, starting with deciding which camps would receive relief aid, and, later, disciplining dissidents and even convincing the camp residents to support certain candidates at election time. The political scientist Adam Branch writes,

> Once the camps were formed, the government stepped up political repression against the newly concentrated population and employed the Homeguard, the UPDF, and other paramilitary forces to that end. Those in the camps who protest[ed] their continued internment, government abuse, or the lack of security face[d] violent repression by state security services. Paralegals and human rights activists [were] particular targets; as one paralegal living in a camp told me, 'when you want to speak freely, the government accuses you of being a rebel.' Local elections that [were] held in the camps [could] also give rise to state violence; in one case, a prominent local government official in conjunction with a UPDF commander organised a paramilitary group among camp inhabitants to ensure that a key election would go their way, threatening the opposition candidate and others known to be critical of the government.[30]

The government was finally able to marshal support from two different sources—Western governments waging a "war on terror" and Western humanitarian agencies wanting to keep their hands clean.

The Humanitarians

It took a full range of humanitarians to keep the camps going. The World Food Programme (WFP) was the lead agency. According to Adam Branch, World Vision International, Oxfam / Accord, the Church of Uganda and the Catholic diocese, Médecins Sans Frontières–Holland, International Committee of the Red Cross (ICRC), Administration of Children and Families (ACF), and UNICEF also assisted. The International Development Committee of the

British Parliament estimated in 2007 that it cost the donors US $200 million per year to run the camps.

Over time, the humanitarians took over more or less the entire function of the camps, from providing relief aid to overseeing a rudimentary civil administration. Prepared to take full charge of camp administration, the relief agencies launched a "camp management" strategy in the mid-2000s, parceling Acholiland between themselves, subcounty by subcounty, all in the name of rendering the camps more sustainable—that is, permanent.[31] The same agencies then chose to bypass the local council system in favor of the new position of "camp commander," the end being to ensure efficiency. Responsible for the distribution of aid to the camps, this administrator set up a bureaucratic machinery for the top-down control of the camp population.[32]

But, despite the aid the humanitarian organizations provided, it took them at least a decade to wake up to the fact that relief work was also political. Amnesty International took ten years to gather the courage to recant earlier reports, which read like apologies for official violence. Writing of the period between October and December 1988, Amnesty International reported that in "one of the most intense phases of the war . . . the NRA forcibly cleared approximately 100,000 people from their homes in and around Gulu town. Soldiers committed hundreds of extra-judicial executions as they forced people out of their homes, burning down homesteads and granaries."[33] The WFP's 1999 report reflected on its moral and political responsibility in the making of the program of "protected villages." In spite of its name, "the programme as a whole was not designed around protection concerns." Even the general assumption that "camps were safer than outlying villages" was not necessarily proven. The report admitted that civilians received no benefit from staying in the camps and lamented "the lack of reasonable steps taken by the authorities first, to minimize displacement and, second, to create conditions in which it can be brought to an end as quickly as possible." The report admitted that "some local authorities were keen to pass by-laws demanding the early return of IDPs [internally displaced persons]." Finally, the report lamented, though late: "WFP may have too readily fallen in line with government policy, in effect becoming both provider and legitimizer of a villagization policy."[34]

Clearly, internment in camps would have been unsustainable without the collaboration of the WFP. Starting with a supply of "emergency food relief" to twenty camps in Gulu in January 1997, the WFP program expanded in steps, from feeding 110,000 people, to 257,000 later that year, to 325,000 by May 1999 and 522,000 by mid-2002, if we add in 81,000 people in five villages in Kitgum.[35] By 2004, the WFP was providing relief distributions to more than 1.5 million internally displaced people. As we have already mentioned, this figure included 80–90 percent of the population in the Acholi subregion, and in addition hundreds of thousands in the Teso and Lango subregions.[36]

The anthropologist Sverker Finnström noted that, in the eyes of many Acholi, there was little to distinguish aid agencies from government violence: "When a truck of the World Food Programme (UN) drove through Gulu town loaded with armed and uniformed government troops . . . people related it to the wider international context, where the United Nations and the international community are said to be allied with the Ugandan government but also with . . . the United States and the rebels of Southern Sudan."[37]

Every time there was an encounter between the army and the LRA, as during Operation Iron Fist, when the army followed the LRA into Sudan, the number of people leaving the countryside increased dramatically. The figures kept rising as old camps were expanded and new ones were built in other locations. But one thing was clear by now: without the LRA, there would not have been justification for keeping the camps going. The central reason for continuing the war was to keep the LRA a live danger. The independence of South Sudan in 2013 seemed to take the border of the War on Terror from the Uganda–South Sudan boundary to the boundary between Sudan and South Sudan. For the Ugandan government, it was a matter of urgency to remain an active partner in the War on Terror in the region.

It is against this backdrop that Uganda's political society began formulating a counterstrategy to promote peace or "reconciliation." The opposition found resonance in parliament, among several high-level government officials who came from the northern districts, and even in the army. A high point of the "peace" or "reconciliation" strategy came with the appointment in late 1993 of Betty Bigombe, an Acholi, as Minister for Pacification of the North. Early in 1994, Bigombe warned, "There are many who do not want peace to prevail. There are those people who are benefiting from the war. There are others who think that if this thing ends, they will have nothing to lean on."[38]

Bigombe's initiative was opposed by both President Museveni and his brother. As talks made progress, the LRA asked for six months to lay down their arms. Museveni responded with an ultimatum—that the LRA must come out of the bush within seven days or be killed. Soon talks collapsed, and there was a surge in violence. The key person facilitating the Bigombe peace talks in 1993–1994, Yusuf Adek, was arrested and charged with treason in 2001; he was detained for over a year. When approached in later years by a range of parties to act as a mediator, not surprisingly, he was uninterested. As Dolan put it, the president had subverted "peace talks" into "war talks."[39] And so the war continued, as did opposition to the war.

In 1996, General David Sejusa (who had changed his name from Tinyefuza) testified to parliament that "the LRA was being needlessly prolonged, that the military budget had become a source of corrupt gains for the government and army insiders, and that soldiers and civilians were suffering horribly as a result."[40] Soon after, Sejusa submitted his resignation, which the president declined to accept. Sejusa went to the courts and won the right to resign. The government appealed, and the Supreme Court reversed the decision—many say on orders from the president. Even though General Sejusa went on to occupy several high offices, he was kept on a short leash, always subject to military discipline wielded by the president as his commanding officer.

But the demand for peace could not be suppressed. In 1996, the opposition's presidential candidate Paul Ssemogerere told voters that he would talk to Kony and urge him to abandon the rebellion; Ssemogerere was then branded a rebel himself. Even those authorized to make contact with the LRA were at times arrested by the UPDF, as happened to three priests who tried to deliver a letter from the Kitgum Resident District Commissioner to LRA Commander Toopaco on August 28, 2002.[41] Whenever religious leaders made attempts to meet with LRA members, they discovered their initiatives to be undercut by the army.

The government found it difficult to rein in its own members from northern Uganda, by now sufficiently outraged to speak publicly of the reality of the camps. The then–Minister for Northern Uganda Reconstruction, the Honorable Owiny-Dollo, commented in a public gathering in Gulu on June 26, 1998: "This insecurity is a greater threat than the abductions. It is present every day but nobody sees it."[42] The member of Parliament for Gulu municipality, speaking of the camps at a rally in Gulu market in January 1999, compared camp life to "living in hell which is full of rape, torture, and other forms of mistreatment." He also observed that "staying in the camp is causing poverty since people have no space for cultivation . . . there is even no protection from the government as instead civilians are used as human shields by the army."[43]

When the local councillor for Awac in Gulu paid a visit to a school for the displaced in July 1999, the parent-teacher association identified two major problems: "soldiers taking pupils . . . [as] house wives and not being followed up by Law," and "parents sending school girls to sell local [alcoholic] brew in the market thus exposing them to the soldiers." Both led to abduction. A youth participant in a conference titled "Youth at the Cross-Roads: Which Way Forward," summed up their common dilemma: "We live by chance, die by design." Among those interned in the camps, despair was widespread. Many turned to suicide—swallowing pesticides or insecticides, either straight from the bottle or from a pack, or by washing seeds which had been sprayed with pesticide and then drinking the water. Also common was hanging, overdoses of medications, and at times even swallowing wristwatch batteries.[44]

Religious leaders joined the growing demand for peace in 1999. The Archbishop of Kampala, Cardinal Emmanuel Wamala, called on Kony "to stop fighting and accept dialogue with the Government." Acholi religious leaders were both more honest and more courageous. They appealed to the government to declare Acholiland a disaster area and immediately enter into direct negotiations with Kony rebels. They also demanded that Parliament revoke its recommendation for a military solution to the twelve-year war "which has devastated northern Uganda."[45]

UNOCHA Critique. In a 2002 publication, the United Nations Office for the Coordination of Humanitarian Action (UNOCHA) acknowledged that the so-called protected villages violated just about all the UN's "Guiding Principles on Internal Displacement": camps were established without due consultation with the people affected (Guiding principle 7.3); lasted longer than required (6); failed to recognize peoples' dependency on their land (9), or to ensure basic standards of living in terms of shelter, water, food, sanitation, clothing, and medical care (18, 19); and infringed on the right "to move freely in and out of camps or other settlements" (14). The camps had not been protected against "rape, mutilation, torture, inhuman or degrading treatment or punishment and other outrages upon personal dignity, such as acts of gender-specific violence, forced prostitution or any form of indecent assault" (11). Camp properties were largely destroyed or looted (21), and camp residents, too, remained liable to attack by the UPDF under suspicion of being associated with the LRA (10.2).[46]

The government claimed this was a rescue mission, but the result was the opposite. Peasants would have had less need of food aid and other provisions if they had had access to their own land and cattle. Without adequate security, the number of people in the camps made them both an easy and a lucrative target, whether for the LRA or for government soldiers. Thus, collective punishment took on a new and grotesque form: "protected villages."

The scale and depth of the problem became clear when the government's own Ministry of Health, along with WFP, found "global malnutrition rates of 32 and 18 per cent among children under 5 in Anaka and Pabo respectively."[47] According to the ministry's report, the excess mortality rate in these camps was approximately one thousand persons per week—inviting comparisons to the numbers killed by the LRA even in the worst year. In other words, more were dying in the camps than were being killed by the LRA. The camps were also tragically unprotected, and accusations that government soldiers failed to protect the camps, refused to respond to LRA incursions, and thus turned civilians into easy targets for the LRA were regularly heard from camp inhabitants.

The army and the LRA seemed to have reached terms of cohabitation—at the expense of "interned" civilians. No longer defined by pitched battles between the adversaries, LRA and UPDF, the hallmark of the "war" was now the burning and bombardment of civilian villages and the internment of people in barricaded camps. The process unfolded with escalating momentum. Still, there was no global outrage. Indeed, impunity had become a defining characteristic of the Museveni government.

President Museveni remained resolutely determined that the problem demanded a "military solution." His brother, Salim Saleh, echoed that same view: "The conflict will be solved by military means, not dialogue." Backing them was the 1997 Report of the Committee on Defence and Internal Affairs on the War in Northern Uganda. The call for a military solution was by now an official chorus.[48]

Determined to find a political solution to enduring mass misery, Parliament introduced a bill in December 1999 offering amnesty to the entire leadership of the LRA, provided they laid down their arms. On January 17, 2000, Parliament passed the Amnesty Act. The president refused to sign it. Two and a half years later, the Gulu diocese Justice and Peace Commission investigated the effectiveness of the amnesty. They found that less than four hundred LRA members had taken up amnesty by April 2002. Even worse, over half of returnees were being pressured to join the UPDF. On February 25, 2004, members of Parliament passed a resolution calling for the North to be declared a disaster zone.[49]

Just when civic and religious leaders in the North had come together behind the call for a blanket amnesty, Museveni was able to muster support from the West for a military solution. The European Union drew up a resolution in July 2000 calling on individual EU member states to ban LRA operations and traveling of LRA representatives within the EU and between EU member states and non-EU Nations. The LRA was placed on the US State Department's Terrorist Exclusion List in December 2001. Soon after, the United States began providing Uganda with military assistance to wage its own war on terror.[50] There was talk of using the Terrorism Act of January 2002 against LRA members in the United Kingdom. In the eyes of the international community, there could be only one perpetrator in this conflict: the LRA.

Uganda passed its own Anti-Terrorism Act in March 2002, which took precedence over the Amnesty Act. So, while the Amnesty Act granted amnesty for engagement in "war or armed rebellion," the Anti-Terrorism Act criminalized peace initiatives, rendering punishable acts carried out for purposes of "influencing the government or influencing the public . . . and for a political or religious . . . or economic aim."[51] In March 2002, the government announced Operation Iron Fist. The Ugandan army would cross the border and invade LRA sanctuaries in Southern Sudan. Abductions increased dramatically, as did night commuting.

The tide turned again in December 2003, when Jan Egeland, the UN's Under-Secretary-General for Humanitarian Affairs, visited the camps. He was left numb, noting that the war waged by the Lord's Resistance Army (LRA) and the Ugandan government had led to the displacement of 1.3 million people. Egeland said to the BBC after visiting the area affected by eighteen years of civil war: "The humanitarian situation in northern Uganda is worse than in Iraq, or anywhere else in the world." "This is not a war where the civilian population is affected through collateral damage, it is a war targeting the civilian population, and especially children," said Egeland. "Nowhere in the world do we have large areas where between 80 and 90 percent of the population [is] terrorised into camps by violence."[52] Even then, despite being over a decade in the making, the situation in northern Uganda attracted little global attention.

International Criminal Court, 2004. With the failure of Operation Iron Fist, the government changed tack. Determined to rule out an amnesty, President

Museveni invited the International Criminal Court (ICC), newly formed in 2002, to charge the LRA leadership with crimes against humanity. Luis Moreno-Ocampo did just that. Joseph Kony became the subject of the ICC's first indictment in 2004. Most civil society organizations in northern Uganda saw the turn to ICC as a measure designed to undercut the provisions of the Amnesty Act of 2000.

As the internment of the civilian population continued into its second decade, there was another attempt at a political solution, now involving the newly independent state of South Sudan (GOSS). This time, the government of Uganda agreed to enter into direct negotiations with the LRA, facilitated and mediated by GOSS. These began in 2006, dragging on for years, but hopes soared as the terms of the agreement, and then its finer details, were agreed on between the two sides. The only thing standing between war and peace was an amnesty for the top leadership of the LRA, specifically Joseph Kony and Vincent Otti. In the words of Otti, the second in command, "To come out, the ICC must revoke the indictment. . . . If Kony or Otti does not come out, no other rebel will come out."

The ICC not only refused, but it now called for a military campaign to target Kony. The call was joined by the Ugandan government, which refused to provide guarantees for his safety. Predictably, the talks broke down and the LRA withdrew, first to the Democratic Republic of Congo and then to the Central African Republic. The government responded with further militarization, seeking to highlight Uganda's centrality in the regional war on terror—starting with the disastrous Operation Lightning Thunder in the Democratic Republic of the Congo in December 2008, which brought combined forces from a number of countries in the region—South Sudan, Congo, and Uganda—with US support to target LRA forces. When that failed, thousands of Ugandan troops poured into the Central African Republic, at the same time calling for support from American advisors. Soon after, the Social Science Research Council of New York charged Ugandan government soldiers in the Central African Republic with atrocities against civilians.[53] The ICC called on Africom, the Africa Command of the US Army, to act as its implementing arm by sending more troops to capture Kony. The United States, under President Barack Obama, responded by sending an unspecified number of advisers armed with drones—

though the United States insisted that these drones were not armed, at least not yet.

No Difference between Government and the Rebels

For those interned in the camps, there was less and less to choose from between the two sides in the war—the government and the LRA. Abduction was no longer a rebel preserve. The NRA had had a tradition of inducting child soldiers—known as *kadogo*—long before the LRA came into being. The Ugandan government went on to support insurgents deploying child soldiers for over a decade. If the LRA abducted villagers numbering in thousands, the government had interned over a million in camps. The internment camps turned into a free-for-all for the adversaries in the war. Both the rebels and the army were implicated in rape and assault, on persons and possessions of those interned. According to the summary of a global report for 2004,

> The government was reported to recruit children into the regular armed forces and into local defence units deployed inside Uganda and also in the Democratic Republic of the Congo (DRC) and Sudan. Until May 2003 government forces supported armed political groups in eastern DRC which extensively recruited child soldiers. . . . Out of an estimated 20,000 children who have been abducted by the LRA, nearly 10,000 were taken since mid-2002. Children coming out of LRA captivity were sometimes recruited into government armed forces or forced to take part in operations against the LRA. [54]

The problem of the LRA did not call for a military operation. And yet, the LRA was given as the reason why there must be a constant military mobilization, at first in northern Uganda, and then in the entire region; why the military budget must have priority; and, finally, why the United States must send soldiers and weaponry, including drones, to the region. Rather than the reason for accelerated military mobilization in the region, the LRA had turned into the excuse for it.

The LRA had been a useful rebel force. Once it was no more, and once the camps had closed and the population had returned to the villages, the government was on the lookout for another useful rebel movement on which to pin the "terrorist" label and thus turn it into a mobilizing tool for global support in Uganda's own "war on terror." In 2021, the year the war in the North ended, a new war on terror was born. This new war was against the Allied Democratic Forces (ADF), which had been active in the Ruwenzori subregion between the mid-1990s and the early 2000s. By the mid-2000s, however, the ADF had been practically defeated.[55] Yet, the government stepped up the war against the ADF. As the ADF went on to develop links with Islamist organizations in the region, it became a more attractive target for UPDF. Could it be that the ADF provided an added advantage? After all, unlike the LRA, which was Christian fundamentalist in outlook, the ADF could easily be labeled "Islamist terrorists."

In the decades that followed 1986, the year the NRA took reins of government in Kampala, its reputation seemed to peel like so many layers of an onion. It started with the claim to have fought a successful guerilla war, and then to boast that it had built a unified nation where all previous regimes had failed. We turn next to the NRM's record on the economic front.

14

FROM NATIONALISM TO NEOLIBERALISM

In independent Uganda, political poison came in three doses. The first was state-directed mass murder: unleashed in the Amin barracks under the guidance of Britain and Israel in 1971, and genocidal acts of violence undertaken in northern Uganda by the Museveni army as part of the US-supported War on Terror in the 1990s. The second was the reversal of Amin's nation-building project and the fragmentation of the polity into multiple tribalized districts. And the third was in the form of privatization, also state-directed.

Privatization ushered in an era of organized state-driven corruption in Uganda: the privatization of Asian-owned assets under Amin and the privatization of state-held assets under Museveni became fixtures of their respective regimes. It became integral to the history of neoliberalism in Uganda. The use of political power for private gain marked the third dose of poison in Ugandan society.

When the NRA took charge of the country in 1986, its leader, Yoweri Museveni, was considered a moralist and a puritan. The Uganda Patriotic Movement he led in the elections of 1980 promised "clean leadership" above all. Much later, in 2022, the same Museveni told the public at a rally in Kampala—whose audience included the inspector general of government (the public ombudsperson)—that it was fine for public officials to steal public money so long as they did not take it out of the country. Museveni went on to repeat this claim in several speeches; different versions can be found on social media.[1] By 2022, Uganda was generally considered "one of the most corrupt countries in the world" by its international allies and by donors, NGOs, and international oversight agencies. Transparency International, for example, ranked Uganda 151 out of 176 countries—in other words, the twenty-fifth most corrupt country in the world.[2]

Many wondered whether the downward slide from 1980 to 2022, from a self-conscious moralism to an amoralism that judges actions only by its results, could have been foreseen. Was Museveni a born opportunist who had managed to hide his true intentions from the people? Or was he a product of his times, making choices under constraint rather than as a free agent, with a yawning gulf between his claims and his practices, as he sought to keep his hold on power?

Some thought Museveni an opportunist. I came to think of him as a weatherman, adept at reading the direction of the wind, and taking advantage of it. Museveni's early puritanism was not a posture, but it was shredded, bit by bit, under the pressure of changing circumstances. To rule, from Museveni's point of view, meant to make compromises and to build alliances. However, instead of keeping in mind that a compromise was just that—something to be corrected, even reversed at the first opportunity—Museveni became increasingly prone to explaining necessity as virtue. His critics kept contrasting the latter amoral Museveni with his former moral self, as evidence of betrayal. Museveni seemed caught in a whirlpool—the structural adjustment program imposed by the Washington Consensus—which he both found impossible to break free from and ended up embracing wholeheartedly. As time passed, the head of state seemed to speak less from conviction and more from a practiced rhetoric.

When the ragtag band of rebels known as the National Resistance Army (NRA) marched into Kampala in 1986, they were said to number roughly 20,000. The leadership included those who had come from the ranks of university students ("academics") and those who had over the years grown through rebel ranks ("fighters"). A few weeks before they entered Kampala, when they had already taken control of the western towns of Fort Portal and Mbarara, Eriya Kategaya, then widely considered Museveni's second in command, wrote to invite me to join them in Mbarara. He said they wanted to establish a university and wanted me to be its vice chancellor. I wrote back saying it would be best to wait until we meet in Kampala. We did meet in Kampala a few weeks later. Kategaya said he had been reading *Mawazo,* a journal at Makerere University that I was then coediting, and wanted to meet students whose work was being published in the journal. I thought about it. Could I really ask my comrades at the university and in town to join a state-building project about which we had little idea and which we would have even less chance to shape after victory? Would we come out any different from Dani Wadada Nabudere, Edward Rugumayo, and Wanume Kibedi, who had joined Amin in 1971? Kategaya sensed my hesitation and decided it was best not to push. I stayed at the university.

During those years, one complaint ran through most of Museveni's speeches: "I have no cadres." As the rebels entered Kampala, the leadership knew they were short on human and financial resources. Their first effort was to reach out to those like-minded and build alliances: they called it "the broad base." The next step was to look for a helping hand outside the country. They began with socialist countries, those they considered "natural allies": Cuba, China, and North Korea, among others. This was no more than a stop gap measure. Then came barter transactions with friendly countries. Next, an outreach to countries they considered neutral, from the Canadians to members of the Organisation of Islamic Cooperation.[3] All responded as if in a chorus: first settle with the International Monetary Fund (IMF) and the World Bank, the leading Bretton Woods institutions, and then come and talk to us.

To work with the Bretton Woods institutions was not possible without implementing their standard structural adjustment program. That agreement was reached in 1987. At the heart of the structural adjustment program was the dismantling of public enterprises. This massive privatization program began with the largest parastatal in the country. It was the first decisive step in the implementation of a neoliberal project over the next several decades.

State-Led Privatization Kick-Starts Neoliberal Reform

Uganda Commercial Bank (UCB), established in 1965 after independence and soon the largest public sector financial institution in the country, was dedicated to providing banking services to the working poor in urban and rural areas. Its sale was prepared by the World Bank—as would be the sale of other large parastatals—through a recapitalization loan of $72 million. The privatization of UCB unfolded in two phases: the first was riddled with widespread individual corruption, and failed; the second phase, pushed by Museveni with close oversight from the World Bank, took place in 2001 with the sale of UCB to Stanbic, a private South African bank.[4]

The process brought to light all the contradictions of the privatization program. On the one hand, privatization was supposed to be an effective antidote to corruption that was said to have paralyzed the entire public sector. On the other hand, privatization mired the country's elite, both those in and out of government, deeply in corruption. It paved their way, so to speak, with gold. The sale itself divided the elite. Parliament passed a resolution "calling for UCB not to be sold into foreign hands." From there followed a national debate on privatization, leading to what many considered a national betrayal. The government decided to go ahead with the sale anyway and celebrated it as a grand national achievement; however, the BBC's *World Business Report* noted that "the Ugandan parliament now wants to approach the constitutional court to try to undo the agreed sale." Decades later, the president admitted he had been wrong but blamed his advisors.

In 1993–1994, the World Bank and the IMF jointly advanced a loan of $100 million to Uganda, to initiate privatization in the financial sector, with special regard given to the privatization of the Uganda Commercial Bank.[5] It took two separate attempts, stretching over almost a decade, to liquidate UCB and sell its assets to a private foreign bank. The first attempt at privatizing UCB, in 1998, involved the sale of a 51 percent stake in the company to a Malaysian Group, Westmont Berhad.[6]

The consortium that sought to purchase UCB through the Malaysian company included many of the high and mighty in government: the president's own brother, Major General Salim Saleh; the president's son, Lieutenant Muhoozi Kainerugaba; and a host of high-level government officials, as well as the head of the Privatisation Unit. At the heart of the scandal was Suleiman Kiggundu, former governor of the Bank of Uganda (1986–1990), then head of the Bank of Greenland. Kiggundu claimed he had been made "the scapegoat in a scam (involving) President Museveni." The scam involved a dubious sale of 49 percent of UCB shares to the Malaysian company Westmont, which then illicitly sold the same to the Bank of Greenland. Kiggundu said the purchase was overseen by Saleh and Muhoozi Kainerugaba, the president's son, with Museveni's approval. Attorney General Bart Katureebe supported Kiggundu's account, but no legal action was taken against anyone but Kiggundu, who was jailed for 6 months, with all his assets confiscated. Agence France-Presse published its own take on these developments in a comprehensive account that dotted every *i* and crossed every *t*.[7]

The sale became the subject of a parliamentary inquiry leading to two separate investigations by two government agencies, the auditor general and the inspector general of government (IGG). Both produced their own reports. The auditor general's 1999 report, sent to the prosecutor, said that Suleiman Kiggundu had lied to a parliamentary committee about Greenland's relation with UCB. For this, Kiggundu faced perjury charges. He also faced fraud charges for denying that Greenland had bought UCB when in fact Kiggundu had been the chief signatory of an Agreement for the Assignment of Shares, signed between Greenland Investments and Westmont.[8]

The IGG report of 1999 investigated the sale of UCB to the Malaysian firm Westmont: "Under Westmont's management, UCBL [Uganda Commercial Bank Ltd] gave out unsecured loans and money placements worth shs [shillings] 40 billion to companies related to Greenland Investments Ltd."[9] The report noted that Major General Salim Saleh had confessed to having secretly bought UCBL from Westmont through the Bank of Greenland but concluded that this was "not sufficient evidence that the deal took place, because the confession was not made under oath."

The only person charged in this scandal, Suleiman Kiggundu, was charged with perjury, of having lied to Parliament under oath. Salim Saleh, who had lied to the inspector general of government, was not charged since he was said not to have lied under oath. Salim Saleh was, however, forced to resign from his post as presidential advisor. President Museveni later said he had sacked Salim Saleh not for his involvement in the scandal, but for "indiscipline and drunkenness" in the army.

Following the scandal, in 1999, the Bank of Uganda took over the main operations of UCB, preparing for a second attempt to privatize it. This set the stage for a national debate over the direction of the country's economic policy. The participants in that debate described the stakes as follows: on one side were "free marketeers," who championed globalization; and on the other side were "nationalists," who called for a central role for the state in shaping the direction of the country's economy.

This debate between free marketeers and statists was over the destiny of the economy. Emmanuel Tumusiime-Mutebile, the then governor of the Bank of Uganda, led the free market forces; Ezra Suruma, the deputy governor, led the statists. The free marketeers preferred to see the debate as between globalists

(Mutebile's side) and nationalists (Suruma's), to use the words of Andrew Mwenda, then an active supporter of the free market option. The free marketeers "argued for efficient allocation of resources," the nationalists "for national control and direction of economic resources."[10] For the free marketeers, what mattered was "the quality of services and goods a business produced" and at what cost, and not the ownership of the businesses, whether local or foreign. The nationalists argued that the key question was the contrary: without the role of the state and local capital, national resources were unlikely to be used for national transformation.

Then a strong proponent of free markets, Andrew Mwenda changed his views a decade later: "True, free markets can give you allocative efficiency but they do not address the problem of structural transformation that lies at the heart of development." This was, however, a limited debate. It did not address the question at the heart of the financial crisis—the question of accountability. To whom would markets be accountable: to business persons, or to bureaucrats? Neither side discussed whether markets needed to be regulated, and how to represent the interests of the vast majority who were neither bureaucrats nor owners of capital. The sides in the debate, free marketeers and statists, seemed to offer a choice between speculation and corruption. Without a form of democratic accountability, this would hardly be a meaningful choice.

Soon, Parliament joined the debate. The main bids to buy UCBL had come from Standard Chartered, Barclays, DFCU (Development Finance Company of Uganda Bank Limited), and Bank of Baroda, all foreign banks with local offices. Members of Parliament (MPs) on the Parliamentary Committee on Finance opposed the sale of UCB to any foreign bank operating in the country: "It seems odd that the Central Bank would contemplate selling UCBL to a foreign bank operating in the local market, an act which would worsen the competitive environment and erode the spirit of affirmative action of its original purpose," argued committee chairperson Professor Ephraim Kamuntu in his report. The report also questioned the rush to sell the bank, which had led to a lack of transparency.[11]

The controversy around the sale of UCB led to a larger discussion on the privatization of public financial institutions. UCB had been one of two enterprises floated in the postindependence era to expand banking facilities to rural areas, and beyond narrow elite circles to the working poor. The other initiative was the sale of Uganda Cooperative Bank. Neither was spared in the broad sweep to privatize public assets. In 1999, the same year it sought to privatize UCB, the National Resistance Movement (NRM) government sold the Cooperative Bank with its twenty-four branches across the country. Once Parliament began discussing the failed attempt to privatize UCB, the discussion spilled over to include the Cooperative Bank: MPs demanded that the Minister of Finance Gerald Ssendaula cancel the sale of the Cooperative Bank and its branches, once again, to the same bank, Standard Chartered of South Africa.[12]

Museveni intervened with a "guidance letter" to Parliament on September 30, 2001. Purporting to accede to Parliament's demand that the bank not be handed over to a foreign entity, the president claimed to offer a compromise. He put forward a two-step proposal: first, sell 80 percent shares in UCB to a private interest; followed by a public issue of 20 percent shares, but only "after the successful core bidder has taken over the bank." Thus, maintained Museveni, the "executive, therefore, is in full agreement with you that UCBL should not become a private sector monopoly."[13] That this was a rhetorical ploy became clear to anyone reading the full letter. The executive was in no mood to compromise. That same day, September 30, President Yoweri Museveni made public his letter to Tumussime-Mutebile, the governor of the Bank of Uganda:

> I have received resolutions passed by Parliament today regarding the privatization of Uganda Commercial Bank. These resolutions do not change my long held view that UCB should be sold as soon as possible, as per our Privatization Plan for the whole parastatal sector. . . . We should not allow our petty internal disagreements to scare away bona fide multinational investors as were in the cases of Coffee Marketing Board, Uganda Airlines and the failed 1997 UCB transaction. Time has come for all of us to appreciate the necessity to harmonize our positions so as to maintain the hard earned credibility with our international partners . . . *in order not to damage our image with the investor community and our development partners, I deem it the duty of the entire government system to be fully involved and supportive of the privatization of the Bank.*[14] (my emphasis)

UCB was sold and Ezra Suruma, the deputy governor of the Bank of Uganda who had led opposition to the sale, was fired. William Pike, the British editor of the government-controlled daily *New Vision,* supported Museveni's view: "Let us avoid misguided nationalism."[15] The editorial called for a dose of "Pan-Africanism" and an appeal to "modernism." Years later, Suruma claimed that the Bretton Woods institutions had forced the privatization option: "The government was pressurized by IMF/World Bank to privatize UCB and other parastatals as a condition for aid."[16]

The government paper celebrated the sale of UCB editorially, reproducing the words of the president: "This is a great day for Uganda. . . . Stanbic has pledged to keep UCB's entire national branch network open. We no longer need fear that the sale of UCB would lead to the disappearance of rural banking."[17] Aware that Parliament could not have forgotten the central role his family had played in the first botched attempt to privatize UCB, Museveni sent the Minister for the Presidency to assure Parliament that neither he nor his family had any personal interest in the deal: "His Excellency and his family have totally zero interest in UCB. . . . We are protecting the interest of over 400,000 UCB depositors."[18] Government assurances turned out to be no more than paper promises. It took Stanbic hardly any time to wind up UCB's network of rural branches. With Museveni's nephew by marriage, Hannington Karuhanga, as its board chair, Stanbic went on to become the most powerful bank in Uganda. Yet, it served hardly 300,000 depositors, mostly the country's wealthy minority. Another foreign bank, Standard Chartered, had about 200,000 depositors. Contrast these figures with 2.1 million depositors served by the two largest local banks in 2016: Centenary Bank serving 1.3 million and Crane Bank 800,000.[19]

Standard Chartered is a UK company, totally foreign owned; Stanbic Bank is South African. According to Andrew Mwenda, they had been one bank, Standard Bank; but during apartheid, they separated. The one in South Africa and Rhodesia became Stanbic, and its London part became Standard Chartered. UCB was eventually bought by Stanbic, which listed 20 percent shares on the Kampala stock exchange. This, to the government and related press, made Stanbic not a foreign but a local, "African" company (even if "South African").

Two decades later, in 2022, speaking at the memorial service of the then deceased central bank governor, Emmanuel Tumusiime-Mutebile, President Museveni said he had been misled by Mutebile to privatize UCB. Instead, he said, he should have listened to Ezra Suruma, then UCB's managing director, who had argued passionately for the bank to remain in the hands of the Ugandan state. Given that privatization continued to define the core of the government's economic policy, these were crocodile tears. It was a characteristic Museveni move, to throw blame on others while portraying himself as a well-meaning public servant who had been misguided by experts.

UCB was, of course, not a solitary case. Between 1992 and 2010, the NRM privatized eighty-three parastatals, including many that had at one time been private companies owned by Asians and Europeans before being seized by Amin.[20]

A Progressive Degeneration

The UCB sale was the heart of a multitude of sales of parastatals. It recast the institutional infrastructure of the economy, ushering in a period marked by bogus transactions. Among those involved was Dr. Speciosa Wandira Kazibwe, who in 1991, as Minister of Agriculture, oversaw a multimillion-dollar World Bank loan to construct fifteen irrigation dams. A few weeks after she reported to Parliament that the dams were nearly complete, an investigative team confirmed that they did not exist. The protest was joined by elders from the area where the dams were supposed to be. This is how the agriculture minister defended herself in parliament: "The valley dams they are complaining about do exist. The problem with Ugandans is they will stand on the dams and then ask you where they are."[21] Dr. Kazibwe went on to become the country's first woman vice president and then a presidential advisor on microfinance. As presidential advisor, she was accused by residents of Busoga—the subregion of Uganda from which she hails—to have withdrawn 58 million shillings (US $23,135) on March 27, 2012, from S'HE Foundation, a microfinance institution, but then failed to refund the money.[22] At each step she demonstrated the capacity for repeated offences in spite of growing popular outrage, and when found out, would go on to commit further offenses, no matter the outrage. For many, Dr. Kazibwe was among the first to benefit from this neoliberal paradise.

The exposure of scandals seemed to make little difference. Rather than eliciting shame and restraint, public exposure led to cynicism. Those involved were usually high-profile leaders in government. Rather than deny charges and plead their ignorance, or admit misconduct and rectify it, they turned to seek pardon from the chief executive, threatening to bring down the entire house if held responsible for their actions. The more I pursued this research, the more I had the feeling of staring down a proverbial black hole. Could it possibly get worse? But it did. Thus followed a progressive breakdown of the civil service, marked by a spread of what has come to be known as a "ghost" culture, and the sale of public resources by those considered its trustees. To cap it all, we were treated to the unseemly sight of the State House seeking first to corrupt and devour Parliament, the one institution that had demanded public accountability and stood in its way, however meekly and sporadically, and then the judiciary. The sale of Uganda Airlines followed, and confirmed there was no stopping the neoliberal juggernaut.

Uganda Airlines

Uganda Airlines was established by the Amin government in 1976. It was rocked by crisis during the Museveni era when it was found illegally ferrying weapons to the breakaway republic of Croatia. One of its fleet, a leased Boeing 707 Reg No 5X-UCM, was seized in Yugoslavia in 1991.[23] Following a World Bank loan of US $500,000 to "trim" it, Uganda Airlines began selling off assets, beginning with a sale of part of its fleet, staff houses, and cars in 1992.[24] Once the government made public its intention to sell the airline, many potential buyers declared their intention to bid: among them were SA Alliance / South African Airways (SAA), Air Mauritius, British Airways, the Johannesburg-based Inter Air, Kenya Airways, and Sabena.

Parliament was outraged by what seemed to have become a regular practice. An entity targeted for privatization would often be stripped of its most lucrative assets, which would be sold first, and only then would the enterprise be offered for sale on the market. This had happened in at least one other instance: the Coffee Marketing Board. The *New Vision* reported that MPs had "grilled the State Minister for privatization, Manzi Tumubweine and a senior Bank of Uganda officials over the impending sale of 73 properties of UCBL. . . . (MP) [Alleluya] Ikote said when the Coffee Marketing Board was stripped of its assets, it became unattractive to buyers. 'And up to this day we are stuck with it.'"[25]

The likelihood that this could be the fate of Uganda Airlines split the board. Following a row in the boardroom, Dickson Turinawe, acting general manager of Uganda Airlines, swore in an affidavit against Investment Minister Sam Kutesa that the latter had threatened his life during the Entebbe Handling Services (ENHAS) board meeting on February 20, 1997.[26] The same day, a board member of ENHAS, which owned ground handling services at Entebbe, swore in an affidavit to the effect that Sam Kutesa, who also served as board chair, had tried to withdraw from the board a financial statement giving the true state of financial affairs of Uganda Airlines. Soon after, the entire list of potential buyers "mysteriously declined to submit bids, leaving SAA as the sole bidder by early 1999."[27]

South African Airways declared its intention to sign on September 30, 1999. The Divestiture Reform and Implementation Committee sanctioned the sale "in a turbulent meeting." Another committee chair, Isanga Musumba, who had opposed the sale, demanded that the contract not be signed before his parliamentary committee had a chance to debate it.[28] At this point, SAA withdrew. The government daily reported that President Museveni and both the Works and the privatization Ministers (the same Sam Kutesa) had met and decided to liquidate the airline following the withdrawal of South African Airways.[29]

There was no clear indication as to what had led to this outcome: was it that asset stripping had left Uganda Airlines a carcass that no serious buyer would any longer be interested in? Or had public feuds, spilling over from the boardroom to Parliament, warned off potential buyers?

The Dawn of the Neoliberal World

With the ongoing privatization of state enterprises, Uganda entered the neoliberal world. Three scandals, involving junk helicopters (1998), jet fighters (2011), and ID Cards (2012), each more outrageous than the previous one, signaled that key regulatory institutions were no longer functioning effectively, which in turn further encouraged impunity.

The first scandal involved the purchase of four Belarusian helicopters for the army by President Museveni's brother, Salim Saleh, who would feature prominently in public reports of one scandal after another. *The Independent* (Kampala) reported that when the initial batch of two helicopters arrived at Kampala Airport, the deputy director of the country's Military Intelligence confirmed that the helicopters had not been overhaul(ed), though it was required in the contract. There were also questions about "the technical history of the second-hand helicopters" as given in the logbooks. British aviation authorities claimed "the helicopters should have cost no more than $700,000 each, whereas the contract price of the helicopter gunships was $1.5 million per helicopter." When the UK-based supplier, Consolidated Sales Corporation (CSC), rejected the report of the official Ugandan investigation, a second independent assessor was mutually agreed upon. And when this independent assessor, a helicopter company from South Africa, deemed the helicopters not airworthy, the Ugandan Defence Ministry terminated the agreement with CSC. But it was too late: the selling company had already cashed promissory notes equal to half the price of the contract.[30] The helicopters had been purchased by Salim Saleh's company for the army, a transaction for which he was said to have received a commission of $800,000. Two years later, the *New Vision* of November 7, 2000, carried the headline "[Kizza] Besigye [leader of the Opposition] Wants Independent Inquiry into Junk Helicopter Deal."[31]

The purchase of junk helicopters set a precedent. A decade later, the *New York Times* reported a wreckage of "two more Ugandan military helicopters that had smacked into Mount Kenya en route to Somalia." According to the *New York Times,* "That means that three of the four Ugandan helicopters that took off from an airfield in Uganda on Sunday evening crashed before ever coming close to the battlefield. . . . In Kampala, Uganda's capital, several people seemed unfazed by the crashes: 'It is now common knowledge that our army often has junk equipment because someone tried to gain from buying cheap stuff,' the *New York Times* cited Allan Brian Ssenyonga, a marketing and media development trainer."[32]

Jet fighters. The largest of the scandals concerned the purchase of jet fighters from Russia. It was also notable because President Museveni took direct ownership, and thus responsibility, for what transpired. In March 2011, President Museveni publicly admitted that "shs 1.7 trillion ($586,004,826)—roughly 4% of Uganda's GDP which stands at shs 40 trillion—had been withdrawn from Bank of Uganda to purchase fighter jets from Russia." According to *The Observer,* "the 740 m shs Uganda is willing to spend on 6 jets could be enough to purchase at least 20 jets."[33]

Parliament debated the allocation for fighter jets and other military hardware, alongside 2.8 billion shillings (US $965,184), for President Museveni's swearing-in ceremony. No other senior government minister seemed willing to share responsibility for this deal with the President. While he defended the jet deal naming the threats Uganda faces, like al-Shabaab, at the same time warning Parliament that such transactions could not be brought to Parliament because the spending is classified, the Minister of Defense, Crispus Kiyonga, was unwilling to take fiscal responsibility for the expenditure, telling Parliament that "shs 1.7 trillion ($586,004,826) to purchase jet fighters should not be reflected in his ministry's budget but in that of Ministry of Finance."[34] According to *New Vision,* he told MPs in a closed-door meeting on expenditure of military aircraft and supplies that, "if included on their budget, it would raise the ceiling and lead to further questions from the donors."[35] The minister seemed to have no compunction pulling a fast one on Parliament, or on the media. His remarks made it clear that when it came to public funds, senior public officials were accountable less to Parliament than to donors.

Museveni defended the purchase of jets, saying that unlike ordinary weapons, they would enable the government to eliminate insurgents swiftly. "We suffered a lot fighting the LRA because of poor equipment. The UPDF was on foot just like the rebels and it became hard to flush them out easily," Museveni added, noting that it would no longer take months to defeat any group of insurgents with the jets in place.[36] The idea that fighter jets were the most appropriate weaponry to defeat armed insurgents on foot was laughable and unlikely to convince anyone, even civilians with the most rudimentary knowledge of ground-level guerrilla fighting. The former army commander, Major General Mugisha Muntu, told *The Observer* that the 1.7 trillion shillings (US $586,004,826) was likely a cover up for something else.[37]

The vote for fighter jets had been doubled with a second vote for 2.8 billion shillings (US $965,184), for President Museveni's swearing-in ceremony. As expected, there was little time to discuss both issues; meanwhile, allocation for the swearing-in ceremony went up from 2.8 billion shillings (US $965,184) to 3.3 billion shillings (US $1,138,000), while the actual expenditure reached an even higher figure, 4 billion shillings (US $1,379,000).[38]

These developments led the highly respected Nairobi-based weekly *The East African* to reveal how military procurement in Uganda had become fertile ground for corrupt official practices: "In 1998, the army procured four M1–24 helicopters, their spares and ammunitions at a cost of $12 million. The Russian-made helicopters were faulty and came to be known as the 'junk choppers.' No official has been prosecuted or convicted over this scam." There was also "a consignment of malfunctioning guns from South Korea and an order of undersize army uniforms." Furthermore, the "army also bought some 90 tanks from Bulgaria, only 10 of which proved operational." This was followed by "the purchase earlier of another set of [Russian-made] MiG jet fighters (which) also followed a similar pattern. They arrived with one wing, had no spare parts nor bomb loading capacity."[39]

The ID Card Project. Officially called National Security Information System, the ID Card project aimed to issue every adult Ugandan with an ID card. This program was justified as part of an anti-terror measure. It also provided yet another opportunity for embezzlement on a mega scale. A Parliamentary report named three former ministers—Ali Kirunda Kivejinja, Alintuma Nsambu, and Kiddu Makubuya—as guilty of having appropriated over a billion shillings (US $99.7 million) without Parliament's approval. Also charged were Internal

Affairs Permanent Secretary Stephen Kagoda and Secretary to the Electoral Commission, Sam Rwakoojo.[40]

The ID project was done in partnership with a German company, Mühlbauer Technology Uganda, a subsidiary of the German-based Mühlbauer Group. In the course of deliberations, Parliament received an external intelligence report that "some (senior) directors" of this company "are ex-convicts with criminal records."[41] President Museveni then entered the dialogue, asking Parliament "to exonerate the officials named in this rip-off arguing that he directed that the Mühlbauer be hired."[42] If he was hoping that presidential immunity would translate into impunity for those working with him, it did not work, at least not this time.

When Parliament rejected the president's appeal, NRM leaders evoked party loyalty to pressure its MPs to support those accused when it came to the parliamentary vote. "The Party wanted us to stand by people who are accused of corruption. To hell with them, enough is enough," Robinah Nabbanja, the woman MP of Kibaale District told the *Daily Monitor*. She revealed that this appeal to party loyalty to cover corruption was not without precedent.[43]

Faced with a parliamentary recommendation that the three ministers (Kivejinja, Nsambu, and Makubuya) be held liable for violating procurement laws, the president appointed a Cabinet subcommittee. Chaired by local government minister Adolf Mwesige, the subcommitte blamed any financial losses on the bureaucracy in government, not on the former ministers.[44] The former ministers were thus absolved and released—once again free to prey on the society at large.

It became customary for ministers facing corruption charges to turn to Museveni, pleading that he intervene on their behalf. Sometimes, there would be an implied warning that failure to do so may lead to an exposure of wrongdoings among high officials. When asked by Parliament's Public Accounts Committee to account for the $200 million the government received from Eastern and Southern Africa Trade and Development Bank (though against the advice of the governor of the Bank of Uganda) to procure medicines and to fund the government's foreign exchange requirements as and when they arise, Finance Minister Matia Kasaija "requested the President to come to his rescue before it is too late."[45] Similarly, when charged with approving payment of 142 billion shillings (US $80,912,000) to businessman Hassan Basajjabalaba without authority, the former attorney general, professor of law Kiddu Makubuya, asked Museveni "to forgive him for any mistakes made in approving shs 142 bn

($80,912,000) claims," at the same time warning that prosecuting him will "open a can of worms over other government transactions."[46] In this case as with the previous one, the request by a minister to his boss was coupled with an implied threat. Ministers seemed to be in the know of a widespread practice of corruption among colleagues, and seemed determined to have their (equal) share of the pie. Next in line was the Minister of Health.

Health Ministry and AIDS

The Minister of Health had publicly maintained that HIV/AIDS could be cured by prayer.[47] The minister's views notwithstanding, the ministry was among the leading recipients of external funds dedicated to a campaign to eradicate HIV/AIDS, and ministry officials seemed content to work under a minister who had publicly questioned the rationale for the entire project.

Meanwhile, funds meant to boost the health infrastructure, including the introduction of accelerated preventive measures for AIDS, were appropriated by senior government officials. By 2012, the police were investigating more than one hundred projects in the Ministry of Health "in which they suspected fraud and corruption," among them "over nine projects including malaria and AIDS control programs, National Health Internship Scheme and Health Insurance Program" amounting to 30 billion shillings (US $11,966,000) in 2012.[48] The Anti-Corruption Court charged former health minister Jim Muhwezi and his two deputies, Captain Mike Mukula and Dr. Alex Kamugisha, with misappropriating 1.6 billion shillings (US $638,000).[49] Also under scrutiny were other senior officers "managing malaria control program funds to the tune of sh 78 billion (US $31,112,000)."[50] Since these funds had come from US government programs, donors were able to call on the US embassy to intervene. That Museveni rode the crisis without any blowback illuminated the degree of global impunity the Ugandan presidency had come to enjoy over the years.

Where in such an institutional environment could one turn for even a modicum of justice? At that time, the answer was often Parliament. The director of the Health Monitoring Unit at the country's principal public hospital, Mulago, informed Parliament of a range of malpractices at the hospital, asking it to intervene and restore some degree of accountability. He said the ministry claimed to have spent 1.4 billion shillings (US $482,000) but could only account for 100 million shillings, less than a tenth of the original sum.[51]

Scandals proliferated.[52] The press covered them, but the public soon realized that the news was one sided—plenty of publicity for those accused, but hardly any news of people held accountable. This new way of thinking was summed up in one sentence: "You eat where you work." To "eat" here meant to put your hands on institutional resources, confirming the spread of an amoral culture.

A "Ghost Culture"

The practice of corruption was referred to as a "ghost" practice in popular parlance. Newspapers first reported of "ghost soldiers." Next came reports of "ghost workers" and then "ghost institutions."

Among the earliest was the report of the privatization of game reserves, which usually bordered larger parks that functioned as sanctuaries for game. The precedent was set when the Ministry of Tourism, Wildlife and Antiquities leased Kyambura Game Reserve to Zwilling Safaris of Switzerland at an annual lease fee of $15,000 in 1991. According to press reports, "the same company may take over Kigezi Game Reserve bordering Queen Elizabeth National Park to the South." Kyambura buffers Queen Elizabeth Park, a major game park in the western part of the country. On its east side there is already a protection zone for wildlife. But the terms of the lease undid this by including "hunting safaris." In a fax message to the minister, the chief executive of Zwilling Safaris AG, Walter Betshel, explained the importance to the company of hunting safaris: "One very important aspect of hunting safaris is to attract wealthy and influential business people to visit Uganda." The press made it clear that there were "no indications that the offer was advertised to attract other interested companies." Indeed, "both the Ministry headquarters and the game department based in Entebbe had kept the deal very secretive." Nor were officials or the board of directors of Ugandan national parks consulted. A workshop on "Man and Biosphere" held in the Queen Elizabeth National Park in November 1991 "pointed out that the lease fee of 15,000 US dollars per year was ridiculously low and wondered how this figure was arrived at." Wildlife experts and conservationists said the arrangement "would be a disaster for the animal population that are at their all time low in the Queen Elizabeth Park." They expressed concern that if there is not enough game to shoot in the game reserve, the company is likely to use unscrupulous means, such as salt licks, to lure the animals from the nearby national park.[53]

As the practice spread, a "ghost college" surfaced in 2011. When the World Bank gave a grant of $23 million to underwrite public service performance, part of it was for the Ministry of Public Service to set up a college to enhance policy implementation and reform. However, when the parliamentary committee set out for an on-site inspection of the college, it was led to "a dilapidated structure owned by the National Fisheries Resources Research Institute (NaFIRRI)."[54] There was no college.

Newspapers further reported on different government departments. The Ministry of Finance discovered an estimated 4,000 ghost workers who had been paid 70 billion shillings (US $27,921,000) over 2012.[55] In the primary school system, declared "free" by the new government, it was reported that as much as 20 billion shillings (US $7,977,000) were lost annually to ghost teachers, also in 2012.[56] According to the auditor general's report for 2022, of the total wages and pension funds sent to local governments in 2021 and 2022, 1.12 billion shillings (US $320,733) were paid to ghost workers.[57]

Over time, theft became institutionalized. Those meant to protect the public, either as guardians or as trustees, began to prey on the same public they were meant to serve. In response, the public perception of public authorities began to change. The most outrageous stories concerned the revenue authorities, the Land Commission, and the police. Officials of the Uganda Revenue Authority were accused of "own(ing) clearing firms . . . vetting some of their own companies to provide services to the authority."[58] In one instance, the police "demanded they should be given a percentage of the money they recover from corrupt people to improve their (own) living conditions."[59] Asked to advance inducements every time they reported a case to the police, residents of one place, Napak District, "said they would rather deal with crime themselves than report it to the police and open themselves to extortion." When a resident, Mr. John Lokut, reported the case of his daughter who had been raped, he "was asked for 30,000 shs (US $10.30) for fuel before police could take action."[60] When I reported the theft of my computer to the police in 2020, I was asked to pay 100,000 shillings (US $31) as "facilitation" money and another 100,000 shillings to meet "transport" costs.

Public Land. The sale of public assets included public land, used by schools or the general public, as playing fields or as conservation sites, all meant to be kept in trust by the state. In each case, the trustee was the Uganda Land Commission (ULC), which made it easy for entrepreneurs seeking valuable land in the centers of cities to bypass school authorities and the education ministry and make deals with individual officials in the land commission. When this happened with a well-known school, it became front-page news—such as when "developers took over prime city land belong(ing) to Nakasero Primary School" in 2013 or when the playing field at Kololo SS "was turned into a housing estate."[61] The pattern was repeated at other places, including public schools in the center of Kampala: Kitante, Buganda Road, and Nakivubo Settlement.[62] A similar fate was faced by golf courses and playing fields in Entebbe, Masindi, and Mbale, as well as by a part of the prestigious Kitante Golf Course in Kampala. Lugogo, a prime recreation site in Kampala, which had been home to seven football (soccer) fields at one time, was by 2013 left with only one football ground. The rest had been replaced by shopping malls—Shoprite, Game, Forest Mall—an expansive parking lot and a customs bond house which held cars yet to be sold.[63]

Soon there were "ghost refugees." In 2018 Uganda claimed to host up to 1.6 million refugees. Rosa Malango, the UN country representative, decided to probe the numbers. Following investigation, she wrote the prime minister, highlighting three issues: doubtful number of refugees in Uganda; abuse of funds and other resources by some officials; and suspected trafficking of girls and women refugees.[64] One day that February, with UN officials in attendance, all refugees, purportedly receiving rations, were asked to turn up; only 7,000 of the registered 26,000 plus did, raising the possibility that there were 19,000 "ghosts" whose monies were being pocketed by some in the Office of the Prime Minister.[65]

Young people who had moved overseas and regularly remitted funds to their families, usually with instructions to build a family home, would find on return home that photographs they had received of houses under construction were a hoax and were really photos of houses that belonged to someone else, "ghost houses." These instances—ghost workers, teachers, refugees, houses, a college—were among the components in the making of a "ghost culture."

State House Corrupts Parliament

Though it had a solid majority in Parliament, the NRM was unable to wield that majority through sheer party discipline. When it came to voting on key constitutional issues, such as removing the two-term limit on the president in office, allowing Museveni to run in the 2006–2011 elections, MPs were paid to remove presidential term limits from the Constitution and "the Museveni campaign was said to have spent an unprecedented amount of money."[66] The following year, 2012, the government introduced a loan scheme of 103 million shillings (US $41,085) for each MP to purchase a car. Since there was no parliamentary vote for the scheme, money was released in "bits and pieces," because they were "cutting and pasting" from other parliamentary votes.[67] A more obvious attempt to corrupt politicians had been in 2011 when the government "wired 20 million shs into accounts of 326 MPs," a payment purportedly to "monitor government programs." Opposition leaders described the money as a "bribe," and sixteen of those 326 MPs returned it to the Treasury. A group called Anti-Corruption Coalition Uganda comprising five civil society groups dragged the attorney general to court, demanding taxpayers' money be returned.[68]

By 1997, just when widespread corruption in Uganda was becoming part of global news, a honeymoon seemed to blossom between the "international community" and the government of Uganda. President Bill Clinton praised President Museveni as one of a "new generation" of African presidents who were willing to bring "African solutions to African problems." When he landed in Uganda, Clinton no doubt had two things uppermost in his mind: Uganda had followed the "conditionalities" laid down by the Washington Consensus; and Uganda was willing to intervene militarily in African countries where domestic considerations prevented the United States from doing so. Human Rights Watch noted, "Because of the close relationship between the U.S. and Uganda . . . U.S. criticism [of Uganda] has become increasingly muted." That would prove to be an understatement.

The year 1998 became a swing year for Uganda. Uganda had been an enthusiastic follower of neoliberal policies, and as Human Rights Watch noted, the country had much to show: "Uganda's economy has rebounded from a complete collapse in the 1970s and 1980s, and between 1994 and 1997 Uganda posted a real GDP growth rate of 8 percent, the highest in Africa." On the negative side was a litany of cases pointing to pervasive corruption and leading to a series of parliamentary inquiries. The World Bank itself shared a confidential report detailing many cases of corruption involving government officials within the Ugandan government. The report was later released to the public at the request of the Ugandan government.[69] As if to ingratiate itself with the Bank, the government hosted a landmark closed-door meeting between World Bank president James Wolfensohn and leaders of twelve African countries in January

1998 to discuss the World Bank's policies in Africa.[70] The meeting showcased Museveni as an enthusiastic neoliberal militant.

The same donors would now shut their eyes to their own reports, and their ears to periodic sermons they were used to giving on the need for accountability. There were already early signs that President Museveni would be amply rewarded by his mentors: Uganda became the first country to benefit from the Heavily Indebted Poor Countries (HIPC) initiative in April 1998, when the World Bank and the IMF agreed to a US $650 million debt relief package for Uganda, effectively reducing Uganda's external debt by 20 percent.[71] Not all that surprisingly, the Consultative Group Meeting ended with Uganda receiving its biggest-yet package of aid: US $2.2 billion, to be dispersed over the following three years.

Human Rights Watch was stunned, incredulous that this had happened in the face of a combination of outrageous practices testifying to a growing disregard for rights combined with a willingness to tolerate flagrant corruption. The United Nations Development Programme (UNDP) report of November–December 1998 echoed similar sentiments in even stronger terms: "Corruption, said to be running rampant in Ugandan government, has been exposed in several banking and privatization deals. A parliamentary select committee's report on Uganda's privatization process has called for the resignation of three Cabinet ministers for using political influence to run down the Uganda Airlines Corporation. The report charged that serious crimes had been committed by a number of individuals, including the brother of Yoweri Museveni, Major General Salim Saleh, who is a joint owner of the Efforte Corporation, which allegedly improperly took over in-flight services. The Uganda police have since opened files on the individuals mentioned in the parliamentary report to see if they 'contravened the law.'"[72]

The donor meeting in 2000 took place at a time that Uganda, along with Rwanda, was openly embroiled in fighting over who would control the diamond city of Kisangani and thus the spoils of war in the neighboring Democratic Republic of Congo. What followed was a remarkable demonstration of how the country's military machine could be wielded as a private instrument by individuals in leadership positions to wage a colossal theft. The whole affair was investigated and exposed by a UN inquiry. To counter it, President Museveni appointed his own inquiry. As if to vouch for its credibility, the inquiry was headed by a white judge. It presaged a decade of crisis for the Museveni regime.

15

THE WAR ON TERROR

The year 2000 began a decade of crisis and survival for the Museveni regime, which faced both internal and external challenges.

Externally, an explosive report from the UN Security Council detailed a regime of loot and plunder by the Ugandan army in eastern Congo. Internally, the courts had questioned the outcome of the 2001 election results. A provision in the 1995 Constitution had limited the presidency to two terms. If the provision held, Museveni would be barred from running in the 2006 elections. The decade closed with US officials issuing Museveni with an ultimatum: withdraw from Congo and prepare a credible transition at home. From the National Resistance Movement's point of view, a renegotiated relationship with the United States was key to cutting off the opposition from external support. For this, there was no limit to the price the president was willing to pay to keep his hold on power.

This was by far the most serious challenge Museveni had faced in more than two decades of presidential rule. He understood that US policy was set around human rights and national security, and he needed to reach out to the US president and the security apparatus if he was to bypass the State Department and its human rights agenda. The NRM offered to join the global War on Terror in return for an assurance of impunity. As the Museveni regime became the front line of the War on Terror, first in Somalia, and then South Sudan, its plunder of Congo became a non-issue.

Congo

The region that ties together Uganda, Rwanda, and eastern Congo is known as the Great Lakes region. Among the Great Lakes are three: Victoria, Tanganyika, and Kivu. This is also the region of the Tutsi diaspora, whose numbers swelled following the 1959 Revolution, which turned the social order in Rwanda upside down. As the reins of power passed from the Tutsi minority to the Hutu majority, Tutsi exiles fled into neighboring countries in the Great Lakes region, beginning a tragic cycle of revenge and counter-revenge. It was in Uganda that Tutsi exiles became embroiled in a contest for power between internal forces. Over four years, they emerged as the leading ranks of the rebel movement, estimated to number 4,000 out of roughly 16,000 in the National Resistance Army (NRA). As the earliest recruits into the NRA, they also provided much of its frontline leadership. When they were denied citizenship in Uganda in 1990, the Rwandese exiles regrouped as the Rwanda Patriotic Front (RPF). With the support of Museveni and the Ugandan army, they planned a return to Rwanda. The background to Uganda's involvement in Congo lay in the 1990–1994 invasion of Rwanda by the Uganda-based Rwanda Patriotic Front (RPF). The scholarship on Rwanda has been driven by a key question: Did the RPF invasion trigger the 1994 genocide of the Tutsi, or did it stop that genocide? In a book I wrote on the subject of the genocide, I argued, both.[1] When the RPF took power in Kigali following the genocidal massacre of nearly 800,000 Tutsi in Rwanda, more than a million Hutu fled into Congo. The RPF followed them into eastern Congo. This was the backdrop to the First Congo War of 1996–1997, which began as a war in eastern Congo and led to foreign invasions that replaced the government of President Mobutu Sese Seko with the rebel leader Laurent Kabila, backed by invading forces from a number of neighboring countries: Zimbabwe, Angola, Rwanda, and Uganda.

In the aftermath of war, Ugandans and Rwandans declared that the new government was failing to meet their urgent security needs. Once Kabila was installed as the new president of Congo, Rwanda pressed on his government to appoint a leading Rwandan military officer, James Kabarebe (my former student at Makerere University, whom I mentioned in chapter 10), as the head of the new Congolese army. Claiming to defend the country's "national" interest, President Kabila dismissed his Rwandan chief of staff, the then leading Rwandan official in Congo, on July 14, 1998. Two weeks later, he asked all Rwandan and Ugandan officials in the Congolese state apparatus to return home. On August 2, another rebellion broke out in eastern Congo, which bordered Uganda and Rwanda and was home to both Congolese Tutsis and refugees from the Rwandan genocide. Rwanda and Uganda immediately offered assistance to the rebels. As the rebels moved toward the capital, Zimbabwe and Angola intervened from the south. The split in the African coalition between those for and against Kabila laid the foundation for the Second Congo War of 1998–2003. In its course, the Uganda Peoples' Defense Forces (UPDF) occupied much of Orientale Province (of which the mineral-rich Ituri region is a part), and worked hand-in-glove with the Kisangani faction of the Rally for Congolese Democracy (RCD-K), a rebel group under the leadership of Ernest Wamba-dia-Wamba (my friend and former colleague at the University of Dar es Salaam, mentioned in chapter 10), to consolidate its control over Ituri. The ensuing Hema-Lendu conflict took on the proportions of a region-wide interethnic battle and led to the deaths of thousands.

The escalating violence politicized and polarized ethnic hostility in the population. Armed groups proliferated, as did small arms. The fighting was said to be between two ethnic groups, Hema and Lendu, the former pastoralists and the latter agriculturalists, historically at odds whenever migrant pastoralists and local cultivators clashed over land. As the conflict between Rwanda and Uganda entered the eastern part of Congo, it politicized and inflamed this ethnic division. The BBC reported that as many as 60,000 people had died in Ituri since 1998. Médecins Sans Frontières put the figure of the dead at 50,000 and of those displaced at more than 500,000. It is against this background that a UN Security Council Panel of Experts report of April 2001 accused Uganda, Rwanda, and Zimbabwe of systematically and illegally extracting diamonds, cobalt, gold, coltan (a rare ore used in cell phones and laptops), and other lucrative resources from the Democratic Republic of the Congo (DRC), in the process feeding and expanding ethnic conflict across Ituri and other regions in eastern Congo.[2]

The UN report used strong language to describe different stages in the involvement of the three countries in Congo: what began as "looting . . . by the armies themselves" led to organized "elite networks" which created "organized systems of embezzlement, tax fraud, extortion, the use of stock options as kickbacks and diversion of State funds conducted by groups that closely resemble criminal organizations." The report focused on the Ugandan-organized network that "exercise[d] monopolistic control over the area's principal natural resources, cross-border trade, and tax revenues for the purpose of enriching members of the network." The report also contrasted the hierarchical looting by Rwanda with the decentralized looting by Uganda. It then went on to identify key names in the Ugandan network, including both chief government officials and leaders of rebel movements supported by the Ugandan government.[3]

The UN report further detailed how the network generated money in the DRC "from the export of primary materials . . . controlling the import of consumables, from theft and tax fraud." The report delineated that the "success of the network's activities . . . relies on three interconnected features . . . military intimidation; maintenance of a public sector facade, in the form of a rebel movement administration; and manipulation of the money supply and the banking sector, using counterfeit currency and other related mechanisms."

The big prize in the battle for Congo's resources was the diamond market in Kisangani: "After the last clash in Kisangani in June 2000, RPA [the Rwanda Patriotic Army] worked through the RCD-Goma administration to funnel all the diamonds in Kisangani through the RCD-Goma administration, by forcing all local diamond traders to sell to a single intermediary with an export monopoly. At stake was also control over other areas containing valuable natural resources like cotton, diamonds, timber, and gold under the control of their respective armies." The report goes on to say that they also "establish[ed] authority in major urban and financial centers, such as Bunia, Beni and Butembo, where they use the rebel administration as a public sector facade to generate revenue, specifically to collect taxes under various pretexts, including licensing fees for commercial operators, import and export duties and taxes on specific products" (para. 101).

This control had been maintained under the personal authority of Lieutenant-General Salim Saleh even after the formal withdrawal of Ugandan troops from eastern Congo.[4] The Ugandan military leaders built two kinds of alliances: the first with Congolese rebel groups they supported financially, and the second with private security venture groups, like the Saracen Group, and its South African director, Heckie Horn.[5] The Ugandan network members received several benefits including exemption from taxation further strengthened through collaboration between "transnational criminal groups"—in particular the group led by Victor Bout, a Russian arms dealer—and leading members of Uganda's ruling circles.[6]

Some of the practices that characterized looting in eastern Congo, such as the theft of cattle, had already been perfected in northern Uganda during the previous decade. The UPDF would appear in several guises, as both raiders and protectors.[7] They would offer to protect the ranchers against their own raids, but for a fee: "The representative of the Food and Agriculture Organization of the United Nations in Bunia has reported the more recent UPDF practice of offering protection to ranchers against attacks that they themselves have orchestrated, in exchange for regular payment in animals." To this, UPDF added the practice of outright extortion from local butchers: "UPDF have also required local butchers to hand over hides from animals butchered locally, and these hides are then transported to Kampala where they are reputedly sold to Bata Shoe Manufacturing."

As the UPDF got bolder, it upped the risk it was willing to take for higher returns. Reminiscent of late nineteenth-century practices when European powers armed both sides in local conflicts, the idea being to subdue one first and the other later, the UPDF armed both sides in the (ethnic) conflict and then supported one against the other. In the conflict between the Hema and the Lendu (purportedly cattle keepers and farmers), the UPDF patronized the Hema, who worked as transporters and businessmen for the UPDF.[8] As the conflict spiraled, the UPDF emerged central to both the problem and the emerging solution. It provided "arms to both sides in the ethnic conflict, the Lendu and the Hema"—and ensured that the side it picked emerged as the winner.[9]

The cycle of violence led to a general breakdown requiring outside intervention. Large numbers of young men joined one or another armed group because they had no other means of finding food or medicine or because they have no one to care for them: "The young men in the Armé Patriotique Congolaise are unpaid but are provided with weapons and a uniform giving them the tools for menacing others. Widespread armed activity is characterized by opportunistic and chaotic encounters. Children are killed, adult victims are eviscerated, women are raped, property is stolen, houses burned, churches demolished and whatever infrastructure exists is laid waste."[10]

The mayhem led to widespread demand for peace, but the resulting peace process institutionalized the presence of the Ugandan army in eastern Congo. For its peacekeeping services, the UPDF received ample returns: it became a signatory to the peace agreement and was promised a hefty monthly income, in addition to a tax-free status for all UPDF-approved enterprises. This role was then institutionalized through a peace agreement.[11]

As soon as the UN report was released, President Museveni appointed the Porter Commission and charged them with investigating the plunder of the Democratic Republic of Congo's wealth by foreign armies who had had help from local rebel groups.[12] The Porter Commission provided a counternarrative that emphasized the role of individuals, but exonerated governments. As would be expected, relations between the UN Panel and the Porter Commission were less than cordial.[13]

From the Ugandan government's standpoint, the Porter Commission had served its main purpose: to exonerate the government, while pointing its finger at individuals.[14] Its report agreed with the Ugandan government that any wrong-doing on Uganda's part must be ascribed to individuals, not the government. Foreign Minister James Wapakhabulo, also the country's third deputy prime minister, said the report "ignored the fact that his country had become involved in the Democratic Republic of the Congo as a result of genuine security concerns." Museveni had told the commission that he had ordered the Ugandan army to help only Ugandan businesses. After being questioned by the commission in Kampala, General James Kazini admitted he had personally written to his field commanders in eastern Congo, instructing them to allow a Lebanese-owned diamond mining company to operate without hindrance. "Maybe that was an oversight on my part, but facilitating Ugandan businessmen working with who?" he asked.[15] Surely, since Ugandan businessmen in Congo were involved in trade, they had to be dealing with other, non-Ugandan businesses, not just themselves. No one answered the question, which was rhetorical.

Justice Porter's 2003 commission absolved the Uganda government of any official involvement; at the same time, it named some top military officials—Major General James Kazini, Jovia Akandwanaho (the wife of Salim Saleh), Major General Kahinda Otafiire, Brigadier Noble Mayombo—for taking part in the plunder in eastern Congo. Action, though, was taken only against Kazini.[16] One name, that of Major General Salim Saleh, was a conspicuous absence on this list. In 2005, Congo sued Uganda in the UN's International Court of Justice for crimes committed by its army during the Second Congo War. The justices concluded that Uganda owed Congo $10 billion in reparations. The debt remains outstanding while Uganda continues to back Congolese proxy armies including the Mouvement du 23 Mars (M23), an armed Congolese group, which the UN has accused of mass rape, looting, summary execution, and other crimes.[17] In December 2021, Ugandan forces returned to eastern Congo, this time mounting air strikes and ground assaults against another group. As in 2001, Uganda said this was for security reasons, in order to attack rebel Allied Democratic Forces (ADF)—now branded "Islamic terrorists," who were said to have carried out several armed attacks in Uganda over the previous months.[18]

After Congo

It was only a matter of time before Congo scandals would intermesh with domestic scandals. In the aftermath of the Congo saga, corruption grew in scale and became blatant. Its perpetrators were confident that, even if found out, they were unlikely to face a demand for accountability so long as they did not directly tread on the interests of the US government or another major power. The exception became clear when the program in question had been launched by President George W. Bush, and the US embassy was obliged to monitor it. The information spilled over into the public domain since there was in this case an American researcher who was able to gather detailed information on wrongs committed and measures suggested, even if not taken. The researcher, Helen Epstein, since 2010 visiting professor of human rights and global public health at Bard College, eventually published her findings as a book, *Another Fine Mess.*[19]

The program in question involved "administering multimillion-dollar grants to Uganda from George W. Bush's new international AIDS program known as PEPFAR [the US President's Emergency Plan for AIDS Relief]." In addition, Uganda "received about $45 million from the Global Fund for AIDS, TB, and Malaria, a Geneva-based program that, like PEPFAR, procured medicine and supported health promotion activities." It, too, was under the oversight of US ambassador Jimmy Kolker. When the ambassador found that programs weren't working, and followed leads, he came upon "evidence to support rumors that Museveni's health minister Jim Muhwezi and two of his deputies had created scores of fake NGOs, into which they were funneling millions of dollars of Global Fund money intended to benefit Uganda's impoverished AIDS, tuberculosis, and malaria victims. Kolker and others believe[d] some of the money was used to enrich the minister and his deputies, but most was diverted to the war chest" for two campaigns—one to lift the two-term constitutional limitation on the presidency, and the other to wage the president's 2006 campaign. Muhwezi was part of the campaign apparatus.

Epstein wrote that "the Global Fund suspended support to Uganda for several years," and "Ugandan taxpayers refunded the money," but "Muhwezi and the others were never punished." The ambassador decided to take what measures he could under US law, which specified that "foreign officials who benefit from diversion of public funds are denied US travel visas." Based on these commission reports, a lawyer on Kolker's embassy staff compiled a list of Ugandans identified as "verifiably guilty" and placed them on a visa ban list. Among these were President Museveni's brother Salim Saleh and Saleh's wife.

Eventually, Kolker decided to take matters into his own hands. According to Epstein, Kolker and UK High Commissioner Adam Wood visited Museveni at the president's country home in Rwakitura in western Uganda in 2005 and offered him a deal: "Retire from office in 2006, and we'll help find you lucrative work as a UN negotiator. The ambassadors also offered to help arrange a deal so that Museveni would not be prosecuted for acts committed in office." The reference was especially to Congo, given that Luis Moreno Ocampo, chief prosecutor of the International Criminal Court (or ICC) established in 2003, "had announced that an investigation into atrocities committed in Congo would be among his first priorities."[20]

What Kolker and Wood did not know was that Museveni had been working with a Washington lobbyist behind the scenes to secure a deal with George W. Bush's administration that would embroil Uganda in yet another bloodbath—this time in Somalia. Museveni was clearly a step ahead of the US ambassador and the State Department.

How Does the Regime Survive?

During an academic staff strike in 1988, a student was killed, and agitation spread among students and staff. I received a call from President Museveni, who wanted to discuss the campus situation. I told him that we, the staff and students, had a just cause. He responded, "Mamdani, this is not about what is right and what is wrong. It is about building a state." This was a clue to Museveni's amoralism, one that separated politics from ethics, reasons of power from notions of right and wrong. As soon as he had acquired power, Museveni's reasons for wanting power seemed to fade into dim memory. He would henceforth be preoccupied with holding power. And, over time, he would evolve a twofold strategy, both external and internal.

The external strategy was a response to the new global situation following the collapse of the Soviet Union. Museveni was among the few African leaders who grasped the opportunities this offered. He had concluded that African leaders had been wrong to choose a side in the Cold War; rather, one must play the drum on both sides and begin by grasping how each side understood its interest. As the dominant power, the United States was most concerned with security; it offered African regimes a way of maintaining order and stability, and thus power. As an insurgent power, China wanted to end Western monopoly control over African resources. It offered the continent and its people the promise of development. There was, however, a downside to both.

Preoccupied with security, Americans were prepared to look the other way as domestic repression increased. The Chinese offer of development aid multiplied opportunities for mega-corruption, particularly by leaders who negotiated official contracts. American and European companies were restrained by domestic legislation that criminalized corruption of foreign leaders; their response was to use local consultants to pay off the same leaders, but on a smaller scale. China had no such legal prohibition, although I have heard from colleagues that China did have administrative regulations setting a limit on what percentage of a contract could be used as financial incentive. Despite that, corruption around mega projects financed by China reached scandalous proportions and was often the subject of local press stories. Making the rounds of the rumor mill a few years ago was speculation about why work on a major dam over Karuma Falls had been halted for years, and why it had finally started. A well-informed friend, who preferred not to be identified, told me that different factions of the ruling family had their own preferred Chinese contractor; each faction had to be paid off for the work to move forward. Chinese aid tended to gravitate to mega projects—highways, dams, rail lines, and so on—each providing an opportunity for mega corruption.

The Secret of Survival

Development, however, cannot guarantee survival. And so Museveni turned to the United States every time his hold on power seemed tenuous; he began his applications to the United States starting in 1987–1989, when the regime was financially unstable; and next in 2001–2006, when the president openly bribed members of Parliament to amend the Constitution and remove the constitutional limit of two terms on the duration of the presidency (thereby proceeding to outrageously rig the election). As his regime gasped for air in the years after it came to power, Museveni enthusiastically joined the Washington Consensus, giving the World Bank total freedom to redesign both the Ugandan economy and its higher education. If the first phase was held together by joining the Washington Consensus, the second phase was defined by equally enthusiastic and unrestrained participation in the regional War on Terror. And so it was, from Rwanda (1994) to Congo (1998), and from Somalia (1996) to South Sudan

(2013), back to what seemed like a replay in Congo (2021). Along the way, he was chastened by the example of Muammar Gaddafi. Gaddafi's example drove home one lesson—that American support is always conditional, in return for loyalty. As a reward, Museveni was admitted among the ranks of the few who enjoyed impunity and protection from the United States—something enjoyed first and foremost by Israel.

The United States speaks two official languages: one is the language of rights, the other is that of war. The United States was willing to exert external pressure in the name of human rights, but it was also prepared to overlook the human rights record of clients or allies for strategic reasons, whether economic or military. As the self-proclaimed custodian of human rights, the State Department issues an annual human rights report, with a global ranking of the worst human rights offenders. Usually, it does not lie; its verdict has reasonable credibility. But when it does lie, it is because of what it ignores, not what it says. National security is the preserve of a second set of agencies, led by the CIA and the National Security Council. They are guided by a different index—one that distinguishes friends from enemies.

Regime Survival and the War on Terror

When Museveni capitulated to the financial discipline demanded of the structural adjustment program, he stood fast against the demand that the country trim its army and cut its military budget. He did everything at his disposal to defend the size of the security budget, even if it meant hiding the real military budget. But this could only be a stop gap measure. Museveni came to realize that a stable relationship with the United States required a sustained participation in the War on Terror. We can divide Uganda's participation in the War on Terror into two phases. The opening period, from Rwanda (1994) to Congo (1998) was a time of learning the language of waging terror, labeling its internal opponents "terrorists" and its repressive measures "anti-terrorism."

The internal challenges, from the Lord's Resistance Army (LRA) in the North to the ADF in the Southwest, were real. But these were also useful enemies. They not only provided a political pretext for a bloated military establishment and for domestic repression, but the language of anti-terrorism also justified prioritizing military over political resolution of conflicts. In the North this meant broadening the conflict to punish the entire population. When it came to Somalia, and then South Sudan, the Ugandan army asserted its unique political advantage. Uganda would use its military arm to help realize American political objectives in the region; in exchange, the United States would ensure that Uganda could use military power with impunity, both locally and regionally.

The turning point in the United States–Uganda relationship was the intervention in Somalia. Museveni glimpsed this opportunity at the time of the 2001 electoral crisis. How these events reshaped Uganda–US relations has been reconstructed by Helen Epstein, with close access to former US embassy officials in Kampala. My account that follows draws generously from Epstein's narrative of events.

The year 2001 posed the first credible electoral challenge to Museveni's position as president. The challenger was Kizza Besigye, a retired colonel who had been Museveni's doctor during the bush war and who now headed a breakaway faction of the NRM called Reform Agenda. Opposition rallies were put down by the personal guards of the president known as the Presidential Protection Unit, and a state-funded militia called Kalangala Action Plan, which beat people with iron bars and sticks. There were widespread charges of kidnapping, torture, and killings. When Museveni was declared the winner, Besigye charged in court that 2.5 million "ghost votes" had been cast in favor of the president. According to accounts by Uganda's leading journalist, Charles Onyango-Obbo, and retired Ugandan Supreme Court judge George Kanyeihamba, the court decided to annul the election 4–1; Museveni warned two of the judges that he would call in the army if they did not revise their opinion in his favor. They thus changed their votes, thereby reversing the tally of Supreme Court votes to 3–2. Besigye was followed everywhere by security men, prevented from traveling within or outside the country, and eventually accused of masterminding a series of grenade attacks in Kampala. Finally, he fled the country for South Africa in August 2001. According to Helen Epstein, US pressure on Museveni mounted over the coming months, with Secretary of State Colin Powell "reading the President the riot act: Get your troops out of Congo, Powell said, and implement real democracy in the next three years, or else."[21]

Museveni looked for a way out. He hired Rosa Whitaker who, according to Epstein, was "a shrewd bible-quoting African-American lobbyist," former assistant trade representative in the Clinton and George W. Bush administrations, to promote his image in Washington by describing the value of his services in the Somalia situation. In 2003, Whitaker sent letters reminding State Department officials that Museveni was "strongly supporting the United States in the global war against terrorism" and arranged for Museveni to visit the White House. Museveni flew to Washington, DC, in January 2003, and met President George W. Bush at the White House. "There's no public record of what they discussed," writes Helen Epstein, her account based on discussions with Jimmy Kolker, the US ambassador to Uganda.

"What should I tell this guy?" Bush asked Ambassador Kolker before the meeting. Kolker suggested Bush urge Museveni to respect Uganda's constitution and not run again.

"I know how much you like your cattle," Kolker says Bush ended up telling Museveni. "I don't know if I'm going to be re-elected even once. But I know I won't be re-elected twice. That's our system. And after my terms are up, I'm going to be happy to get back to my ranch. Isn't that what you want too? To get back to your cattle?" Museveni just stared straight ahead. "It was like there were daggers coming out of his eyes," Kolker told Epstein.

Museveni's internal problem did not disappear with the 2001 election. His ambitions were still impeded by the 1995 Constitution, which limited the tenure of a president to two five-year terms; Museveni would have to retire in 2006. In response, he mobilized support through means fair and foul, as the expression goes, to pass a constitutional amendment to lift the two-term clause and run again. The Kisanja Project—Kisanja is a Luganda word for both "banana leaves" and "term" (as in a presidential term)—began with the president appointing a Constitutional Review Commission and then "brib(ing) its members to support scrapping term limits." The next step was to "fire anti-Kisanja cabinet ministers and replace anti-Kisanja Parliamentary Speaker Francis Ayume with the more accommodating Edward Ssekandi."[22] But Museveni wouldn't have to fire Ayume. The president had ordered Ayume, who had been playing golf in the northern town of Arua, to appear for an early morning Cabinet meeting the next day, making Ayume travel at night. That evening, Ayume would die in a car crash on the road back to Kampala.

Women parliamentarians were mobilized to support constitutional change; a Cabinet minister praised Museveni as a revolutionary who should rule for life, in the manner of Fidel Castro and Muammar Gaddafi. Two moves cleared the way to the parliamentary vote; each MP who voted for the Kisanja amendment was given an "inducement" of US $2,500: "No one would have known of this had one pro-Kisanja MP, told to wait for his payout, not revealed the scam in parliament. . . . Anti-Kisanja MPs were sent out of the country on study tours on the day of the vote and the amendment passed in June 2005, opening the way for Museveni to run again in 2006."

With Kolker's ultimatum hanging over his head, Museveni desperately needed an American nod. The opportunity came with a changing regional situation, especially in Somalia. After the Union of Islamic Courts, an Islamic reform group, took over the Somali capital Mogadishu from an Ethiopian-backed group, the new rulers implemented a reform agenda and enforced civic order, and the country began to stabilize. Six months later, Ethiopia launched a disastrous invasion with US support. The following month, the African Union authorized African peacekeepers for Somalia while the country trained its own army. There was little support for this initiative around the African continent. But the United States and its European allies "had already been preparing Museveni's troops for months. In November 2006, two months before the invasion, American, French, and British instructors were in Uganda training Museveni's troops in urban combat techniques in preparation for deployment to Somalia. In December, a trainload of food, tents, tanks, rockets, and assorted artillery began making its way from Uganda to Somalia at US government expense. Thousands of Ugandan soldiers followed within days of the Security Council resolution," wrote Epstein.

For the first three years (2007–2010), troops of the African Union Mission in Somalia (AMISOM), a multinational peacekeeping operation in Somalia, were easy targets for al-Shabaab, a Jihadist group whose origins lay in a commitment to constitutional change; when thwarted by the US-backed Ethiopian invasion, it retaliated with a campaign of suicide bombs, killing seventeen AMISOM soldiers, including the Burundian deputy force commander. Museveni demanded more resources and an authority to go on the offensive. He told US officials in Entebbe and on the sidelines of the UN Security Council, "Give me more weapons, more money, more troops and a mandate to fight al-Shabaab, or I'll pull my men out of Somalia." Al-Shabaab claimed AMISOM soldiers were targeting civilians indiscriminately in Somalia; then al-Shabaab suicide bombers targeted a Kampala restaurant and a nearby rugby stadium where crowds were watching the World Cup soccer final on July 11, 2010.

Seventy people were injured and seventy-four died, including an American aid worker. The Americans and Europeans agreed to increase funding for AMISOM and changed its mandate from "peacekeeping" to "peace enforcement." According to a UN report cited by Epstein, "a third to a half of all weapons and ammunition delivered to AMISOM by the U.S. ended up in the hands of Al-Shabaab, presumably sold by disgruntled Ugandan soldiers." Epstein concludes, "Thus, the U.S. has effectively been arming both sides of the conflict, guaranteeing its continuation."[23] Over these years, Uganda became a crucial transport and logistics hub for Africom, with at least three installations in the country, at Entebbe, Kitgum, and Kasenyi.

After Somalia, Uganda became a fallback option for the United States whenever it was in need of intervention in the East African region. The most prominent of these was South Sudan. The day Ugandan troops invaded South Sudan, I received a call from the American embassy asking me to come to the embassy to meet the ambassador. I said the ambassador was welcome to my office at Makerere Institute of Social Research. When the ambassador came, she wanted to know whether there was likely to be public opposition to Uganda's intervention in South Sudan. I had little to say.

Ugandan forces returned to Congo in November 2021, when Uganda mounted air and artillery raids in Operation Shujaa, the word for bravery in Kiswahili, ostensibly to target Allied Democratic Forces (ADF), the counterpart of LRA in the North a decade before. Unlike in 2001 when Ambassador Kolker had given Museveni an ultimatum to withdraw from Congo, this time, there was no American response, even though the Congolese had sued the Ugandan government at the International Court of Justice for damages worth $14 billion suffered during the Second Congo War. A *New York Times* article on the invasion said nothing of official American silence, only citing critical voices from the region, including those in the Ugandan Parliament concerned that the operation had been mounted without the consultation of Parliament.[24] The article cited experts and NGOs in the region and expressed concern that "Mr. Museveni has long exploited Western fears of Islamist terrorism—including overplaying the A.D.F.'s connection to jihadist movements—to advance his own interests," at the same time asking why the operation should have targeted "an area where violence by the A.D.F. is no longer rampant," and questioning the need to advertise "quick wins." With widespread knowledge that

Ugandan troops had been involved in plunder the last time they had entered Congo, many worried that "the latest incursion will allow Uganda to plunder their nation's resources again." The *New York Times* cited Denis Mukwege, the Congolese gynecological surgeon awarded a Nobel Peace Prize, saying the joint operation was "unacceptable": he concluded that "the same errors will produce the same tragic results." Besides the inevitable plunder of resources, a military approach would bypass the more serious and fundamental question of seeking lasting solutions to persistent violence in eastern Congo.

CONCLUSION

Idi Amin Dada and Yoweri Kaguta Museveni were both responsible for shaping the postindependence Ugandan state. Both were forced to craft futures from cloth not of their own making.

Theirs is a story that addresses several predicaments. The first is the meaning of independence. Both Amin and Museveni believed they were continuing the struggle for independence. But their understanding of independence changed as they tasted its fruits. For Amin, the challenge of independence was to make Black rule meaningful by nurturing Black millionaires in place of wealthy Asians. Museveni used a different language to convey the same meaning: Uganda had to develop a "Black middle class" to safeguard its independence and develop the country.

This is also a story of leaders who realized at precisely their moment of triumph that they lacked the resources to translate their vision into reality. The German philosopher Friedrich Engels, Karl Marx's close collaborator, had once remarked on this type of bittersweet fate. Faced with a choice between continuing the struggle or abandoning their vision, Amin and Museveni made opposing choices—Amin fighting to the finish and Museveni yielding, first accommodating and then capitulating to circumstances. It took Amin less than a year to realize that he lacked the means to exercise independence. Most African states gave Amin no more than six months to survive. And Museveni faced more of a financial than a military impasse in 1986. The national treasury had hardly any money, and he lacked the requisite human resources to manage the state.

Neither Amin nor Museveni were model members of the nation-state. Like the "Asians" Amin targeted and Museveni found useful, both were marginal men. Each went about redefining the nation in different ways. Amin was a Nubi, a people considered as foreigners or even worse. And Museveni has been accused of being a Rwandese Tutsi for most of his political life. Amin could have gone one of two ways: into the King's African Rifles (KAR), the British colonial regiment in East Africa, following his father's legacy, or into an Islamic education and preaching following his mother's path. Amin drew his inspiration ("Africa for Africans") from his mother, Ama Aate (of the West Nile Lugbara people), and the Yakan order to which she belonged. Museveni also could have gone one of two ways: as a political organizer or as a military man. He went both ways. Both Amin and Museveni promised decolonization. Whereas Amin failed in his endeavor, he could not be accused of failing to try. Museveni dropped the project as a romantic dream of a youth long spent.

Amin and Museveni came to power in the teeth of growing opposition and the constraints of a narrow social base. They responded with extreme state violence and widespread institutionalized corruption. Both top-down solutions were designed to suppress the opposition and to seek supporters. If violence coerces support, corruption tries to achieve the same goal through temptations. Both corrode moral character and social solidarity.

There were also important differences between Amin and Museveni. The main difference was political. Amin may rightly be considered the father of the Ugandan nation, whose birth was a consequence of the Asian expulsion. Amin racialized the nation as Black, but his nation-building project was limited in two ways. First, the property appropriated from Asians never became public property; it was distributed to a narrow group of private persons. Second, these persons were mainly army officers, not members of the local entrepreneurial class. They were the least qualified to run private enterprises. Many thought they were running the economy into the ground. Amin accused the men and women who ran these officer-owned enterprises of being "Black Asians" and charged them with "economic crimes." These limitations notwithstanding, Amin retained the support of the Black nation until the end of his regime.

Where Amin racialized the nation, Museveni tribalized it. And where Amin promised dignity for the Black nation, Museveni promised life, by which he meant peace. Amin saw the cohesiveness of the nation as a source of strength;

Museveni saw cohesiveness as a potential threat. In politicizing ethnicity, Museveni fragmented the nation. Museveni dismantled the nation, dividing it into an increasing number of minorities, tribe by tribe.

Amin's core support remained civilian. His Achilles heel was a divided army—on one side the Nubi-West Nile group, his original support base at the time of the 1971 coup; on the other, the South Sudanese (Anyanya), who joined him mainly after the 1972 Addis Ababa Agreement. The split between the two first came to light as early as 1974, when Charles Arube attempted to displace Amin. Two years later, an assassination attempt was made on Amin. The Cabinet meeting of June 14, 1976, congratulated Amin on escaping an attempt on his life at Nsambya in Kampala on June 10.[1] Two years later, the division fueled the Kagera War and split open the ranks of the army at the Battle of Lukaya in the Uganda–Tanzania War, when Lieutenant Godwin Sule was killed by "friendly fire." Coinciding with an external war, the break turned out to be fatal to both the supporters and opponents of the regime inside the country.

Museveni tried to translate his peace dividend into a license to rule without a time limit: he promised peace to the population, but only so long as he ruled. The price of continuing peace would be political servitude. Museveni rationalized that Uganda is a premodern collection of tribes which can only be ruled with a strong hand guided by a sound iron will. Like the colonial power, Museveni set out to create the Uganda of his imagination. The more the tribes, the merrier the ruler.

Violence

Both Amin and Museveni made violence central to their political project. Each had learned violence in a different school: Amin as part of the colonial (British) school of counterinsurgency, and Museveni, in the anti-colonial armed struggle. Once a student at the University of Dar es Salaam, Museveni had gone to Mozambique and trained with FRELIMO (Mozambique Liberation Front). Though both Amin and Museveni emerged as professional organizers of violence, their approach to violence was radically different.

Recruited as a child soldier in the British colonial army, Amin was trained in methods of counterinsurgency in a variety of campaigns, mainly against anti-colonial Mau Mau guerrillas in the White Highlands in Kenya and nomadic populations of northern Uganda and Kenya. Counterinsurgency was a clinical name for unleashing state terror. Museveni saw himself as a lifelong devotee of violence, a "professional revolutionary." Characteristic of our generation of radical scholars, Museveni embraced violence as central to the politics of emancipation. His guiding star was Frantz Fanon, the Martinican revolutionary theorist who had joined the Algerian national liberation struggle led by the Algerian National Liberation Front, and written *The Wretched of the Earth,* the manifesto of the postcolonial African Left intellectuals. The book was both a call to arms and a cautionary warning about the pitfalls of national consciousness.

From as early as his student days at the University of Dar es Salaam, Museveni wrote about violence with missionary fervor. In his undergraduate thesis "Fanon's Theory of Violence," Museveni eulogized Fanon's embrace of violence as "the highest form of political struggle," necessary "to bring about total and authentic decolonization."[2] The "armed struggle" that brought him to the seat of the presidency of Uganda was the five-year-long bush war in the Luwero Triangle, an area with an ethnically mixed population, mostly consisting of Baganda and Banyarwanda (both ethnically Bantu), as well as other northerners. For Fanon, the purpose of revolutionary violence was to defend the people against settler violence. When and how Museveni saw violence as a state-making project and not just an anti-state project—as an end in itself, moving away from a "problematique" formulated by Frantz Fanon to one associated with Georges Sorel—is an issue I have grappled with in this book.

During the five-year bush war against Obote from 1981 to 1986, the Front for National Salvation (FRONASA) joined with the Uganda Freedom Fighters, a group led by Yusufu Lule, and morphed into the National Resistance Army (NRA). Once it took control of the capital city, Kampala, the NRA organized a "broad base" among parties in the south, and unleashed a massive campaign of retaliation, massacre, and plunder as it followed the retreating state army up north. What seemed to be calculated revenge at the outset turned into more of a colonial-type war over two decades from 1986 to 2005. At its heart was the forced internment of over 90 percent of the Acholi, a Luo-speaking ethnic group from northern Uganda, in concentrated and enclosed camps, and of many in the adjoining areas of Lango in northern Uganda and Teso in the east. If comparisons can be made, this protracted humiliation, brutalization, and expropriation of a people was much worse than the violence Amin soldiers had meted out in the barracks in 1971, or anything experienced by Ugandan Asians in 1972. But, whereas the British propaganda machine turned Amin into a monster and Asians his global victims, Museveni became a Washington poster boy. Even when the UN's Under-Secretary-General for Humanitarian Affairs, Jan

Egeland, was horrified by what he witnessed in the camps in northern Uganda in December 2003, describing them as "one of the worst humanitarian situations in the world . . . worse than Iraq," few in the human rights industry stirred. Instead, the "international community" conferred impunity on Museveni and protected him from being branded a perpetrator. They assumed that when it came to the War on Terror—which they supported without qualification—there could only be one set of perpetrators, all on the same side.

Both the Amin and the Museveni governments reorganized the state's armed forces with their eyes set on fighting enemies rather than ensuring civic law and order. In the process, they turned to the army to manage public order, pitting sections of the army against the police. Under the Amin regime, the Public Safety Unit (PSU) and the military police lorded it over other police; under Museveni, a number of military generals—Edward Katumba Wamala, Edward Kale Kayihura, and Geoffrey Katsigazi Tumusiime—were made superintendents of police, and military units were integrated into the police. Both regimes were known for targeting prominent public figures who were said to have "disappeared" under Amin and been "poisoned" under Museveni.

However, Amin's relationship to state violence differed from that of Museveni. Amin appointed the postwar world's first truth commission. It deserves our attention for one reason. Unlike other truth commissions, which focus on the actions of previous governments or eras, the focus of Amin's commission on "disappearances" was limited to his own regime, and the commission was tasked with suggesting reforms that would address this problem. Museveni, on the other hand, appointed a truth commission at the start of his rule, with its scope limited to pre-Museveni regimes. Despite a growing public outcry against illegally authorized violence by state forces, Museveni never appointed a commission to look into the use of such violence under his own regime, let alone acknowledge the problem publicly.

Expulsions

Amin carried out three expulsions—of Israelis, Asians, and British—in 1972, his second year in power. We have looked at each in detail. Amin saw the first expulsion, of Israelis, as necessary for the very survival of his regime, since nearly a third of the army had fled into exile with Obote and many of them were now in training camps in Sudan and Tanzania. But when he turned to Israel, and then to Britain, for military hardware to nip this threat in the bud, not only were his pleas ignored but he was humiliated, treated like a child who needed attention and given candy. The Israeli expulsion was a final act in a swap mediated by Libya's Muammar Gaddafi between Gaafar Nimeiry, Sudan's president, and Idi Amin. Amin persuaded the South Sudan rebels (the Anyanya) to sign the 1972 Addis Ababa Agreement and, in return, Nimeiry closed Obote's training camps in Sudan. The Anyanya dissolved after the agreement: roughly half joined the Sudan state army, whereas the rest were integrated into Amin's army, and the expulsion of Israelis followed. Amin told Ugandans and the rest of the world that this was part of a wider struggle against Zionism and imperialism.

Amin came to see himself as a messiah called upon to ensure true independence for Uganda. He said Uganda was a country of Black people and it was only right that Black people take control of the country. This was the vision he had inherited from Ama Aate, his mother. This was also the vision he shared with his brother-in-law, Wanume Kibedi, his foreign minister, and the "brother president" of Libya, Muammar Gaddafi. It was this vision that Amin pursued to the end. After Amin expelled Asians as a British colonial asset and their postcolonial responsibility, his next target was Great Britain: Amin forced Britain to accept responsibility for Asians—of whatever nationality. Britain would respond by treating all Asians, whether or not they held British passports, as "refugees." This casual gesture disenfranchised Asians with British nationality, but it was applauded by "the international community" as a grand "humanitarian" commitment.

The expulsion had two faces. Claiming to rid Uganda of any vestiges of British colonialism, Amin presented the Asian expulsion as a decolonizing move, the opening phase in "the economic war," meant to end the domination of the country by a nonnational minority. Amin said this would be the first step to redistributing their property to the nation of "Black Ugandans" and setting the country on the road to liberation. But that was not to be. Amin's vision began with a large-scale expropriation of Asians. The "economic war" had begun spectacularly, by shattering to smithereens the dome of privilege baked in the colonial oven. This was followed by privatization, creating a class of wealthy Black residents known to ordinary people as the "*mafuta mingi,*" those dripping with much fat. Thus began the era of wealth creation whereby expropriated wealth was distributed to individuals with direct connections to the state.

Organized elites such as Baganda landlords and their merchant offsprings, as well as northern military officers around Amin, gave enthusiastic support to the "economic war."[3] The former had economic clout and management skills, but the latter held the gun. They would come to dominate the committees in charge of distributing Asian properties, but they lacked the organizational and managerial skills to run a modern economy. A struggle ensued between the new military elite and the old civilian one, punctuated by the killing of prominent Baganda, such as of the wealthy entrepreneur Michael Kawalya Kaggwa, when he was burned to death trapped inside his Mercedes-Benz. Amin promised the UN Secretary-General there would be no nationalization of Asian property. Instead, it would be and was privatized. The "economic war" turned into a neoliberal jamboree with army officers as its main beneficiaries.

The promise to create a land of opportunity would become mired in a swamp of sharp business practices, leading to commodity scarcities and rising prices. It was a world about which neither Amin nor his officers knew much. Bewildered, Amin would only make sense of it as the rebirth of "Black Asians." In a cruel twist of fate, many of the beneficiaries of the "economic war" would later be hauled before "economic war tribunals" and charged with "economic crimes."

In 1986, Museveni had big aspirations—"national liberation" and "Pan-Africanism"—but not the resources to realize them. The Americans put the noose around him, and seemed bent on tightening it. What was he to do? As the terrain of battle changed, from the military to the economic, Museveni, too, found himself, as had Amin, on unfamiliar turf. His repeated lament "I have no cadres" expressed this impossible situation. Museveni took the easier route. Unlike Amin, who kept his eye on the goal, Museveni looked to change goal posts. Instead of a Mao-style long march through wilderness as he marshalled resources bit by bit, he looked for a quick fix, embracing the package of neoliberal reforms known as the Washington Consensus (Structural Adjustment). Instead of explaining this as a tactical retreat necessitated by difficult circumstances, he claimed to have discovered a new truth. Like Saul on the road to Damascus, a biblical story he was fond of referencing repeatedly, this son of evangelical born-again Christians would swallow each new truth with the enthusiasm of a convert. Leading a population tired of war and yearning for peace, Museveni would turn the promise of "national liberation" into a wholesale national capitulation.

At the heart of this capitulation was privatization of state assets, from financial institutions to industries. Privatization would provide many opportunities for crass accumulation by the leader's family and its coterie of followers.

Amin had called for a nation of "Black millionaires" but without seeking to become one himself. In contrast, Museveni and his family proudly led the new *mafuta mingi.* Others followed, accumulating wealth by means fair and foul. Washington applauded the regime for having risen from the ashes and achieved one of the highest growth rates of any African economy in a decade. But the figures did not tell the whole story, which was made up of two contradictory developments: growth of an enriched minority alongside an increasingly impoverished majority. Rates of monetization grew as peasants were forced to meet emergencies by selling their assets—from land to food crops—as a survival strategy in the face of impoverishment. State and International Monetary Fund statistics pooled together both mass impoverishment and the enrichment of the new *mafuta mingi* into a single statistic: rates of economic activity known as growth. This figure combined two rapid but contradictory developments, enrichment and impoverishment. Figures highlighted growth in the monetary economy, but not necessarily in people's livelihoods. Punch-drunk with World Bank–inspired rhetoric, Museveni would tell an astounded but by now numbed audience at a public rally in Kampala in 2022—and in subsequent rallies—that there was nothing wrong with official corruption so long as its beneficiaries kept the loot within the country.[4] The fire-breathing young revolutionary would settle into old age respectability after nearly four decades in power. Theft would become society.

A similar perverse outcome disfigured the regime's "Pan-Africanism." Starting with the Rwandan Patriot Front's (RPF) invasion of Rwanda whereby the regime exported its internal crisis to its neighbor, Pan-Africanism ceased to be an anti-imperialist rallying cry. Instead, it turned into a rhetorical banner waved by an army that mounted one invasion after another—from Rwanda to Somalia, from South Sudan to eastern Congo, even the Central African Republic—in the service of and with the blessing of empire. The African Union hailed this turn, of doing the empire's dirty work with less cost and great efficiency, as providing "African solutions for African problems" still financed by the empire. The costs were high and the outcome grim, from the genocide in Rwanda to successive massacres in eastern Congo. Decades ago, Ali Mazrui had called on African leaders to give up the rhetoric of national independence and use their armies to put out flames of civil war in countries like the Democratic Republic of Congo. He was then lambasted by many African scholars, including the Nigerian Nobel Prize winner Wole Soyinka, for seeking to undermine Africa's hard-won sovereignty. Museveni would now lead the way, with hardly a critical note from the same scholars.

Museveni had learned from failure. The invasion of Uganda in the thick of the 1972 expulsion had been a disaster. The promise to Tanzania's first president, Julius Nyerere, that Uganda was ripe for revolution and that FRONASA would lead it turned out to be an empty boast, even a hoax. From then on, Museveni would look for a patron—first Tanzania, then Washington—rather than go it alone. The result was a state project joining nationalism to neoliberalism, becoming the West's golden boy, a junior version of Israel that enjoyed the license to dish out violence indiscriminately and with impunity, both in the region and at home—always, of course, within reason. But, I ask, has it been worth it? Karl Marx says in *The Eighteenth Brumaire* that all important events in history, as it were, happen twice, the first time as tragedy, the second time as farce. If the redistribution of Asian properties after expulsion turned into a tragedy for Amin, Museveni enacted a farce following his reconciliation with the United States.

Politics

The main difference between Amin and Museveni lay in their politics. Amin created the Ugandan nation, though he racialized it. Museveni dismantled the nation Amin had built, but without deracializing it. He invited Asians to return, but as "investors" and not "citizens." Amin brought peace to the nation after an interlude of infighting. Museveni ushered in a period of stability, but followed it with a period of disorder in large parts of the country—not only the North but also the South. Amin was opposed to tribalization. Museveni embraced tribalization as both an instrument of rule and as a consequence of indirect rule, another "tactical" ploy to prolong his stay in power.

For both Amin and Museveni, the army became a substitute for a political organization. Afraid that political organization would provide ground for factions to stabilize themselves, Museveni refused to build one. In both cases, the result was similar. Those who followed Amin could neither define nor defend nor build on his legacy. Museveni is likely to leave behind a similar predicament for his followers. If the Baganda heralded Amin for removing Obote, they are likely to welcome the demise of Museveni despite his claim to have rescued them from the clutches of Obote.

Amin was brought to power by Britain and Israel, and was widely seen by his peers as an imperialist stooge. The moment he realized he was expected to be grateful for his new station in life, to celebrate his place under the imperial sun and to govern as a grateful stooge, Amin turned his back on his erstwhile sponsors, and began to push for something different. Museveni, on the other hand, came to power without direct support from imperial centers. But, once in power, flummoxed by the lack of resources and sanctioned by American power, he succumbed to their demands. Unlike Amin, who refused to govern as a grateful stooge, Museveni comfortably settled into that role.

Also unlike Amin, Museveni began with an anti-imperialist rallying cry. His moment of glory was in the Luwero Triangle, where he put in place a mode of governance based on Resistance Committees, dismantling the regime of "indirect rule" by treating locals and migrants as equals—that is, as residents. But Museveni never understood the theoretical or strategic significance of what he had achieved in Luwero. Like most things that he did, good or bad, he confused strategy as tactics and tactics as strategy. For him, Luwero had been no more than a stepping stone to power. He remained uninterested in drawing lessons from the experience of Luwero, never recognizing the lasting value of what the NRA had achieved there, crystallized in the mode of organization (the Resistance Committee system) they had pioneered in Luwero. His formal repudiation of the lessons of Luwero was inscribed in the 1995 Constitution. This was his moment of surrender to local reaction in Buganda.

Every tactical innovation Museveni introduced, or embraced, after 1995 turned out to be a Pyrrhic victory. Whether he "won" an election, or managed to revise the constitution to prolong his stay in power, he paid a price. Each "victory" generated more cynicism than celebration. To ensure the continued subservience of the population, the regime upped both the level of corruption and of violence. The price kept rising with each "victory." As he tightened his grip over the country, Museveni looked for opportunities to make his army and himself indispensable to the service of "the international community," the code name for big powers.

The Road to Reform

The Museveni era has corroded the morals of an entire generation, and there is unlikely to be an easy solution to the problem. An all-pervasive corruption and cynicism clouds the country like a fog. It will take no less than a generation for the country to come out of it, to nurture a political culture that can provide an effective antidote.

Corruption has in fact become so rampant that the existing vocabulary can no longer capture it. A regime insider told me, "We are beyond corruption, which is usually discrete. Our public posture is now more that of prostitutes, who display their wares in public, for all the world to know these are for sale to the highest bidder." If Amin organized theft without corruption, today there is no line between theft and corruption as we witness the level of devastation of an entire society. The consequences are immense. Unlike Amin, Museveni has no social base. The regime has clients, but hardly any followers. It is an argument that it is possible to rule without followers.

A political culture produced by the lethal combination of widespread violence, deep-seated corruption, and an ever-fragmenting population cannot be replaced with a mere change of leadership, or of constitutions. Old habits die hard. Rather than reforming existing political practices, new constitutions and the new safeguards they promise are more likely to appear as paper promises. They cannot give the country a pain-free reform. New constitutions do not produce new political cultures, which are more likely to take a generation to change.

Besides institutionalized corruption and state repression, the colonial power introduced a political culture based on a political fiction, that the communities they conquered had long lived as isolated "tribes," each in their own "homelands." When it built colonial Uganda as home to a collection of tribes, it claimed to respect and reproduce this tradition. In reality, colonialism turned the precolonial legacy inside out, changing an assimilationist political culture into a segregationist one. It undermined a historical practice of integrating "migrants" with "indigenes," and replaced it with a convention that turned "migrants" into "non-indigenes" who were permanently excluded from political society. Neighbors became strangers. Immigrants became outsiders. This claim had informed the 1962 Constitution, which sanctioned two forms of discrimination: one based on race ("affirmative action"), the other on tribe ("customary rights" of indigenes). With this classification, even many of those born in the country were presumed to be strangers or guests entitled to no more than a conditional welcome.

Whether large or small, precolonial political communities had been open to immigrants, whether voluntary or forced. While it is true that Uganda did not exist as a single political community before colonialism, no local society made a rigid distinction between historical and nonhistorical members. The political community we know as Uganda today was produced by conquest. Is it possible to transform the basis of this political community from conquest to consent?

At the time of colonization, Uganda was a collection of separate autonomous communities in both a political and cultural sense. Each of its components had its own system of decision making and adjudicating conflicts, its own rules for admission of adults into the existing political community, and its own education designed to incubate the young. The introduction of three colonial institutions destroyed the autonomy of these communities: a hierarchal system of administration emulating Buganda's monarchical structure; a rule of law that blended a British system of hierarchical courts with subordinate "customary" courts; and an English language–based, missionary-dominated education system designed to create a new elite among the colonized. Crosscutting these "traditional" societies was an enduring system of migrant labor that provided cheap wage labor for the modern economy (plantations, factories, market-based rich peasant production) and for repressive institutions of the modern colonial state (army, police, prisons). In sum, colonial Uganda became a single polity but remained a multicultural society governed through a colonially sanctioned notion of "custom" that turned each cultural community ("tribe") into an administrative district and divided the population into two separate groups—"indigenes" and "migrants"—each subject to a different disciplinary regime.

In this setup, all "migrants" were defined as minorities, and all were targeted as such at one time or another. Migrants were subdivided racially at independence. Asians, most of whom had no passport, were presumed to continue their colonial status as "British" subjects, who were required to apply for Ugandan citizenship, and at the same time renounce their presumed "right" to a British passport, should they wish to be part of the new Ugandan political community. This difference separated them from the resident "African" population, who were not presumed to be British subjects at independence. Obote's 1967 expulsion of all "Africans" who had originated from outside only reinforced this logic; Amin's expulsion of Asians in 1972 was a culmination of this logic. Museveni's 1995 Constitution created a statutory list of "indigenous" tribes. Though subject to revision over time, it excluded all "non-indigenous" residents of Uganda from a birthright to Ugandan citizenship.

If the first privatization under Amin had liquidated Ugandan Asians, the second privatization under Museveni ushered their reentry into the economy, this time not as citizens, but as "investors." It set them up as likely targets of an anticipated storm in the aftermath of another failed project. If the first privatization under Amin was demonized by the "international community" as a rule of savages, the same "international community" applauded the second privatization as evidence of a capacity to reform—feting, garlanding, and welcoming the leadership of the Museveni regime into the civilized community of nations.

Amin first, and then Museveni, turned to nativist notions to build a political community, with a nuanced difference. For Amin, the political community was race-based. For Museveni, it would be narrower—not just racial, but also tribal.

Museveni enthroned the colonial notion of indigeneity as political identity in the 1995 Constitution. He also restored the monarchy, albeit as a "cultural institution," and returned *mailo* land to those on whom the British had bequested them—without any popular consultation. By contrast, Amin's most ambitious initiatives—both the Asian expulsion of 1972 and the appointment of the 1974–1975 Commission of Inquiry to restore the supremacy of civil institutions—responded to popular demand and made room for popular participation.

How could Amin, who had come to power with the support of Israel and Britain, go on to expel these same powers—and local Asians—and still persist as leader? Furthermore, how could Amin, brought to the presidency through a foreign-supported coup, survive both the 1972 external invasion and an externally supported coup in 1974, and then again in 1975?

Amin's coup to remove Obote in 1971 would earn him a popular base in the south of the country, particularly among the Baganda; and the Asian expulsion would consolidate this base, which he never lost. Amin did not fall because of a narrowing of his civilian base; he fell because of the widening rift inside his army between, on the one hand, its Nubi and Kakwa/West Nile sections who had made the 1971 coup, and, on the other, the section of the army that would be drawn from South Sudan after the Addis Ababa Agreement of 1972.

In spite of inheriting empty state coffers, Museveni would begin with political capital he had accumulated over a decade in the Luwero Triangle (1981–1986). It would take him less than a decade to squander this capital as he developed a new colonial-style model of rule. That model threw overboard lessons of Luwero that had treated locals and migrants as political equals in village-level Resistance Committees, which would forge alliances between locals and migrants. Once in power, in a startling turnaround, the same NRA would resurrect an extreme version of the colonial "indirect rule" model—this time stretched to entrench indigeneity as a birthright for citizenship—in the 1995 Constitution. The National Resistance Movement (NRM), the ruling party in Uganda since 1986, would combine this constitutional innovation with a legislative program to multiply administrative districts and kingdoms, while at the same time introducing reserved seats for women at all levels of governance. The project had been designed to fragment the population to the maximum, but it faced stiff opposition in Buganda, a powerful kingdom comprising the largest region in the country.

Buganda

Throughout this book, I have asserted the centrality of Buganda in shaping Ugandan politics, for better or worse, starting with the alliance between British colonialism and Protestant Baganda chiefs at the outset of the colonial period. The terms of this alliance were embedded in the 1900 agreement, whereby Britain granted a total of eight thousand square miles to one thousand landlords, the size of their individual estates corresponding to their position in the social hierarchy. As commander of the army, Amin had inherited the eternal opposition of the Baganda landed aristocracy and their kabaka (king) when he led the assault on the kingdom headquarters in Mengo in 1966. It is a testimony to Amin's political astuteness that he was able to reverse this liability over the short period of a half decade.

An Asian commercial class had been a predominant feature of the market economy in the whole of East Africa—not just in Uganda, but also in Kenya and Tanzania. Why, then, was the Asian expulsion limited to Uganda? Many have suggested that it was uniquely Amin's undertaking. I find this claim wanting. The proposal to register Asians was discussed as early as the Obote period, before Amin came to power. Only in Uganda did there exist an indigenous entrepreneurial class with sufficient historical depth and experience to challenge and displace the class of Asian entrepreneurs. This indigenous class had its origin in the 1900 land agreement. The Baganda landlords who had since moved into commerce, and some into manufacturing in later decades, were already beginning to challenge the commercial supremacy of Asian business during the interwar period. By contrast, the development of an African entrepreneurial class in Kenya and Tanzania was mainly a post–World War II phenomenon. To imagine a Uganda without an Asian presence was more realistic in Buganda than anywhere else in East Africa.

To appreciate this fact is also to acknowledge Amin's "mistake" in the aftermath of the expropriation of Asian property. Baganda entrepreneurs were best qualified to manage these properties, but army officers, though least qualified for the job, turned out to be the main beneficiaries when these properties were distributed. Those who have considered Amin and his regime a curse that befell Uganda have focused on the inept running of the economy after Amin's expulsion of Asians. Rather than look to politics, they have looked for an answer in race, starting with Amin, and then the Black nation he spoke for.

Amin did not just seek to passively "represent" the interests of the Baganda elite. While developing an alliance with them, he avoided becoming their instrument. When necessary, Amin reined them in. Several instances support this assertion. Key to forging an alliance with the Baganda—not just the minority of entrepreneurs—was the expulsion of the Asian entrepreneurial class in 1972. So strong was the bond between Amin and the Baganda elite that it withstood several assaults on Baganda interests. The first was on the morrow of the 1971 coup. Then, Amin played up to the Baganda landed elite by bringing the kabaka's body home for burial; but at the same time, he buried any ideas of resuscitating either kingship or kingdom in Buganda. The second was when Amin decided to expel the British in the wake of the Asian expulsion, showing scant regard for their landlord protégés in Buganda. In a third hit, Amin clipped the wings of the landed gentry in Buganda in 1975, when he nationalized all land in the country, including *mailo* land in Buganda. Amin's singular internal success was to retain broad support of ordinary Baganda throughout his rule.

Museveni's singular political failure has been his inability to cultivate support among the Baganda, in spite of having overthrown Obote. This could not have been for lack of trying since Museveni went out of his way to woo the royal house of Buganda. In the latter days of the war in Luwero, he brought Prince Mutebi, the heir apparent in Buganda, to Luwero. In a joint address to peasants, Museveni, unlike Amin, is said to have promised to restore kabakaship in Buganda when in charge of the country. To those in the NRA leadership, especially its Baganda members, who were startled by this proclamation, he promised that this restoration would be cultural, not political. He went on to distinguish between two kinds of kingships—cultural and political—claiming that culture was every person's birthright. But Museveni politicized culture. Unlike Amin, he ended up restoring both the king and the kingdom as political institutions.

Disillusioned, many of the leading members of the NRA drifted away. Among these was Serwanga Lwanga, a colonel in the NRA bush war. Slowly, Museveni removed one restraint after another, put in place by Amin to curb the ambitions of the Baganda landed elite. As part of the adoption of the 1995 Constitution, he made three critical concessions: First, Museveni reversed the nationalization of land by Amin and restored the *mailo* land grants given to chiefs by the British. Second, in the 1995 Constitution, Museveni institutionalized the difference between two kinds of citizens, indigenous and immigrant, making the first a citizen by birth and the second a citizen at the pleasure of the state. In doing so, he acceded to a key demand of Baganda royalists on the question of political identity. And, third, Museveni restored kingship.

Every concession was said to be a tactical necessity. But as tactical retreats accumulated, their significance became strategic, making for a radically different style of governance. The end result was that Museveni was unable to drive a wedge between the Baganda elite (*baami*) and their tenants (*bakopi*), without which he could not reform land relations in Buganda. The Baganda elite were able to point to land seizures by the NRA in the North as a warning to Baganda peasants of their likely fate should they be tempted to take seriously the promises of the Museveni regime that it would likely guarantee them security of tenure. When it came to the land question in Buganda, Museveni was checkmated.

Museveni moved the battlefront from land to local administration (governance), attempting to fragment Buganda into many districts so the central government could deal separately with each. In response, the elite around the kabaka named after the kingdom's capitol—known as Mengo—called on peasants to rally against the impending partition of Buganda to defend both the institution of the kabaka and the integrity of the kingdom. The popular agitation that followed, culminating in the Buganda riots of 2009, targeted non-Baganda in Buganda. With it, the politics of indigeneity exploded. Museveni embraced it over the next decade.

Uganda after Museveni

Uganda has had two major political successions since independence in 1962. Both have been engineered by soldiers: the first was Amin overthrowing Obote in 1971; the second, the NRA's displacement of Obote's second regime (and the Lutwa extension) in 1985–1986. Each resulted from a split in the army. Both were testimony to the failure of the regime in office to forge a durable citizenship by building a common political community. Uganda is not a solitary case. In the 2020s, civil peace in Uganda's two neighboring states—Ethiopia first, and now Sudan—has been undermined by civil wars triggered by factions in the army. We cannot rule out yet another split in the Ugandan army. Is there an antidote?

And who will rule after Museveni? At first sight, there seem to be a few possibilities: Rule may come from within the NRM, though it lacks any durable structure—from charismatic individuals, initially Kizza Besigye; or, since 2019, Robert Kyagulanyi (Bobi Wine), both of whom have registered impressive election-time mobilizations against Museveni; or from longtime regional opposition based in Buganda.

Buganda is the heart of the opposition. It is also likely to provide the answer to the question, Who will lead Uganda after Museveni? One contender is the Baganda landlord-commercial class mobilized around the person of the kabaka. Will Buganda turn inward, as has been its customary response at times of crisis, or will it open up to the rest of the country and take on the challenge to provide national leadership? Will there be a second Asian expulsion? The possibility is raised by Baganda scholar-activists such as the historian Samwiri Lwanga-Lunyiigo in his book *Uganda: An Indian Colony.*

Our challenge is to look for an antidote to this long colonial legacy. Where do we begin? We begin with the primacy of the political. What is an adequate political roof for a multicultural mix? I have suggested a federal roof with a common citizenship, so that membership in each of the federated units is derived from common residence, and not from separate cultural identities based on birth. The ongoing debate in Buganda between two alternatives—*federo* (which accents indigeneity and ethnicity) versus *federation* (with its accent on common residence)—provides a useful framework for our starting point. *Federo* freezes the cultural identity of each unit in the period before colonialism, but ignores subsequent changes. It turns migration into a politically salient fact. It thus equates cultural identity with political identity. *Federo* is thus conceived at the expense of migrants, especially those who moved during the colonial period and after, setting up colonial and postcolonial migrants as adversaries of "indigenes." By contrast, *federation* bases the notion of political belonging on where one lives, rather than where one came from. By making residence—rather than "indigeneity"—the basis of political identity, *federation* makes for a more elastic understanding of political community.

The political community the British pieced together as Uganda was marked by state-enforced violence, institutionalized corruption, and fragmentation into politicized cultural (tribal) identities. I have suggested political reform as the first step to reverse this corrosive mix: a federal arrangement that can reverse Museveni's political project to fragment the entire country into tribalized districts, each divided into indigenes and migrants, one a majority and the other a minority, creating two polarized and permanent political identities unable to come together around a common political project. It is this ongoing fragmentation of the country, reinforced by state-sponsored violence and institutionalized corruption, that is the "slow poison" gradually but surely eating away at the political fabric of the country.

In closing this book, we ask: What lessons can we draw for intellectuals and academics on the margins of corridors of powers? What does it mean to be in conversation with those who are or will be in power and at the same time keep a "safe distance" from power? Can one engage power without being corrupted by it? How can we learn to live with "dirty hands"? There is no single answer, no one textbook solution in the range of alternatives between saint and sinner. For now at least, we explore for an answer in the realm of practice.

Notes

Acknowledgments

Index

Notes

1. IDI AMIN: THE PARENTAL HERITAGE

1. Abudul Mahajubu, "Identity, Indigeneity and Citizenship: The Nubi Ethnic Minority in Uganda" (PhD diss., Makerere University, 2021).

2. Mahajubu, "Identity, Indigeneity and Citizenship," 39.

3. Omari H. Kokole, "The 'Nubians' of East Africa: Muslim Club or African 'Tribe'? The View from Within," *Institute of Muslim Minority Affairs Journal* 6, no. 2 (1985): 420–448.

4. Bernd Heine, *The Nubi Language of Kibera: An Arabic Creole* (Berlin: Dietrich Reimer, 1982).

5. Douglas H. Johnson, *The Root Causes of Sudan's Civil Wars* (Kampala: Fountain, 2003), 83.

6. These were Brigadier Shaban Opolot, an Etesot from Teso district; his deputy, Idi Amin; the commanding officer of the 1st Battalion, Lieutenant-Colonel Juma Musa, who had a Lugbara father and a Munyoro mother; and commander of the 2nd Battalion, Lieutenant-Colonel Suleiman Hussein, a Nubi Alur. Kokole, "The 'Nubians' of East Africa," 431. In 1971, when Obote was in Singapore, three administrators—all Nubi—had planned to arrest Amin before Obote's return: Juma Musa, the then Air Force chief of staff; Suleiman Hussein, the Army chief of staff; and Suleiman Dusman, the chief police constable of Buganda. Similarly, Brigadier Charles Arube, Amin's first chief of staff of the Armed Forces and a Roman Catholic Kakwa, who was one of the four coup leaders in April 1974, was fluent in Kinubi. Kokole, "The 'Nubians' of East Africa," 432. See also L. M. Passmore Sanderson and Neville Sanderson, *Education, Religion and Politics in South Sudan 1899–1964* (Khartoum: Khartoum University Press, 1981), 85, 136; cited in Douglas H. Johnson, "The Structure of a Legacy: Military Slavery in Northeast Africa," *Ethnohistory* 36, no. 1 (1989): 72–88, at 82.

7. Samuel White Baker, *Ismaili'a* (London: Macmillan and Co., 1874), 2:242, cited in Amii Omara-Otunnu, *Politics and the Military in Uganda 1890–1985* (New York: Palgrave Macmillan, 1987), 14.

8. C. H. Stigand, *Equatoria: The Lado Enclave* (1923; London: Cass, 1968), 165–166.

9. Kokole, "The 'Nubians' of East Africa," 443–444.

10. Omara-Otunnu, *Politics and the Military in Uganda,* 14–15.

11. Frederick D. Lugard, *The Rise of Our East African Empire,* 2 vols. (Edinburgh: William Blackwood & Sons, 1893), 2:134; Omara-Otunnu, *Politics and the Military in Uganda,* 15, 17, 21.

12. Stigand, *Equatoria.*

13. Samwiri Karugire, *A Political History of Uganda* (Nairobi: Heinemann, 1980), 116.

14. Mahajubu, "Identity, Indigeneity and Citizenship," 69.

15. Mahajubu, "Identity, Indigeneity and Citizenship," 59, 60.

16. Judith Listowel, *Amin* (Dublin: IUP, 1973), 14–15.

17. I interviewed Jaffar Amin in Kampala several times between 2018 and 2020. After that, he sent me his biography of his father. Unpublished, this typed manuscript runs over six hundred pages. Often repetitive, it is a mix of fact and fable. I have used and cited it to fill in gaps in Idi Amin's life story, but also used it whenever it offers an alternative account of key events. Jaffar Amin and Margaret Akulia, "Idi Amin: Hero or Villain; His Son Jaffar Amin and Other People Speak" (manuscript, Kampala, 2010), 68.

18. J. Amin and M. Akulia, "Idi Amin," 68.

19. Mahajubu, "Identity, Indigeneity and Citizenship," 7.

20. J. Amin and Akulia, "Idi Amin," 82–84.

21. J. Amin and Akulia, "Idi Amin," 49–52.

22. Iain Grahame, *Amin and Uganda: A Personal Memoir* (London: Granada, 1980), 134.

23. Ronny Bai supplied Jaffar Amin with the conscription numbers of the three: N-14610/Idi Amin Dada-Kakwa/Lugbara; N-14611/Ozo-Ayiyu of Jiako Village; and N-14612/Ronny Bai-Kakwa, cited in J. Amin and Akulia, "Idi Amin," 88–90.

24. J. Amin and Akulia, "Idi Amin," 93.

25. Listowel, *Amin,* 20.

26. J. Amin and Akulia, "Idi Amin," 93.

27. J. Amin and Akulia, "Idi Amin," 119–120.

28. Listowel, *Amin,* 22.

29. Listowel, *Amin,* 177.

30. Listowel, *Amin,* 23.

31. J. Amin and Akulia, "Idi Amin," 107–108.

32. J. Amin and Akulia, "Idi Amin," 113.

33. Listowel, *Amin,* 141.

34. Listowel, *Amin,* 27.

35. Grahame, *Amin and Uganda,* 19.

2. GOOD ASIAN, BAD ASIAN

1. Mahmood Mamdani, "The Sidis: An Introduction," in Ketaki Sheth, *A Certain Grace: The Sidi, Indians of African Descent* (New Delhi: Photoink, 2013).

3. THE BREAK WITH ISRAEL

1. Judith Listowel, *Amin* (Dublin: IUP, 1973), 30–41.

2. Listowel, *Amin,* 29.

3. Arye Oded, "Israeli-Ugandan Relations at the Time of Amin," *Jewish Political Studies Review* 18, nos. 3–4 (Fall 2006): 65–79, at 66.

4. "Uganda: Who Put Gen. Idi Amin in Power?," *The Monitor* (Kampala), March 31, 2002, excerpted in *The Foundation of Life* (Kampala: Monitor Press, 2009); https://allafrica.com/stories/200203310131.html.

5. Oded, "Israeli-Ugandan Relations," 68.

6. Helen Epstein, "Idi Amin's Israeli Connection," *New Yorker,* June 27, 2016.

7. "Uganda: Who Put Gen. Idi Amin in Power?"

8. The barter deal involved two separate transactions: the sale of gold and other valuables, with at least some of the proceeds deposited in Amin's account in Uganda; and the purchase and distribution of arms bought using funds in this account. As knowledge of bank deposits became public, it fueled the parliamentary squabble between the Obote and the Kabaka-allied factions in parliament, followed by an inquiry conducted by three East African judges. The Inquiry concluded that both Obote and Amin were innocent of charges of corruption.

9. Norman S. Mivambo, *Black Star News,* July 30, 2006 (accessed April 4, 2022).

10. Jaffar Amin and Margaret Akulia, "Idi Amin: Hero or Villain; His Son Jaffar Amin and Other People Speak," manuscript, Kampala, 2010, 165.

11. Oded, "Israeli-Ugandan Relations," 9, 10.

12. J. Amin and M. Akulia, "Idi Amin," 206–207.

13. North Koreans were involved in setting up a bullet munitions factory in Nakasongola.

14. *Times* (London), February 24, 1972, cited in Oded, "Israeli-Ugandan Relations," 72.

15. According to Jaffar Amin, his father received a telegram from Col. Baruch Bailey at the Israeli embassy announcing the birth of twin boys to the agent he had met in Cairo. At the same time, Amin received photographs of the twins on a more or less regular basis from 1973 to 1978, in spite of the break in relations between Israel and the Amin regime during that period. J. Amin and M. Akulia, "Idi Amin," 208–209, 389.

16. Epstein, "Idi Amin's Israeli Connection."

17. J. Amin and M. Akulia, "Idi Amin," 215.

18. "Israelis Helped Amin to Topple Obote When He Turned Anti-Israeli," *Ha'aretz*, July 18, 1976.

19. Thomas James Lowman, "Beyond Idi Amin: Causes and Drivers of Political Violence in Uganda, 1971–1979" (PhD diss., Durham University, 2020), 42–43, http://ethesis.dur.ac.uk/13439/.

20. Lowman, "Beyond Idi Amin," 45–46, 72.

21. Lowman, "Beyond Idi Amin," 43.

22. "Uganda: Who Put Gen. Idi Amin in Power?"

23. Richard Dowden, "Revealed: How Israel Helped Amin to Take Power," *The Independent* (London), August 17, 2003.

24. Testimony of Macimino Ochen, Uganda Commission of Inquiry into Violations of Human Rights (1986), 10247, Uganda Human Rights Commission (UHRC), cited in Lowman, "Beyond Idi Amin," 26–27, 37–38, 67.

25. "Uganda: Who Put Gen. Idi Amin in Power?"

26. Lowman, "Beyond Idi Amin," 63.

27. Listowel, *Amin*, 79.

28. Aggrey Awori, former Minister of Information and Communications Technology in the Museveni government, interview with author, April 24, 2014, Kampala.

29. Minutes of the 5th Meeting of the Cabinet, March 5, 1971 (CT 1971), Minute 51, "16th Session of the OAU Council of Ministers, Addis Ababa, February 26, 1971," 20–25.

30. Minutes of the 32nd Meeting of the Cabinet of the 2nd Republic of Uganda, Tuesday, September 28, 1971, 10:00 AM, in the Cabinet Room in the West Wing of Parliamentary Buildings, Kampala, Minute 329 (CT 1971): "A Ten-Man Delegation to the Republic of South Africa," 12–13.

31. Listowel, *Amin*, 94.

32. *Davar*, October 15, 1972, and *Foreign Report of the Economist Intelligence Unit*, October 4, 1972, cited in Listowel, *Amin*, 94.

33. Listowel, *Amin*, 95–96.

34. Jaffar Amin, interview with author, March 4, 2020, Kampala.

35. Jaffar Amin, interview with author, March 4, 2020, Kampala.

36. Listowel, *Amin*, 133–134.

37. Listowel, *Amin*, 137, 142–143.

38. Minute 404 [CT 1972]: "Visit of HH Majesty King of Saudi Arabia," 31st Meeting of the Cabinet, November 17, 1972; "King Faisal of Saudi Arabia Visits Uganda," Reuters, record no. 189724, November 15, 1972, https://reuters.screenocean.com/record/189724.

4. THE ASIAN QUESTION

1. Constitution of the Republic of Uganda, September 8, 1967, Article 20 prohibited discrimination on grounds of "race, tribe, place of origin, political opinion, colour or creed" (3) except for the "application in the case of members of a particular race or tribe of customary law" (4(e)). https://www.worldstatesmen.org/Uganda-Const-1967.pdf.

According to the Constitution of Uganda, 1962, Article 74 (4), customary law "shall not apply to any person who is not an African." A similar exception appears in Article 75 (4). https://www.worldstatesmen.org/Uganda-const-1962.pdf.

2. The 1967 Constitution of Uganda, Article 20, introduced several provisions pertaining to grounds for positive discrimination (affirmative action), particularly concerning "land or other property" (4(f)), "privilege or advantage . . . reasonably justifiable in a democratic society" (4(g)), and "the employment of a proportion of African citizens of Uganda in any trade, business, profession or occupation" (4(h)).

3. Godfrey Asiimwe, "The Roots and Dynamics of the Indian Citizenship Question, Relations and Contestations in Uganda" (unpublished manuscript, Dept. of History, Makerere University, 2006), 5–6.

4. Constitution of Uganda, April 15, 1966, Chapter II ("Citizenship"), Article 12 (1), stated on the subject of "dual citizenship":

> Any person who upon the attainment of the age of twenty-one years, is a citizen of Uganda and [is] also a citizen of some other country other than Uganda [*sic*] shall, subject to the provisions of Clause 7 of this article, cease to be a citizen of Uganda on the specified date unless he has renounced his citizenship of that other country, taken the oath of allegiance and, in the case of a person who is a citizen of Uganda by virtue of clause (2) of article 7 or article 10 of this Constitution, made and registered such a declaration of his intentions concerning residence as may be prescribed by parliament.

5. Judith Listowel, *Amin* (Dublin: IUP, 1973), 112.

6. Republican Constitution of Uganda, 1966, Chapter II, Article 7, defined citizenship as a right of birth: "Every person born in Uganda, [who] is on 8th October 1962 [a] citizen of the U.K. or a British Protected Person, shall become a citizen of Uganda on 9th October, 1962." But then followed a clause that canceled this right for most of its Asian residents: "Provided that a person shall not become [a] citizen of Uganda by virtue of this clause if neither of his parents were born in Uganda." It was unlikely that at independence more than 5 percent of Asian residents of Uganda would have a parent born in Uganda. The 1967 Constitution enshrined the right to citizenship of an indigenous person defined as one born in Uganda of "whose parents or grandparents is or was a citizen of Uganda" (1967: 4 (1) (b))—(1962: 7 (1)).

7. J. B. Kakooza, "The Asian Ugandan Question," *Sunday Vision,* August 11, 2013.

8. Listowel, *Amin,* 114.

9. "The Asian Problem in East and Central Africa," January 9, 1973, Foreign and Commonwealth Office (FCO) 37: South Asia 37/1300, National Archives, Kew, UK, pp. 95–96, cited in Ian Sanjay Patel, *We're Here Because You Were There: Immigration and the End of Empire* (London: Verso, 2021), 225.

10. Application of immigration control to citizens of the UK and Colonies who do not belong to the UK, Home Office memorandum, September 20, 1967, p. 77, FCO 37: South Asia 37/19, National Archives, Kew, UK, cited in Patel, *We're Here,* 226.

11. James Read, "Some Legal Aspects of the Expulsion," in *Expulsion of a Minority: Essays on Ugandan Asians,* ed. Michael Twaddle (London: Athlone, 1975), 193.

12. Patel, *We're Here,* 253.

13. Kampala to FCO, September 15, 1972, FCO 50/404, National Archives, Kew, UK, p. 54; cited in Patel, *We're Here,* 253; Kindle p. 340.

14. Deb. Aug 7, 1972, vol. 842, cols. 1261, 1264, cited in Patel, *We're Here,* 250; Kindle p. 337.

15. Edward Heath, *The Course of My Life: My Autobiography* (London: Hudder and Stoughton, 1998), 457.

16. Cited in Patel, *We're Here,* 252.

17. Patel, *We're Here,* 272, 275.

18. "Diplomatic Offensive," September 28, 1972, FCO 31/1391, National Archives, Kew, UK, cited in Patel, *We're Here,* 97.

19. Yumiko Hamai, "'Imperial Burden' or 'Jews of Africa'? An Analysis of Political and Media Discourse in the Ugandan Asian Crisis (1972)," *Twentieth Century British History* 22, no. 3 (2011): 415–436, at 424.

20. UK Cabinet Papers; UK Mission, NY, to FCO, September 29, 1972, FCO 31/1391, National Archives, Kew, UK; "British Asians in Uganda: Background

Information to the Issue," Uganda Mission to the UN, September 28, 1972, FCO 31/1392, National Archives, Kew, UK, p. 132, cited in Patel, *We're Here,* 81.

21. Patel, *We're Here,* 270. In addition, there were those who had gone to India (1,500) and Pakistan (800).

22. Bob Astles, "Asians Plight and How British Diplomat Faked His Kidnap," *The Monitor* (Kampala), May 4, 2019.

23. Bernard Weinraub, "Briton in Uganda: A Tangled Drama," *New York Times,* August 10, 1970.

24. *The Times* (London) article [date unknown], cited in Bernard Weinraub, "Briton in Uganda: A Tangled Drama," *New York Times,* August 11, 1970; see also statement on Mr. Brian Lea by the Secretary of State for Foreign and Commonwealth Affairs, Mr. Michael Stewart, in Parliament, HC Deb. May 4, 1970, vol. 801, cc33-533.

25. On the Lea affair, see "Bob Astles Memoir," *The Monitor* (Kampala), May 4, 2019.

5. PRELUDE TO THE EXPULSION

1. Judith Listowel, *Amin* (Dublin: IUP, 1973), 108–109, 113. Listowel writes that the speech was transcribed by a white Kenyan settler who spoke excellent Kiswahili and who was present in the meeting.

2. Minutes of the 27th Meeting of the Cabinet . . . held on Thursday, 2nd September, 1971, Minute 278 [CT 1971]: "Promotions of Africans in Trade," pp. 10–17; Minute 280 [CT 1971]: "Census of Asians in Uganda," pp. 17–21.

3. And yet, according to Hasu Patel, a Ugandan Asian academic, "it was widely suggested during his last months in office that in a UK-Ugandan agreement Obote was prepared to discount technical irregularities in granting citizenship to Indians, particularly to the 12,000 who were reputed to have applied for citizenship but whose papers had been left unprocessed year after year." Hasu H. Patel, "General Amin and the Indian Exodus from Uganda," *Issue: A Journal of Opinion* 2, no. 4 (1972): 12–22, at 12.

4. Patel, "General Amin and the Indian Exodus," 13.

5. Listowel, *Amin,* 118–119.

6. Patel, "General Amin and the Indian Exodus," 15.

7. Vali Jamal, vali.jamal@yahoo.com, email communication on "Passing away of Mohinder Dhillon," March 10, 2020, at 11:32:18 PM GMT+3, sent to editors@awaazmagazine.com and many recipients.

8. Manzoor Moghal, *Idi Amin: Lion of Africa* (Central Milton Keynes, UK: Authorhouse, 2010), 72.

9. Listowel, *Amin*, 120–122.

10. Mark Leopold, *Idi Amin: The Story of Africa's Icon of Evil* (New Haven, CT: Yale University Press, 2020), Kindle, L4515, L4521, L4532; Kindle p. 230.

11. Ngũgĩ wa Thiong'o, "Asia in My Life," *Chimurenga*, July 21, 2012, https://chimurengachronic.co.za/asia-in-my-life.

12. Alfred Friendly, Jr., "Slick African Magazine Gains a Wide Following," New York Times, August 11, 1968, cited in Gerard McCann, "Rajat Neogy (1938–95)," from *East Africa's Global Lives*, part of the "Another World? East Africa and the Global World" project, funded by Leverhulme Trust, https://globaleastafrica.org/global-lives/rajat-neogy.

13. The same group that produced *Transition* also produced public debates on issues of public interest between government intellectuals and Makerere dons, in particular between Attorney-General Adoko Nekyon and Professor Ali Mazrui, at the clock tower in the city, outside the university campus. Rajat Neogy "was a key sponsor and behind-the-scenes organizer of the landmark 1962 Makerere Conference for African Writers of English Expression, which attracted renowned literary figures from America and the Caribbean such as Langston Hughes and Arthur Drayton," Dennis Brutus, and Nadine Gordimer from South Africa, to name a few. Neogy's wife, Barbara Lapchik, an American artist, went on to found and become the first director of the Nommo Art Gallery, which survives to this day in Kampala. McCann, "Rajat Neogy (1938–95)."

14. Paul Theroux, "Tarzan Is an Expatriate," *Transition* 32 (August–September 1967): 12–19.

15. Paul Theroux, "Hating the Asians," *Transition* 33 (October–November 1967): 46–51.

16. Paul Theroux, "Rajat Neogy," unpublished manuscript (1995) courtesy of Tayu Neogy.

17. For this and other quotes, see Barbara Lapček-Neogy, "A Matter of Transition," *Transition* 38 (1971): 43–48; repr. 1997, no. 75/76, https://www.jstor.org/stable/2935413.

18. Mr. Mohammed Saied would become known as a man of integrity, who had the courage to issue verdicts against the express will of the government. Saied would reappear in 1974 as chair of the Commission of Inquiry into "disappearances" appointed by Idi Amin.

19. "After the prayers, Buganda's Prince Badru Kakungulu, who was serving as the Imam at the mosque, stood up to inquire if Professor Mazrui was in the congregation. When I confirmed, the Imam asked me to move to the front of the mosque. That was the first time I knew that Rajat had made advance preparations for his public conversion. I whispered urgently to Rajat at my side that this was not the right way of making such a momentous transition. As we walked towards

Prince Badru, Rajat fortunately whispered the reassuring words: 'I will do whatever you say.' When Imam Badru handed the microphone to Rajat, expecting him to request the rituals of conversion, I snatched it away and gave a different message. I recounted that Rajat had suffered in Uganda under the regime of Milton Obote and that Rajat considered me as the friend who had risked the most to stand by him. Now that Obote was gone, and Rajat was back in Uganda, he had decided to join his old friend, Ali Mazrui, in a prayer of thanksgiving at our mosque. . . . Prince Badru was greatly perplexed, but the congregation swallowed my story quite happily." Ali Mazrui, "The Day I Stopped Rajat Neogy from Becoming a Muslim," unpublished manuscript (1995), courtesy of Tayu Neogy.

20. Wole Soyinka, "Memories of Rajat," unpublished manuscript (1995), courtesy of Tayu Neogy.

21. Djamila Anne McNutt, untitled, unpublished manuscript (1995), courtesy of Tayu Neogy.

22. Soyinka, "Memories of Rajat."

6. THE EXPULSION

1. Wanume Kibedi, open letter to Idi Amin, Paris, June 21, 1974, Supplement 1, in International Commission of Jurists, "Violation of Human Rights in Uganda," 1974, https://www.icj.org/resource/violations-of-human-rights-and-the-rule-of-law-in-uganda/.

2. Cited in Mark Leopold, *Idi Amin: The Story of Africa's Icon of Evil* (New Haven, CT: Yale University Press, 2020), 230.

3. Judith Listowel, *Amin* (Dublin: IUP, 1973), 146–147.

4. Listowel, *Amin,* 148.

5. Jaffar Amin and Margaret Akulia, "Idi Amin: Hero or Villain: His Son Jaffar Amin and Other People Speak," manuscript, Kampala, 2010, 268–269.

6. Listowel, *Amin,* 150, 171.

7. Minutes of the 3rd meeting of the Cabinet of the 2nd Republic of Uganda, February 19, 1971, Minute 20a (CT 1971): "Relations between the Government of the 2nd Republic of Uganda and Asians," pp. 23–25.

8. Minutes of the 13th meeting of the Cabinet of the 2nd Republic of Uganda, May 25, 1971, Minute 123 (CT 1971): "Hon. Shafiq Arain: East African Minister for Communications, Research and Social Services," p. 6.

9. Minutes of the 3rd meeting of the Cabinet of the 2nd Republic of Uganda, February 19, 1971, Minute 20a (CT 1971): "Relation between the Government of the Second Republic of Uganda and Asians," pp. 23–25; Minutes of the 13th meeting of the Cabinet, May 25, 1971, Minute 125 (CT 1971): "Hon. Shafique

Arain, East African Minister for Communications, Research and Social Services," p. 5.

10. Minutes of the 15th meeting of the Cabinet of the 2nd Republic of Uganda, June 3, 1971, Minute 135 (CT 1971): "1971/72 Admissions to Makerere University, Kampala," p. 3.

11. Minutes of 18th meeting of the Cabinet of the 2nd Republic of Uganda, June 24, 1971, Minute 123 (CT 1971): "Uganda Citizenship," pp. 1–6.

12. Minutes of the 13th meeting of the Cabinet of the 2nd Republic of Uganda, May 25, 1971, Minute 154 (CT 1971): "Hon. Shafiq Arain, East African Minister for Communications, Research and Social Services," pp. 1–6.

13. Minutes of the 27th meeting of the Cabinet of the 2nd Republic of Uganda, September 2, 1971, Minute 278 (CT 1971): "Promotion of Africans in Trade," pp. 10–14.

14. Minutes of the 26th meeting of the Cabinet of the 2nd Republic of Uganda, August 17, 1971, Minute 336 (CT 1971): "The Decision of the Government to Remove All Non-Uganda Citizens from Uganda," pp. 2–5, 14–15; Minutes of the 24th meeting of the Cabinet of the 2nd Republic of Uganda, August 6, 1972, Minute 327 (CT 1972): "The Decision of the Government to Remove All Non-Citizen Asians from Uganda," pp. 1–6, 8–9.

15. Minutes of the 24th meeting of the Cabinet of the 2nd Republic of Uganda, August 6, 1972, Minute 327 (CT 1972): "The Decision of the Government to Remove All Non-Citizen Asians from Uganda," pp. 1–10.

16. On the process of distribution of properties, see Minutes of the 32nd meeting of the Cabinet of the 2nd Republic of Uganda, November 21, 1972, Minute 407 (CT 1972): "Allocation of the Businesses of Departing Asians to Ugandans," pp. 1–10.

17. Minutes of the 31st meeting of the Cabinet of the 2nd Republic of Uganda, November 17, 1972, Minute 407 (CT 1972): "Allocation of the Businesses of the Departing Asians to Ugandans," p. 2; Minutes of the 32nd meeting of the Cabinet of the 2nd Republic of Uganda, November 21, 1972, Minute 401 (CT 1972): "Transfer of Economic Power into Hands of Ugandans," pp. 2, 3.

18. Minutes of the 26th meeting of the Cabinet of the 2nd Republic of Uganda, August 17, 1972, Minute 337 (CT 1972): "Government Arrangements for the Acquisition of Property of Non-Citizen Asians and Any Other Matters Connected Therewith," pp. 4–15.

19. Minutes of the 26th meeting of the Cabinet of the 2nd Republic of Uganda, August 17, 1972, Minute 336 (CT 1972): "The Decision of the Government to Remove All Non-Citizens from Uganda: Cancellation of Exemption Statutory Instrument No 124, 1972," pp. 1–4.

20. "With regard to the Senegalese businessmen, it was pointed out that their ability to import goods by air and sell them at competitive prices in Uganda was mainly because they smuggled those goods from their countries of origin . . . they smuggled fish from Uganda waters to the Republic of Zaire." See Minutes of the 13th meeting of the Cabinet of the 2nd Republic of Uganda, April 27, 1972, Minute 178: "The Difficulties Caused to Ugandan African Traders by Senegalese Living in Uganda," pp. 6–7.

21. Minutes of the 27th meeting of Cabinet of the 2nd Republic of Uganda, September 29, 1972, Minute 349 (CT 1972): "Doctors Who Leave Government Service," p. 6; Minutes of the 32nd meeting of the Cabinet of the 2nd Republic of Uganda, November 21, 1972, Minute 408 (CT 1972): "The Recruitment and Replacement of Foreign Personnel Who Were Employed in Both the Public Service and Industries and Who Have Left the Country," pp. 10–13.

22. Minutes of the 1st meeting of the Cabinet of the 2nd Republic of Uganda, January 9, 1975, Minute 18 (CT 1975): "A Decree to Set Up a Special Tribunal to Try Persons Charged with the Offense of Overcharging, the Penalty for Which Shall Be Death," pp. 9–15.

23. See, Cabinet Minutes, July 10, 1976, pp. 11, 19; and Cabinet Minutes, January 12, 1978, pp. 8, 13.

24. Minutes of the 23rd meeting of the Cabinet of the 2nd Republic of Uganda, June 2, 1976, Minute 195 (CT 1976): "Misappropriation of Tax Revenue by Government Operated Companies," p. 10. See also Minutes of the 20th meeting of the Cabinet of the 2nd Republic of Uganda, June 2, 1977, Minute 142 (CT 1977): "Amendment to the Assets of Departed Asians Decree, 1977," pp. 11, 17, 19.

25. Listowel, *Amin,* 163.

26. Listowel, *Amin,* 160.

27. Letter to author, privately circulated at Makerere University, November 1972.

28. Manzoor Moghal, *Idi Amin: Lion of Africa* (Central Milton Keynes, UK: Authorhouse, 2010), 103.

29. Cited in David Hebditch and Ken Connor, "The Kampala Strangler: Uganda 1971," *How to Stage a Military Coup: From Planning to Execution* (London: Greenhill, 2005), 131.

30. Moghal, *Idi Amin,* 4.

31. Neema Shah, *Kololo Hill* (New Delhi: Picador, 2021).

32. This is discussed in detail in Mahmood Mamdani, *Saviors and Survivors: Darfur, Politics, and the War on Terror* (New York: Pantheon, 2009).

33. Leopold, *Idi Amin.*

7. THE REGIME STABILIZES

1. Rev. Prof. John Mbiti to Mr. J. A. Okodoi, Secretary to the Ministerial Committee on the Setting up of the Ministry of Religious Affairs, Kampala, February 17, 1971. Minutes of the 2nd meeting of the Cabinet, February 8, 1971, Minute 19a (CT 1971): "The Proposed Ministry of Religious Affairs," p. 23; Minutes of the 12th Meeting of the Cabinet, May 14, 1971, Minute 110 (CT 1971): "Report by the Ministerial Committee of Cabinet to Set Up and Recommend to Cabinet about the Proposed Establishment of the Ministry of Religious Affairs," pp. 1–6; Minutes of the 13th Meeting of the Cabinet, May 25, 1971, Minute 110 (CT 1971): "Report by the Ministerial Committee of the Cabinet to Recommend to Cabinet about Proposed Establishment of the Ministry of Religious Affairs," pp. 1–2; Minute 121 (CT 1971): "Conference of Religious Leaders," p. 1.

2. Mbiti to Okodoi, February 17, 1971, 1–2.

3. Mbiti to Okodoi, February 17, 1971, 2–4.

4. Mbiti to Okodoi, February 17, 1971, 5.

5. Thomas James Lowman, "Beyond Idi Amin: Causes and Drivers of Political Violence in Uganda, 1971–1979" (PhD diss., Durham University, 2020), https://etheses.dur.ac.uk/13439/.

6. Even then, Amin was taken unawares when it came to the Entebbe raid, orchestrated by Israel in July 1976. Key to the success of Israel's operation then was close collaboration with its agents in Uganda and neighboring Kenya, in particular Bruce McKenzie, minister of agriculture and advisor of Jomo Kenyatta, the Kenyan president. McKenzie was widely believed to have been an agent of the Israeli, South African, and British intelligence services. McKenzie died two years later, when his flight from Entebbe to Nairobi was blown up by a bomb believed to be hidden in the state gift he was carrying for the Kenyan president at Amin's behest. He had made it possible for Israeli pilots to refuel their planes in Kenya on the way to and return from Entebbe. Ugandan collaborators were individuals Israel had cultivated over its decade-long presence in Uganda.

7. Jan Jelmert Jørgensen, *Uganda: A Modern History* (London: Croom Helm, 1981), 277, cited in Lowman, "Beyond Idi Amin," 109.

8. *Kampala Domestic Service in English,* "Briefs," 1000 GMT, January 27, 1974, radio, cited in Lowman, "Beyond Idi Amin," 109.

9. Jaffar Amin and Margaret Akulia, "Idi Amin: Hero or Villain: His Son Jaffar Amin and Other People Speak," manuscript, Kampala, 2010, 320, 324.

10. Minutes of the 2nd meeting of the Cabinet of the 2nd Republic of Uganda, February 8, 1971, Minute 26 (CT 1971): "The Return and Burial of the Body of the Late Sir Edward Frederick Mutesa, First President of Uganda and Former Kabaka of Buganda," pp. 33–34; Minutes of the 8th meeting of the Cabinet of the 2nd Republic of Uganda, March 29, 1971, Minute 87 (CT 1971): "The Return and Burial of

the Body of the Late Sir Edward Frederick Mutesa, First President of Uganda and Former Kabaka of Buganda," pp. 4–6 (end of kabakaship); Judith Listowel, *Amin* (Dublin: IUP, 1973), 81–84, 86–87, 90; Mark Leopold, *Idi Amin: The Story of Africa's Icon of Evil* (New Haven, CT: Yale University Press, 2020), Kindle edition, L3952.

11. Minutes of the 3rd meeting of the Cabinet of the 2nd Republic of Uganda, February 19, 1971, Minute 26 (CT 1971): "The Return and Burial of the Body of Late Sir Edward Frederick Mutesa, First President of Uganda and Former Kabaka of Buganda," pp. 33–34; Minutes of the 8th meeting of the Cabinet of the 2nd Republic of Uganda, March 29, 1971, Minute 87 (CT 1971): "The Return and Burial of the Body of the Late Sir Edward Frederick Mutesa, First President of Uganda and Former Kabaka of Buganda," pp. 3–6.

12. Minutes of the 28th meeting of the Cabinet of the 2nd Republic of Uganda, May 22, 1975, Minute 209 (CT 1975): "A Decree to Provide for the Nationalisation of Unused Land," p. 4.

13. "Report of the Commission of Inquiry into Disappearances of People in Uganda since the 25th January, 1971," Kampala, signed and submitted June 13, 1975, p. 4. Links to sections of the report from a copy at Amnesty International available at https://www.usip.org/publications/1974/06/truth-commission-uganda-74.

14. "Report of the Commission of Inquiry."

15. Joanna R. Quinn, *The Politics of Acknowledgement: Truth Commissions in Uganda and Haiti* (Vancouver: University of British Columbia Press, 2010); Alicia Decker, "Idi Amin's Dirty War: Subversion, Sabotage, and the Battle to Keep Uganda Clean, 1971–1979," *International Journal of African Historical Studies* 43, no. 3 (2010): 489–513; Alicia C. Decker, *In Idi Amin's Shadow: Women, Gender, and Militarism in Uganda* (Athens: Ohio University Press, 2014). Cited in Lowman, "Beyond Idi Amin," 31–32.

16. Kampala Domestic Service in English, "Commission of Inquiry Begins Work," 1000 GMT, July 1, 1974 (radio), cited in Lowman, "Beyond Idi Amin," 129.

17. "Report of the Commission of Inquiry," 132–133.

18. "Soldiers may be only too ready and willing to try to assist, by force if necessary, their relatives or even friends, who may complain to them against other people." "Report of the Commission of Inquiry," 698.

19. "Report of the Commission of Inquiry," Subject no. 84, Eriyah Byaruhanga, 243.

20. "All the cases of soldiers, with which we dealt, barring a few exceptions, could be ascribed to the logical and natural consequences of the takeover of the Government by the army on the 25th of January, 1971 which, in effect means that they were all opposed to the change-over and were either known to the authorities and were arrested or put up active resistance and died in the shoot-out. Those 500 odd soldiers as mentioned in Ex. 124 and detained under Decree No. 7/71 also came under the same category." "Report of the Commission of Inquiry," 776.

21. "Report of the Commission of Inquiry," 711.

22. "Report of the Commission of Inquiry," 714.

23. "Report of the Commission of Inquiry," 734, 748, 732, 742.

24. "Report of the Commission of Inquiry," 743–744.

25. "Report of the Commission of Inquiry," 266.

26. "Report of the Commission of Inquiry," 715.

27. "Report of the Commission of Inquiry," 720.

28. "Report of the Commission of Inquiry," 565.

29. "Report of the Commission of Inquiry," 697.

30. "Report of the Commission of Inquiry," 764.

31. "Report of the Commission of Inquiry," 715–717. Asked "why the police were unable to resist the interferences about which they were complaining," the former Minister of Internal Affairs, Mr. Obitre-Gama responded that "it was beyond their control . . . probably because of force of arms" (767).

32. "Report of the Commission of Inquiry," 754, 761.

33. "Report of the Commission of Inquiry," 709.

34. "Report of the Commission of Inquiry," 138, 149, 318.

35. See Mahmood Mamdani, *Neither Settler Nor Native: The Making and Unmaking of Permanent Minorities* (Cambridge, MA: Belknap Press of Harvard University Press, 2021), ch. 3.

36. "Report of the Commission of Inquiry," 799.

37. "Report of the Commission of Inquiry," 801.

38. US Institute of Peace, http://www.usip.org/publications/truth-commission-uganda-74, cited in Decker, *In Idi Amin's Shadow,* Kindle locs. 2857–2862, 4327–4329, 6446–6447.

39. Cited in Lowman, "Beyond Idi Amin," 143.

8. THE REGIME IMPLODES

1. Ali A. Mazrui, "Violation of Human Rights in Uganda: Is It a Case for International Sanctions?" Testimony prepared for Congressional hearings on US policy toward Uganda before the subcommittees on Africa, International Economic Policy and International Organizations, of the US House of Representatives, Committee on International Relations, Washington, DC, February 1978, 2, 4, 13. See "Violation of Human Rights in Uganda: Is It a Case for International Sanctions?," prepared for US Congressional hearings, February 1978, box 5, Ali A. Mazrui Papers, Bentley Historical Library, University of Michigan.

2. On Mo Dhilllon, Mo Amin, and Ali Mazrui, see, Vali Jamal, vali.jamal@yahoo.com, email communication on "Passing away of Mohinder Dhillon," March 10, 2020 at 11:32:18 PM GMT+3, sent to editors@awaazmagazine.com, and many recipients.

3. International Commission of Jurists, "Violation of Human Rights in Uganda," 1974, 61, https://www.icj.org/resource/violations-of-human-rights-and-the-rule-of-law-in-uganda/.

4. David Hebditch and Ken Connor, *How to Stage a Military Coup: From Planning to Execution* (London: Greenhill, 2005), ch. 3, section "The Kampala Strangler: Uganda 1971," pp. 125–132, at 125.

5. Hebditch and Connor, *How to Stage a Military Coup,* 131.

6. Moses Serugo, "The Myths Surrounding Idi Amin," *Daily Monitor* (Kampala), May 28, 2007.

7. Mark Leopold, *Idi Amin: The Story of Africa's Icon of Evil* (New Haven, CT: Yale University Press, 2020), L349.

8. Leopold, *Idi Amin,* L349n45.

9. Leopold, *Idi Amin,* L349n43.

10. Leopold, *Idi Amin,* L583.

11. Leopold, *Idi Amin,* L457–463.

12. Leopold, *Idi Amin,* L451.

13. Hebditch and Connor, *How to Stage a Military Coup,* 125–132.

14. Dominic Casciani, "Despot Planned 'Save Britain Fund,'" BBC News, January 1, 2005, http://news.bbc.co.uk/2/hi/africa/4132547.stm.

15. Casciani, "Despot Planned 'Save Britain Fund.'"

16. Leopold, *Idi Amin,* L5241.

17. And, then, of course, was the outrageous, even despicable telegram to the UN Secretary-General, responding to the Munich massacre of athletes, praising Hitler for killing six million Jews. "Amin Praises Hitler for Killing of Jews," *New York Times,* September 13, 1972, p. 4.

18. Leopold, *Idi Amin,* L5241.

19. "Today in History," *Daily Monitor,* April 6, 2021.

20. The genocide of the Banyoro people is the part of the subject addressed in Mary Muhuruzi's doctoral thesis (forthcoming, Makerere Institute of Social Research) on the historiography of Bunyoro-Kitara in the colonial period.

21. Thomas James Lowman, "Beyond Idi Amin: Causes and Drivers of Political Violence in Uganda, 1971–1979" (PhD diss., Durham University, 2020), 45–46, 48–50, 58, http://etheses.dur.ac.uk/13439/.

22. Moses Ali, 1986 Uganda Commission of Inquiry into Violations of Human Rights (CIVHR), p. 13502, Uganda Human Rights Commission (UHRC), cited in Lowman, "Beyond Idi Amin," 48.

23. Cited in Lowman, "Beyond Idi Amin."

24. During 1969–1970, the Obote government carried out May Day nationalizations. These, too, left property under private control.

25. Godfrey Asiimwe, "The Roots and Dynamics of the Indian Citizenship Question, Relations and Contestations in Uganda," 2006, unpublished manuscript, 2006, Makerere University, Kampala, 14, 17.

26. "MPs Probe Ownership of 460 Asian Properties," *Daily Monitor,* August 9, 2019, 4, 14.

27. "MPs Probe Ownership," 4, 14.

28. Joe Oloka-Onyango, "Legal and Political Dynamics of the Asian Question," Commentary at Asian African Association (AAA), August 6, 2013, *Sunday Monitor* (Kampala), August 11, 2013.

29. "Report of the Subcommittee of the Committee on Statutory Authorities and State Enterprises (COSASE) on the Investigation into the Operations of the Departed Asians Property Custodian Board (DAPCB)," Office of the Clerk to Parliament, April 2021, 21.

30. "Some formerly compensated properties [for] by government had ended up in the hands of unscrupulous individuals who had later transferred the same to bona fide purchasers for value without notice. Some Asians had obtained repossession, yet they had been compensated." "Report of the Subcommittee of the Committee on Statutory Authorities and State Enterprises," Uganda Parliament, Kampala, (unpublished), 66, 15, 10–11.

31. Asiimwe, "The Roots and Dynamics," 17.

9. NAMING THE WAR

1. Yoweri Museveni, *Sowing the Mustard Seed: The Struggle for Freedom and Democracy in Uganda* (London: Macmillan, 1997), 54.

2. See Andrew Rice, *The Teeth May Smile but the Heart Does Not Forget: Murder and Memory in Uganda* (New York: Metropolitan, 2009).

3. Museveni, *Sowing the Mustard Seed,* 52.

4. Museveni, *Sowing the Mustard Seed,* 55–56.

5. Museveni, *Sowing the Mustard Seed,* 59, 62.

6. Museveni, *Sowing the Mustard Seed,* 88.

7. Museveni, *Sowing the Mustard Seed,* 106.

8. Museveni, *Sowing the Mustard Seed,* 99, 105, 103, 110, 114.

9. Pecos Kutesa, *Uganda's Revolution: 1979–86: How I Saw It* (Kampala: Fountain, 2006), back of jacket.

10. Museveni, *Sowing the Mustard Seed,* 110, 148, 121.

11. Museveni, *Sowing the Mustard Seed,* 151.

12. Museveni, *Sowing the Mustard Seed,* 129, 121.

13. Charles Onyango-Obbo, interview with author, February 16, 2020, Kampala-Toro Road.

14. Kutesa, *Uganda's Revolution.*

15. Charles Onyango-Obbo interview.

16. John Kazoora, "Betrayed by My Leader," *The Monitor* (Kampala), January 10, 2021.

17. Charles Onyango-Obbo interview.

18. Charles Onyango-Obbo interview.

19. Charles Onyango-Obbo interview.

20. Museveni, *Sowing the Mustard Seed,* 121.

21. "Editorial Postscript," *Forward: A Call for a Democratic Uganda,* no. 2, April 1979, 1.

22. Museveni, *Sowing the Mustard Seed,* 99.

23. Issa G. Shivji, *Development as a Rebellion: A Biography of Julius Nyerere,* vol. 3, *Rebellion Without Rebels* (Dar es Salaam: Mkuki na Nyota, 2020), 249.

24. Cited in William Pike, *Combatants: A Memoir of the Bush War and the Press in Uganda* (Nairobi: William Pike, 2019), 61.

25. Shivji, *Biography of Julius Nyerere,* 3:251, 254.

26. Shivji, *Biography of Julius Nyerere,* 3:250.

27. Cabinet Minutes, UK Government. CAB 128/64/18—Cabinet: Minutes CM and CC Series—Record type: Conclusion. Former Reference: CM (78) 38. Attendees: J. Callaghan, Michael Foot, D. Healey; . . . 09 November 1978.

28. Shivji, *Biography of Julius Nyerere,* 3:260.

10. RETURN HOME: WORKING ABOVE GROUND

1. Barbara D'Amato, *The Doctor, the Murder, the Mystery: The True Story of the Dr. John Branion Murder Case* (Chicago: Noble, 1972), 90.

2. D'Amato, *The Doctor, the Murder, the Mystery,* 92–93.

3. "John Marshall Branion Trial: 1968," Encyclopedia.com, https://www.encyclopedia.com/law/law-magazines/john-marshall-branion-trial-1968.

4. D'Amato, *The Doctor, the Murder, the Mystery,* 210.

5. Charles L. Sanders, "Saga of a Man on the Run: Chicago Doctor Flees U.S., Works for Idi Amin," *Ebony,* July 1984, 112–126.

6. Kenan Heise, "John Branion, Recently Freed in Wife's Slaying," obituary, *Chicago Tribune,* September 14, 1990.

7. On Amwoma, see Mahmood Mamdani, "Forms of Labour and Accumulation of Capital: Analysis of a Village in Lango, Northern Uganda," *Mawazo: The Makerere Journal of the Arts and Social Sciences* 5, no. 4 (1984). On Kitende, see Mahmood Mamdani, "Analyzing the Agrarian Question: The Case of a Uganda Village," *Mawazo* 5, no. 3 (1984).

8. Kirunda Kivejinja, Bidandi Ssali, and Kintu Musoke, *The Sapoba Legacy: A Story of Ideals and Idealism in Ugandan Politics and Family Life* (Kampala: Menha, 2014).

9. A total of four editorial boards were set up: the first included Hope Baingana and Sarah Mukasa for the Luganda edition (Central region), and was called *Kitangala* (light); the second included John Musinguzi, John Nuwagaba, Staliko Tibanyendera, and Byarugaba for the the Runyankole-Rukiga version (western Uganda), called *Mushana* (sunshine). The two other boards were set up to begin preliminary work to launch a couple of editions: one (Okello Yubo and Obong) to launch a Luo (Northern region) edition; and a one-person committee headed by Charles Ocan, also the editor of the local Ateso edition of the government paper *Voice of Uganda,* to begin work toward an Ateso edition for the East. The first meeting was held at Ntare School on September 9, 1984. See *Minute,* December 3, 1984. All minutes found at the Mamdani Papers, Makerere Institute of Social Research, Archives, Kampala.

10. Mahmood Mamdani, *Imperialism and Fascism in Uganda* (Nairobi: Heinemann Educational Press, 1983; Trenton, NJ: Africa World Press, 1984).

11. Below is a September 1983 list of the Society's chapters by region:

- **Kampala**: 1. Nsambya Railway Workers; 2. Kampala South Teachers; 3. St. Benedict Primary School; 4. Lusaka Primary School; 5. Makerere University; 6. Women Journalists; 7. Uganda Commercial College, Nakawa; 8. Uganda Technical College, Kyambogo; 9. Old Kampala Secondary School; 10. Kampala Secretarial College; 11. United Garment Industries Ltd. (UGIL); 12. Dairy Corporation
- **Eastern**: 13. Busia Secondary School; 14. Dabani Girls College; 15. Dabani Town; 16. Mbale Secondary School; 17. Mbale Town; 18. Iganga Secondary School; 19. Iganga Town; 20. Soroti Secondary School
- **Central**: 21. Sanje Secondary School; 22. Sanje Town; 23. Bishop Willis T.T.C., Iganga; 24. Kawete Primary School, Iganga
- **Western**: 25. St. Charles Secondary School, Bwera; 26. Kasanga Primary School, Bwera; 27. Ndongo S.D.A. Integrated School, Kasese; 28. Mundongo Old Boys Society, Bwera; 29. Ruwenzori Saad Islamic Institute, Bwera; 30. Bwera Primary

School, Bwera; 31. Mpondwe Primary School, Bwera; 32. Kamaiba Primary School, Kasese; 33. Mbarara Secondary School; 34. Ntare School; 35. Mbarara Town; 36. Kabale Secondary School; 37. Kabale Town; 38. Kisoro Secondary School; 39. Kisoro Town

• **Northern**: 40. Gulu Secondary School; 41. Gulu Town.

12. In 1982–1983, the average official shilling value of the dollar was 111.14.

13. Our core group would recommend individuals for each post. NEC members were usually happy to approve these recommendations. The UKFS confirmed four coordinators at the NEC meeting of November 19, 1983: Mathew Ojiambo, a railway worker, for Kampala; John Musinguzi, a university student, for the Western region; Okot Nyormoi, a pathologist in Mulago, for the Northern region, and Dagera Suza, a Mbale-based lawyer, for the Eastern region. The main responsibility of coordinators was to organize regional conferences for delegates.

14. Uganda-Korea Friendship Society Report, 1982, delegation to attend the 35th anniversary of the founding of DPRK p. 2; UKFS documents found at Mamdani Papers, Makerere Institute of Social Research, Archives, Kampala.

15. The cost per delegate for each meal of the day was 100 shillings; with the average Ugandan shilling value to the US dollar at 111.14, it cost a total of 20,000 shillings (roughly $180) for meals per delegate for all three days. Materials (paper, pens, folders) cost roughly 26,700 shillings ($240); tea, over 5,300 shillings ($48); and the closing reception, limited to evening tea, over 11,000 shillings ($100).

16. Uganda-Korea Friendship Society (UKFS) Report, 1982.

17. The first lesson concerned the doctor. We began with Dr. John Busingye (Dr. John Branyon), our African American colleague at Makerere. Guided by Wabwire, Busingye was thrilled to spend the day treating peasants in the village. At the end of the day, Busingye asked for *waragi,* then a woman companion. It was the end of our arrangement with Busingye. Since Busia was 120 miles from Kampala, we found a local doctor who could be part of the cooperative.

11. THE WORLD BANK ENTERS THE UNIVERSITY

1. Mahmood Mamdani, *Scholars in the Marketplace: The Dilemmas of Neoliberal Reform at Makerere University, 1989–2005* (Cape Town: HSRC Press, 2007), 45, table 5.

2. Three distinct positions emerged at Dar. A radical camp, mostly non-Tanzanian, wanted a complete transformation of the curriculum and the university's administrative structure; above all, they wanted to abolish discipline-based departments. A moderate majority, including most Tanzanian members of staff, agreed that there should be a radical review of the curriculum but no abolition of departments. A conservative minority resisted any change in the curriculum and argued for the separation of disciplines. At the same time, the demand for an interdisciplinary approach,

like the appeal to relevance, seemed to compromise the principles of scholarship. An astute review of the program by a subcommittee of the university council, appointed at the end of 1970, suggested that interdisciplinarity was likely to focus on solving problems rather than understanding method, and went on to ask whether this wouldn't produce "technocrats" rather than "reasoning graduates."

3. The debate around Shivji's book is collected in Yash Tandon, *University of Dar es Salaam: Debate on Class, State and Imperialism* (Dar es Salaam: Tanzania Publishing House, 1982).

4. For a broader discussion, see Mamdani, *Scholars in the Marketplace,* 208–220.

5. According to work done by Professor Abdu Kasozi at the Makerere Institute of Social Research, taken as a percentage of annual GDP, Uganda spent roughly a third on public universities in the decade from 1997–1998 to 2007–2008; this stands in contrast to Kenya and Tanzania, which spent 1 percent and 0.9 percent, respectively. Government contribution to Makerere University's budget declined from 100 percent in 1993–1994 to a meager 41 percent in 2005. See Abdu Kasozi, "The Impact of Governance on Research in Ugandan Universities," MISR Working Paper no. 30, Makerere Institute for Social Research, July 2017; and Abdu Kasozi and Mahmood Mamdani, "MISR Views on the National Discussion on Makerere University," MISR Working Paper no. 29, Makerere Institute for Social Research, December 2016.

6. Mamdani, *Scholars in the Marketplace.*

7. The inaugural professorial lecture and three critical reflections were published as a symposium. Sylvia Tamale, "Nudity, Protest and the Law in Uganda," *Feminist Africa* 22 (2017): 52–86; Lyn Ossome, "The Public Politics of Nudity," 168–179; Samson A. Bezabeh, "Post-Structuralism in Tamale's Text," 180–185; and Mahmood Mamdani, "History, Nudity and Protest," 186–193, in *MISR Review,* no. 2 (September 2018). Sylvia Tamale, "Nudity, Protest and the Law in Uganda," Inaugural Professorial Lecture (Kampala: Makerere University, 2016). Commentaries on Professor Tamale's inaugural lecture by Lyn Ossome, Samson A. Bezabeh, and Mahmood Mamdani, MISR Working Paper no. 28, Makerere Institute of Social Research, Kampala, February 2017.

12. HOW THE NATIONAL RESISTANCE MOVEMENT GOVERNED

1. See *Report of the National Commission of Inquiry into Local Government System* (Ministry of Local Government, Kampala, 1987).

2. "He [Otafiire] said they had started organizing the Resistance Committees in September 1981 and there had been over 1000 Councils operating in the Luwero Triangle by the time the UNLA started its offensive in 1983." See William Pike, *Combatants: A Memoir of the Bush War and the Press in Uganda* (Nairobi: indepen-

dently published, 2019), 120. This is likely to be an overstatement, given the conditions of the time.

3. Mahmood Mamdani, *When Victims Become Killers: Colonialism, Nativism, and Genocide in Rwanda* (Princeton, NJ: Princeton University Press, 2014).

4. Joe Oloka-Onyango, "From Expulsion to Exclusion: Citizenship and the Ethnicity Conundrum in Contemporary Uganda," *Mawazo: The Makerere Journal of the Arts and Social Sciences* 12, nos. 1–2 (2017).

5. More recently in his new year address on December 31, 2021, President Museveni advanced a vision that separated Muslims from "indigenous Ugandans": "It is pathetic to listen to the sick talk of these disoriented young people, claiming to be fighting *Bakafiiri* (us Ugandans), in order to make Uganda a country governed by 'Sharia law.' . . . Uganda is a land of my ancestry and no foreigner or foreign agent, will ever take this land from the indigenous people of Uganda. Yes, since the 1840s, foreign religions, starting with Islam, started coming to our area" (12). "New Year Address 2022" by His Excellency Yoweri Kaguta Museveni President of the Republic of Uganda," December 31, 2021.

6. *Number of districts by region in 2022:* Northern = 41; Western = 38; Central = 27; Eastern = 40. Source: Government of Uganda (September 23, 2022). Florence Nakayaki, "Uganda's Districts since Independence," *New Vision* (Kampala), August 28, 2010. "Uganda Bureau of Statistics, 2022 Statistical Abstract, http://www.ubos.org/wp-content/uploads/publications/05_20232022_Statistical_Abstract.pdf.

7. The letter is cited in "Why Museveni Wants 36 New Constituencies," *The Observer* (Kampala), May 18–19, 2015.

8. "Ruwenzori Clashes Betray Our Sense of Nationhood," *The Observer* (Kampala), July 14–15, 2014.

9. Thus, in the Ruwenzori region, the president blames the majority (Bakonzo) king, the Omusinga Mumbere, of "imposing a cultural institution on other ethnic groups in the region such as the Bamba, Basongora and Banyabindi." He thus stood for the right of these minorities to create their own kingdom as a "cultural institution." Similarly, in Bugisu, a cultural leader was "installed with the rather intriguing, if meaningless, title of *Umukuka* (literally meaning 'the grandfather')." Moses Khisa, "Museveni Shouldn't Pass the Buck in Ruwenzori," *The Observer* (Kampala), July 11–13, 2014.

10. Ssemujju Ibrahim Nganda, "President Museveni to Blame for Crisis in Ruwenzori," *The Observer* (Kampala), July 16–17, 2014.

11. The general discussion brought out the following facts: Only 5.5 percent of seats in the open election were contested by women. The Constitution of the Republic of Uganda, 1995, Article 78, 1(b), specifies "one woman representative for every district." Also, a designated woman's seat is a district seat; mainstream representation is tied to electoral constituencies created by Parliament.

12. For AAA's Founding Declaration, see Mamdani Papers, Makerere Institute for Social Research, Papers, Kampala.

13. "Makerere Professors Want Citizenship for Minorities," *New Vision,* July 20, 2015, 6.

14. For an expanded discussion, see Mahmood Mamdani, "An African Reflection on Tahrir Square," *Globalizations* 8, no. 5 (2011): 559–566.

15. John Nagenda, "To Walk or Not to Walk," *Saturday Vision* (Kampala), April 16, 2011, 8.

16. Nagenda, "To Walk or Not to Walk," *New Vision,* http://www.newvision.co.ug/news/1013131/walk-walk.

17. Milton Olupot and Cyrpian Musoke, "Opposition Wants Chaos—Gov't," *New Vision,* April 15, 2011, 1 and 3. See also John Njoroge, "Besigye Not Giving Up on Walk-to-Work Campaign," *Daily Monitor* (Kampala), April 14, 2011, 2.

18. "Govt Concedes Police Have No Prerogative over Demonstrations," *Daily Monitor,* April 20, 2011.

19. Njoroge, "Besigye Not Giving Up on Walk-to-Work Campaign," 2.

20. "Mayor Elect Issued with Criminal Summons," *Daily Monitor,* April 20, 2011.

21. "Corridors of Power—They Said It," *New Vision,* April 14, 2011, 14. When the opposition insisted on continuing to Walk to Work, every Monday and Thursday, the official Communications Commission (UCC) sent verbal instructions directing radio and television stations to stop running live coverage of the events. Richard Wanambwa, "Govt Bans Live Broadcast of Events," *Daily Monitor,* April 15, 2011, 3.

22. "MPs Plot Hunger Strike," *The Observer* (Kampala), April 14–17, 2011, 3.

23. Samuel Okirir, "Uganda Condemned for 'Shameful' Decision to Close UN Human Rights Office," *Guardian* (Kampala), February 8, 2023.

13. REVENGE IN THE NORTH

1. Peter Clottey, "Ugandan Opposition Candidate Accuses President of Genocide," VoA Africa, January 4, 2011, https://www.voanews.com/a/ugandan-opposition-candidate-accuses-president-of-genocide--112978964/157161.html.

2. This is my main difference with Chris Dolan's otherwise brilliant work, which limits the understanding of the northern war to mainly internal factors. Dolan does not sufficiently take into account the fact that the Ugandan government needed to keep the LRA a live danger in order to make a credible claim that the government was a necessary participant in the War on Terror, and thus needed continuing support from Western government and agencies. Chris Dolan, *Social Torture: The Case of Northern Uganda, 1986–2006* (New York: Berghahn, 2009).

3. Willet Weeks, "Pushing the Envelope: Moving Beyond 'Protected Villages' in Northern Uganda," unpublished report, for United Nations, Office for the Co-

ordination of Humanitarian Affairs (OCHA), March 2002, 49, 8; and "Patterns of Global Terrorism 2001," US Department of State, May 2002, 124, https://2009-2017.state.gov/documents/organization/10286.pdf, both cited in Dolan, *Social Torture,* 112.

4. "Appeal for Uganda's Abducted Children," December 8, 2000, cited in Dolan, *Social Torture,* 113.

5. "Abductions in Northern and Southwestern Uganda, 1986–2001: Result of the Update and Verification Exercise," Kampala, UNICEF, 2001, 8, cited in Christopher Gerald Dolan, "Understanding War and Its Continuation: The Case of Northern Uganda" (PhD diss., London School of Economics and Political Science, 2005), 113, 124.

6. Michael Mubangizi, "Arrested, Tortured, Dismissed, for Fighting Ghost Soldiers," *Weekly Observer* (Kampala), March 15, 2007; also see Aili Mari Tripp, *Museveni's Uganda: Paradoxes of Power in a Hybrid Regime* (Boulder, CO: Lynne Rienner, 2010), 144.

7. Tripp, *Museveni's Uganda,* 143, 144; Helen C. Epstein, *Another Fine Mess: America, Uganda and the War on Terror* (New York: Columbia Global Reports, 2017), 141. In his minority report, which tried to provide a historical rationale for this practice, Salim Saleh claimed the problem went as far back as the 1987 conflict against Alice Lakwena. As AIDS spread and soldiers died, there was a failure to remove their names from the roster. It sounded more like a ruse than an explanation. Mubangizi, "Arrested, Tortured, Dismissed."

8. Wafula Oguttu, "What Does the Imprisonment of Former Army Chief Maj Gen James Kazini Mean?" *New Vision* (Kampala), April 5, 2008; Edris Kiggundu, "Kazini Was Reckless, Says Museveni," *The Observer,* November 12, 2009; Tripp, *Museveni's Uganda,* 144.

9. The Kazini story is detailed in Tripp, *Museveni's Uganda,* 143–145.

10. Kiggundu, "Kazini Was Reckless"; Tripp, *Museveni's Uganda,* 145.

11. Moses Sserwanga, "Kazini's Life: An Officer with Extraordinary Skills," *Daily Monitor* (Kampala), 2009.

12. Chris Obore, "Tumukunde in U.S.," *Daily Monitor,* September 7, 2007.

13. Alex Atuhaire, "Did Officers Sell Arms to LRA Rebels?" *Daily Monitor,* March 31, 2008, cited in Tripp, *Museveni's Uganda,* 170.

14. "Ugandan Leader Warns Army Officers against Land Grabbing," *BBC World Monitoring Africa,* August 18, 2008, cited in Tripp, *Museveni's Uganda,* 170.

15. Dolan, "Understanding War," 75.

16. "The Beasts of Burcoro: Recounting Atrocities by the NRA's 22nd Battalion in Burcoro Village in April 1991," Justice and Reconciliation Project, Field Notes XVII, July 2013 (Gulu, Uganda), https://justiceandreconciliation.com/wp-content/uploads/2013/07/Burcoro-Final_SM-2013-07-25.pdf.

17. "The Beasts at Burcoro," 26, 3, 9, 7–8. According to another male respondent, "I believe that this Operation took place because of a desire for revenge by the soldiers. When they were here they kept telling us that the Acholis killed a lot of people in the Luwero Triangle and that the same thing that happened in Luwero is what they were going to do here" (7–8).

18. Theresa Auma Eilu, email to author, February 8, 2023.

19. Dolan, "Understanding War," 92, 76.

20. Ian Drury, "UK Aid Cash Helped African Dictator Buy Himself a £30m Jet," *Daily Mail* (London), June 10, 2011.

21. Robert Gersony, "The Anguish of Northern Uganda: Results of a Field-Based Assessment of the Civil Conflicts in Northern Uganda," submitted to US Embassy and USAID Mission, Kampala, August 1997, 38–44, cited in Dolan, "Understanding War," 470.

22. Dolan, "Understanding War," 71.

23. Dolan, "Understanding War," 480.

24. "12 Die in UPDF Protected Villages," *The Monitor* (Kampala), October 30, 1996, cited in Adam Branch, "Humanitarianism, Violence, and the Camp in Northern Uganda," *Civil Wars* 11, no. 4 (2009): 477–501, 499n30. Mahmood Mamdani, "What Jason Didn't Tell Gavin and His Army of Invisible Children," *Daily Monitor,* March 13, 2012.

25. World Food Programme, Weekly Report 47/1996, November 29, 1996, 482–483, cited in Branch, "Humanitarianism," 483.

26. Dolan, "Understanding War," 162.

27. Mamdani, "What Jason Didn't Tell."

28. Dolan, "Understanding War," 158, 78.

29. Mahmood Mamdani, research notes from the field, 2011–2012; Dolan, "Understanding War," 225, 223, 221; Heike Behrend and Mitch Cohen, "Alice Lakwena and the Holy Spirits: War in Northern Uganda, 1986–97," NED-New edition, Boydell & Brewer, 1999. JSTOR, https://doi.org/10.2307/j.ctv136c09s, 7.

30. Authors' interviews at the camps, 2011–2012; Branch, "Humanitarianism," 486.

31. Branch, "Humanitarianism," 484.

32. Branch, "Humanitarianism," 490n20.

33. Amnesty International, "Breaking the Circle: Protecting Human Rights in the Northern War Zone," AFR 59/1999, March 1999, 17, https://www.amnesty.org/fr/documents/afr59/001/1999/en.

34. "WFP Assistance to Internally Displaced Persons: Country Case Study of Internal Displacement. Uganda: Displacement in the Northern and Western

Districts," World Food Programme, Rome, 1999, cited in Dolan, "Understanding War," 158–159.

35. Anna Jefferys, "Giving Voice to Silent Emergencies," *Humanitarian Exchange Magazine* 20 (April 2002), Article 2, https://odihpn.org/publication/giving-voice-to-silent-emergencies/; "WFP Assistance to Internally Displaced Persons," 6, cited in Dolan, "Understanding War," 158–159.

36. Dolan, "Understanding War," 159.

37. Sverker Finnström, *Living with Bad Surroundings: War, History, and Everyday Moments in Northern Uganda* (Durham, NC: Duke University Press, 2008), 158–159.

38. Cited in Dolan, "Understanding War," Annex E, 110.

39. Dolan, "Understanding War," 147, 76, 150.

40. Epstein, *Another Fine Mess,* 200.

41. "Let Us Vote on the Kony War," *The Monitor,* May 16, 1998, cited in Dolan, "Understanding War," 45, 88.

42. Dolan, "Understanding War," 33.

43. Dolan, "Understanding War," 161.

44. "Youth at the Cross-Roads: Which Way Forward?" Youth Conference, District Council Hall, 22 January 1999, cited in Dolan, "Understanding War," 232, 243, 269.

45. "Acholi Want Disaster Zone," *New Vision,* January 20, 1999, cited in Dolan, "Understanding War," 102.

46. Weeks, "Pushing the Envelope"; 22–25, 49; United Nations, Office for the Coordination of Humanitarian Affairs (UNOCHA), *Uganda Case Study: Conference on Internally Displaced Persons, Lessons Learned and Future Mechanisms* (Oslo: UNOCHA), 14; UNOCHA, *When the Sun Sets We Start to Worry: An Account of Life in Northern Uganda,* cited in Dolan, "Understanding War," 229.

47. Dolan, "Understanding War," 237.

48. Dolan, "Understanding War," 82n52.

49. Dolan, "Understanding War," 85, 87, 105.

50. "US Lists ADF, LRA as Terrorists," *New Vision,* December 8, 2001; "Uganda Pledges to Support USA in Combating Terrorism," *New Vision,* December 12, 2001; "Ambassador Brennan Termed an LRA Attack a 'Pure Terrorist Act against Humanity,'" "US Ambassador Condemns LRA Rebel Attack in the North," Radio Uganda, Kampala, 10:00 GMT, March 21, 2002; "USA Gives $3M to Fight Kony," *New Vision,* January 10, 2003, all cited in Branch, "Humanitarianism," 481–482.

51. "Uganda Rebels Face UK Courts," *New Vision,* January 20, 2002. Under of the Uganda Anti-Terrorism Act (2002), Section 7, these include placing explosives

or other lethal devices in public places with intent to cause death or serious bodily injury, direct involvement or complicity in the murder, kidnapping or maiming, or attack on a person or group of persons, and seizure or detention of hostages in order to compel a State, an international or intergovernmental organ, a person or group of persons, to do or abstain from doing any act. According to Sections 7(1) and (2), persons found guilty of these acts (a) "shall be sentenced to death if the offence directly results in death of a person" or (b) "in any other case, be liable to suffer death." https://ulii.org/akn.ug/act/2002/14/eng@2024-12-23. Section 10, as well as the Second Schedule thereto. Dolan, "Understanding War," 88.

52. "Uganda War 'Worst Forgotten Crisis,'" *Al Jazeera*, November 11, 2003; BBC News, November 10, 2003, http://news.bbc.co.uk/2/hi/africa/3256929.stm (accessed May 12, 2025); "Interview with Jan Egeland, UN Under-Secretary General for Humanitarian Affairs," *New Humanitarian,* April 4, 2006, https://www.thenewhumanitarian.org/news/2006/04/04/interview-jan-egeland-un-under-secretary-general-humanitarian-affairs (accessed on May 12, 2025).

53. Mamdani, "What Jason Didn't Tell."

54. "Child Soldiers Global Report 2004: Uganda," Child Soldiers International, summary by RefWorld, Global Law and Policy Database, https://www.refworld.org/docid/49880620c.html.

55. Moses Khisa, "Museveni Shouldn't Pass the Buck in Ruwenzori," *The Observer* (Kampala), July 11–13, 2014.

14. FROM NATIONALISM TO NEOLIBERALISM

1. The last citation I saw was on the internet site maintained by Yoga Adhola. Nicholas Sengoba, "Museveni's 'Good Thieves' Give Him a Bad Name," *Daily Monitor* (Kampala), August 15, 2023, https://www.monitor.co.ug/uganda/oped/columnists/nicholas-sengooba/museveni-s-good-thieves-give-him-a-bad-name-4336354.

2. Cited in Yash Tandon, *Common People's Uganda* (Kampala: independently published, 2019), 138.

3. Helen C. Epstein, *Another Fine Mess: America, Uganda, and the War on Terror* (New York: Columbia Global Reports, 2017), 96.

4. David Ouma Balikowa, "The Double Edge of Winnie Saga," *The Monitor* (Kampala), March 14, 2002, cited in Aili Mari Tripp, *Museveni's Uganda: Paradoxes of Power in a Hybrid Regime* (Boulder, CO: Lynne Rienner, 2010), 92.

5. International Monetary Fund External Relations, "IMF Approves Third Annual ESAF Loan for Uganda" (press release), https://www.imf.org/en/News/Articles/2015/09/14/01/49/pr9656. See also George R. Clarke, Robert J. Cull, Michael J. Fuchs, "Bank Privatization in Sub-Saharan Africa: The Case of Uganda

Commercial Bank," policy working paper, no. WPS 4007 (Washington, DC: World Bank Group, 2007), https://documents.worldbank.org/en/publication/documents-reports/documentdetail/539991468310727480/bank-privatization-in-sub-saharan-africa-the-case-of-uganda-commercial-bank.

6. "Uganda's Biggest Bank for Sale," BBC News, October 17, 2001, http://news.bbc.co.uk/2/hi/business/1604100.stm.

7. "Major General Salim Saleh resigned from his post as presidential security adviser for using a Malaysian company, Westmont, as a front to buy the Uganda Commercial Bank (UCB). In a three-page statement, he confessed that Greenland Investments, a company of which he was a major shareholder, used Westmont as a front to buy a 49 percent share in UCB after he failed to secure the deal through Greenland Investments directly because of longstanding liquidity problems. Then he persuaded Westmont to sell the shares to Greenland Investments after which Greeland Investments received US $44 million in loans from UCB to bail **it** out of its liquidity problems of which US $1.8 million went to Efforte Corporation. The parliamentary select committee has ordered his investigation and prosecution for his illegal take over while several members of parliament have called for his imprisonment for corruption. Saleh has maintained that he acted without the knowledge of the president. . . . The timing of Saleh's confession and the parliamentary probe is linked to the upcoming foreign donors' conference in Kampala, which has corruption high on the agenda. Meanwhile, President Museveni reiterated his commitment to fighting corruption." Agence France-Presse, December 6–8 and 10–14, 1998, cited in "Horn of Africa—Monthly Review, 11–12/98," African Studies Center, University of Pennsylvania, https://www.africa.upenn.edu/Hornet/hoa_dec.html.

8. "UCB Sale Report Sent to Prosecutor," *New Vision* (Kampala), February 18, 1999.

9. The Uganda Commercial Bank Ltd is abbreviated as either UCB or UCBL.

10. Mwenda followed with his own apology: "I write this article with a lot of humility because I was, at the time, a strong believer in the free market and stood shoulder to shoulder with Mutebile." Andrew Mwenda, "The Museveni-Mutebile Conundrum," *The Independent* (Kampala), February 14, 2022, https://www.independent.co.ug/the-museveni-mutebile-conundrum/.

11. "MPs Oppose UCB Sale," *New Vision,* October 5, 2001.

12. "Bank: Sendawula Faces Censure," *New Vision,* August 3, 1999.

13. Richard Mutumba, "MPs Refuse to Consider Movt Budget over UCB" and Felix Osike and John Odyek, "Nsibambi Queried on UCB Bids," *New Vision,* October 3, 2001, p. 5.

14. "Museveni on Sale of UCB," *New Vision,* October 5, 2001, https://www.newvision.co.ug/news/1024720/museveni-sale-ucb.

15. "UCB Sale Is Great," *New Vision,* October 17, 2001, https://www.newvision.co.ug/news/1023814/ucb-sale.

> The Bank of Uganda has sold 80 per cent of Uganda Commercial Bank to Stanbic. Let us avoid misguided nationalism. Make no mistake. This is a great day for Uganda. Stanbic is the foreign arm of Standard Bank of South Africa, the largest bank in Africa with operations in 17 countries and assets of $38 billion. Stanbic has pledged to keep UCB's entire national branch network open. We no longer need fear that the sale of UCB will lead to the disappearance of rural banking. Indeed the rural network may have been the real attraction of UCB for Stanbic because it gives access to a large population with limited competition. Now the rural population will have access to modern sophisticated banking services that previously have been restricted to Kampala and the main urban centres.

16. "Museveni Fired Me for Opposing Sale of UCB—Prof Suruma," *The Observer* (Kampala), May 13, 2019, https://observer.ug/news/headlines/60665-museveni-fired-me-for-opposing-sale-of-ucb-prof-suruma.

17. The banking saga was reported in some detail by Andrew Mwenda (email with Mwenda, Kampala, August 31, 2025).

18. Then, in 1999, General Salim Saleh had been reported in the press "attack(ing) MPs over UCB Sale," saying he had been misunderstood; he only wanted "to make money and loan it to ordinary people, not to steal it." See "Saleh Attacks MPs over UCB Sale," *New Vision,* August 4, 1999. See also "Bukenya Defends UCB Sale," *New Vision,* October 5, 2001.

19. Mwenda, "The Museveni-Mutebile Conundrum."

20. Privatized parastatals and when they were privatized:

1. Nile Breweries Ltd (sold in April 1992)
2. East African Distilleries (November 1992)
3. Uganda American Insurance (November 1992)
4. Shell (Uganda) Ltd (December 1992)
5. Lake Victoria Bottling Co. Ltd (February 1993)
6. Uganda Securiko Ltd (August 1993)
7. Agricultural Enterprises Ltd (October 1993)
8. Uganda Tea Corporation Ltd (May 1994)
9. TUMPECO (August 1994)
10. White Horse Inn (August 1994)
11. Blenders (Uganda) Ltd (August 1994)
12. Hotel Margherita (August 1994)
13. Mt. Moroto Hotel (November 1994)

14. Rock Hotel (November 1994)
15. Uganda Cement Hima (December 1994)
16. Lira Hotel (January 1995)
17. Soroti Hotel (January 1995)
18. Hilltop Hotel (May 1995)
19. Uganda Fisheries Enterprises (May 1995)
20. Mt. Elgon Hotel (May 1995)
21. White Rhino Hotel (May 1995)
22. Acholi Inn (May 1995)
23. Uganda Leather and Tanning (July 1995)
24. Uganda Meat Packers Ltd (August 1995)
25. Lake Victoria Hotel Ltd (August 1995)
26. Mweya Safari Lodge (August 1995)
27. Uganda Meat Packers Ltd (August 1995)
28. Uganda Hardwares Ltd (October 1995)
29. Winits (Uganda) Ltd (October 1995)
30. Uganda Cement Tororo (October 1995)
31. Uganda Motors Ltd (November 1995)
32. Kampala Auto Centre (November 1995)
33. Uganda Hire Purchase Co. (November 1995)
34. Republic Motors (December 1995)
35. African Textile Mills (March 1996)
36. Total (Uganda) Ltd (March 1996)
37. NYTIL (March 1996)
38. Fresh Foods Ltd (May 1996)
39. Agip (Uganda) Ltd (May 1996)
40. Foods & Beverages Ltd (May 1996)
41. African Ceramics Co. (May 1996)
42. Uganda Pharmaceuticals Ltd (July 1996)
43. Motorcraft and Sales Ltd (September 1996)
44. Kibimba Rice Co. Ltd (September 1996)
45. Stanbic Bank (Uganda) Ltd (December 1996)
46. ITV Sales (December 1996)
47. Comrade Cycles (Uganda) Ltd (January 1997)

48. Uganda Ind. Machinery Ltd (May 1997)
49. Uganda Crane Estates Ltd (June 1997)
50. Second National Operator (March 1998)
51. Entebbe Handling Services (April 1998)
52. Lango Dev. Co. (May 1998)
53. Barclays Bank of Uganda Ltd (October 1998)
54. PAPCO Industries Ltd (February 1999)
55. Ug. Consolidated Properties (April 1999)
56. BAT Uganda "phase 1" (September 1999)
57. Uganda Clays Ltd (October 1999)
58. NEC Pharmaceuticals Ltd (December 1999)
59. Masindi Hotel (February 2000)
60. Uganda Telecom Ltd (June 2000)
61. BAT Uganda "phase 2" (June 2000)
62. Central Purchasing Company (July 2000)
63. Kakira Sugar Works (July 2000)
64. Steel Corporation of EA (July 2000)
65. Uganda Garment Industries (August 2000)
66. Apollo Hotel Corporation Ltd (March 2001)
67. Associated Match Company (June 2001)
68. Transocen 1998 (Uganda) Ltd (July 2001)
69. Uganda Commercial Bank (February 2002)
70. Rwenzori Highland Tea Co (May 2002)
71. Bank of Baroda (November 2002)
72. Uganda Electricity Generation Co (November 2002)
73. Nile Hotel International Ltd (January 2004)
74. DFCU (July 2004)
75. New Vision (September 2004)
76. Uganda Spinning Mills (sold in 2004)
77. Uganda Electricity Distribution (May 2005)
78. National Housing (June 2005)
79. Uganda Railways Corp (October 2005)
80. Dairy Corporation (August 2006)
81. Kinyara Sugar (October 2006)

82. Uganda Grain Milling (December 2009)

83. National Insurance Corp (March 2010)

T. Kalyegira, "20 Years of a Privatised Uganda," *Daily Monitor,* August 20, 2011, https://www.monitor.co.ug/uganda/news/insight/20-years-of-a-privatised-uganda-1498630. J. Mugunga, "Tackling Questions on Privatised Companies," *New Vision,* March 18, 2016, https://www.newvision.co.ug/news/1419925/tackling-questions-privatised-companies.

21. "Kazibwe Ready to Resign over Dams," *New Vision,* January 14, 1991.

22. "Kazibwe Accused of Embezzling shs 58 m from Foundation," *Daily Monitor,* January 31, 2013. See also Roger Tangri and Andrew Mwenda, *The Politics of Elite Corruption in Africa: Uganda in Comparative African Perspective* (London: Routledge, 2013), 58; Human Rights Watch, "'Letting the Big Fish Swim': Failures to Prosecute High Level Corruption in Uganda," October 21, 2013, https://www.hrw.org/report/2013/10/21/letting-big-fish-swim/failures-prosecute-high-level-corruption-uganda.

23. "Ug Airlines Nears Bankruptcy," *New Vision,* October 10, 1991.

24. "Should Ug Airlines Be Revived?" *Business Vision* (Kampala), April 19, 2012. Around that same time, it was reported that President Museveni had asked for a second plane to be purchased for him since his Gulfstream 4 jet was due for servicing at the manufacturer's headquarters in the United States.

25. In his interview with the IGG, Saleh had first bought 8,000 shares in Garment Industries Limited (GIL) and then "raised US $980,000 from Geneva towards buying UCBL." "IGG Releases UCB Report," *New Vision,* February 9, 1999; also see "UCB Asset Sale Inflames MPs," *New Vision,* December 17, 1999.

26. "Sam Kutesa Threatened to Kill Me," *New Vision,* March 1, 1999.

27. "Kutesa Named," *New Vision,* March 1, 1999.

28. "MPs Block Airlines Sales Deal," *New Vision,* September 30, 1999.

29. "Uganda Airlines to Be Liquidated," *New Vision,* March 30, 2000.

30. "How UPDF Bought Junk," *The Independent* (Kampala), April 30, 2010, https://www.independent.co.ug/updf-bought-junk/. Also see Epstein, *Another Fine Mess,* 140; Tripp, *Museveni's Uganda,* 132.

31. Felix Osike, "Besigye Wants Independent Inquiry into Junk Helicopter Deal," *New Vision,* November 7, 2000, 4.

32. Jeffrey Gettleman and Josh Kron, "Crashes Underline Uganda's Spotty Record with Helicopters," *New York Times,* August 14, 2012.

33. "Fighter Jet Secrets Out," *The Observer* (Kampala), April 11–13, 2011.

34. "Fury as MPs Debate Fighter Jets, Swearing-in Budget," *Saturday Monitor* (Kampala), April 28, 2011.

35. "Minister Grilled over shs 1.7 Trillion Jet Cash," *New Vision*, April 20, 2011.

36. "Fighter Jets: Museveni Says No More War Hurdles," *Daily Monitor*, August 16, 2011.

37. "Fighter Jet Secrets Out."

38. "Why shs 3.3 Billion Swearing-in Should Be shs 30 Million (or Less)," *Daily Monitor*, April 19, 2011.

39. "$740 m Fighter Jet Scam Sneaks under the Radar," *The East African* (Kenya), April 4–10, 2011.

40. Morgan Mbabazi, "Uganda's ID Project: $100m lost in latest scam," *The East African*, July 21, 2012.

41. "Report Says ID Firm Run by Ex-Convicts," *Daily Monitor*, April 4, 2012.

42. Dicta Asiimwe, "Uganda's ID Project: $100M Lost in Latest Scam," *East African*, July 23–29, 2012, 5.

43. "NRM Won't Acquit Ministers," *Daily Monitor*, July 12, 2012.

44. Sulaiman Kakaire, "Kivejinja, Nsambu Held Liable for ID Project Mess," *The Observer* (Kampala), July 3, 2012.

45. "Museveni Refuses to Shield Kasaija on Censure Motion," *Saturday Monitor*, February 3, 2018.

46. Tabu Butagira, "I Need Your Mercy, Makubuya Pleads with Museveni," *The Monitor* (Kampala), February 8, 2012.

47. Flavia Lanyero, "Minister's Comment on HIV/AIDS Careless, Say Experts," *The Monitor* (Kampala), July 2, 2011.

48. Simon Masaba and Steven Candia, "Detectives Probing Government Bodies over Fraud," *New Vision*, December 5, 2012.

49. "Court Rules on Muhwezi Graft Case Today," *Daily Monitor*, July 31, 2012.

50. "Detectives Arrest Health Ministry Officials in Corruption Crackdown," *Daily Monitor*, July 31, 2012.

51. "Health Ministry Fails to Account for sh 1.4 b," *New Vision*, August 27, 2011.

52. According to an investigation by one paper, officials in the Office of the Prime Minister received 15.6 billion shillings on private accounts in the 2010–2011 financial year. "Fresh Details Emerge in OPM Investigations," *Daily Monitor*, August 7, 2012.

53. Uganda Wildlife Authority, "Ministry of Tourism, Wildlife and Antiquities-General Management Plan 2011–2021," *New Vision*, Dec 10, 1991.

54. "MPS Pin Public Service Staff over 'Ghost' College," *New Vision*, August 5, 2011.

55. "Shs 70 bn Paid to Ghost Workers," *Daily Monitor,* June 22, 2012.

56. "More Decay in UPE, New Report Reveals," *Daily Monitor,* May 22, 2012.

57. "Districts Spend over shs 1 B on Ghost Workers," *New Vision,* February 3, 2022.

58. "URA Whistleblowers Run to the President," *Sunday Vision,* February 4, 2018.

59. "Police Ask for Share of Stolen Money," *New Vision,* August 17, 2012.

60. "Napak Residents No Longer Report Crimes," *Daily Monitor,* March 26, 2013.

61. "Ed Ministry, ULC Officials in Fight over School's Playground," *Daily Monitor,* February 26, 2013.

62. "Kampala Continues to Lose Playing Fields to Investors," *Sunday Monitor,* March 10, 2013.

63. "Kampala Continues to Lose."

64. "OPM Hit by Refugee Corruption Scandal," *Daily Monitor,* February 5, 2018.

65. "OPM Hit by Refugee Corruption Scandal."

66. Charles Onyanto-Obbo, "Uganda the Bribe Republic and the World of Its Visionary-in-Chief," *Daily Monitor,* July 11, 2012.

67. "MPs Receive shs 103 m for New Vehicles," *Daily Monitor,* January 7, 2012.

68. "Named: MPs Who Took shs 20m," *Daily Monitor,* July 25, 2011.

69. Inspectorate of Government, *First Annual Report on Corruption Trends in Uganda: Using the DTM [Data Tracking Mechanism],* November 1, 2010, https://www.igg.go.ug/publications/?page=7. Human Rights Watch, "Hostile to Democracy: The Movement System and Political Repression in Uganda," Part IX: The Role of the International Community, August 1999, https://www.hrw.org/reports/pdfs/u/uganda/ugan998.pdf.

70. Stephen Buckley, "African Leaders Ask World Bank for More Aid," *Washington Post,* January 25, 1998.

71. "Uganda to Receive U.S. $650 Million in Debt Relief," press release, International Monetary Fund, April 8, 1998, https://www.imf.org/en/News/Articles/2015/09/14/01/49/pr9813. Since 1987, the World Bank has provided an estimated US $790 million in adjustment support, in addition to an estimated US $1 billion in project support in the agriculture, infrastructure, and social sectors.

72. Horn of Africa, Monthly Review, Regional Issues, "Uganda: Corruption in Government," United Nations Development Programme, covering November–December 1998, https://www.africa.upenn.edu/eue_web/hoa1298.htm.

15. THE WAR ON TERROR

1. Mahmood Mamdani, *When Victims Become Killers: Colonialism, Nativism, and Genocide in Rwanda* (Princeton, NJ: Princeton University Press, 2014).

2. "Final Report of the Panel of Experts on the Illegal Exploitation of Natural Resources and Other Forms of Wealth of the Democratic Republic of the Congo," United Nations Security Council, S/2002/1146, October 16, 2002, https://www.securitycouncilreport.org/atf/cf/%7B65BFCF9B-6D27-4E9C-8CD3-CF6E4FF96FF9%7D/DRC%20S%202002%201146.pdf.

3. "Final Report," para. 98: "The Uganda network consists of a core group of members including certain high-ranking UPDF officers, private businessmen and selected rebel leaders/administrators. UPDF Lieutenant General (Ret.) Salim Saleh and Major General James Kazini are the key figures. Other members include the Chief of Military Intelligence, Colonel Noble Mayombo, UPDF Colonel Kahinda Otafiire and Colonel Peter Karim. Private entrepreneurs include Sam Engola, Jacob Manu Soba and Mannase Savo and other Savo family members. Rebel politicians and administrators include Professor Wamba dia Wamba, Roger Lumbala, John Tibasima, Mbusa Nyamwisi and Tomas Lubanga."

4. "Final Report," para. 101: "Uganda has recently agreed to withdraw all UPDF troops except for a reinforced battalion in Bunia and a small number of units on the slopes of the Ruwenzori Mountains. In anticipation of this withdrawal, a paramilitary force is being trained under the personal authority of Lt. General Saleh which, according to the Panel's sources, is expected to continue to facilitate the commercial activities of UPDF officers after UPDF have departed."

5. "Final Report," paras. 102, 19: "This military group draws on dissidents from Jean-Pierre Bemba's MLC (Movement for the Liberation of the Congo), members of the Uganda-supported RCD-Congo including its leaders Professor Kinkiey Mulumba and Kabanga Babadi, and others in the northeastern Democratic Republic of the Congo who have supported UPDF in the past. It has been reported that Lt. General Saleh discreetly provides financial support for this new rebel group."

See also "Final Report," para. 102: "The Panel's sources have indicated that Heckie Horn, Managing Director of Saracen Uganda Ltd., is a key partner with Lt. General Saleh in supporting this paramilitary group and that Lt. General Saleh himself is a 25 per cent owner in Saracen."

6. "Final Report": "As in the past, the network continues to involve the transnational criminal group of Victor Bout. Mr. Bout recently purchased the Uganda-based non-operational airline company Okapi Air. The purchase of the company allowed Victor Bout to use Okapi's licences. The company was subsequently renamed Odessa. The Panel is in possession of a list of outbound flights from 1998 to the beginning of 2002 from Entebbe International Airport, which confirms the op-

erational activities of Mr. Bout's aircraft from Ugandan territory. Currently, Mr. Bout's aircraft share the flight times and destinations (slots) with Planet Air, which is owned by the wife of Lt. General Salim Saleh and which facilitates the activities of Mr. Bout by filing flight plans for his aircraft" (para. 107). The report quotes the panel's sources "in Bunia, Kisangani and Kampala" as recognizing "Lt. General Saleh . . . as the founder and director of the Victoria Group and as the mastermind of its operations" (para. 112).

7. "Final Report," para. 117: "Many of the cattle removed have been forcibly taken from villages that have been the objects of attack by Hema militia supported by UPDF troops. The Panel has received reports from ranchers in areas to the south of Bunia as well as to the north in Mahagi detailing the removal of large numbers of cattle by UPDF troops."

8. "Final Report," para. 121: "The Hema fill an important niche in the operation of the criminal enterprises as truck owners and businessmen. They transport shipments of primary products from Ituri across the border to Uganda under the protection of UPDF troops and return with gasoline, cigarettes and arms, all exempt from taxation. They benefit from the trade and the generous profit margins, and from their association with the Trinity Group's Ugandan patrons." All along, the winning group in the local conflict—Hema in this case—secured no more than marginal earnings. "But their niche has remained marginal. They control none of the primary product exports themselves. They remain peripheral to the alliance between RCD-K/ML leaders, the Ugandan patrons and UPDF."

9. "Final Report," para. 124: "UPDF military operations have contributed to the arming of large numbers. UPDF have trained the militia of their Ituri commercial allies, the Hema, and provoked the need for the victims of Hema attacks to defend themselves."

10. "Final Report," para. 125.

11. "Final Report," para. 122: "The consequent increase in ethnic fighting has resulted in UPDF being urged to assist in furthering the peace process in Bunia. This function was formalized in an official Protocole d'Accord signed on 22 February 2002 by Mbusa Nyamwisi and John Tibasima as President and Vice-President of RCD- K/ML and by Colonel Noble Mayombo as an official representative of the Government of Uganda. The Protocole d'Accord gave UPDF official responsibility for reducing the *conflits armés inter-ethnique en Ituri* and for assisting in bringing about a *retour de la paix* by keeping a contingent in place for observation and for negotiating an eventual long-term solution. In exchange, UPDF were promised a monthly stipend of $25,000 from the RCD-K/ML public treasury, and all Ugandan enterprises that were approved by UPDF were accorded exoneration from all duties and taxes due to the rebel administration. This has given UPDF a legitimate cover for continuing military support for the elite network's activities in the area."

12. Alfred Wasiki, "Justice Porter Presents Report Today," AllAfrica, January 31, 2002, https://allafrica.com/stories/200301310224.html.

13. "Final Report": In the words of the UN panel, "The Panel's many efforts to establish a constructive relationship with the Commission have mostly been met with attempts to dismiss its credibility." The panel complained further: "During a specially arranged hearing aimed at corroborating the authenticity of certain documents transmitted by the Panel, the Porter Commission submitted one of the Panel's informants to an unusually aggressive questioning designed to frighten the individual and discredit his testimony" (para 135). At the same time, according to the UN report, the Porter Commission acknowledged that "the Commission's investigations, ongoing now for more than a year, were stymied primarily because of a 'conspiracy of silence' within UPDF" (para 133).

14. "Final Report," para. 137: In his last meeting with the UN panel, "Justice Porter explained that any recommendation by the Commission to refer an individual for criminal prosecution as the result of its enquiries must first be approved by the Minister for Foreign Affairs and President Museveni. A criminal investigation would then be necessary before the authorities could determine if grounds for prosecution existed." The commission further explained that its "terms of reference restrict[ed] the scope of its enquiries into the activities of military personnel. It is not empowered to obtain military records and documents from the Defence Ministry. Nor can it conduct audits of individual officers' finances."

15. "Uganda Army Chief 'Lied' over Congo," BBC News, World Edition, May 21, 2002, http://news.bbc.co.uk/2/hi/africa/1999913.stm.

16. Aili Mari Tripp, *Museveni's Uganda: Paradoxes of Power in a Hybrid Regime* (Boulder, CO: Lynne Rienner, 2010), 68.

17. Helen C. Epstein, *Another Fine Mess: America, Uganda, and the War on Terror* (New York: Columbia Global Reports, 2017), Kindle, 128–130.

18. Halima Athumani, "Uganda Sends Ground Troops into the Democratic Republic of Congo," VoA Africa, December 2, 2021, https://www.voanews.com/a/ugandan-troops-deploy-in-eastern-democratic-republic-of-congo/6336537.html.

19. Epstein, *Another Fine Mess,* Kindle, 149–151.

20. Epstein, *Another Fine Mess,* Kindle, 145–148.

21. Epstein, *Another Fine Mess,* Kindle, 147.

22. Epstein, *Another Fine Mess,* Kindle, 145–147.

23. Epstein, *Another Fine Mess,* Kindle, 35.

24. Abdi Latif Dahir, "Why Did Uganda Send Troops into Congo?," *New York Times,* December 31, 2021.

CONCLUSION

1. See Minutes of the 26th Meeting of the Cabinet of the 2nd Republic of Uganda, June 14, 1976, Minute 209 (CT 1976): "The Cabinet Message to His Excellency the President Congratulating Him on His Miraculous Escape on 10th June, 1976," p. 4.

2. Yoweri T. Museveni, "Fanon's Theory on Violence: Its Verification in Liberated Mozambique," in *Essays on the Liberation of Southern Africa,* ed. N. M. Shamyurira, 1–24 (Dar es Salaam: Tanzania Publishing House, 1971), 1–2.

3. Minutes of the 32nd Meeting of the Cabinet of the 2nd Republic of Uganda, November 21, 1972: Minute 407 (CT 1972): "Allocations of the Businesses of Departed Asians to Ugandans," 32nd meeting, November 21, 1972. On p. 10, the minutes record a call for "armed forces from Kampala and Jinja to assist in distributing businesses."

4. Video footage of several of these can be seen on social media, for example, on a site run by Yoga Adhola.

Acknowledgments

I have benefited from colleagues and friends who had the generosity to read and comment on my book at some stage of its development: Joe Oloka-Onyango at Makerere University School of Law; Charles Onyango-Obbo, the veteran and itinerant Ugandan journalist; Manan Ahmed and Gil Anidjar at Columbia University; Suren Pillay at the University of Cape Town; Harko Bhagat in Dar es Salaam; Ibrahim Abdullah at Fourah Bay College in Sierra Leone; and Yahya Sseremba and Okello Ogwang at Makerere Institute of Social Research (MISR). To all, my heartfelt gratitude.

Frank Muhereza, the director of the Centre for Basic Research (CBR) in Kampala, and Joe Oloka-Onyango helped in locating official documents otherwise hard to find. I had the support of research assistants: Brian Musinguzi in Kampala; Roland Gillah (Spring 2024), Shahrukh Mohamed (Fall 2023), and Shana Pareemamun (Fall 2024) at Columbia University. Olivia Kayizzi, my secretary at MISR, was invaluable throughout my tenure at MISR. David Ngendo-Tshimba, at Uganda Martyrs University, provided fact-finding assistance.

This book was written over the twelve years (2010–2022) that I spent as director of Makerere Institute of Social Research, concurrent with my tenured position at Columbia University. I want to thank Nick Dirks, who as executive vice president of Arts and Sciences at Columbia gave me official permission to spend an extended period at Makerere. I also want to thank Professors Venansius Baryamureeba and Barnabas Nawangwe, vice chancellors at Makerere who helped me negotiate formidable bureaucracies at the university at the beginning and toward the end of my term as director.

I leaned on the goodwill of comrades and friends over endless conversations that spanned decades. I dedicate this book to comrades who worked selflessly "above ground" in Uganda after we returned from Dar es Salaam in 1979–1980.

Index